Christopher Turner.

1 9 5 9.

Native Peoples of South America

Cuzco man blowing a conch shell trumpet.
(Courtesy of Abraham E. Guillém.)

NATIVE PEOPLES OF SOUTH AMERICA

Julian H. Steward
RESEARCH PROFESSOR OF ANTHROPOLOGY
UNIVERSITY OF ILLINOIS

Louis C. Faron
RESEARCH ASSOCIATE IN ANTHROPOLOGY
UNIVERSITY OF ILLINOIS

McGRAW-HILL BOOK COMPANY, INC.
New York   Toronto   London   1959

NATIVE PEOPLES OF SOUTH AMERICA

THE MAPLE PRESS COMPANY, YORK, PA.

PREFACE

Until comparatively recent years native South America was ethnographically the least understood of all major world areas. The aboriginal people had been described at length by scores of explorers, Spanish administrators, missionaries, and historians and by a few ethnographers, but the data were scattered in obscure sources published in a dozen languages. During the 1930s, a group of leading anthropologists sought to remedy this situation through the preparation of a *Handbook of South American Indians*. The *Handbook* was to assemble all available information on South American physical anthropology, linguistics, archaeology, and ethnology so as to provide the general student with a convenient summary of the salient facts and the scholar with a springboard for future research.

The opportunity to make the *Handbook* a reality came in 1939, when the Bureau of American Ethnology of the Smithsonian Institution undertook the task, in collaboration with the Department of State, as one of the projects under the broad program of "Cooperation with the American Republics." The work was carried out under the direction and editorship of the senior author of the present volume. Truly cooperative in nature, the *Handbook* drew upon the expert and specialized knowledge of more than ninety contributors from many different nations.

Begun in 1940, the manuscript of the *Handbook* was completed in 1945, but publishing costs delayed its appearance so that it was brought out in six volumes between 1946 and 1950. The completed work fulfills the original hope of assembling all the essential information on South American Indians in a single source. But its very size and comprehensiveness make it unsuited to the needs of the student and general reader. Moreover, a cooperative work by so many authors, while following a general plan, necessarily lacks an integrating point of view. The *Handbook* is essentially descriptive; theory and interpretation had to be kept at a minimum.

The present volume is an effort to meet the need left by the *Handbook*. In a sense it is a general summary of the *Handbook;* and the authors wish to express their great gratitude to all the *Handbook* contributors, whose labors made this volume possible. But the present volume is also an interpretative work, written according to a general theoretical point of view which may differ somewhat from that of the authors of the *Handbook* and also from that of persons who have previously written about South American Indians.

Another qualification of our book must be stated. While the *Handbook* did a fairly thorough job of summarizing and synthesizing information about the South American Indians available in the early 1940s, since its completion a tremendous amount of research has been carried on in South America. This presents any author of a single, concise volume a formidable problem; for the hundreds of articles and monographs as well as the ongoing but unpublished research accumulating each year make any volume out-of-date even before it is published.

North American anthropology confronted this dilemma of excess of riches twenty years ago, when current research disclosed so many new facts, cultural relationships, and interpretations that few persons since have had the temerity to write a general book about North American Indians. South American anthropological research is approaching, if it has not reached, the same point of frustration for the general writer. Within the last ten years, hundreds of books, monographs, and articles have been written on South American Indians.

The present book does not pretend to take all of these publications into account—this could be done only by another *Handbook of South American Indians*. It docs, however, offer a general description of South American Indian cultures and an interpretation of how these cultures developed, subjects which, we believe, will not be greatly affected by current research. It offers an interpretation of cultural development, beginning with very primitive man, as exemplified by the various nomadic hunters and gatherers, passing through various types of communities and states based upon agriculture, and culminating in the Central Andes in fairly sophisticated militaristic empires supported by irrigation farming. We hope that the insights and understandings of human development provided by these chapters will throw light on human history in other parts of the world, even though future research in South America will undoubtedly require modification of our particular interpretations.

The present text occasionally cites references on specific points. Otherwise the basic information will be found in the six volumes of the *Handbook*, which constitute Bulletin 143 of the Bureau of American Ethnology, Smithsonian Institution. These volumes are:

The Marginal Tribes. Volume 1, 1946.
The Andean Civilizations. Volume 2, 1946.
The Tropical Forest Tribes. Volume 3, 1948.
The Circum-Caribbean Tribes. Volume 4, 1948.
The Comparative Ethnology of South American Indians. Volume 5, 1949.
Physical Anthropology, Linguistics, and Cultural Geography of South American Indians. Volume 6, 1950.

The authors wish to express their gratitude to those who have read the manuscript of this book and given helpful criticisms concerning both facts and interpretations. We are especially indebted to Dr. Robert Carneiro of the American Museum of Natural History for his painstaking perusal of the entire manuscript, to Dr. Donald Collier of the Chicago Natural History Museum and Mr. Junius Bird of the American Museum of Natural History for reviewing the sections on Andean prehistory, and to Dr. Betty J. Meggers and Dr. Clifford Evans of the United States National Museum for various helpful suggestions concerning the archaeology of the northern Andes and the tropical forests.

Our debt to the ninety contributors to the six-volume *Handbook of South American Indians* will be obvious throughout this book. For use of unpublished material on the Warrau Indians of the Orinoco River we thank Dr. Johannes Wilbert of Venezuela.

We wish also to thank the persons and institutions which have furnished the photographs reproduced here. These include Dr. Abraham E. Guillém of the Museo de Arqueología of Lima, Peru, Dr. Paul Fejos of the Wenner-Gren Foundation for Anthropology, Dr. Irving Goldman of Sarah Lawrence College, Mr. John Collier, Jr., of Taos, New Mexico, Dr. Robert Murphy and Mr. Seth Leacock of the University of California, Mrs. Marion Tschopik of New York, Dr. Alfred Métraux of UNESCO, Mr. Junius Bird of the American Museum of Natural History, and Mr. Sol Miller of the University of Illinois. Many of the photographs were made available to us through the kindness of the American Museum of Natural History, the University Museum of Philadelphia, Cornell University, and the Bureau of American Ethnology of the Smithsonian Institution.

Above all, we are indebted to Jane Steward for relieving us of much of the toil of preparing manuscript and illustrations and reading proof.

Julian H. Steward
Louis C. Faron

CONTENTS

INTRODUCTION

The Indians of South America are widely known through popular tales and legends. Everyone is familiar with the gold of the Inca—the fabulous wealth of native Peru—which motivated a handful of men under Pizarro to conquer an empire of 3,500,000 people in 1532. Today one still frequently reads of expeditions seeking El Dorado and buried treasures. The mystery that clings to the many incompletely explored regions of South America provides a backdrop for stories based partly upon fact, such as those of head-hunting in Ecuador and the "white Indians" of Panama, and tales of pure fancy, such as those of the "pygmies" of Colombia or of lost cities and civilizations.

In the present volume we undertake to present a simple, straightforward description of the native cultures of South America. While there are several good books about South American Indians in general and about the Indians of particular localities, the information in the *Handbook of South American Indians* now makes it possible to delineate the various cultures more accurately than in the past. But, more importantly, we go beyond factual or descriptive accounts that follow the conventions of ethnography; we offer interpretations and explanations that are not usually found in the literature.

First, we attempt to recognize the several types of native South American cultures as the results of particular causes or processes. For this reason we pay special attention to subsistence or food-getting activities and the ways in which societies had to organize themselves for such activities. We also ask whether surplus production was possible in local areas and, if so, how such features as groups of special artisans, social classes, priesthoods, militarism, and political leaders were related to surplus.

1

We are not indifferent to questions of the origins and history of particular inventions and traits or elements of a culture. Every society borrows heavily from its neighbors, and no culture can be explained without reference to the spread or diffusion of the many features that make up a culture. It is, rather, that we are interested in the different roles or functions of these traits in the various cultures. Many domesticated plants, for example, had a very wide distribution in America, but in some societies, such as those of Amazonia, they barely sufficed to feed a sparse population of simple villagers, whereas many of the same crops cultivated by irrigation in the Central Andes supported classes of specialists and castes of rulers in an elaborate empire. Head-hunting among the Jívaro Indians of Ecuador, to take another example, was carried out for revenge and to obtain supernatural power, but it was one of several means by which the Colombian chiefdoms provided sacrificial victims for their temples and accorded prestige to individual warriors.

The corollary of the fact that a particular element may serve different functions is that different elements may serve the same function. Thus the chiefdoms of Venezuela, the Greater Antilles, and eastern Bolivia consisted of a number of villages bound together through common religious worship. But the particular features of religion differed in each case: in the Greater Antilles, there was a hierarchy of guardian spirits that ranged from those of the lowliest commoners to that of the high chief, which was the supreme god of the chiefdom; in Venezuela, there were a temple cult and a high priest; and in eastern Bolivia, a men's ceremonial house, based upon the Amazonian pattern, was magnified to state significance.

Second, our interests lead to a treatment of archaeology that differs in emphasis from that of our colleagues; for in prehistory as well as in ethnology we endeavor to extract all possible sociological meaning from the data. It is not that we are indifferent to the sequence of types and styles in ceramics, architecture, and other antiquities or fail to take into account the territorial distribution of these features at different periods in history. It is that our point of view invites interpretation—admittedly often speculative—about the larger patterns.

We ask, for example, why the desolate coast and the high, cold interior of Peru had one of the world's great ancient civilizations—one that compared favorably with those of China, Mesopotamia, Egypt, and Meso-America. Our broad answer is that the exceptional farm productivity based upon irrigation led, through several millennia, to enlarged hydraulic works which required strong managerial controls and a bureaucratic authority. The surplus production enabled a portion of the population to become specialists who developed metalworking, ceramics, weaving, construction, and the other material arts.

In considering the northern Andes of Ecuador and Colombia and the southern Andes of Chile, we ask why, since both areas borrowed many culture elements from the Central Andes, they not only differed from the Central Andes but from each other. Our tentative answer is that potential production in both areas might have supported state organization and classes of specialists. But the chiefdoms of the northern Andes were integrated by their constant warfare, which supplied the sacrificial victims demanded by the state temples, whereas these patterns were completely absent in Chile. In the case of the northern Andes, the "explanation" of the chiefdoms involves not only productive efficiency but patterns of warfare, human sacrifice, and state temples, idols, and priests. This is not to say that warfare "diffused" in the usual meaning of the term. Once conquest for sacrificial victims originated elsewhere, the victims of conquest would fight in self-defense and, if they had an adequate population, would adopt the religious sacrifices of their neighbors.

Whereas the northern Andes, between Meso-America and South America, were exposed to warfare and the pattern of the priest-temple-idol cult, the southern Andes were rather isolated from cultural contacts by the deserts on their northern frontier. Whether or not their productive basis might have supported chiefdoms, they did not receive the military or religious stimuli.

Answers to questions of these kinds come partly from archaeological data. In the Central Andes, the evolving settlement pattern so well analyzed by Willey in the Virú Valley shows clearly how independent farm villages with their local shrines increased in number and began to cluster around temple mounds until small multicommunity theocratic states were formed. Finally, warfare amalgamated these states into militaristic empires. In the northern Andes, certain early prehistoric remains strongly suggest local theocratic states, whereas late prehistoric sites fit quite well the Spanish chroniclers' accounts of the warring native chiefdoms. The data relevant to the answers of these and many other questions will be presented in this volume.

Our third interest is the interaction of the European conquerors and colonists with the Indians in South America. This interaction had great importance to the nature of Spanish and Portuguese settlement and policy. In the early colonial period, the Europeans were interested in gold rather than in conquest and settlement of lands in order to produce export crops. In the densely populated Andes, the Spanish Empire at first replaced the Inca Empire only at the top. So long as gold was the Spaniards' objective, native farm production theoretically remained little altered, owing to the Spanish crown's restrictions on trade within the Empire. The Spanish King and his representatives supposedly ruled through the personnel and political structure that were traditional in the local society, although exaction of tribute in the form of new produce and enforced labor in mines and public works badly violated the ideal.

But when the Andean colonies became more self-sufficient, and especially after they became independent American republics, greater freedom of trade stimulated new kinds of land use, which began to alter the role of the Indian. While modern censuses state that 40 to 50 per cent of the Andean people are "Indian," these Indians are very different from their pre-Columbian ancestors. We endeavor to trace the changes in the native culture from prehistoric to modern times and to specify some of the factors that have caused these changes.

The consequences of European conquest to both the Europeans and the Indians in other parts of South America differed from those in the Andes. In Amazonia and other tropical-rain-forest areas, there was never sufficient gold to satisfy the early colonial objectives. When crops that might be produced locally, such as ginger, sugar, coffee, and cacao, became the basis of plantations, the Europeans found no settled, immobile population, such as that of the Central Andes, from which to draw their labor supply. Since the Indians fled from the Europeans, these plantations could be operated only by slave labor, either imported African slaves or captured Indians.

In the areas of aboriginal nomadic hunting-and-gathering bands, especially in the southern pampas, Patagonia, and the Chilean archipelago, the Europeans brought a herding economy to many of the districts where farming was impossible. The aboriginal population, however, had very little value to European settlers. European policy regarding some of these Indians constitutes one of the darker chapters of human history. In Tierra del Fuego, the great island off the southern tip of South America, the Indians were at first shot down like wild game; no more than twenty or thirty survive today. In Patagonia and the pampas to the north, the Indians acquired horses from the Spanish settlers and organized themselves in predatory bands which raided the new colonies until the settlers defeated them. The survivors of these Indians now constitute a large portion of the Gaucho and farming population of Argentina, and native culture has virtually disappeared.

While the Indian biological contribution is markedly evident everywhere, South America today has some 7 million persons who are classified as "Indians" but represent different types of subcultures within the modern republics. Most of the "Indians" of the Andes are peasants, not Indians in an aboriginal cultural sense. Of the several hundred thousand Indians of the tropical rain forests, some are farm workers, some are peasants, and a very few retain their aboriginal culture. In the Gran Chaco, the pampas, and Chile, there are remnants of native culture but no genuinely aboriginal societies.

one

SOUTH AMERICAN CULTURE IN PERSPECTIVE

1. SOUTH AMERICA AT THE EUROPEAN CONQUEST

The sixteenth-century European conquest of South America was limited largely to the coasts and rivers, except in the Andes, where the lure of gold stimulated rapid subjugation of the highland Indians.

In the Central Andes, the Spaniards found an aboriginal empire which exerted absolute control over more than 3,500,000 people in an area extending some 2,000 miles north to south from southern Colombia through Ecuador, Peru, and western Bolivia to northern Chile. This empire was controlled by the Inca of Peru and had one of the world's truly high indigenous civilizations. It compared favorably with similar ancient civilizations in Mexico, Yucatán, China, India, and the Near East. It was based upon intensive cultivation of more than sixty species of domesticated plants, which were grown on agricultural terraces constructed on steep mountainsides, irrigated by an incredibly vast and complex system of canals and ditches, and extensively fertilized. The Inca were skilled in the arts of metallurgy, pottery, basketry, weaving, and stone carving. They were masters of construction on a large scale, and by use of sheer manpower they compensated for what they lacked in knowledge of engineering principles. Their roads, bridges, mounds, temples, and megalithic structures were not surpassed by any native peoples of the world.

In social, religious, and political affairs also the Inca exhibited an organizing genius that matched their competence in the material arts, and their empire was one of the most thoroughly regimented societies the world has ever known. In the sixteenth century, the dense population of this empire supplied miners and servants for the gold-greedy Spanish colonists. Later, the native people provided laborers and artisans for farms and towns.

The Spaniards also subjugated the Indians of most of Central America, Colombia, northern Venezuela, and the Antilles early in the sixteenth

Farming in the high Andes: Vicos, Peru. (Photo by John Collier, Jr., courtesy of Cornell University.)

century, but they encountered great local differences in native wealth, population, settlement stability, and aboriginal culture. Owing to the quantities of gold and emeralds found in Colombia, the Indians of the northern Andes bore the brunt of conquest, and most were soon assimilated to Spanish culture. The early chronicles, however, describe the native societies of Colombia and parts of Central America as warlike states or chiefdoms which were ruled by priests and warriors and were sharply divided into social classes. These chiefdoms maintained temples which sheltered village and state idols, they kept large armies, and they took war captives whom they sacrificed in religious rites and then made trophies of the heads, bones, and even whole bodies of their victims. They also had classes of highly skilled artisans who manufactured beautiful products of gold, copper, textiles, precious stones, and other materials for their ruling classes.

In northern Venezuela and the Greater Antilles, the conquistadors found chiefdoms that were somewhat like those of Colombia, except that they were less militaristic and produced less gold.

The chiefdoms found around the Caribbean Sea shared many culture elements with the Central Andes, but they fell far short of the Inca Empire in the political integration of a huge population in a vast area and in technological and aesthetic achievements. Moreover, many societies which resembled the simple farm villages of the Amazon were interspersed among the chiefdoms of the Circum-Caribbean area, and the western tip of Cuba was inhabited by primitive hunters and gatherers.

While the Spanish Conquest eliminated native culture in much of the Circum-Caribbean area and absorbed the Indians into a Hispanic way of life far more rapidly and completely than in the Central Andes, a few modern villages in isolated areas are much like the aboriginal communities. Since these villages are much like those of the Amazon, anthropologists were misled for many years into classifying most of the native population with the independent farm villages of the tropical rain forests. It had long been known that the Chibcha, or Muisca, who controlled a portion of highland Colombia and whose capital was Bogotá, the modern Colombian capital, had formed a powerful state or realm in aboriginal times. The Chibcha were regarded as a kind of northern outpost of Central Andean civilization, but not as today as a distinctive cultural type that was widely distributed mainly around the Caribbean Sea.

It is only recently that, thanks to the investigations of Lothrop, Kirchhoff, Hernández de Alba, and others, who searched the Conquest-period chronicles for ethnographic information, that we now know that many simple villagers of today are descended from once-powerful chiefdoms. Among the more important native chiefdoms are those of several Chibchan-speaking peoples of Colombia, the Cuna and others of Panama and Central America, the Timotean-speaking people of northern Venezuela, and the Arawak of the Greater Antilles.

The relationship of these chiefdoms to prehistoric remains in the Circum-Caribbean area and the extremely interesting process of deculturation, or culture loss, after the Spanish Conquest will be discussed subsequently in Chapter Six, which deals with this area in detail.

European contact with the Indians of the lowland tropical rain forests was very different from that with Indians of the Andes and the Circum-Caribbean area. In the rain forests, the Europeans found a sparse population of simple farm villages and no important mineral wealth. The native culture disappeared very quickly, for the Indians were

Spearing fish, upper Xingú River. (Courtesy of the University Museum, Philadelphia.)

enslaved, killed, or fled into the interior. In the hinterlands, between the main rivers of the tropical lowlands, there were somewhat more primitive farm communities and bands of hunters and gatherers, whose inaccessibility to the Europeans has left them with an aboriginal culture to the present day.

These tropical-rain-forest Indians lacked most of the technological skills and sociopolitical complexities characteristic of the Central Andean empire and the Circum-Caribbean chiefdoms. They were a simple village people whose lives were primarily devoted to exacting bare subsistence from their dense, humid forest habitat. They grew root crops in clearings which had to be hewn from the jungle anew every few years. They utilized the fish, reptiles, and mammals of the rivers, and they hunted in the forests. They lived in pole-and-thatch houses and manufactured fairly simple pots, hammocks, cloth, wooden stools, mortars, and other objects for domestic use. These Indians had no full-time specialists skilled in production of particular goods, they knew nothing of metallurgy, and there were no upper classes for whom such products might be produced. Society was based largely upon kinship ties.

Religion among these Indians lacked temples, priesthoods, and ethical systems which gave meaning to Central Andean and Circum-Caribbean religion. It was concerned more with supernatural practices related to birth, puberty, sickness, and death. Instead of a class of priests who had hereditary rank and who performed group rites, the rain-forest villagers had shamans whose own spirit-helpers enabled them to cure sickness and perform other supernatural deeds. Only occasionally, the shamans led simple village ceremonies in addition to helping individuals. Since political ties never united different villages, there was no over-all chief or class of rulers. Owing to his control of supernatural powers, the shaman was often village chief.

In the pampas of Argentina, the Europeans found scattered bands of guanaco hunters, but virtually all descriptions of these people were written after the Indians had acquired horses from the Spaniards and had become organized in bands which not only hunted on horseback but which raided the colonists. In the extremely cold and rainy islands of southern Chile, the Europeans encountered only small, wandering families which subsisted principally on shellfish.

In both the pampas and the Chilean islands the Indians had no knowledge of farming, metallurgy, pottery, weaving, and other characteristic skills of the people of the tropical rain forest or the Andes. The absence of these features is readily explained by two factors. First, because the Indians were forced to constant nomadism, they not only lacked time for the material arts but were unable to transport a large number of objects. Second, they were so far from the Central Andean center of inventions that little knowledge was passed on to them.

Nomadic hunting-and-gathering Indians as primitive as those of the pampas and the Chilean archipelago were also encountered dispersed in isolated regions among the tropical-rain-forest farm villagers. All of these nomads have been described as "marginal" in culture, since they were marginal, or peripheral, to the main centers of culture that had developed. Father John Cooper aptly designated the enclaves of hunters in the tropical forest "internal marginals."

The types of aboriginal society encountered by the first European explorers or conquerors form the basis for the delineation of the native cultures in subsequent chapters of this volume (see page 13). These types are the Central Andean irrigation civilization, the chiefdoms, the tropical-forest farm villages, and the several types of nomadic hunters and gatherers. The types only partly represent territorial units. The Central Andean civilization was found in a single block of territory extending from Ecuador through Bolivia. The chiefdoms were best represented in what has been called the Circum-Caribbean area: Central America, Colombia, Venezuela, and the Antilles. But the chiefdoms of the northern Andes, northern Venezuela, and the Greater Antilles represented three different local subtypes, while certain Indians of eastern Bolivia, who had also developed to the cultural level of multicommunity, class-structured chiefdoms, can be considered a fourth subtype.

Yagua house, upper Amazon. (Courtesy of Paul Fejos, Wenner-Gren Foundation.)

The tropical-rain-forest farm villages had a fairly homogeneous culture, despite considerable variation in details and despite their far-flung distribution, which followed the humid, lowland jungles. Away from the coasts and main rivers, however, the more characteristic features of these villages were lost, and the culture shaded off to a type more like that of the nomads or what have been called the internal marginal societies of the remote hinterlands.

These are the principal types and subtypes of aboriginal South American culture, but they do not in all cases represent the Indians at their first contact with whites; for European settlement initiated changes even before direct contact was made with the Indians. Refugee coastal people mingled with native societies in the interior. In Chile, some 40,000

Araucanians fled from the Spaniards to cross the Andes into the pampas. In the rain forests, steel axes and machetes from Europe were traded from one group to another until they reached people not yet visited by whites. These tools enormously facilitated clearing the jungle, constructing houses, and building canoes, and thus led to larger, more permanent settlements. To offset this technological advantage, epidemics of European origin not only decimated societies that had settled at European missions and towns but took a toll among those who remained in the bush.

2. SOUTH AMERICA IN RELATION TO ABORIGINAL NEW WORLD CULTURES

The native cultures of South America were largely the independent products of the New World. It is possible that particular features or elements were contributed to the New World by the people of the Pacific or beyond, but few students of the American Indians believe that such contributions materially affected the course of indigenous developments. The problem of transoceanic diffusion will be dealt with later. First, we shall view South America in the perspective of the Western Hemisphere.

Within the New World there was clearly a far-reaching exchange of cultural features, each group of Indians being indebted to others for many of their cultural accomplishments.

At the time of the discovery of the Americas, three or four of the cultural types of South America had counterparts in Mexico and North America (see page 12). In Mexico, the civilizations of the Aztec of the Valley of Mexico and of the Maya of Yucatán had attained a level of cultural development equal to that of the Inca of Peru. All three were based on intensive farming, which, in the arid portions of the Andes and Mexico, required extensive irrigation works. All had dense populations, large towns and cities, religious mounds and temples, priesthoods, organized armies, and extensive empires.

These features are not peculiar to the New World; they characterize various civilizations in other parts of the world.[1] The Andean and Meso-American civilizations were, however, historically connected with each other in at least some specific features. The common use of such farm staples as maize, beans, and squash is indisputable evidence of diffusion. There is some question as to how elements of the total inventory of these civilizations diffused between the Americas. Certain archaeological evidence, which will be presented in a subsequent chapter, strongly suggests that there was a great deal of cultural interchange at an early period, when the civilizations were in their formative phases

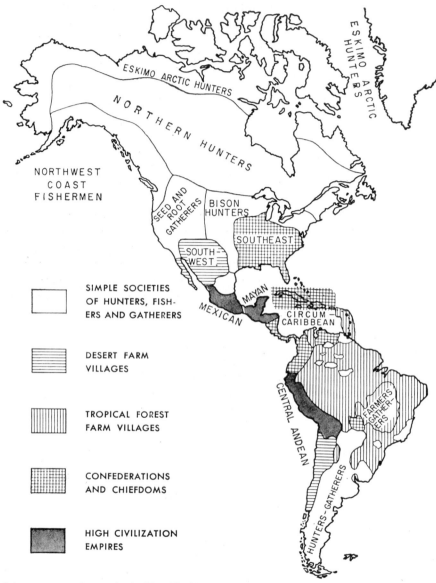

Culture areas and types in the New World.

and when the societies seem to have maintained fairly peaceful relations. But during this Formative Era, the Mexican and Andean cultures were more similar to each other than they were at the discovery of the New World by the Europeans, when each had developed in somewhat distinctive ways. At the Spanish Conquest, the Maya had theocratic states, phonetic writing, mathematics, the calendar, and religious art and archi--

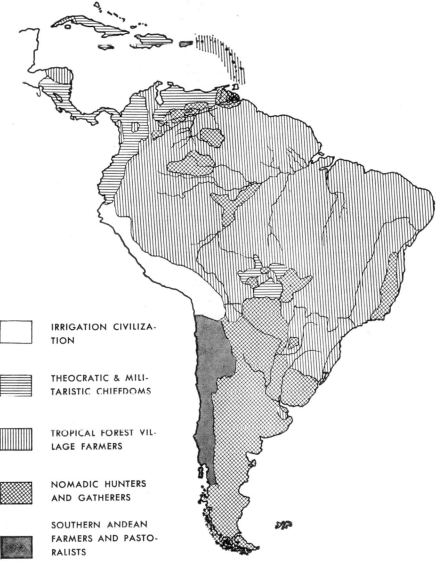

IRRIGATION CIVILIZA-
TION

THEOCRATIC & MILI-
TARISTIC CHIEFDOMS

TROPICAL FOREST VIL-
LAGE FARMERS

NOMADIC HUNTERS
AND GATHERERS

SOUTHERN ANDEAN
FARMERS AND PASTO-
RALISTS

Culture types of native South America.

tecture. Highland Mexico shared some of the Maya achievements but
emphasized warfare and conquest, and their religion reflected their
warfare in its bloody rites. The Inca were empire builders, organizers,
and engineers on a grand scale, rather than intellectuals, aesthetes, or
bloodthirsty ritualists.

The distribution of the Circum-Caribbean chiefdoms in the northern
Andes and Central America, which separate the high civilization of

Meso-America from that of the Andes, is further evidence of a break in the free interchange of the highest cultural achievements of the two centers of American civilization at the Conquest. Central America lacked the writing, mathematics, calendars, and aesthetic accomplishments which characterized the Maya and the advanced metallurgy, megalithic construction, militaristic prowess, and political organization of the Central Andes. The similarity of the Circum-Caribbean cultures to the two centers of civilization consists of general features which had probably attained an inter-American distribution at an earlier period—basic farm crops, ceramic and weaving styles, mounds and temples, and a class-structured society. The precondition of these features was a dense, stable population, which was absent among some of the peoples of Central America, who remained largely on a village level.

The Meso-American, Circum-Caribbean, and Central Andean civilizations must therefore be regarded as specialized cultures which developed from a rather similar basis in the Formative Era but which became distinctive as time passed. Moreover, the Circum-Caribbean culture was strongly adapted to a rain-forest environment, part of it in a very rugged, mountainous terrain and part of it along seacoasts. Such rain-forest features as pole-and-thatch houses, hammocks, dugout canoes, and others link it with Amazonia rather than with high civilizations.

To the north and the south of the areas of the nuclear, or high, civilizations there were secondary or peripheral agricultural people, who had received most of their principal cultural traits from the nuclear areas. But the North American and South American peripheral farm cultures differed because each was adapted to a distinctive environment.

The eastern United States is an area of deciduous hardwood forests and a temperate climate. In prehistoric times, cultures with complex ceremonialism centering in temple mounds were distributed along the alluvial lowlands of the Mississippi River and its tributaries. The general patterns and many elements of these cultures at certain periods were strikingly similar to those of the Circum-Caribbean peoples, although some particulars, especially a few art motifs, link this area with the Valley of Mexico. It is not now possible to say whether these cultures represent some kind of diminished Meso-American culture or a temperate hardwood-forest variant of the Circum-Caribbean type.

The Greater Southwest of the United States and northwestern Mexico and the Calchaquí and Diaguita area of northwestern Argentina are both regions of mountains, high plateaus, and deserts which are peripheral to high civilizations. Both adopted many architectural, religious, and technological features from their civilized neighbors—the Southwest from Meso-America and northwest Argentina from the Central Andes. But neither developed great states, chiefdoms, or empires. Many of the villagers of the Southwest were intensive farmers, but none, except the prehistoric Hohokam people of the Salt and Gila Rivers of southern Arizona, employed irrigation on a large scale. The Greater Southwest has many striking similarities to Meso-America in ceramics, stonework, ritual, and other features, but it lacked the religious mounds and temples of the latter, and, with the possible exception of the Hohokam, it also lacked the priesthood, armies, states, and class-structured society which characterized the Mexican high civilizations.

Northwestern Argentina acquired many Central Andean features, just as the Southwest drew upon Meso-American culture. But it also lacked the states, social classes, and temple mounds of the Andes. It seems to have resembled the Pueblo Indians of Arizona and New Mexico, but, since these Argentine Indians were assimilated long ago by the Spaniards, the extent of these similarities is not clear.

There has been some tendency to schematize American cultural history in such a way that the Pueblo Indians of Arizona and New Mexico and the Indians of northwest Argentina are represented as peripheral survivals of an early inter-American stratum or period which antedated and underlay the later growth of the nuclear, or high, civilizations. Such schematizing ignores the impossibility that cultures which were adapted to steppes and deserts would have existed in the rain forests of the northern Andes and Central America. The similarities between the North American Southwest and northwestern Argentina developed because of the marginal relationship of these cultures to the great irrigation cultures. Instead of representing ancestral stages of the Andean and Meso-American civilizations, they must be considered as later, derived cultures, which repatterned their borrowed features in somewhat similar ways.

The rich, fertile valley of central Chile is strikingly like that of California. But the Indians of California, despite their proximity to the Southwest, never adopted farming and remained hunters and gatherers until the coming of the white man, whereas the native Chilean Indians were intensive farmers. The Araucanians of the Chilean central valley borrowed not only farming but a considerable repertory of culture traits from the Central Andes. They did not, however, irrigate on a large scale, for this was not necessary in their rainy climate, and they did not adopt any of the social, political, and religious patterns of the Central Andes. The vast area of almost waterless desert which cuts across the Andes from northern Argentina to southern Peru was inhabited only by very small villages located at the few oases. Social and political organization as well as many culture elements of the Andean type failed to spread across this desert and reach the densely populated central valley of Chile.

The tropical rain forests of the Amazon Valley, the coast of Brazil, and portions of the Circum-Caribbean area have no counterparts in North America. Closer parallels to the specialized culture of the tropical-rain-forest farm villages occurred in portions of the Pacific, Southeast Asia, and Africa, where similar environments and cultural ecological adaptations have occurred.

Nomadic hunting and gathering people of North and South America are broadly similar to one another principally in a negative sense. Characteristically, they all lacked farming, pottery, metallurgy, loom weaving, permanent settlements, priests, social classes, and state organization. The nomads occupied principally the extreme northern and southern latitudes of each continent, but their environments were extremely varied, and a considerable number of cultural types can be distinguished. Socially, the hunting people of southern California and of Tierra del Fuego were similar in their patrilineal band patterns, and the shellfish-gathering Indians of the Chilean archipelago resembled the seed-gathering Shoshoneans of Nevada in their simple family groups. The bison hunters of the high plains of North America were apparently much like the guanaco-hunting Puelche of the pampas and Tehuelche of Patagonia in Argentina, especially after both peoples acquired horses from Europeans. But there are no parallels in South America to the specialized arctic culture of the Eskimo, the caribou-hunting bands of the northern Athabaskan and Algonquian peoples, and the fishing villages of the northwest coast of Alaska and British Columbia. Although the Chilean archipelago resembles the Northwest Coast of North America, it has very few fish. On the other hand, in South America a number of specialized nomadic types are represented among the Ge Indians of the arid east Brazilian plateau and by the seed gatherers of parts of the Gran Chaco.

3. NATIVE GROUPS AND LANGUAGES

The classification of South American Indian groups and the reconstruction of their culture history are aided by knowledge of their linguistic affiliations, but the classification presents certain difficulties. A complete tribal map would contain two or three thousand names, many of them of dubious significance. Such a map, moreover, would encounter the problem of the many synonyms for each tribe found in the literature. The figure on page 18 shows the location of most of the tribes mentioned in the text, and it employs the *Handbook* names.

A map showing the linguistic relationships of most South American Indian groups is presented on page 23. This map, based on Greenberg's provisional classification,[2] has four main groups of families and thirteen lesser groups, or subfamilies—a great simplification of the *Handbook* classification, which has sixty-five main groups and twenty-two small, unclassified language groups. Many South American Indian societies are so incompletely known linguistically that different authorities have assigned them variously to one or another family. Some of these languages are now extinct.

"Tribes" and other sociolinguistic groups. Anthropologists have never reached agreement on the meaning of "tribe," although this is one of their most common terms. Among the nomadic hunters and gatherers and tropical-forest villages, the small band or village was generally independent, and presumably it was somewhat distinct in dialect and culture from its neighbors. It has been customary, however, in connection with these people, to designate groups of similar bands and villages as "tribes." On the other hand, in some areas, as among the Arawakan and Tucanoan peoples of the northwest Amazon, small, independent villages are called "tribes." This practice is very confusing, for the villages were named after headmen of transient authority and they often split and re-formed. Elsewhere, "tribe" might be applied to a large block of independent villages, which were linguistically and culturally similar, although not necessarily identical. The Tupinambá "tribe," for example, consisted of dozens of independent villages scattered along more than 1,000 miles of the coast of Brazil. Many of these villages were at war with one another.

More often than not anthropological usage in South America, as in other continents, employs "tribe" to designate a group of bands or villages that are related in culture and language, but it carries no implication as to how close these relationships must be nor does it imply political unity. It does not, in fact, follow any hard and fast rule, except that, if the dialects are not mutually intelligible, the sociocultural groups are usually said to belong to different "tribes."

Use of "tribe" to designate the social units making up more developed sociocultural systems is fraught with greater difficulties. In a sociological sense, "tribal society" usually means a small, independent folk society. In the Circum-Caribbean and Andean areas, however, there were more complex sociopolitical systems, which ranged from small states and confederacies to huge empires. When the local society retained a measure of dialectal and cultural distinctiveness, despite being a dependent part of a larger political unit, it would be justifiable to consider it a folk society or subsociety. In the case of the small states, such as the Cuna chiefdoms of Panama, the Timotean chiefdoms of western Venezuela and the confederacy of the Fincenú, Pancenú, and Cenufaná of northern Colombia, society returned to a folk or village level when the states disintegrated following the Spanish Conquest. In Peru, however, the

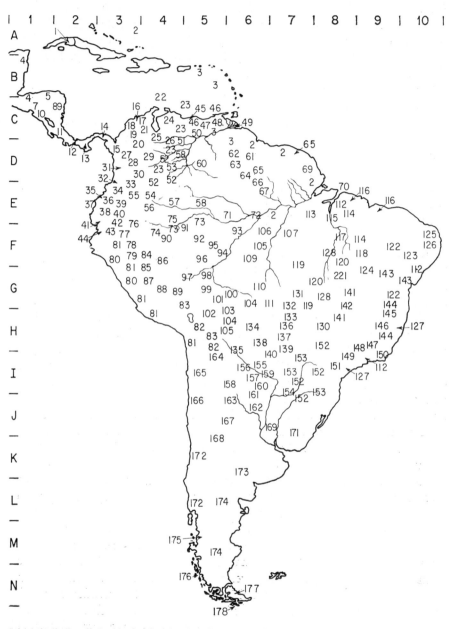

Principle "tribes," that is, local sociocultural groups of South America.

Alphabetic List of Tribes and Locations

Abipón, 162, J-5-6
Acawai, 61, D-6
Achagua, 52, D-4
Acroa, 142, H-8
Alacaluf, 176, M-4
Amoipira, 124, G-8
Amuesha, 87, G-3
Apinayé, 117, F-8
Arara, 113, F-7
Araucanian, 172, J,K-4
Arawak, 2, A-3-4,
  B-3-4-5, D-6-7, E-6-7
Arinagato, 63, D-6
Arua, 70, E-7
Aruaki, 72, E-F-6
Ashluslay, 155, I-6
Atacama, 165, I-4-5
Atorai, 66, E-6
Aymara, 82, H-4-5
Bacaïri, 132, H-6
Barbacoa, 32, D-E-3
Bora, 56, E-4
Bororo, 133, H-6
Botocudo, 147, H-I-8
Caeté, 127, H-9
Cágaba, 17, F-8
Caingang, 152, H-I-7
Calibí, 68, D-7
Camacán, 145, H-9
Camaracotó, 62, D-5-6
Campa, 88, G-4
Cañar, 43, E-3
Caquetio, 23, C-4
Cara, 39, E-3
Caraca, 45, C-5
Carajá, 128, F-8
Carib, 3, B-C-D-5
Carijona, 54, E-4
Caripuna, 98, G-5
Cariri, 122, F-H-9
Catukina, 92, F-5
Catukino, 86, F-4
Cayapá, 36, E-3
Cenufaná, 20, D-3
Chacó, 15, D-3
Chacobo, 99, G-5
Chaima, 48, C-5
Chané, 137, H-6
Charrua, 171, J-6
Chébero, 78, F-3
Chibcha, 29, D-4
Chimane-Mosetene, 102,
  H-5
Chimu, 80, F-G-3
Chiquito, 134, H-6
Chiriguano, 135, H-5

Cholón, 79, F-3
Chono, 175, L-4
Ciboney, 1, A-1, B-2
Cocama, 74, F-4
Colorado, 38, E-3
Comechingón, 167, J-5
Conibo, 85, F-3
Coroado, 149, I-8
Cuna-Cueva, 14, C-3
Diaguita, 166, I-4
Dorasque, 12, C-2
Esmeralda, 35, E-3
Evéjico, 27, D-3
Fincenú, 18, C-3
Fulnio, 123, G-9
Goajiro, 22, C-4
Guahibo, 53, D-4
Guaitaca, 150, I-8
Guamontey, 50, D-5
Guanahatabey, 1, A-1,
  B-2
Guaraní, 153, I-6-7
Guató, 136, H-6
Guayakí, 154, I-6
Guayaná, 151, I-7
Guaymí, 13, C-2
Güetar, 11, C-2
Huancavilca, 41, E-2
Huarpe, 168, J-5
Inca, 81, F-G-H-3-4
Ipuriná, 96, F-5
Itonama, 100, G-5
Jeicó, 118, G-8
Jicaque, 5, B-2
Jirajara, 24, C-4
Jívaro, 77, F-3
Lenca, 7, C-1
Lipe, 164, H-5
Lule, 158, I-5
Macú, 58, E-5
Macusi, 65, E-6
Manao, 71, E-5
Mangue, 10, C-1
Maniteneri, 97, G-4
Manta, 37, E-2
Mascoi, 89, G-4
Mashacalí, 146, H-8
Mataco, 156, I-5
Maué, 106, F-6
Maya, 4, B-1
Mayoruna, 90, F-4
Mbayá, 139, H-6
Minuané, 169, J-6
Mocoví, 161, I-5
Mojo, 103, H-5
Mompox, 21, C-4

Mosquito, 9, C-2
Motilones, 25, D-4
Móvima, 101, G-5
Mundurucú, 108, F-6
Mura, 93, F-5
Nambicuara, 110, G-6
Northern Cayapó, 119,
  G-H-7
Omagua, 73, F-4-5
Ona, 177, N-5
Páez, 33, D-3
Palenque, 47, C-5
Palicur, 69, E-7
Pancenú, 19, C-3
Panzaleo, 40, E-3
Paressí, 111, H-6
Parintintin, 109, F-6
Pasto, 34, E-3
Patángora, 28, D-3
Patashó, 144, H-9
Paumari, 95, F-5
Paya, 6, B-2
Payagua, 140, H-I-6
Pijao, 30, D-3
Pilagá, 159, I-6
Potiguara, 125, F-10
Puelche, 173, K-5
Purí, 148, I-8
Puruhá, 42, E-3
Querandí, 170, J-4-5
Quiriquire, 46, C-5
Sáliva, 59, D-4
Setebo, 84, F-3
Shacriaba, 141, H-8
Shavante, 120, G-8
Sherente, 121, G-8
Shipaya, 107, F-7
Shirianá, 60, D-5
Sirionó, 104, H-5
Southern Cayapó, 130,
  H-7
Sumo, 8, C-2
Tairona, 16, C-3
Tapirapé, 129, G-7
Taulipang, 64, D-E-6
Teheulche, 174,
  K-L-M-4-5
Tembe, 115, F-8
Teremembe, 116, E-9
Timbira, 114, F-8
Timoté, 26, D-4
Toba, 160, I-5-6
Tonocoté, 163, I-5
Trumai, 131, G-7
Tucano, 57, E-4
Tucuna, 91, F-4

Tumbez, 44, F-2
Tupina, 143, G-9
Tupinambá, 112, F-8,
  G-9, I-8
Tupinikin, 127, H-9, I-8
Uru, 83, G-4, H-5

Vilela, 157, I-5
Waiwai, 67, E-6
Warrau, 49, C-D-5
Witoto, 55, E-3
Yagua, 75, E-4
Yahgan, 178, N-4-5

Yaruro, 51, D-4
Yuma, 94, F-5
Yuracare, 105, H-5
Yurumango, 31, D-3
Zamuco, 138, H-6
Záparo, 76, E-3

Legend to Numbers of Tribal Map

1. Guanahatabey or Ciboney
2. Arawak
3. Carib
4. Maya
5. Jicaque
6. Paya
7. Lenca
8. Sumo
9. Mosquito
10. Mangue
11. Guetar
12. Dorasque
13. Guaymí
14. Cuna-Cueva
15. Chocó
16. Tairona
17. Cágaba
18. Fincenú
19. Pancenú
20. Cenufaná
21. Mompox
22. Goajiro
23. Caquetío
24. Jirajara
25. Motilones
26. Timoté
27. Evéjico
28. Patángora
29. Chibcha (Muisca)
30. Pijao
31. Yurumango
32. Barbacoa
33. Páez
34. Pasto
35. Esmeralda
36. Cayapa
37. Manta
38. Colorado
39. Cara
40. Panzaleo
41. Huancavilca
42. Puruhá
43. Cañar
44. Tumbez
45. Caraca
46. Quiriquire
47. Palenque
48. Chaima

49. Warrau
50. Guamontey
51. Yaruro
52. Achagua
53. Guahibo
54. Carijona
55. Witoto
56. Bora
57. Tucano
58. Macú
59. Sáliva
60. Shiriana
61. Acawai
62. Camaracotó
63. Arinagoto
64. Taulipang
65. Macusi
66. Atorai
67. Waiwai
68. Calibí
69. Palicur
70. Arua
71. Manao
72. Aruaki
73. Omagua
74. Cocama
75. Yagua
76. Záparo
77. Jívaro
78. Chébero
79. Cholón
80. Chimu
81. Inca (Quechua)
82. Aymara
83. Uru
84. Setebo
85. Conibo
86. Catukino
87. Amuesha
88. Campa
89. Mascoi
90. Mayoruna
91. Tucuna
92. Catukina
93. Mura
94. Yuma
95. Paumari
96. Ipuriná
97. Maniteneri

98. Caripuna
99. Chacobo
100. Itonama
101. Móvima
102. Chimane-Mosetene
103. Mojo
104. Sirionó
105. Yuracare
106. Maué
107. Shipaya
108. Mundurucú
109. Parintintin
110. Nambicuara
111. Paressí
112. Tupinambá
113. Arara
114. Timbira
115. Tembé
116. Teremembé
117. Apinayé
118. Jeicó
119. Northern Cayapó
120. Shavante
121. Sherente
122. Cariri
123. Fulnio
124. Amoipira
125. Potiguara
126. Caeté
127. Tupinikin
128. Carajá
129. Tapirapé
130. Southern Cayapó
131. Trumai
132. Bacaïri
133. Bororo
134. Chiquito
135. Chiriguano
136. Guató
137. Chané
138. Zamuco
139. Mbayá
140. Payaguá
141. Shacriaba
142. Acroa
143. Tupina
144. Patashó
145. Camacán

146. Mashacalí
147. Botocudo
148. Purí
149. Coroado
150. Cuaitaca
151. Guayaná
152. Caingang
153. Guaraní
154. Guayakí
155. Ashluslay
156. Mataco

157. Vilela
158. Lule
159. Pilagá
160. Toba
161. Mocoví
162. Abipón
163. Tonocoté
164. Lipe
165. Atacama
166. Diaguita
167. Comechingón

168. Huarpe
169. Minuané
170. Querandí
171. Charrua
172. Araucanian
173. Puelche
174. Teheulche
175. Chono
176. Alacaluf
177. Ona
178. Yahgan

Inca Empire was imposed upon a large number of local states, and each of these, although somewhat distinctive in language and culture before the Inca leveled local differences and imposed the Quechua language, had long since developed beyond what could properly be called folk or tribal society.

The term "tribe," thus having no clear meaning, will be generally avoided in this volume.

The linguistic map. This map (see page 23) is based upon the territorial distributions of the tribal and linguistic map prepared by J. Alden Mason and Julian H. Steward for the *Handbook of South American Indians* and upon Joseph Greenberg's provisional linguistic classification. It shows the more important languages, but several limitations of such a map should be kept in mind.

First, the country was not completely occupied by an evenly distributed population, and the language groups were not bounded by clean lines. A detailed map based on adequate information would show blank areas, and, where languages interpenetrated one another or where peoples were bilingual, it would have overlapping shading.

Second, locations would be given with dates in each case, because white occupation set up a series of dislocations which often caused groups to move hundreds of miles before they were first encountered. In effect, the present map shows the whereabouts of the various social, linguistic, and cultural divisions when they were first known to Europeans. Some Indians of the upper Xingú River first became known only a half century ago, whereas those on the Brazilian coast were discovered some 400 years ago.

The linguistic map approximates aboriginal conditions. Today, many Indians have lost their native speech and adopted a European language —in continental South America, usually Spanish or Portuguese—or they are bilingual. In certain parts of South America, aboriginal languages have spread since the European conquest. Quechua, the language of the Central Andes, has replaced many aboriginal languages in the Montaña and upper Amazon to the east, owing partly to its use by

Linguistic Classification of South America

Legend

This classification follows the tentative scheme presented by Joseph Greenberg, to be published in the *Proceedings* of the 1956 International Congress of Americanists.

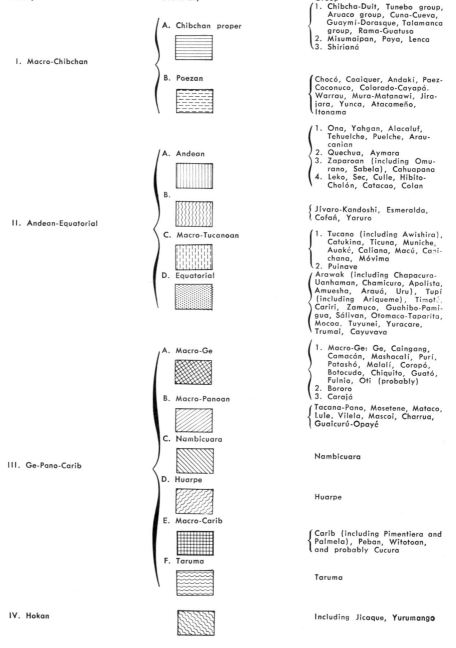

Family	Subfamily	Group
I. Macro-Chibchan	A. Chibchan proper	1. Chibcha-Duit, Tunebo group, Aruaco group, Cuna-Cueva, Guaymí-Dorasque, Talamanca group, Rama-Guatuso 2. Misumaipan, Paya, Lenca 3. Shirianá
	B. Paezan	Chocó, Coaiquer, Andakí, Paez-Coconuco, Colorado-Cayapá. Warrau, Mura-Matanawi, Jirajara, Yunca, Atacameño, Itonama
II. Andean-Equatorial	A. Andean	1. Ona, Yahgan, Alacaluf, Tehuelche, Puelche, Araucanian 2. Quechua, Aymara 3. Zaparoan (including Omurano, Sabela), Cahuapana 4. Leko, Sec, Culle, Hibito-Cholón, Catacao, Colan
	B.	Jívaro-Kandoshi, Esmeralda, Cofań, Yaruro
	C. Macro-Tucanoan	1. Tucano (including Awishira), Catukina, Ticuna, Muniche, Auaké, Caliana, Macú, Canichana, Móvima 2. Puinave
	D. Equatorial	Arawak (including Chapacura-Uanhaman, Chamicuro, Apolista, Amuesha, Arauá, Uru), Tupí (including Ariqueme), Timoté, Cariri, Zamuco, Guahibo-Pamigua, Sálivan, Otomaco-Taparita, Mocoa, Tuyunei, Yuracare, Trumai, Cayuvava
III. Ge-Pano-Carib	A. Macro-Ge	1. Macro-Ge: Ge, Caingang, Camacán, Mashacalí, Purí, Patashó, Malalí, Coropó, Botocudo, Chiquito, Guató, Fulnio, Oti (probably) 2. Bororo 3. Carajá
	B. Macro-Panoan	Tacana-Pano, Mosetene, Mataco, Lule, Vilela, Mascoi, Charrua, Guaicurú-Opayé
	C. Nambicuara	Nambicuara
	D. Huarpe	Huarpe
	E. Macro-Carib	Carib (including Pimentiera and Palmela), Peban, Witotoan, and probably Cucura
	F. Taruma	Taruma
IV. Hokan		Including Jicaque, Yurumango

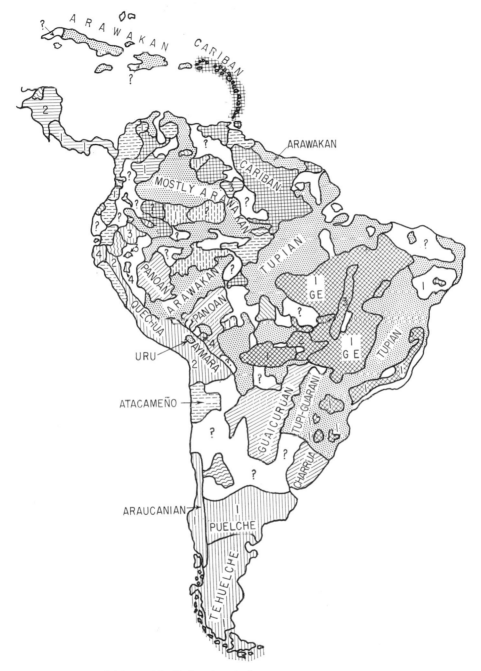

Major language divisions of South American Indians.

Spanish missionaries. A simplified form of Tupian has become the lingua franca in much of Amazonia.

Linguistic divisions. The ultimate linguistic division is the dialect. Among the more primitive societies, the dialect of each village or band was often slightly distinctive, although wholly intelligible to members of other villages or bands speaking the same language. Even dialects that were mutually unintelligible might nonetheless be fairly closely related. Despite the small amount of linguistic research in South America, the resemblance between certain dialects is sufficiently convincing to produce general agreement on many larger groups, some of the better known being Chibchan, of the northern Andes; Quechua and Aymara, of the Central Andes; Atacameño, Araucanian, Alacaluf, Chono, and Yahgan, of the southern Andes; Arawakan and Cariban, both found scattered from the Antilles through large portions of Amazonia; Tupian, of the Amazon and southern Brazil; Panoan, of the western and southwest Amazon; Ge, of the eastern Brazilian highlands; Guaycuruan, of the Gran Chaco; and Puelche and Tehuelche, of the pampas and Patagonia.

Proposals for the classification of many small groups with these larger divisions and the affiliation of these divisions with one another have, however, made most linguists hesitate. Most authorities have listed between sixty and one hundred major, unrelated language groups, and they have been reluctant to postulate larger groupings for two reasons. First, they have assumed that lexical resemblances—similarities in word forms and roots—have only limited value in establishing genetic relationships between languages. Inaccurate phonetic recording of words has made it difficult to identify basic forms, and it has been assumed that similarities might be merely superficial results of crude transcriptions. Moreover, many lexical similarities result from word borrowing between wholly unrelated languages; modern Peruvian Spanish, for example, has many Quechua words, and Brazilian Portuguese has drawn from Tupian dialects. Second, it was believed that genetic relationship between long-separated languages could be proved only by similarity of basic structure or morphology.

The history of language classification in South America somewhat parallels that of North America. The early Powell map of North American languages published by the Bureau of American Ethnology showed fifty-seven unrelated families. Subsequent research has demonstrated basic similarities between so many of these families that the total number of unrelated families has now been reduced to six. While this number is somewhat tentative, it is likely that it may be reduced further rather than increased. Moreover, it now seems probable that some of these six divisions are related to certain Asiatic languages, a matter formerly regarded with great skepticism.

Successive classifications of South American languages did little to decrease the large number of seemingly unrelated or unaffiliated families until Greenberg advanced his bold simplification, which presents a picture comparable to that of North America. While Greenberg's classification is provisional in certain respects, it is an expectable reduction of what was obviously a greatly excessive number of families. It is interesting, too, that this classification is based upon vocabularies rather than upon morphology, special importance being ascribed to commonly used and stable words such as personal pronouns.

The trend in South American linguistic classification is shown by the following data:[3]

Date	Authority	Number of families
1891	Daniel G. Brinton	60
1913	Alexander Chamberlain	84
1924	Paul Rivet	74
1926	Wilhelm Schmidt	no total
1935	Cestmir Loukotka	94
1950	J. Alden Mason	65 plus innumerable un- affiliated groups
1956	Joseph Greenberg	4 families, 13 subfamilies

South American linguistic classifications, unlike most of those of North America, have suffered from disagreement as to the affiliation of many languages. A given language may be classed in four or five different families by as many authorities. This has rather serious implications for cultural-historical reconstructions. For example, Arawakan, one of the most widespread languages, has been classed with Chibchan, the language predominant among the northern Andean chiefdoms, by some persons and with Quechua, the language of the Inca Empire, by others. Both classifications were related to an effort to prove that the Arawak originated, or at least spread, the basic ingredients of South American cultures. Mason, while classifying Arawakan as independent, believed it might be related to Cariban. Greenberg classifies Arawakan with Tupian and several other languages in the Equatorial subfamily of the Andean-Equatorial family, which includes Quechua, Aymara, Araucanian, Ona, and others along the Andes, but he places both Chibchan and Cariban in separate families.

A word should be said regarding the terminology of language divisions. Linguists have used the terms "family," "stock," "phylum," and "macro-group" for their major divisions. In the present volume, we have designated the major divisions as families, subdivisions of families as subfamilies, and subdivisions of these as groups. While the classification implies that the languages of groups are most closely related to one another, that members of subfamilies are less closely related, and that subfamilies are rather distantly related within families, the divisions are not necessarily comparable since a fixed quantity or degree of relationship can never be stated.

Language and culture. The distribution and affiliation of the South American languages have certain implications for culture history. It should be stressed, however, that there is no direct relationship between language groups and culture. Degree of cultural development has no connection with the type of linguistic structure, and there is no reason other than historical circumstance why people of a particular cultural type should speak certain languages. Vocabulary expectably reflects the complexity and nature of the culture—the kinds of phenomena of interest to the people, the cultural concepts, and the variety of things to be distinguished—but the vocabularies upon which Greenberg's classification is based involve words that are little affected by culture.

The principal value of linguistic classifications to cultural studies is that of supplying a basis for inferences concerning how long members of families, subfamilies, and groups have been separated from one another. When glottochronological studies of the kind being carried on by Morris Swadesh have been applied more generally to South American languages, we shall have reasonably good estimates of the number of centuries or even millennia since members of the groups separated. Meanwhile, the present classification gives some clues to the movement of people and to culture history.

In the Amazon-Orinoco area, most of the societies with a tropical-forest-village type of culture belong to a comparatively few, widely distributed, and fairly undifferentiated language groups—Cariban, Arawakan, Tupí-Guaraní, and Panoan. The homogeneity of these language groups and the comparative uniformity of their cultures suggest that the wide distribution of these people was brought about by fairly recent and rather rapid migrations. The case for the Tupí-Guaraní migrations is even supported by historical documents, as described in a subsequent chapter. Any linguistic and cultural predecessors of these major tropical-forest villagers either were absorbed or remain as fairly isolated small, atypical enclaves. The migrations seem to have been principally along the waterways, and the culture is essentially a farming and riparian one.

More nomadic hunters and gatherers survived in areas which were too swampy, mountainous, cold, or dry for the tropical-forest villagers —areas such as the Orinoco Delta, the upper Orinoco River, the plains of eastern Colombia, the divide between the Orinoco and Amazon Rivers, parts of the Ecuadorian, Peruvian, and Bolivian Montaña, Mato Grosso, and portions of eastern Brazil. The Tupí-Guaraní, Arawakan, and Cariban languages are not represented by major blocks of people in these peripheral areas. Instead, each of these areas contains a number of fairly small language groups, most of which were formerly considered to be linguistically isolated. While these groups are now classified by remote affiliations with the larger families, they seem to represent early migrants who became linguistically and culturally isolated in the hinterlands.

Many of these small groups belong to several larger subfamilies or families. Within a fairly small area of southern Venezuela on the Orinoco-Amazon watershed are the Calianans, Macuans, and Auakeans of the Macro-Tucanoan subfamily of the Andean-Equatorial family, and the Shirianá of the Macro-Chibchan family. Along the upper Orinoco River are the Sáliva, Guahibo, Otomaco, and Taparita, representing the Equatorial subfamily of the Andean-Equatorial family, the Yaruro and Puinave of the Macro-Tucanoan subfamily, and members of other subfamilies. In the northwest Amazon of eastern Ecuador and southeast Colombia are the Witoto of the Macro-Carib subfamily of the Ge-Pano-Carib family; the Záparo of the Andean subfamily of the Andean-Equatorial family; the Panoans of the Macro-Panoan subfamilies; and others.

Eastern or silvan Bolivia has, in addition, a number of small linguistic groups: Itonaman, Canichanan, Cayuvavan, Móviman, Mosetenean, Lecan, Yuracarean, Chapacuran, and Mascoian, whose larger affiliations are very diversified. A considerable cultural diversity also characterizes this area, but the language groups just mentioned were doubtless predecessors of the culturally more developed Arawakan-speaking Mojo, Bauré, Saraveca, and Paressí and the Chiquitoan-speaking people. In eastern Bolivia also are the Nambicuara, Bororo, and Guató, who represent different subfamilies of the Ge-Pano-Carib family.

The highlands of eastern Brazil are exceptional among the peoples with simpler cultures in that the principal language is Ge of the Ge-Pano-Carib family. East of the Ge, on and near the coast, were a number of simple groups, now largely extinct, who spoke several languages closely related to Ge: Mashacalí, Purí, Patashó, Coroado, Fulnio, and others.

While linguistic diversity was greatest among the simpler societies in the general area surrounding the Amazon Basin, there was a remote relationship of most of these languages to those spoken by more developed societies. For example, Macro-Chibchan languages were spoken not only among most chiefdoms of the northern Andes but by such simple Amazonian canoemen and farmers as the Mura and by the hunting-and-gathering Warrau of the Orinoco Delta. Since the Warrau, however, are culturally anomalous among hunters and gatherers in having a priest-temple-idol cult, which is a characteristic of certain chiefdoms, it is interesting to speculate whether their membership in the Páezan subfamily of Macro-Chibchan, which is represented in Andean Ecuador and northern Venezuela, indicates an eastward migration from the northern Andes where the temple cult was strongly developed. Perhaps glottochronology will help solve this particular problem. But there are limitations to linguistic aids to historical reconstructions, as is exemplified by the Mura, who show no trace of Andean culture and, indeed, lack many tropical-forest features.

A more cogent example of the disparity between linguistic and cultural classification is the distribution of the Andean subfamily of the Andean-Equatorial family. This subfamily was spread from the Peruvian highlands, which had the most developed culture in South America, to the simpler Araucanian farmers of Chile and the sea-food gathering Alacaluf, Chono, and Yahgan of the south Chilean archipelago. The most one can say of this distribution is that the Andean subfamily is presumably more recently differentiated from the Andean-Equatorial family than its other subfamilies and that it tended to remain in the highlands and along the Pacific Coast. If true, this would suggest that the archipelagic peoples are fairly recent arrivals in the far south—at least, that they differentiated from the Quechua after the tropical-forest Arawak and Tupí and the Ecuadorian Esmeralda had split off—even though their historic cultures show considerable continuity with the early archaeology of the region and differ completely from the culture of the Central Andes.

But these are largely speculative observations. One could also guess the possible significance of the affiliation of the Yurumango (Yurumangui) of the southern Colombia coast with the widespread North American Hokan family. By and large, however, it is the closer language relationships, those that imply fairly recent separation of peoples, that are now most helpful in reconstructing culture history. Such cases are the migrations of the Tupí-Guaraní, previously mentioned, or of the Arawak, who, by the evidence of archaeology and history as well as language, migrated fairly recently to the Greater Antilles.

In a limited and cautious way, one may also relate language to political development. In modern times, the Spanish, Portuguese, English, Dutch, and French languages have been imposed upon the native peoples. In aborignal times, political domination also carried a certain degree of linguistic domination. According to Inca tradition, there were some ninety local languages or dialects—we have no idea of their classificatory significance—before the imperial conquest, but, with the exception of Yunca-Puruhan of the north coast, where the Chimu Kingdom had existed, and Ayamara of highland Bolivia, most of these languages seem to have been superseded by Quechua at the Spanish Conquest. The Quechua language had even extended into the northern frontier of the empire in Ecuador and Colombia, and into northern Chile. In both cases, the people had become bilingual.

No Chibchan language became so widely dominant in the northern Andes as Quechua in the Central Andes; for there were no empires in the northern Andes that forced their national institutions, including speech, upon the common or local peoples.

These linguistic inferences may even corroborate seeming implications of archaeology in the Central Andes. A later chapter discusses how a Tiahuanaco style of art, architecture, and artifacts, originating about A.D. 1000, probably at Lake Titicaca in the Bolivian highlands, became superimposed on local artistic and religious styles throughout the Central Andes, suggesting some kind of centralized control of the entire area. But these widespread stylistic features did not last very long, and local styles regained their vigor before the later Inca conquest. Meanwhile the local languages or dialects seem to have persisted under the Tiahuanaco regime. It was not until the Quechua-speaking Inca, a group at first living in the region of Cuzco, began their conquest that linguistic uniformity approached the political and cultural uniformity imposed by the empire. Quechua, which was originally spoken by only a half dozen small states near Cuzco, was forced, along with Inca political controls, on all the native people from Ecuador to northern Chile.

That local languages or dialects survived the Tiahuanaco Empire, if this was an empire, surely indicates that the Tiahuanaco rulers achieved no domination of the local states comparable to that of the Inca. By the same reasoning, the linguistic diversity among the chiefdoms of the Circum-Caribbean area suggests that these people never had such large and enduring political entities as the Central Andes.

Relations of South American languages to those of other areas. It would seem expectable that some South American languages should show relationships to those of North America. At present, however, evidence of close ties is limited. Jicaquean, of Nicaragua, and Yurumango (Yurumangui), of the southern Colombia coast, are members of the widespread North American Hokan-Souian family. Scattered through Central America are a number of very small enclaves of Uto-Aztecan, one of the principal North American families. These included Nahuatl, which was probably introduced by fairly early migrants from Mexico, and Aztec, which was evidently brought in by traders.

Since the discovery of the New World, there have been many claims that American Indian languages are related to certain ones of the Old World. Except for the North American–Asiatic connections previously mentioned, few of these claims merit mention. One serious scholar, however, has postulated that Hokan-Souian is related to Malayo-Polynesian of the Pacific and that Chon (Tehuelche-Ona) is related to Australian. These relationships have not been accepted by linguists, and they do not accord with cultural-historical facts. Hokan-Souian is obviously much older in America than the settlement of Polynesia, which was accomplished by canoe voyages less than 2,000 years ago, and it is not imaginable that the Australians could have crossed the Pacific at any time, let alone many thousands of years ago when the Andean-Equatorial family, of which Tehuelche and Ona are members, began to differentiate.

Isolated canoes of Polynesians may have reached American shores and introduced a few elements of culture. They did not, however, implant their language anywhere.

NOTES

1. Julian H. Steward (ed.), *Irrigation Civilizations: A Comparative Study,* Social Science Monographs, Pan American Union, Washington, 1955.
2. Joseph Greenberg, "Tentative Linguistic Classification of Central and South America." A paper presented to the International Congress of Americanists at Philadelphia in September, 1956, to be published in the *Proceedings* of the Congress. While provisional and subject to some modification, this general classification can be accepted with reasonable confidence.
3. The South American Indian classifications of these and other persons are discussed in the *Handbook,* vol. 6, by J. Alden Mason.

two

FOUNDATIONS OF
NEW WORLD CULTURES

1. THE ANTIQUITY OF THE AMERICAN INDIAN

Mankind entered the New World as a fully evolved variety of Homo sapiens, equipped with the mental and physical capacity to carry out any kind of cultural activity. The hypothesis that mankind evolved from the higher primates in the Western Hemisphere has never been taken seriously, for there is neither zoological nor paleontological evidence that such primates ever existed in America. The New World monkeys are of a fairly low order of primates, and there are no authenticated remains of lower types of mankind. The question of when mankind first inhabited America is, however, open to some difference of opinion.

At one time, before any substantial amount of scientific archaeology had been done, it was thought that man was comparatively recent in the New World. An antiquity of 5,000 years seemed certain; but 10,000 was considered excessive. More recent finds have shown that human remains were associated with extinct species of animals and with geological remains which belong to the late phases of the last Ice Age, that is, at the close of the Pleistocene period. Some human remains may date from the last interglacial period. This period antedates by many thousands of years the earliest inscribed Mayan monuments, which provide a fairly exact chronology for associated archaeological remains. Until recently the only method of establishing their age was by geological techniques. It was considered that the last Ice Age ended some 10,000 to 20,000 years ago and that the interglacial period may have occurred 50,000 years ago.

A new dating technique has been made available to archaeology as the result of studies in atomic physics. It has been found that living organisms contain a certain amount of radioactive carbon, which has an atomic weight of 14, and hence is called radiocarbon or carbon 14. If, upon death, the organism becomes buried and protected against cosmic rays, this type of carbon is not replenished, and the radioactivity decreases at a known rate. Measurement of the radioactivity of such archaeological specimens as bones, plant remains, wood, charcoal, and other objects made of plant or animal materials indicates within a margin of error of perhaps 5 or 10 per cent—a small error as compared with that of earlier methods of dating—the time of death of the organism from which the specimen came. This technique has by no means replaced previous guess dates, but it has shown that some guesses were too early and some were too late,[1] and it has put the dating of remains which are no more than 10,000 or 20,000 years old on an unexpectedly sound basis.

In North America, where the greater part of research on early man in the New World has been carried out, the oldest dates established by radiocarbon for late Pleistocene man are surprisingly recent, few being earlier than 9000 B.C. There are probably older human remains, and the question of whether man was in America in interglacial times is still unsettled. The search for ancient man in South America has yielded only sporadic finds. The geological technique of dating these finds by association with Pleistocene remains is precluded by the absence of glacial evidence, except in the extreme south, but in several instances human bones or man-made artifacts have been found in association with giant mammals which belonged to the Pleistocene fauna and became extinct after this period. One of the most interesting finds is that of human bones and cultural remains associated with the extinct giant ground sloth in Palli Aike Cave in southern Chile. This find by Junius Bird has been dated by radiocarbon at about 6690 B.C. Another site yielded human and sloth remains, seemingly contemporary, from 8880 B.C. These are approximately the same dates that are assigned the cultural materials that were associated with sloth remains in Gypsum Cave, Nevada, a desert site which had previously been dated geologically as belonging to the closing phases of the Pleistocene.

This evidence shows beyond doubt that South America was inhabited by Indians at least 10,000 years ago, and future discoveries may extend the antiquity. Ten thousand years, however, seems ample time for the South American Indians to have developed the remarkable culture which culminated in the civilization of the Inca and their Andean predecessors. Previous reckoning, which placed the beginnings of Andean, and South American, agriculture at about the time of Christ, seemed to allow too little time; the developmental picture was too cramped. Such reckoning was based on a rough comparison of Andean and Mayan periods, the latter being dated fairly exactly through inscribed stone monuments. These monuments, however, represent a comparatively late and sophisticated culture. The undated and possibly long developmental beginnings of the Mexican and Andean high cultures could only be guess-dated. Radiocarbon has now provided dates which fit most of the evidence rather comfortably. The lowest levels of Huaca Prieta, a mound over 40 feet deep on the north coast of Peru, which contains stratified pre-Ceramic remains of an agricultural people, has a radiocarbon date of about 2300 B.C. The fairly developed farming culture known as Cupisnique flourished at about 870 B.C., and other well-developed cultures, such as Paracas and Nazca A, belong in the first half millennium before Christ.

It is clear, therefore, that South America was inhabited by man at least 10,000 years ago. This is not to say that all of it was inhabited nor that any part was at first very densely populated. In the preagricultural periods, there must have been comparatively small numbers of hunting-and-gathering peoples who occupied the more favorable regions. At present, the culture of these people is known only through sporadic finds—the Chilean remains belonging to the sloth period, finds in Ecuador of man possibly associated with mastodons, the remains at Lagoa Santa, in Brazil, where man and several extinct species were contemporaneous. Upon the basis of this early and simple hunting-and-gathering culture were built the different farming cultures of later periods. We now turn to the problem of the origins of South American cultures.

2. THE ORIGINAL HERITAGE

The pre-Columbian inhabitants of America came from Asia, and it is fairly certain that the original migrations crossed from Siberia by way of Bering Strait, which was a land bridge during the several periods of Pleistocene glaciation. At the time of the first migrations, the Old World already had a cultural history of perhaps half a million years. The migrations to North America began no less than 10,000 years ago, when the Old World was nearing the end of the Paleolithic hunting-and-gathering cultures but no less than 2,000 years before farming began in the Near East. It is out of the question that farming was known to the first immigrants or that, had it been known, it could have survived the slow movement through the far north to be resumed thousands of years later in the more favorable climate of lower latitudes. Radiocarbon dates place the first farmers of the Near East at 7,000–8,000 B.C. These migrations were probably a slow infiltration, extending over hundreds of years, not a steady, purposeful march toward a known destination.

The eastern Asiatic Paleolithic cultures of 10,000 B.C. are little known, except that some of the simple though important technological inventions had been made. The first Americans undoubtedly knew how to make fire, to manufacture knives, scrapers, and projectile points of chipped flint, to make projectiles or spears tipped with a stone point, and probably to use skin robes for clothing. This list of cultural traits is very small and obviously does not fairly represent what the original American culture was like, but it would be hazardous to reconstruct more from the simple archaeological remains left by these people. The sloth-period remains of Chile afford little more evidence of the general nature of the culture, though they do have distinctive forms of worked flints and other objects.

Some anthropologists have attempted to reconstruct the earliest, or "archaic," American culture through the "age-area" method of comparing the cultures of the more recent marginal, or peripheral, hunting-and-gathering tribes, which, at the time of the discovery of America, survived in the far north and the far south. These people were undoubtedly somewhat similar to the first immigrants in the simplicity of their lives, in the predominance of kinship bonds in their social relations, and in a religion based on shamanism, birth, puberty, and death rites, and belief in magic, but they cannot be taken as living fossils of an earlier era. They had many technological skills, such as the bow and arrow, basketry, and other devices, which represent fairly late inventions, and their sociopolitical organization had distinctive patterns that resulted from adaptations to their different environments.

Of the original cultural heritage of South American Indians, therefore, we can say little. The early cultures of Chile and elsewhere will be described in subsequent sections. By far the greater part of the content of South American cultures consisted of inventions, practices, and beliefs that appeared long after the original migrations. Much of this content is clearly indigenous, but so many basic features and trends are strikingly similar to those of the Old World that the question of transoceanic influence has presented a constant challenge to Americanists.

3. TRANSOCEANIC INFLUENCES

After the original migrations from Siberia to America, communication with Asia was not entirely cut off, but most Asiatic influence did not penetrate far beyond the extreme northwest of North America. No one seriously believes that any of the features of the American agricultural civilizations could have diffused from Asia via Bering Strait.

The question of transoceanic influence on the New World, however, has been the subject of lively controversy for many years, and recent finds of many quite detailed cultural similarities between the hemispheres have reopened the question. Disputants marshal their arguments in support of three extreme positions. First, most North American anthropologists have held that New World cultural developments subsequent to the original migrations were almost entirely autochthonous and that contributions from the Eastern Hemisphere were negligible. Second, a number of Europeans, some Latin Americans, and a few dissenters within the ranks of the North Americans believe that the similarities in the cultural development of the two hemispheres are too great to have been achieved independently, and they postulate that oceanic voyages of one sort or another introduced the basic features of Old World civilizations to the New World. They generally claim that these voyages originated in Southeast Asia, Melanesia, or Polynesia, rather than in Africa or Europe, for it is these former areas which most closely resemble America. No one has found any evidence to support the contention that Africa or Europe were the sources of American culture, and even Gladwin,[2] who attributes American high civilizations to the sailors of Alexander the Great, claims that after Alexander's death his fleet sailed eastward, via India, Malaya, Melanesia, and Polynesia. The third position reverses the second and holds that civilizations originated in America and that features of it were transmitted westward, across the Pacific, to Asia. Because of the demonstrable chronological priority of Old World civilizations, few scientists consider this possibility worth serious attention, although it contains a sufficient grain of truth to have warranted a comprehensive presentation of the evidence in its favor in a recent issue of a scientific journal.[3] When, after World War II, a group of Norwegians made the east to west trip from Ecuador to the Tuamotu Archipelago in an aboriginal-type balsa raft,[4] public interest in this theory was renewed.

These discrepant interpretations of the contribution of the Old World to the cultural development of native America have great importance to an interpretation of the origin of South American cultures and of cultural development generally. The great majority of features alleged to have an Asiatic or Oceanic provenience are found in South America, some of them in the Andes, especially in Peru, and others in the northern and western portions of the tropical forests. Conclusions about these features, however, depend more upon theoretical point of view than upon fact, although certain new evidence has come to light in recent years which has forced the most intransigent supporters of American cultural independence to concede that at least some influence probably reached the New World from across the Pacific. The theoretical assumptions which enable different persons to attach conflicting meaning to the same evidence will be considered briefly.

A century ago, before anthropology had developed a coherent method and theory or made a systematic collection of facts, the similarity of many Indian customs to Old World practices was the subject of much comment and speculation. The usual explanation was that some Old World group had migrated to America, and many persons identified this group as the ten lost tribes of Israel. In time, there were devised many other popular, pseudoscientific explanations, including postulated lost continents, which were supposed to have been the cradle of all world civilizations—Atlantis in the Atlantic Ocean and Mu in the Pacific. The important thing about these claims is that all assumed that actual migrations of people must account for cultural similarities in different parts of the world.

During the latter half of the nineteenth century, when anthropology began to develop scientific concepts and methods, it was shown that migrations were not necessary to explain the spread or diffusion of culture. Migrations do, of course, occur, but one group may come to resemble another because it has borrowed or imitated the other's culture. A study of the cultures of the New World showed that a very large number of items, such as the bow and arrow, house types, ceramics, domesticated plants, and social and religious practices had attained a very widespread distribution, which could be explained best by tribe to tribe diffusion. Diffusion, in fact, became so important an explanation that the first decades of the present century found American anthropologists devoting considerable effort to plotting the distribution of various cultural features in order to ascertain the probable center of origin and the direction and extent of diffusion of each.

Americanists gradually attained virtual unanimity in the assumption that native America represented a cultural unit as compared with other world areas. Some Indians, like those of Meso-America and the Andes, had far outstripped the others in their cultural growth, but all had built on a common basis, which consisted of features that had spread widely within the hemisphere after man settled America. Features which distinguished more restricted areas were simply interpreted as later inventions, which had not had time to spread or which environmental and local cultural factors would not permit to spread. The Stone Age cultural heritage of the original migrants from Siberia was replaced, modified, or heavily overlaid by distinctively American traits. It survived principally among some of the marginal, or culturally backward, nomadic hunting-and-gathering societies in peripheral and isolated spots.

Both diffusion and migrations were ruled out as explanations of similarities between the Old and New Worlds, because the oceanic barriers were assumed to have prohibited contacts or movements of people during the time when American civilizations were already fairly well developed in the millennium before Christ. In fact, radiocarbon dates place the earliest Peruvian agriculture at over 2300 B.C. The Polynesian migrations, to judge by genealogies and migration legends, however, had not begun at this time, and the chance that voyagers from the Asiatic mainland could have reached America early enough to contribute to the basic civilization seems remote indeed.

The improbability that any Old World peoples undertook to make or could make transoceanic voyages as early as 2000 B.C. is still the greatest obstacle to attributing important American cultural features to an Asiatic source. But certain protagonists of transoceanic influence have kept the controversy alive, and it now appears that some features might have been brought across the ocean. This is not to say that a case has been made for the wholesale importation of Asiatic culture to America. While it follows that if one vessel could cross the Pacific many could do it, American archaeology shows that there was no single period when massive cultural influence suggesting a migration reached America. Instead, the various cultural elements common to South America and Asia first appeared in South America at different periods. It is as if stray boatloads of Oceanic or Asiatic people arrived intermittently at intervals of fifty or one hundred years. We shall first review the list of features of possible Old World origin and then discuss their significance to the development of American cultures. The features include cultural practices and botanical species.

The culture elements are much more difficult to assess than the plants, because the question of what constitutes similarity is open to difference of opinion. The blowgun of Malaysia and South America is a fairly well-defined object, consisting of identical parts and used in about the same way. Can the same be said of the Greek scroll, metallurgy in copper, a clan organization, or the general idea of plant domestication? Father W. Schmidt, a German anthropologist, formulated quantitative and qualitative criteria for measuring similarities: the cultural feature must consist of a sufficient number of unique parts to be considered identical. But having decided that identity exists, the question of mankind's inventive ability remains unanswered. The extreme diffusionists, such as G. Elliot Smith, W. J. Perry, and H. S. Gladwin believe that most basic inventions, such as pottery, weaving, metallurgy, farming, and the like, involve a series of technological processes which are so difficult to imagine at a time when they are wholly unknown that it is remarkable that they were invented at all and virtually out of the question that they should have been independently invented twice or more. In the opinion of most Americanists, who hold the line for American cultural independence, these basic inventions were made twice, once in the Old World and again in America, but probably not a third time. They tend to attribute similarities within each hemisphere to diffusion from a single source or invention.

The identity of domesticated plants is somewhat less a question of subjective judgment, although it is subject to uncertainty. Plant taxonomy is based on the identification of genetic characteristics in each species or variety, characteristics which are thought not to reproduce themselves independently in different places. If it can be shown that a plant of the Old and New Worlds belongs to the same variety or species, there is presumed to be no question that, wherever found, the plant was derived from a single origin. The only question is when and how it spread.

The anthropologist, however, may believe with some justification that quantitative and qualitative criteria apply to plants no less than to culture and that the question of independent evolution versus genetic derivation from a common ancestor allows considerable latitude for subjective judgment. Recently, a distinguished geographer and a botanist argued whether the New World *Canavalia* bean was derived from the Old World. The crux of the matter was the significance of the relative lengths of a small ridge along one edge of the bean. Since other characteristics were virtually identical, the geographer argued that the few millimeters difference in the ridge did not matter and that therefore the New World variety must have been derived from the Old World. The botanist ascribed such importance to this small difference that he concluded that the New World bean was domesticated independently and in no way derived from the Old World.

The *Canavalia* bean, however, is an exception. The genetic relationship between most plants has been established with reasonable certainty.

The evidence of domesticated plants

There are several domesticated plants which appear to have been used by the peoples of Southeast Asia and certain islands of the Pacific and by American Indians prior to the voyages of Columbus. The case for the pre-Columbian, interhemisphere distribution of cotton and bottle gourds is fairly strong but that for sweet potatoes is less so. A much weaker case has been made for maize, coconuts, and certain beans. When the techniques of plant genetics have been more extensively used, perhaps other food plants can be added to this list.

The probable explanation of the distribution of these plants is that human beings carried them from one place to another. It is possible, of course, that some were spread by natural means, such as ocean currents or birds, but such an assumption is a last resort of antidiffusionists. Coconuts, for instance, might have been carried by ocean currents, washed ashore, and then grown, but to judge by the experience of the Norwegians, who carried coconuts on their raft, the plants would have sprouted before reaching land. Most domesticated plants, however, are highly dependent upon man. Their seeds must be carefully preserved, they must be planted in suitable soils and climates, they must be properly cultivated, and the crop must be harvested, stored, and prepared as food in particular ways. Some of the plants are propagated by means of shoots. Often they are known by very similar names.

The bottle gourd (*Lagenaria siceraria*) is a native of the Old World, where it had a wide distribution and respectable antiquity, being known in China in the fifth or sixth century B.C. It has been found in many pre-Columbian archaeological sites in America, including a Peruvian site, Huaca Prieta, which belongs to the very beginning of the Era of Incipient Agriculture. At Huaca Prieta, it was dated at 2307 B.C. by carbon 14, and thus it has become one of the earliest known plant domesticates in America. Since there is considerable doubt that man could have navigated across the Pacific at this time, some persons assume that the gourd was carried by ocean currents. This explanation, however, becomes less likely if the case for cotton is accepted.

Cotton (*Gossypium* sp.) has a somewhat complicated history. The Old World wild and domesticated species have 13 large chromosomes; American wild species have 13 small chromosomes; and American cultivated and Hawaiian wild species have 13 large and 13 small chromosomes, a total of 26 chromosomes. The 26-chromosome American domesticate is almost certainly a cross between the Old World domesticated cotton and the New World wild form. The simplest historical interpretation is that 13-chromosome cotton was first domesticated in the Old World, where it appeared during the Bronze Age and spread very widely. The domesticate was introduced to the New World, where it crossed with the 13-chromosome wild variety, producing the 26-chromosome domesticate. The latter type occurs in the lowest levels of the Peruvian site just mentioned, along with the gourd. In America, it spread widely and became differentiated into various species and varieties. Meanwhile, it also spread to certain islands of the Pacific, where its cultivation was abandoned for some undisclosed reason, and it became the 26-chromosome Polynesian wild cotton. It is presumed that human beings must have spread these varieties of cotton, for seeds could scarcely have been carried by natural means. Moreover, the early co-occurrence of cotton and gourds in Peru strengthens the case for both.

The sweet potato (*Ipomea batatas*) is clearly a native American domesticate, but it was also cultivated in Melanesia and Polynesia according to some of the earliest historical accounts of those islands.

It is possible that it was carried to the Pacific by whites after the voyages of Columbus, but legends of the Maori of New Zealand attribute it considerable antiquity in their culture, possibly as early as A.D. 1000. The evidence for the sweet potato, in contrast to cotton and the gourd, suggests travel from east to west.

The yam (*Dioscorea alata*) has been cultivated in Southeast Asia since the time of Christ, and it spread to Melanesia and Polynesia as a staple crop. Apparently it was one of the root crops which were found and described in the West Indies early in the sixteenth century. This evidence is certainly far from conclusive, but certain species of *Dioscorea* are widely cultivated among the tropical-forest tribes of South America. When this plant is better understood distributionally, historically, and genetically, its significance will be clearer.

Maize (*Zea mays*) presents the most complicated case of all. Long considered the typical native American crop, which was supposed to represent a domesticated form of teocintli or teosinte, a wild plant of Mexico, it is now known through new archaeological evidence and genetic studies that its history is exceedingly complex. Teocintli (*Euchlaena*) is now recognized to be merely a cross between a domesticated pod corn and a wild American species, *Tripsacum*. Although pod corn was not found in the lower levels of the previously mentioned Peruvian site, there are several surprisingly early dates for it elsewhere. Pod corn found in Bat Cave, New Mexico, was grown in 1000 B.C., radiocarbon shows, and it was probably known by at least 4000 B.C. At Perra Cave, Tamaulipas, radiocarbon proves an antiquity to 2500 B.C. for this grain. Fossil maize pollen has been found in drillings 200 feet under Mexico City. While an antiquity of 60,000 years, which has been claimed for this pollen, is impossibly great, existence of this evidence supports the contention that maize or its ancestors are indigenous to America.[5] It is true that the wild ancestor of the pod corn has not yet been located in America, and that in Southeast Asia there are several genera which are related to pod corn. But the argument for an Asiatic origin of maize becomes weaker as each new archaeological find shows its great antiquity in America.

Several other plants which appear to have occurred both in islands of the Pacific and in America before the time of Columbus include hibiscus and a number of common weeds. Inconclusive in themselves, they simply add to the bulk of evidence interpreted to indicate that trans-Pacific voyages did take place.

The difficulty in accepting the theory of trans-Pacific voyages is that they are not mentioned in any written history or in Oceanic oral history, despite the extraordinary detail of the Polynesian migration legends which describe events back to A.D. 500 or 1000. It is not unlikely that individual boatloads of Polynesians did reach America. We know that they reached Easter Island, only 2,000 miles off the coast of South America. The plants which genetic evidence most strongly suggests to have been transmitted across the Pacific, however, appear in both hemispheres by 2000 B.C., long before the Polynesian migrations.

If we accept the evidence in favor of diffusion, we must conclude that, impossible as it seems, man somehow crossed the Pacific before 2000 B.C., bringing domesticated cotton and gourds and possibly an ancestor of maize from Asia. Much later, he brought yams and on return voyages took the new hybrid cotton, sweet potatoes, hibiscus, and perhaps several weeds to Polynesia. It should be stressed that his failure to transmit other domesticated plants and animals from Asia is not explained. He did not bring rice, sorghum, wheat, sugar cane, chickens, or pigs to America, although the last two were common to Polynesia, and he did not take squash, beans, maize, tomatoes, potatoes, quinoa, or any of the large number of other native American domesticates to the Old World.

The cultural evidence

The interpretation of cultural similarities between peoples of the Old and New Worlds has not claimed a scientific methodology which has the rigor of biological genetics; and yet, as we have seen, perhaps it is not really a great deal more subjective. There are a number of cultural elements so strikingly alike in the two hemispheres that the possibility of their transoceanic spread to America must be seriously considered. These features have been discussed at length by Roland Dixon,[6] and we shall mention here only some of the more notable ones.

The blowgun is a weapon which kills by injecting a small amount of a powerful poison into its victims, and it would be nearly useless without the poison. In Southeast Asia and the northwest Amazon, the blowgun consists of a long tube constructed of two half tubes carefully worked and fitted inside a larger, covering tube or sheath. The missile is a slender dart 8 or 10 inches long, its tip coated with poison and its butt wrapped with lint to fit snugly in the bore of the gun. A slight expulsion of breath propels the dart with considerable accuracy up to 100 feet. The slightest wound is generally fatal to the victim.

There is no way of knowing for certain whether so remarkable a weapon was independently invented twice. Stirling reviewed early Spanish sources and found, interestingly, that, while the blowgun was probably native to eastern Ecuador, it seemed to have spread rapidly during historic times to other parts of the tropical forests.[7] The blowgun —or perhaps a tube for shooting pellets rather than darts—is also known from the Mochica culture, circa 200 B.C. to A.D. 450, of Peru. The pre-

Columbian occurrence of the blowgun in South America does not, of course, prove that it was invented in the area. It may have been introduced by some unknown migrants from Asia, a possibility that is strengthened by the occurrence of a number of other Oceanic and Asiatic traits in the same general area as the blowgun.

These other elements, none conclusive in itself, simply provide cumulative evidence of historical connections of some kind. Some of the elements are fairly specific, such as the penis cover, the chewing of lime or ashes with a narcotic, and the Panpipes. The last appeared in Peru between 500 and 200 B.C. Von Hornboestel showed that the scale of certain Panpipes from Oceania and from South America was identical. Moreover, in Southeast Asia and South America they were often played in joined, complementary pairs. In evaluating this evidence, it must be recognized that the music of these peoples was probably not so sophisticated that they used a standardized scale. In a large collection of specimens, a few might readily be identical in scale through pure chance.

Bark cloth, which is made by pounding together thin layers of bark, is another feature shared by the northwest Amazon and Oceania. In South America, however, it was known by 2000 to 3000 B.C., and probably antedates the settlement of the Pacific; for pieces of bark cloth have been found in the lowest levels of Huaca Prieta in Peru, where they date from the third millennium B.C., while stone bark-cloth pounders are found in the earliest periods of Central America.

Oceania and South America have other similar features, but they do not seem so distinctive as to suggest the strong possibility of diffusion. The pole-and-thatch house, dugout canoe, slash-and-burn farming, and other technological traits are perhaps inventions that any sedentary tropical-forest people would make.

There are a great many more typically Andean traits which also have parallels in Asia. These include such specific items as star-headed war clubs (between 200 B.C. and A.D. 450) fishhooks of special shapes, tie-dyed cloth (A.D. 1000), litters (by A.D. 500), and umbrellas (Inca period). They also include more generalized features, such as irrigation farming, ceramics, coiled and twilled basketry, metallurgy, mound construction, and terraced farm lands.

It is impossible at present to provide a definitive answer to the question of how much influence Asia exerted upon South American cultures. Isolated similarities might be explained away as parallel developments, but it seems unlikely that the rather imposing list of botanical and cultural similarities does not show some kind of transoceanic influence. It should be noted, however, that we are dealing here with culture elements, not with basic cultural patterns. A fairly strong case can be made for the Oceanic or Asiatic origin of a considerable number of culture elements, but this proves nothing whatever about the origin of the various American culture types or patterns.

Each New World pattern represents the adaptation of cultural elements, especially of the exploitative technology, to a specialized environment. The density and distribution of the population over the land, the specific forms of cooperation between individuals, and the political and religious controls are all functionally related to land use. It is conceivable that the entire technology and, in fact, a preponderance of cultural traits might have been derived from Asia; and yet the social and political forms would still have to develop locally as the population increased and evolved new types of interpersonal arrangements. These could not be imported unless there were mass migrations of peoples who already had such patterns, but mass migrations are entirely out of the question. New World archaeology shows a steady development from small villages through more complex social forms that can only have been indigenous. That the native upper classes adopted litters, stools, or umbrellas as insignia of status, that certain art motifs found local appeal, that specific religious concepts were accepted, and that technological processes were found useful is quite understandable. Such traits diffused within the New World, and very likely some may have found their way across the Pacific. But they did not create the basic patterns. They constituted no more than superficial embellishments.

NOTES

1. W. F. Libby, *Radiocarbon Dating*, 2d ed., University of Chicago Press, Chicago, 1955. *Radiocarbon Dating: A Report on the Program to Aid in the Development of the Method of Dating*, assembled by Frederick Johnson, Society for American Archaeology Memoir 8, 1951.
2. Harold S. Gladwin, *Men Out of Asia*, McGraw-Hill Book Company, Inc., New York, 1947.
3. Gilbert N. Lewis, "The Beginning of Civilization in America," *American Anthropologist*, vol. 49, pp. 1–24, 1947.
4. Thor Hyerdahl, *Kon-Tiki*, Rand McNally & Company, Chicago, 1950.
5. Paul C. Mangelsdorf, "New Evidence on the Origin and Ancestry of Maize," *American Antiquity*, vol. 9, pp. 109–110, 1954. Herbert Dick, "The Bat Cave Pod Corn Complex: A Note on Its Distribution and Archaeological Significance," *El Palacio*, vol. 61, pp. 138–144, 1954.
6. Roland B. Dixon, *The Building of Cultures*, New York, London, 1928.
7. Matthew Williams Stirling, *Historical and Ethnographic Material on the Jívaro Indians*, Bureau of American Ethnology Bulletin 117, 1938.

three

ENVIRONMENT, PRODUCTION, AND CULTURE

1. ENVIRONMENT AND SUBSISTENCE

There is considerable correspondence in South America between environment and cultural types. The Central Andean coastal desert and high, moist mountain massif were the seat of the great irrigation civilizations. The warm tropical and subtropical areas that are covered by rain forests correspond to an extraordinary degree with the distribution of village slash-and-burn farmers. In the varied environment of the broken highlands of the northern Andes, Central America, Venezuela, and the Greater Antilles, chiefdoms, farm villages, and nomadic hunters and gatherers were all found within small areas, although chiefdoms predominated. In the southern Andes, where deserts and scrub steppes limited farming to small oases and streams, only small-scale irrigation and pastoral villages occurred.

Farther south, environmental factors prevented farming entirely. The sodding grasses of the pampas could not be turned with digging sticks. The scrub steppes which extend along the eastern flank of the Andes from the Gran Chaco of Paraguay south into Patagonia were too arid. And the wet, cold beech-conifer forests of the Chilean archipelago—the tundra of the far south—completely prohibited farming.

Wild animal resources

The Chilean archipelago south of the island of Chiloé, which is the southern limit of farming, is predominantly an area of wild food collecting. The main resources are such shellfish as limpets, *Fissurella*, mussels,

HIGHLAND FARMING,
SMALL-SCALE IRRIGATION

RIVER HUNTING, FISHING

SLASH-AND-BURN TROPICAL
FOREST FARMING—FISH
IMPORTANT ON MAIN RIVERS—
WILD GAME INCLUDES
DEER, PECCARIES
ARMADILLOS, MONKEYS

GALLERY-FOREST FARMERS

WILD FOOD (PALM) COLLECTORS
AND FARMERS

INTENSIVE
IRRIGATION
FARMING

SMALL-SCALE
IRRIGATION FARMERS
AND PASTORALISTS

SLASH-AND-
BURN FARMERS

XEROPHYTIC
SEED COLLECTORS

RHEA, PECCARIES, TAPIRS, FISH

HUNTERS

GUANACO AND RHEA

LITTORAL SHELL-
FISH GATHERERS
AND MARINE
HUNTERS

Subsistence areas of native South America.

sea urchins, and giant barnacles, sea game, including sea lions, otters,
an aquatic rodent called "coypu," and various birds, especially cormorants and penguins. Land game and wild plants are unimportant.

By contrast, the steppes, deserts, and grasslands which extend from
Patagonia north to the Gran Chaco are an area where wild game predominated but was limited in quantity. By far the most important was

the guanaco, a wild relative of the llama and alpaca, but it did not occur in large migratory herds of thousands of individuals, like the North American bison and caribou, or in vast numbers, like the many game species of East Africa. The pampas also offered rheas (often mistakenly called the "ostrich"), skunks, armadillos, and tuco tucos (*Ctenomys*), all native foods. Several thousand years ago, the Indians also hunted certain large, slow-moving, and now extinct members of the sloth family, remains of which have been found associated with human artifacts in the far south. After the Spaniards introduced horses and cattle, both species became feral. Hunted like wild animals, these became the principal foods. Although horses were ridden, they were also eaten, their blood was drunk, and they were ritually sacrificed.

In the eastern Gran Chaco, there were peccaries in addition to the pampean species. To the north, throughout the humid, hot lowlands of Amazonia and Central America, several species of land fauna provided meat: peccaries, often called "pigs" (puercos), tapirs, monkeys, iguanas, deer, and anteaters. These animals, however, were sparse and hard to kill. Many of the South American deer are extremely small, while monkeys living in the high trees are killed only with difficulty. Peccaries and tapirs, which are larger and tend to herd, are perhaps the most important land game and reward the efforts of a skilled hunter.

In the tropical rain forests, water resources are more rewarding than land game, especially along the main courses of the Amazon and Orinoco Rivers and their tributaries. The rivers afford innumerable fish, including the dangerous piranha, sting ray, and electric eel, and they formerly yielded vast numbers of turtles and thousands of turtle eggs, which were of major importance. There were also giant-scaled fish, manatees or sea cows (peixe boi, or ox fish), river dolphins, caymans, and their close relatives crocodiles. The last, owing to their great size and carnivorous habits, also presented a hazard to human beings.

Domesticated animals

Prior to the introduction of European horses, cattle, sheep, pigs, burros, and chickens, few South American Indians had a basic pastoral economy. The Western Hemisphere as a whole lacked wild species suitable for domestication, and while many South American Indians kept birds and animals as pets, few of these were genuinely domesticated.

The principal development of animal domestication was in the Central Andes, but herds became only a supplement to the essentially non-pastoral economy. The two most important species, llamas and alpacas, are American cameloids. These were distributed from southern Colombia to northern Chile and northwest Argentina, not quite overlapping the territory of their wild cousin the guanaco of the pampas. They were pastured mainly in the cool, open highlands, and served as beasts of burden, sacrificial animals, and a source of wool and meat. Three other animal domesticates were also found in the Andes: dogs, guinea pigs, and Muscovy ducks (so named from having been taken to Russia and reintroduced to America).

Far to the south, the Alacaluf of the Chilean archipelago had partially domesticated the flightless steamer duck (*Tachyeres pteneres*), but they had no other domesticated animals.

The native people of the northern Andes had obtained domesticated animals from three sources: Muscovy ducks and guinea pigs from the Central Andes; a "mute dog" that was eaten and may have been domesticated locally in Colombia or Venezuela; and turkeys and honey-bees that probably originated in Mexico.

None of these domesticated animals were more than supplements to plant foods. In the rain forests, they were much less important than wild game, fish, river mammals, and reptiles.

Wild plant foods

The South American Indians made very extensive use of edible wild plants. Moreover, in the areas of farming, experimentation with wild species had brought many under partial domestication. Among the wild food plants, two groups have outstanding importance: the xerophytic or drought-resisting species of the Gran Chaco; and the palms, nuts, and fruits of the hot rain forests.

The Gran Chaco, especially the more arid western portion where thorny scrub forests predominate, afforded exceptional resources in its algorroba pods (*Prosopis*), tuscas (*Acacia moniliformis*), chañar fruit (*Gourliea decorticans*), mistol (*Zizyphus mistol*), and palms. The eastern Chaco shades off into a moister climate and a swamp-palm savanna, and farther east are the rain forests of southern Brazil and the campos, or high savannas, of east central Brazil. In the swamplands of the upper Paraguay River wild rice (*Oryza perennia*) was a staple food, and it was collected from canoes much as the wild rice of the North American Great Lakes region was collected.

Palms were important not only in the Chaco but throughout the trop-ical-forest areas, where several species were domesticated. This multi-purpose plant supplied edible shoots, fruits, and pith, it could be fer-mented to make chicha, the aboriginal beer, its bark was used for cordage, some species supplied bow wood, and in others edible larvae could be raised. The tropical forests also afforded various nuts, of which the Brazil nut is best known.

Domesticated plants

If the Western Hemisphere was deficient in domesticable animals, it was compensated by a wealth of potential domesticable plants. Its list of contributions to world farm production is impressive. Such plants as corn or maize, kidney beans, lima beans, squashes (*Cucurbita*), tomatoes, white potatoes, sweet potatoes, peanuts, manioc, possibly yams, and various fruits have enriched and augmented the diet of every continent so greatly that they contributed to the rapid increase of world population after 1650.

An explanation of New World plant domestication is not simple. Fundamentally, domestication means that a wild species has been selectively bred to develop desired qualities but at the same time has acquired a vulnerability to competition with wild species since it is adapted to artifical or man-made conditions. Feral plant domesticates usually cannot survive very long in a state of nature. It is, of course, conceivable that once the general concept of domestication was grasped it spread from one society to another. There is little doubt, however, that the Western Hemisphere originated domestication independently of the Old World. Moreover, there were several American centers of plant domestication. For example, a number of grains, such as quinoa, came from the high, cold Central Andes. White potatoes, which belong to one of the two classes of root crops, came from the cold climates of the high Andes and central Chile. Sweet potatoes, manioc, and yams, included in the second group of root crops, were grown in the tropical rain forests.

The tropical fruits constituted another special class of plants, including papayas, avocados, custard apples, and many others little known outside South America. The fruits were most common in northern South America, although many spread into portions of the tropical forests.

The Central Andes and the Circum-Caribbean areas offer a great range of altitude and climate; consequently, they can produce a large variety of crops, including most of the plants mentioned above, many of which are adapted to special climates. These areas had other advantages, which partly followed the need to irrigate and to terrace the hillsides. First, their soils are less subject to destructive leaching than the tropical rain forests, where cultivated plots must be shifted every few years. Second, watering of the fields could be controlled by irrigation. In addition, the Central Andean Indians made greater use of fertilization, for they had access to the enormous offshore guano deposits which were imperially controlled under the Inca.

In addition to foods, special plants were cultivated for drugs (coca, the source of cocaine), narcotics (tobacco), and stimulants, which included several species in the northwest Amazon and mate, or "Paraguay tea." Other plant domesticates provided arrow shafts (cane), paint (urucú and genipa), bow wood (chonta palm), fish drugs (barbasco and many others), containers (gourds and calabashes), and fibers (cotton). The list of wild plants used for these purposes is enormous; for example,

TABLE 1: *Domesticated Plants in Aboriginal South America*

	Central Andes	Northern Andes	Central America	Southern Andes	Tropical forests	Antilles
Grains						
Maize (*Zea mays*)	x	x	x	x	x	x
Quinoa (*Chenopodium quinoa*)	x			x		
Lupine (*Lupinus tauris*)	x					
Cañahua (*Chenopodium pallidicaule*)	x					
Amaranth (*Amaranthus* sp.)	x					
Beans						
Kidney (*Phaseolus vulgaris*)	x	x	x	x	x	x
Lima (*Phaseolus lunatus*)	x	x	x	x	x	
Jack (*Canavalia ensiformis*)	x			x	x	
Scarlet runner (*Phaseolus multiflorus*)		x	x			
Fruits						
Pineapple (*Ananas sativus*)	x	x	x		x	x
Soursop (*Annona muricata*)	x	x	x			
Papaya (*Carica papaya*)	x	x	x		x	x
Avocado (*Persea americana*)	x	x	x		x	x
Cherimoya (*Annona cherimolia*)	x	x	x		x	x
Guava, Guayava (*Psidium guajava*)	x	x			x	x
Pepino (*Solanum muricatum*)	x	x				
Surinam cherry (*Eugenia uniflora*)					x	
Lucuma obovata					x	
Pacae (*Inga* sp.)	x				x	
Fruta de lobo (*Solanum lycocarpum*)					x	
Tumbo (*Passiflora guadrangularis*)	x					
Granadilla (*Passiflora popenovii*)	x					
Mangaba (*Hancornia speciosa*)						
Roots						
Potato (*Solanum tuberosum*)	x		x	x		x
Potato (*Solanum andigenum*)	x	x		x		
Oca (*Oxalis tuberosa*)	x	x		x		
Ulluco (*Ullucus tuberosus*)	x			x		
Mashua (*Tropaeolum tuberosum*)	x					
Achira (*Canna edulis*)	x					
Arracacha (*Arracacia xanthorrhiza*)	x	x			x	
Yacon (*Polymnia edulis*)	x	x		x		
Sweet potato (*Ipomoea batatas*)	x	x	x	x	x	x

TABLE 1: *Domesticated Plants in Aboriginal South America* (*Continued*)

	Central Andes	Northern Andes	Central America	Southern Andes	Tropical forests	Antilles
Peanut (*Arachis hypogaea*)	x				x	x
Bitter manioc (*Manihot utilissima*)			x		x	x
Sweet manioc (*Manihot aipi*)	x	x	x		x	x
Yam, cará (*Dioscorea sp.*)					x	x
Yautia (*Xanthosoma sagittifolium*)					x	x
Arrowroot (*Maranta arundinacea*)					x	x
Mito (*Carica condicans*)	x					
Miscellaneous Foods						
Squash (*Cucurbita maxima*)	x	x	x	x	x	
Peppers, ají (*Capsicum annuum*)	x	x	x	x	x	x
Cacao (*Theobroma cacao*)	x	x	x			
Cashew (*Anacardium occidentale*)					x	
Hualusa (*Colocasia esculenta*)					x	
Caimito (*Chrysophyllum caimito*)	x					x
Mate					x	
Palms						
Pejibaye (*Guilielma gasipaes*)			x		x	
Bocaiúva (*Acrocomia sp.*)					x	
Babassú (*Orbigni speciosa*)					x	
Tucum (*Astrocaryum sp.*)					x	
Burití, mirití (*Mauritia flexuosa,* M. *vinitera*)					x	
Drugs and Narcotics						
Coca (*Erythroxylon coca*)	x	x	x		x	
Tobacco (*Nicotiana tabacum*)	x	x	x		x	x
Tobacco (*Nicotiana rustica*)	x					
Miscellaneous						
Gourds (*Lagenaria siceraria*)	x	x	x		x	
Calabash (*Crescentia cuiete*)	x	x	x	x	x	
Cotton (*Gossypium*)	x	x	x		x	x
Urucú (*Bixa orellana*)					x	
Genipa (*Genipa americana*)					x	
Barbasco (*Lonchocarpus nicon*)					x	
Clebadium vargasii					x	
Reeds (*Arundo donax*)					x	
Uba cane (*Gynerium sagittatum*)					x	

several hundred species were used for fish poisoning. In the Amazon, latex from wild rubber was used for balls and syringes, but rubber trees were not domesticated.

The preceding table gives some idea of the distribution of the more important of these plants. Knowledge of the native distribution of these species is, however, still far from complete. Blanks, therefore, do not necessarily indicate absences.

2. DEMOGRAPHY

Aboriginal population

Population measured in terms of density per unit of territory is a rough index of productivity and therefore of cultural development. But more important than mere density are the distribution of the people within their territory and the nature of their social units. This subject will be discussed in the following section.

Estimates of the native population of the Americas of the Conquest period made by competent scholars have an incredible range of difference. Kroeber (1939) estimated 8,400,000 for the hemisphere, while Rivet and Sapper (1924) placed the figure at 40,000,000 to 50,000,000 and Spinden (1928) 50,000,000 to 75,000,000. Totals for South America, including Central America and the Antilles, range from Kroeber's 4,500,000 to Rivet's 25,000,000, while Means (1931) thought there were 16,000,000 to 32,000,000 in the Andes alone. Rosenblat's figure of 13,-385,000 for the hemisphere, 4,750,000 for the Andes, and 2,035,000 for the remainder of continental South America is more modest, even though it nearly doubles Kroeber's estimate.[1]

The problem of demography involves various difficulties. The Spaniards clearly tended to exaggerate their census figures. In many areas, it was impossible to count isolated societies, of which the officials knew virtually nothing. Moreover, in many groups European diseases caused the population to decline before estimates of their numbers could be made.

The data in Table 2 are only approximations, but in two respects they are fairly reliable. First, comparative densities, such as that of the gaunaco hunters of Patagonia or the tropical-forest farm villagers compared with the Central Andes, are certainly significant. Second, South America as a whole had a surprisingly low population density compared with other world areas. The density of 10 persons per square mile obtaining in the Central Andes is lower than the figure for most of Africa, except for the Sahara and Kalahari Deserts. East Africa, whose societies have never developed beyond chiefdoms, has 53 persons per square mile northwest of Lake Victoria, while the kingdoms from

Native Indian population densities in South America: number of persons per square mile.

Nigeria to the Ivory Coast have 45 to more than 60 persons per square mile. Today, Indonesia as a whole has more than 135 persons per square mile, which is immeasurably greater than the figure for the Central Andes, even allowing for an increase of severalfold in Indonesia in the last century. In India and China a density of 25 is sparse, while maximum concentration exceeds 500 persons per square mile in large areas.

Much of the Central Andes, however, are exceptionally inhospitable owing to the proportion of the country that is either complete

TABLE 2: *Native Population Densities in South America about 1500*

Area	Population	Persons per square mile
Inca Empire		
Central Andes	3,500,000	10.0
Chiefdoms		
Northern Andes	1,500,000	6.6
Central America	736,500	4.8
Northern Venezuela	144,000	1.1
Antilles	225,000	2.5
Southern Andes		
Atacama-Diaguita	81,000	0.38
Southern Chile: Araucanian	1,050,000	7.0
Tropical Forests	2,188,970	0.6
Hunters and Gatherers		
Chilean archipelago	9,000	0.2
Patagonia: Guanaco hunters	101,675	0.12
Western Chaco	186,400	1.1
Eastern Chaco	80,250	0.5
Eastern Brazil	387,440	0.3
	10,190,235	

desert or that lies in the tundra and alpine zones of the high mountains. In modern Peru, not over 2 per cent of the land is farmed, and the portion cultivated in native times cannot have been much greater. The Central Andes lack broad, temperate plains or great fertile river valleys comparable to those of the Ganges, Indus, Nile, Hwang, or Yangtze Rivers. Nevertheless, the Central Andes sustained great local concentrations of people, a situation which created a very high density in the inhabited portions and a great contrast between this area and the northern Andes, where a smaller percentage of the terrain precludes occupation.

The accompanying tabulation and map bring out some of the contrasts in aboriginal South American population densities. It will be noted that, while central Chile (density 7 persons per square mile) about equals the northern Andes (density 6.6), the Atacama and Diaguita of the deserts of northern Chile are about the same (density 0.38) as most of the nomadic hunters and gatherers. The western Chaco, owing to its wealth of wild seeds, was more heavily populated (density 1.1) than the tropical forests (average density 0.6).

The tropical forests, however, should be considered an area where the people were concentrated principally along the main rivers and coasts. The interfluvial forests had little value to most of these canoe-using, fishing people and were used principally for slash-and-burn farm plots near the rivers. Concentrations were several times greater along the Amazon and the portion of the Brazilian coast occupied by the Tupian people, where the density reached 2 persons per square mile as against an average of 0.6 for the forest area as a whole. Densities were also greater among many peoples of the Montaña and eastern Bolivia adjoining the Andes.

In comparative terms, the density of the Central Andes was about two hundred times that of the guanaco hunters, forty times that of the archipelagic shellfish gatherers, about twenty times that of the tropical-forest farmers, and half again that of the Araucanians of Chile and of the Circum-Caribbean chiefdoms.

Post-Conquest population trends

The aboriginal population of continental South America is estimated to have been over 10 million, of which more than one-third was in the Central Andes. Today, nearly 7 million persons are classed, largely for cultural reasons, as Indians. (Some estimates double this figure.) There are several million caboclos (the backwoodsmen of Brazil), criollos, and mestizos of various sorts, who, though predominantly Indian in race, are not classed as Indians in the census. Biologically, therefore, there are considerably more than 7 million persons of Indian ancestry. In fact, the Indian race is undoubtedly as numerous as at the time of the Conquest, and it has probably made a substantial net gain. The gain, however, is attributable entirely to the Andes, an area in which population declined sharply after the Spanish Conquest but recovered and increased. Elsewhere, the population has declined, although not always to the extent that the census indicates. The loss, which is primarily a function of the intensity and duration of European contact and of the aboriginal population density, varies in each area.

The greatest decline was along the coasts and large rivers, where the Europeans, water-borne and maintaining contact with the homeland, came with overwhelming force. The Indians of the coasts of Brazil, the Guianas, Venezuela, Colombia, Central America, and Ecuador, though very numerous, soon died, fled, or were assimilated. Along the Amazon and Orinoco, they also suffered a rapid decline. In these areas, their place was partly taken by Negro slaves from Africa, who met the Europeans' need for laborers. In many of the coastal and fluvial areas, the very identity of the native Indians is in doubt. In the Antillean islands, the Indians were nearly extinct culturally within a century and a half. Las Casas, a critic of Spanish policy, estimated that the native population of Puerto Rico and Jamaica had shrunk from 3 million (a figure that is much too high) in 1509 to 200 in 1542. Actually, the Indians' biological heritage in the Antilles is very marked, even though it is mixed with Negro and white.

As the Europeans penetrated inland along the Amazon and Orinoco, the Indians gradually succumbed, some perishing, others becoming culturally assimilated and adding their blood to that of the whites and Negroes to form mixed populations. Today the Indians survive mainly in the areas beyond easy navigation, that is, in the great U which surrounds the Amazon Basin and includes the Amazon-Orinoco watershed, the northwest Amazon, the Montaña, Mato Grosso, parts of the Chaco, and the eastern Brazilian plateau. This was precisely the area of enclaves of nomadic hunting-and-gathering people and of simpler farming villages, who in pre-Columbian times had remained comparatively uninfluenced by the more characteristic tropical-forest-village type of culture, which also was water-borne. Elsewhere in the tropical forests and around the Caribbean Sea, the Indians who survive today live mainly in areas that are unsuited for European occupation, such as the swamps of the Orinoco Delta and of the Mosquito Coast in Nicaragua and the mountainous areas of western and southern Venezuela and Central America.

In Argentina and Uruguay also, where the native population was sparse, the coastal Indians were first to succumb. Later, the Europeans swept inland, and, finding the country suitable for their Old World pastoral economy, they exterminated the Indians or absorbed them as Gauchos. In Chile, the story was the same, except that some of the Araucanians crossed the Andes into the pampas, while others, driven south but not surrendering, were finally isolated on reservations.

There were numerous factors in this decline, and their effect in different localities is reflected in very unlike population curves. European diseases, which were most devastating where the Indians were concentrated, as in missions or forced settlements, wiped out some groups within a century or two, whereas immediate neighbors in the forests survive in some strength to the present day. Warfare, both with the whites and with other Indians dislocated by the Conquest, took a terrific toll. Moreover, slaving expeditions that sent Indians against their neighbors to supply workers for the whites wiped out many groups. The Indians also suffered from disrupted economic and cultural life. While better health measures and reservation systems will undoubtedly check this decline, we can be sure that assimilation of the native societies as subcultural groups in the modern nations will eventually remove the category "Indian" from the censuses.

By contrast to the remainder of South America, the Andes, especially the Central Andes, have more "Indians" today than at the time of the Conquest. As elsewhere, the coast suffered most from European contacts, but later the whites penetrated the interior and the total population was probably halved. Aboriginally numerous, culturally stable, and comparatively unaffected by epidemics, the highland population has recovered and is now larger and increasing. But it too is destined to lose the characteristics that make it "Indian."

3. DEMOGRAPHY AND COMMUNITY SIZE

Productivity was more important in its relationship to community size (see page 52), than mere population density. While no communities among the chiefdoms were as large as some in the Central Andes, which have been called "cities" and which sometimes reached 100,000 or more inhabitants, the former commonly had 500 to 3,000 persons. Such size is unusual in the tropical rain forests, except along the Amazon and Brazilian coast, where population density was also unusually great and communities sometimes had 2,000 persons. Many rain-forest villages consisted of only a single lineage or household of 15 to 200 persons.

The correlation between population density and maximum community size, however, breaks down in the case of central Chile. While the population density of the latter equaled that of the northern Andes, its settlements were no larger than the bands of pampean nomadic hunters. Like their northern Chilean neighbors of the nearly waterless deserts, the central Chilean settlements had only 50 to 150 persons, even though their population was nearly twenty times greater than in the northern deserts. These Chilean settlements remained small despite the high productivity of the area because there were no factors that caused local lineages to cooperate and concentrate in fewer but larger communities.

Settlement size, although indicative of the level of social development, must also be related to settlement pattern. In the Central Andean highlands, the rural population tended throughout all periods to be dispersed over farm and pasture lands which were productive more because of rainfall than irrigation. Concentration of population in Peru started with agglutinated settlements, that is, started when religious centers attained

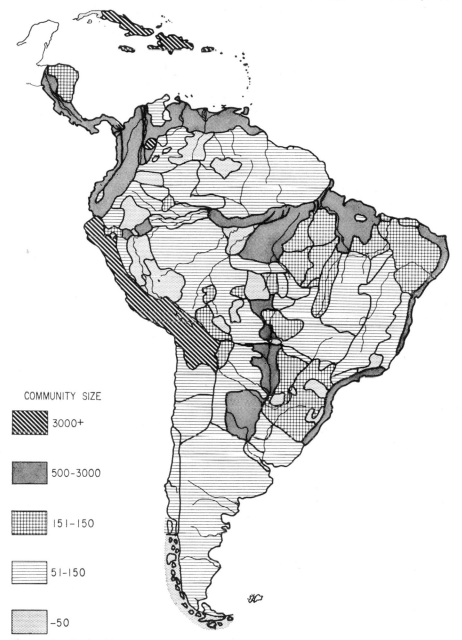

COMMUNITY SIZE

3000+

500-3000

I5 I-I50

5I-I50

-50

Community size in different areas of native South America. (Steward, **Handbook**, vol. 5.)

considerable size and importance and the common people began to live close to them. Highly agglutinated or nucleated towns, that is, settlements of closely spaced and ordered houses, temples, and palaces, developed for two reasons. First, the great number of administrative, religious, and military specialists, which proliferated particularly after the growth of imperial institutions, became concentrated in large towns or cities. Possibly, as Kidder[2] contends, the idea of such centers originated in the Tiahuanaco culture of the highlands. This culture, which began about A.D. 1000, probably represented the first empire. In any event, urban centers unquestionably were a functional response to the needs of new centralized institutions. Second, urban centers became more numerous, larger, and better planned on the coast. This fact is undoubtedly related not only to the demands of imperial institutions but to the prevalence of irrigation, the limited amount of farm land, and the utter aridity of the terrain outside the river valleys. It was good sense to settle in concentrated towns which had a common source of water rather than on the precious farm lands or in the desert.

The settlement patterns in highland Ecuador and Colombia were similar in their functional basis to those of the Central Andean highlands, except that there was far less need for strong administrative centers. Irrigation, although practiced to some extent, was not a major factor in concentrating the population. A general dispersal of houses and small settlements prevailed throughout most of these highlands. Common religious devotion brought people from fairly wide areas to worship at central temples or shrines, while needs for defense were met by mountain forts in which the common people found refuge. The clustering of houses in rural communities was comparatively small, and these communities were generally situated in hilly places or in intermontane basins.

In many chiefdoms, especially those in the rain-forest areas, however, the people lived in very tightly nucleated, or concentrated, towns. Typically, these towns had a central plaza which was dominated by the temple with its idols and ceremonial paraphernalia and often by the chief's house. The plaza was surrounded by ordered rows of dwellings, and the towns were protected by palisades, which prevented dispersal of dwellings.

Why these two unlike settlement patterns existed in the northern Andes invites speculation. Both developed in the face of rather brutal warfare, human sacrifice, and cannibalism, which obviously called for some means of defense. The similarity of the southern Colombian and Ecuadorian highland dispersed settlements to those of the Central Andean highlands might be explained partly as the extension of a Peruvian highland pattern through borrowing. But the environmental factor must also be considered. The northern Andean settlements of dispersed houses occurred largely in the high, grassy paramos, while the palisaded villages were more common in the lower forested country, where timbers for palisades could be cut. Timber was not readily available in most of the Colombian and Ecuadorian highland paramos, and it was almost completely absent in the Central Andean highland. The eucalyptus trees found today in the highland were brought from Australia in post-Columbian times. In timberless areas, fortification was accomplished in two principal ways: hilltop redoubts, especially in the Central Andean highlands; and towns and cities protected by high massive walls of adobe, as in the later communities on the north Peruvian coast.

It should be noted that the need for protection against raids also differed in the chiefdoms of the northern Andes and in the Inca Empire. After the latter was well established, it required local garrisons to maintain order among its mixed population rather than elaborate defense against mass attack from the outside, except on its borders. The chiefdoms, on the other hand, were so small territorially that attack from enemy groups was always imminent. In addition, they were so loosely organized that their own component communities or territorial subdivisions might at any time threaten their rulers. Even the Chibcha, the largest and most tightly organized chiefdom, never brought their many villages and districts as thoroughly and safely into line as the Inca.

The correlation between highland chiefdoms and a dispersed rural population, on the one hand, and lowland chiefdoms and palisaded villages, on the other, is not complete. The Chibcha towns in the Colombian highlands, for example, were palisaded, as were the settlements in northern lowland Colombia and most of northern Venezuela.

Among the tropical-forest villages, the people living on the lesser tributaries of the principal rivers had a sparse population and single-house communities. The house was typically a structure of poles and thatch, and it seems usually to have sheltered an extended patrilineal lineage, a group of kin related through the male line. Households had 15 or 20 to a maximum of 200 or 300 persons. In more densely populated areas, as along the middle Amazon, such houses were closely spaced but not clearly grouped in villages. Definite village aggregates of several households were most strongly developed where warfare brought palisading, and some of these villages exceeded 1,000 persons in population. The social importance of these different settlement patterns will be discussed in Chapter Eleven.

The hunters and gatherers had the most sparse population in South America. The nature of subsistence activities precluded permanent settlements and limited the social aggregates to nomadic groups which consisted of single families among the shellfish gatherers of the Chilean archipelago and lineages that rarely exceeded 150 persons among the hunters of the pampas and the hunters and food collectors of the forests.

4. SURPLUS PRODUCTION AND SOCIAL TYPES

The interrelationship of environment, land use, population, and socio-cultural type may also be examined in terms of surplus production and socially integrating factors. While sociocultural types are not determined solely by the amount or kind of food production, there is an important relationship between the two. A minimum of surplus production was necessary to support classes of part-time or full-time non-food-producing specialists, but the character of the specialists was determined also by the nature of productive activities and by certain diffused patterns. Before examining these latter, however, it is necessary to consider surplus production in detail.

It is clear that, among the chiefdoms of the Circum-Caribbean area and eastern Bolivia and among the states and empires of the Central Andes, there was sufficient food surplus to support classes of military, religious, political, and craft specialists who were entirely relieved from food production. On the other hand, the tropical-forest-village farmers and the nomadic hunters and gatherers had no such specialists, for they lacked the economic basis to support them. The Araucanians of central Chile also lacked specialists, although they were seemingly capable of potential surplus food production. It would seem therefore that while some societies lacked the minimum productivity necessary to develop an internally specialized society, it does not necessarily follow that the possibility of surplus production will lead to full-time specialists.

The nomadic hunters and gatherers barely met minimum subsistence needs and often fell far short of them. Their population of 1 person to 10 or 20 square miles reflects this. Constantly on the move in search of food, they clearly lacked the leisure hours for nonsubsistence activities of any significance, and they could transport little of what they might manufacture in spare moments. To them, adequacy of production meant physical survival, and they rarely had surplus of either products or time. Moreover, since their communities usually consisted of lineages, internal differentiation into specialists was nearly impossible.

The tropical-forest-village farmers had a much denser population—0.5 to 1.0 person per square mile—and more stable communities than the nomadic hunters and gatherers, but they also typically lacked social classes and groups of specialists. Every family produced its own food, manufactured nearly all of its domestic articles, and met its other needs.

There were, no doubt, many instances wherein village leaders or shamans among the tropical-forest people received a portion of their keep through community obligation. This partial specialization was less common among the smaller communities that consisted of a single lineage than in the larger multilineage villages. In any kin group or lineage, old people are gradually relieved of work obligations, partly because they become feeble, partly because status tends to increase with age. In multilineage communities, such as those in the more densely populated sections along the Amazon River and its major tributaries and on the Brazilian coast, leadership was much less commonly based on kinship and age status, and the chief or shaman-chief was more fully supported by the common folk. The Cocama of the upper Amazon may even have had hereditary ruling classes, which were perhaps maintained by a surplus derived from the unusually rich resources of such river foods as turtles and their eggs, caymans and fish, together with game, wild plants, and farm products.

Most cases of class specialization among both the tropical-forest villages and the nomadic hunters and gatherers evidently resulted from the changed economy that followed European conquest. In the Gran Chaco and pampas, superior classes of warriors attained considerable importance after livestock and horses were introduced and the Indians formed predatory bands. As Oberg[3] has shown, these new classes of warriors—for example, those among many of the Guaicuruan peoples of the Chaco—pertained solely to the new predatory activities and had no other function in the society. After European settlement, many tropical-forest people specialized in the production of farinha, or manioc flour, and the gathering of rubber, turtle eggs, and other products for trade with the Portuguese. The exchange of these foods was at first managed by the village chiefs, who thereby acquired great importance. But later, as described in Chapter Twelve, trade eliminated the chiefs, destroyed native social organization, and transformed the native culture. After European settlement, the Indians of Amazonia also carried on slaving expeditions among their fellow Indians in order to sell the captives to the Portuguese and Spanish settlers. In some cases, slaving resulted in the addition of a kind of servile class to their own society.

Several facts, however, indicate that the aboriginal societies of the tropical forests could not produce sufficient surplus—or at least surplus of a balanced diet—to support more than an unstratified village society. First, Inca efforts to conquer and extract tribute from their tropical-forest neighbors to the east or to colonize their area were consistently unrewarding because stable villages that might produce a surplus could not be established. Second, the prehistoric remains of the Marajoara culture on the island of Marajó at the mouth of the Amazon, discussed subsequently, certainly represents some kind of class-structured chiefdom which was on a higher cultural level than that of the neighboring tropical-forest farmers. Betty Meggers and Clifford Evans have shown that these sites must represent an intrusive culture with Andean features which came down the Amazon from the Napo River in Ecuador and the Putamayo River in Colombia and was briefly established on Marajó.[4] This culture did not survive because, as Meggers and Evans suggest, it was in a foreign environment and lacked a productive basis adequate to support its specialists. Third, Johannes Wilbert (see Chapter Fourteen, section 5) has found traces of a genuine temple-idol-priest cult among the Warrau of the Orinoco Delta. Since the Warrau who lived in historic times in the marshes of the Delta, an area not unlike the island of Marajó, have been so primitive in most respects as to be classifiable with the nomadic hunters and gatherers, it seems likely that they are a deculturated people. Formerly, they may have lived among or in contact with the chiefdoms not far to their west in northern Venezuela and shared their culture patterns, but they migrated into an area which would not support these patterns. If this interpretation is correct, the history of the Warrau was comparable to that of the early inhabitants of Marajó, except that the Warrau did not disappear as a cultural entity and preserved the priest-temple-idol cult of former times. Fourth, mounds, roads, and other prehistoric structures associated with states or chiefdoms have been reported east of the Andes in Bolivia, Ecuador, and Colombia, while the Caribbean lowlands of Nicaragua and Honduras, in Central America, occupied in historic times by a tropical-forest-village type of culture, contain archaeological remains apparently associated with state organization. Finally, as Oberg points out, the people of Amazonia had mechanisms, such as infanticide, for preventing population increase beyond the means of subsistence.

Such evidence can be taken to mean that a society consisting of social classes and specialists could not be sustained in most of these tropical-forest areas. In support of this inference is the fact that the tropical-forest-village enclaves in the Circum-Caribbean area occurred largely in the rain-forest lowlands while chiefdoms tended to follow higher terrain. The flimsy productive basis of the tropical-forest villagers was further undermined when the spread of warfare made dispersed communities so vulnerable that they had to cluster in small palisaded villages. Warfare, even though carried out to take sacrificial or cannibalistic victims or to obtain human trophies rather than to conquer, curtailed economic activities since the villagers could not travel daily to farm plots too far from the community.

Additional factors served to inhibit the development of classes and specialists in the tropical forests. The rapid leaching of the soils prevented intervillage federations or alliances by requiring frequent shift of the farm plots and in many cases also of the villages. In addition,

incursions of ants and destruction of the house at the death of an occupant might cause the people to move their settlement.

To judge by population density, food productivity was much greater
among the chiefdoms and among the Araucanians of the central valley
of Chile than among the people of the tropical forests (see Chapter
Three, section 2). There is, of course, not a complete correspondence
between population and food, for many nonsubsistence factors determine
life and death. But we may reasonably assume that the Araucanians no
less than the chiefdoms had potential surplus production to support
classes of specialists. In fact, under the fairly brief prehistoric Inca
domination and for a short period after the Spanish Conquest, the
Picunche division of the Araucanians did support classes of foreign overlords. These social classes, however, did not last after the invaders were
gone since the internal organization of the Araucanians was kin-based.
The high productivity of the Araucanians had merely brought about the
multiplication of small, independent lineage villages which had no social
classes or important groups of specialists.[5]

There seem to be circumstances under which productivity falls short
of its potentiality. The modern, Guaraní-speaking rural population of
Paraguay, described by Elman and Helen Service[6] and discussed at
greater length in Chapter Twelve, section 4, need to spend comparatively
little time providing what they consider adequate food, clothing, and
housing. They accept wage labor only briefly and irregularly in order
to meet some special need such as supplying food, drink, or clothing
for a festival or wedding. Possibly the Araucanians had also achieved
adequate production and surplus or leisure time. The extent to which
each individual devoted this time to craft production or other activities
is difficult to say. Among primitive peoples who lack classes of specialists,
there is a high correlation between excellence of technical achievement
and surplus time.

To judge by a comparison of the Araucanians and the chiefdoms, it
does not follow that the mere possibility of supporting full-time classes
of non-food producers will necessarily bring about such classes. The
difference is evidently that among the chiefdoms the spread of warfare
to take captives and sacrificial victims afforded a basis for social status
and its accouterments and caused them to cross the threshold from
adequacy of production to surplus production and rather marked class
specialization. The warfare and priest-temple cult may have come either
from the Central Andes or Meso-America. To recognize diffusion as a
factor that helped crystallize class structure in the Circum-Caribbean
area, however, is not to say that this area is a poor copy of the civilizations by which it was influenced or that it represents a stage through
which these civilizations had passed. The diffused patterns acquired

distinctive local character in the area of chiefdoms partly because farming in this area was not essentially based upon irrigation and partly because social status and specialization were not strongly fixed by heredity.

NOTES

1. These population estimates and the demography of South American Indians are discussed by Julian H. Steward in the *Handbook*, vol. 5.
2. Alfred Kidder, II, "Settlement Patterns—Peru," Gordon R. Willey (ed.), in *Prehistoric Settlement Patterns in the New World*, Viking Fund Publications in Anthropology, no. 23, 1956.
3. Kalervo Oberg, "Types of Social Structure Among the Lowland Tribes of South and Central America," *American Anthropologist*, vol. 57, 1955.
4. Betty J. Meggers and Clifford Evans, *Archeological Investigations at the Mouth of the Amazon*, Bureau of American Ethnology Bulletin 167, 1957.
5. Oberg, *op. cit.*, discusses some of these problems and points out that the possibility of producing surplus food is a precondition of specialization and social classes but does not of itself necessarily cause classes.
6. Elman Service and Helen Service, *Tobatí: A Paraguayan Town*, University of Chicago Press, Chicago, 1954.

▶ **four**

THE CENTRAL ANDEAN

IRRIGATION CIVILIZATIONS:

PREHISTORIC ERAS

1. THE ANDEAN CULTURAL ACHIEVEMENTS

Central Andean cultural development had probably fulfilled its native potentialities by the time of the Spanish Conquest. It is very doubtful that it could have acquired any radically new patterns through internal evolution alone. When first encountered by the Spaniards, the Inca Empire represented the culmination of at least 4,000 years of development, during which simple farm villages were followed by expanding states based upon irrigation agriculture. There is an essential continuity in this long cultural tradition. The farm crops and the methods of raising them became well adapted to the distinctive environments of the arid coast and somewhat rainy highlands of the Central Andes of Peru and Bolivia. The cultural ecological adaptations of the people—the social forms that developed in response to land-use patterns—took shapes characteristic of an irrigation civilization despite some local distinctiveness in stylistic features, regional emphasis, and certain lags.

The basic pattern that characterized the Central Andean irrigation civilization became fairly definite at least 3,000 years ago, when the principal plants and animals had been brought under domestication. By the time the Inca Empire was founded in the fifteenth century the limits of population growth attainable under the prevailing agricultural system seem to have been reached. The basic technologies were also invented or acquired early in Andean prehistory, but, with the exception of metallurgy, they showed little essential change during later eras. The vast militaristic empire of the Inca represented the culmination of an irrigation civilization which had seemingly reached its demographic limits, yet which was unable to create a new productive technology or land use. The Central Andean empire was destined to experience cycles of rise and fall until radically new economic and social patterns were introduced from Europe.

The Spanish Conquest profoundly altered the course of Andean cultural history because it imposed wholly new national economic and social institutions upon the native population and introduced features of an iron age technology. The self-contained, noncommercial Inca state was replaced by a mercantilistic empire. Overseas trade was superimposed upon a system of subsistence farming, local barter, and tribute. Spanish mercantilism called for the production of special cash commodities, the importation of manufactured goods, the introduction of cash and credit, and, eventually, private ownership of the means of production. Spanish political, military, and religious institutions were geared to the commercial pattern. The Inca Empire became an economic and political colonial dependency.

The growth of the native Andean civilization can now be traced in broad outline, which is not very different from that of other early irrigation civilizations. Seen in greater detail, however, the Central Andes as a whole show a certain individuality in their cultural emphasis, while the local regions are distinguishable by the ways in which they stylized the fundamental ingredients of this civilization.

Table 3 presents a general development scheme for Andean prehistory. Between columns listing dates at the left and major changes at the right, periods of local development in various portions of the Central Andes are named; they constitute subdivisions of both area and time. These local periods are based primarily on the distribution and sequence of ceramic styles, which provide a general chronological framework for the area as a whole. Other archaeological materials, such as mounds, villages, house types, and manufactured goods, are presumed to be correlated in time by their association with ceramic types and are now also being dated by radiocarbon.

When attention is shifted, however, from the ceramic styles to the other materials and an attempt is made to draw inferences concerning the basic cultural trends, it is extremely difficult to decide what features are most diagnostic and how the lesser periods should be grouped into major developmental eras. The answer to this depends largely upon one's point of view, and it is not surprising that there is still disagreement. Different authorities may be primarily interested in technological progress, artistic development, religious growth, or social patterns. Although Americanists are not yet in agreement as to criteria of major eras, they have broken from the long-standing European custom of using single technological criteria, such as Old Stone Age, New Stone Age, and Bronze Age. The development schemes which Larco Hoyle, Bennett, Willey, Strong, and Steward[1] have suggested for the Central Andes all attempt to give due weight to sociological as well as technological trends; that is, they attempt to view the culture of each period as a whole and not to characterize it soley by some minor feature. There is still room for disagreement about how to characterize whole cultures.

TABLE 3: *Prehistoric Periods and Eras of the Central Andes**

Date	Local periods	Eras and cultures
1532	Spanish Conquest	European empire
1450	Inca Empire	Founding the Inca Empire
1200	Local periods	Cyclical conquests: prehistoric empires
1125	Black-white-red style	
1000	Tiahuanaco	
450	Early Lima; Nazca-B; Mochica-B; Racuay-B	Regional florescent states: priests, warriors, artisans
A.D.		
B.C.		
200	Paracas; Pucara; Nazca-A; Recuay-A; Mochica; Early Tiahuanaco	
500	Chanapata; Chiripa; Gallinazo; Salinar; Chancay; Huaraz	Regional differentiation of local states
	Ancón; Chavín; Cupisnique; Guañape	Formative: emergence of theocratic states
1000	Aspero Upper Huaca Prieta	Incipient farming: folk communities
2300	Lower Huaca Prieta; Cerro Prieto	
8000?	North coast sites	Hunters, gatherers, and fishers

* The local periods are conventional archaeological divisions. The eras and cultures are the developmental sequences described in the subdivisions of the present chapter.

The developmental scheme used in Table 3 is based primarily upon sociological patterns as they were related to productive technology in an area requiring irrigation. These patterns represent cultural types, rather than lists of cultural elements, and they have counterparts in other centers of irrigation civilization, despite many features which are unique to the Andes. This scheme is, of course, subject to revision.

Extensive archaeological research being carried on in Peru has disclosed new ceramic types and subtypes, new cross-associations of types, and conflicts in carbon 14 datings. The schema of Local periods in Table 3 will be modified again and again in years to come.[2] Perhaps some modification of the developmental interpretations will also be necessary. As yet, however, no one has offered reinterpretations of cultural processes or new formulations of developmental eras based upon the new findings.

The archaeological materials of the Central Andes are exceptionally rich in implications of sociological features. As yet, however, it is impossible to utilize these to the fullest, because for many years archaeology was concerned almost exclusively with the more spectacular materials representing artistic and architectural achievements and inventive genius. Reports describe mounds, temples, forts, and irrigation works; museums are full of beautiful pottery, textiles, goldwork, and sculpture. The great structures are state works, and the more handsome museum pieces are largely grave offerings. The dwellings of the common people and the household ceramics, textiles, and other goods are little known. It does not at all follow that products made for ceremonial use were similar to those intended for everyday use. In fact, the very few excavations of dwellings and studies of domestic goods suggest that throughout Andean history the latter were generally simpler, cruder types. A sharp contrast between domestic and temple goods strongly suggests a class-structured society.

Another factor that handicaps efforts to interpret the archaeological materials is the overshadowing importance attached to ceramics. Pottery has of necessity been studied for its own sake because the sequence and distribution of ceramic styles has come to form the chronological framework by which other antiquities are dated. Emphasis upon pottery, however, had often led to deemphasis of the other features of culture which, from a broad social-science point of view, are the more important.

The present description and analysis attempt primarily to interpret the sociological significance of archaeological materials and often pass lightly over things which preoccupy archaeologists. Many interpretations, of course, must remain speculative; yet the Andean data show quite clearly the evolution of theocratic and militaristic states from folk communities and the final amalgamation of states into empires.

Peruvian prehistory starts with an era of hunting, fishing, and gathering. Little evidence of this primitive culture has been found, largely for want of searching, and it is impossible to sketch the social patterns. The sparse and probably mobile population left only the scantiest remains at a few camp sites.

Archaeological sites and areas of the Central Andes. (Revised for the **Handbook** from A. L. Kroeber, "Peruvian Archaeology in 1942," Viking Fund Publications in Anthropology, no. 4, 1944.)

The next era was one of small villages of incipient farmers. Inconspicuous and quite unexciting as compared with later sites, these villages have received comparatively little attention. The people of this era farmed along the riverine plains without irrigation. They lived in sedentary villages but lacked sufficient leisure to develop the basic technologies and social forms which later characterized the Central Andes.

The Formative Era is marked by the introduction of factors that brought about the emergence of local states. A substantial number of new crops grown by means of irrigation supported an increasing population, which lived in small communities dispersed around temple mounds. The temples were the centers of theocratic states under the control of a priestly class, which coordinated the efforts of the several communities in agricultural ritual and probably also directed cooperative irrigation.

The most basic inventions in man's control of nature appeared at this time: irrigation, terracing, fertilizers, farm tools, ceramics, loom weaving, metallurgy, architecture, stone carving, and probably boats, roads, and bridges. Subsequent improvements in the material appurtenances of living consisted of refinements of the major productive processes and technologies rather than any new basic inventions. A large number of plants were domesticated during subsequent eras, but these resulted from an experimental zeal in applying the earlier idea of domestication to new species. New kinds of cloth were woven during later periods, but no fundamentally new invention, such as the foot loom or power loom, was made. Ceramics were improved through greater skill in modeling and painting, and production was increased by use of pottery molds, but the potter's wheel was never known. Mounds and temples were made larger, but no new architectural principles, such as the arch, came into general use. Later, also, metallurgy advanced in that new metals were utilized—copper, silver, and tin, in addition to gold—and they were alloyed. Bronze, a tin-copper alloy developed in the Era of Cyclical Conquests, is thus not new in principle. A more fundamental discovery of the later era was smelting.

From a sociological point of view, the Formative Era is significant because it represents the first tentative step toward state formation. Although there is room for some difference of opinion in interpretation of the religious complex of this era, it is clear that some kind of supracommunity sociocultural integration emerged. During the Era of Incipient Farming, society was organized solely on the basis of the community, which probably consisted of a kinship group. In the Formative Era, embryonic state institutions are represented by the intercommunity social cohesion involved in participation in the temple cult and in cooperation in irrigation, and the specialized priesthood which served the temples constitutes the first appearance of social classes. The essential patterns of the folk community were not destroyed, but communities were modified to the extent that they became functional parts of a new form of organization.

The development of states and empires during Andean prehistory must be understood as the result of essentially local processes and not diffusion or borrowing from other areas, even though diffusion and probably population movements were important during the Formative Era. Because rather strong chiefdoms and states, together with a substantial number of culture elements, have a wide inter-American distribution, there has been some disposition among anthropologists to postulate a single origin and diffusion for the political patterns as well as the culture elements. There is no question that culture elements diffused on a large scale, and diffusion is particularly evident in the Formative Era. Several sites in Ecuador, Colombia, Meso-America, and even in the Mississippi Valley are strikingly similar to Formative Era sites in Peru. They share not only maize farming, basketry, and mound construction but a rather distinctive style of pottery decoration. Recent radiocarbon dates support other evidence that all these Formative-like cultures flourished about 1000 B.C. Evidence of this kind proves beyond doubt that farming and the technological basis for statehood attained their wide distribution through diffusion. It also suggests that particular integrating concepts, such as the religious organization represented by temple mounds, also diffused. But state growth cannot be thought of in terms of diffusion unless there is actual migration of whole populations making up states. A state presupposes that in any locality there are enough people having enough in common to necessitate some pattern of sociocultural integration and coordination superseding the folk community. When the conditions for statehood exist, supracommunity institutions will begin to appear, though they may utilize diffused concepts as nucleating factors. In the Central Andes, a large number of small states evidently crystallized around the nucleating concepts of the temple and the feline god.

The Formative Era was a Pan-Andean and, in a broader sense, a Pan-American culture. It was followed in the Central Andes by the emergence of local styles which laid the basis for the subsequent Era of Florescent Local States. The appearance of regionalism probably came about when lands which were first brought under cultivation during the Formative Era were well settled and each region began to develop its own distinctive traditions and styles. Pan-Andean traditions did not appear again until the Era of Cyclical Conquests, when they were spread by imperial conquests rather than by the processes of free cultural borrowing that operated during the Formative Era.

There are various ways of grouping the periods during which regionally distinctive states developed. The scheme presented in Table 3 groups the local cultures of the first phase—Chanapata, Chiripa, early Paracas Cavernas, Salinar, Gallinazo, Chancay, and Huaraz—in a Regional Developmental Era because localism was initiated at this time, and it includes the subsequent late Paracas, Nazca-A, Mochica, Pucura, Recuay-A, and early Tiahuanaco cultures in a single era when local states came into full flower. There would be some justification for including the Regional Developmental Era with the preceding Formative Era inasmuch as there was still some technological development and the states had not yet taken full form. It seems best, however, to include these cultures in a separate era in order to emphasize the appearance of regionalism.

The Era of Regional Florescence, also called the Classical of Era of Master Craftsmen, is characterized by the production of goods, which, judged by any standards, were superlative—especially those made for the state institutions. Modeled and painted pottery was produced in an intriguing variety of realistic and geometric shapes and painted in excellent designs of many colors. North-coast vessels are modeled and molded in forms showing houses, plants and animals, deities, and all kinds of human activities including even sex life and its aberrations. Painted pots, more characteristic of the south, have greater pictorial possibilities and depict intricate scenes of everyday life, warfare, and religion. One vessel, perhaps more subjective or autobiographical than most, shows the fire demon breaking a pot that is in the process of baking. Textiles had a fineness of weave, a range of technique, and a richness of ornamentation unsurpassed anywhere in the world by people of comparable culture. Ornaments and ritual objects of precious metals were made with consummate skill. Mounds, temples, irrigation works, roads, and bridges were larger than in any other period. Religious structures were richly decorated with carved stone, stucco, and painting. These products manifest infinite care, effort, and artistic imagination, but they required no fundamentally new inventions.

The cultural florescence of this era must be regarded as a state or national rather than a folk achievement. The farm practices, village pattern, house types, and domestic pottery and other household goods were very similar to those of previous eras. On the north coast, where strong, class-structured states had developed, master craftsmen produced especially fine goods for the state religious and military institutions, that is, for the ruling classes. This distinction between simple domestic products and costly aesthetic state products has been found the world over in strongly class-structured societies. The finest of Chinese jades, bronzes, porcelains, and silk were for the state or the ruling class, just as the greatest paintings of Michelangelo developed religious themes and were placed in state churches while the exquisite goldwork of Benvenuto Cellini was created for his patrons, the feudal lords.

In the south of Peru, where statehood was much weaker, the best cultural products were destined for mortuary use in a cult of the dead.

During the final prehistoric era of the Central Andes, beginning about A.D. 1000, the distinctive local achievements were replaced by the first Pan-Peruvian style, which originated first at Tiahuanaco in Bolivia and typically depicted puma gods, condors, and weeping anthropomorphic deities. The Tiahuanaco style disappeared and was followed by a brief resurgence of localism, after which the Inca undertook and completed their conquest of the Andes between 1438 and 1532, when the Spaniards arrived. As native Peru had neither written records nor a reliable oral tradition that accurately recounts much more than 200 years, there is no way of knowing precisely what happened during the Tiahuanaco period and the subsequent return to localism. The number and size of the communities of that time suggest that the population had approached its possible limits under the native economy, while the great number of forts, weapons, and other indications of warfare during the previous era as well as this era shows that the states were becoming strongly militaristic. The Old World centers of irrigation civilization, which have written records, entered an era of militarism and empire building at a time when population pressure brought regional florescence to an end and created competition for available food and other products. The evidence from the Central Andes points to a similar trend.

It is not certain that the spread of Tiahuanaco styles was the result of actual conquest. We know, however, that the Inca forced their own styles, customs, language, religion, and sociopolitical organization upon the people throughout their vast empire, and it is reasonable to suppose that the Tiahuanaco styles were introduced by a similar conquest. The return to localism, not only in art styles but in religion, and the resurgence of local states, however, show that the Tiahuanaco Empire had no such far-reaching effect as the Inca upon the local populations.

The Era of Cyclical Conquests differed culturally from previous eras principally in features contingent upon imperialism. Militarism overshadowed religion, although a state religion was an essential feature of empire. Imperial government entailed extreme regimentation of the population of the conquered states in order that they should contribute goods and services to the government, church, and army. Class, occupational, and other status differences were strengthened. Cities developed as religious and administrative centers. Regimentation was at the expense of creative initiative. Goods were mass produced in standardized styles and lost their aesthetic freedom, while no important new productive processes, except the manufacture of bronze, were invented. Public works requiring sheer manpower, however, were carried out on a larger scale than ever before.

True bronze, an alloy of about 90 per cent copper and 10 per cent tin, was first made during this era. Bronze was invented at a similar stage of cultural development in the Near East, whose great civilizations are quite ineptly called the "Bronze Age." Bronze, however, was a relatively unimportant item in all of these cultures. Too scarce to be made into tools for tilling the soil or for meeting other basic, everyday needs, it was reserved principally for weapons, ornaments, and a few relatively unimportant artifacts. The cultural role of bronze was wholly unlike that of iron, which was discovered later in the Old World. Produced in abundance, iron was made into tools which enabled men first to cope with the hardwood forests of Europe, where they created new centers of civilization, and later to invent machines which led to the industrial era.

Native America never knew the use of iron, partly, perhaps, because of the absence of ores in the high civilization areas. Without mass production of an ore comparable in hardness to bronze and iron, without new plant or animal resources, and without commerce with areas producing goods not found in the Andes, it is difficult to see how aboriginal Andean cultures could have changed in basic patterns. The era of expansion, fusion of local states, and imperialism was destined to be cyclical so long as the productive technology remained unchanged. Had there been no Spanish invasion, it is probable that conquest and empire building would have ridden a crest of expanding population until the empire reached its limits; then, as in Egypt, Mesopotamia, and China, it would have collapsed under internal stresses brought about through overpopulation and inequitable distributon of goods and would have disintegrated into local states. New conquests and alliances would initiate a new cycle.

The Peruvian national achievements, although broadly comparable to those of other native American irrigation civilizations, differ somewhat in local emphasis. In general, the Inca were men of action as compared with the intellectual and aesthetic Maya of Meso-America. This is perhaps because the Inca were farther along as empire builders than the Maya, who remained in a florescent phase until the Toltec invasions from highland Mexico. The Inca were builders, engineers, and organizers. Their art was definitely inferior to that of Meso-America, they had no writing whatever, they lacked the complicated calendar of the Maya, and they were able to make only simple mathematical calculations with knotted strings, or quipus. It should be noted, however, that during the Florescent Era the Mochica people may have inscribed ideographs on beans, although the practice was soon abandoned, and that the aesthetic developments of the Central Andes at this time compare best with those of Meso-America, although the former excelled in ceramics and weaving, whereas the latter are best known for sculptured stone.

Before discussing Peruvian prehistory in detail, it is necessary to explain the present status of its chronology. Inca oral traditions cover only some 200 years before the Spanish Conquest in 1532. In the absence of written records, dendrochronology, and other methods of establishing absolute dates, pre-Inca periods had been estimated by the probable amount of time required to develop the culture of each local period. The different local cultures, however, are now cross-dated with reasonable accuracy by two methods. First, widely distributed ceramic styles such as Ancón-Cupisnique-Chavín, white-on-red, negative painting, Tiahuanaco, and black-white-and-red give points of reference for earlier and later periods in the same valleys. Second, intrusive or trade pieces serve to show the contemporaneity of associated materials in different localities.

Ceramic studies, supported by other evidence, have furnished a general chronological framework for the Central Andes, but they have provided no absolute dates and consequently have left the temporal relationship of the Central Andes to other areas in doubt. It was surmised that certain general features, such as modeled or negative-painted pottery, stirrup-mouth jars, metallurgical techniques, and others which have an inter-American distribution, would appear in the different areas at times which were not very widely separated. The evidence, however, did not add up to a very consistent picture.

The method of dating through radiocarbon began only in 1949, and it has provided comparatively few Peruvian dates as yet. It is time-consuming, difficult, and expensive, but in coming years it can be expected to clarify many problems of American prehistory. Meanwhile, the few tentative dates available for Peruvian materials show that the beginnings of agriculture and especially the growth of the Formative and Florescent Eras occurred much earlier than had generally been supposed. The Formative Era was once thought to have begun at about the time of Christ. This seemed to compress all of Andean prehistory into too short a time. It now appears that the Era of Regional Florescence began before the time of Christ and that the Formative Era may have begun about 1000 B.C. Since the lowest level at Huaca Prieta, a deep midden of stratified remains on the north coast of Peru, which contains the earliest known agricultural evidence, furnishes a date about 2300 B.C., 3000 B.C. is perhaps not too early for the beginnings of Central Andean agriculture.

It is only recently that the many local periods of the Central Andes have been cross-dated and arranged in an over-all historical scheme.

New finds will certainly revise the picture, just as research since the war has already required revision of the *Handbook* scheme. The best general relative chronology at present is Bennett's, which is followed here. Absolute dates, however, are based on recent radiocarbon research.

2. THE ERA OF HUNTERS, GATHERERS, AND FISHERS[3]

There is no doubt that early migrations brought hunting, fishing, and gathering peoples to Peru as they did to other parts of South America. It is probable that when Peru was first inhabited the Andes were moister and colder than at the present time and the flora and fauna were different. The means of subsistence of the first inhabitants, however, is not clear. Rock shelters near Huancayo in the highlands and a few north-coast sites, such as Pampa de los Fosiles, contain chipped flint implements, which perhaps indicate a hunting culture. Shellfish along the seacoast were no doubt also consumed, but it is not always possible to distinguish the shell middens of the early hunting-and-gathering cultures from the temporary coastal sites used by later agricultural peoples. Where ceramics are present in the middens, as at Ancón, the sites clearly belong to later eras. The coastal waters of Peru abound in fish, but it is by no means certain that the first inhabitants had techniques for taking them.

Percussion-flaked implements, such as core choppers and scrapers, have been found in early hunting-and-gathering sites. More finely made, pressure-flaked implements, though part of the original American cultural heritage and made by hunters and gatherers of southernmost South America, are more characteristic of later, farming people. Pressure-flaked projectile points, however, have been found at several pre-Ceramic and possibly prefarming sites.

It is imposible to say how long the hunting-and-gathering culture lasted in the Central Andes. If we assume that the area was inhabited as early as southern Chile, the era must have lasted some 5,000 years or more, from circa 8000 B.C. to 3000 B.C. More complete evidence will doubtless show that there were differences between local cultures and successive periods.

3. THE ERA OF INCIPIENT FARMING: FOLK COMMUNITIES

This era is now known only through a few sites in the Central Andes, all of them on the north coast: Puemape, Milagro, Aspero, Cerro Prieto, and Huaca Prieta. The last, at the mouth of the Chicama Valley, has yielded the fullest information, thanks to Junius Bird's thorough excavation of its 39 feet of deposits and to the radiocarbon dating of materials from several levels. As the Era of Incipient Farming covers some 2,000 years, it is certain that more complete information will disclose regional variations and sequential differences.

The people who settled the lowest levels of Huaca Prieta, which radiocarbon dates around 2300 B.C., grew domesticated gourds, cotton, two species of squash, *Canavalia* beans, chile peppers, achira (*Canna edulis*), and a fruit known as lúcuma, plants which are still known in the locality but never attained importance elsewhere. These were almost certainly farmed without irrigation along the moist alluvial plains bordering the river. Wild foods were still of some importance and included fish, shellfish, waterfowl, and plants from the river banks. There is little evidence that land mammals were hunted, and this is not surprising if coastal Peru was as completely arid then as it is today. As there were no ceramic containers, food was probably roasted and baked, hot stones being used to retain the heat.

During the last half of the occupation of Huaca Prieta, dwellings were single- and double-room structures, dug partly in the ground and the pit faced with boulders. Similar houses with wall facings of adobe were found in the pre-Ceramic sites in the Virú Valley.

Domesticated cotton supplied the principal material for textiles, which were generally woven with a twined or "finger" technique, since the heddle-equipped loom was not yet known. This technique requires a pair of weft strands to pass over and under each warp element and to be twisted by hand before passing around the next warp. Occasionally fabrics with woven patterns were produced, yet it can be deduced that these were made without the use of heddles. A twined technique was also used in making baskets and mats. Fish nets were made with a knotted technique, and pouches were created by means of looped coils and knots.

In its later phase, the Incipient Farming culture acquired several new features, all indicating a more settled and thoroughly agricultural life. Llama bones were found at Aspero, but it is uncertain whether they are from the domesticated animal. If, as some authorities believe, the llama was a distinct species during the Pleistocene period, or Ice Age, this wild ancestor has now become extinct. It is difficult to say at what point the llama could be considered domesticated.

Unpainted cooking jars ornamented only with appliqué and pinched or notched ribs initiated the art of ceramics at Aspero during the later phase of this farming culture, although pottery did not appear at Huaca Prieta until the Formative Era. The heddle loom also was introduced. Jet mirrors, bone and shell beads, and various bone ornaments show some degree of technical skill in handling new materials. Dwelling construction foreshadowed later methods in that walls were sometimes built up by means of lumps of adobe, which are typically cylindrical or conical in shape. The distribution of houses indicates small, loosely knit villages, but a room at Aspero, 12 feet square, connected with two smaller rooms, and having a platform in the center, may be the forerunner of the later ceremonial center or temple. The incipient farmers interred their dead, and Ceramic-period burials contain a few mortuary offerings.

It is uncertain that the Central Andes can claim the invention of any of the ingredients of this early farming culture. Nor can the elements be traced to any single source. Like most cultures, it is a composite of features of various origins. Bottle gourds, the domesticated ancestor of cotton, and *Canavalia* beans might have come from Asia (cf. supra), while Peru possibly supplied the wild ancestor of cotton. Squashes are native American domesticates, whose history is still incompletely understood but which probably had several origins.

The semisubterranean house has a scattered distribution throughout America, Europe, and Asia, and it is found in the Era of Incipient Agriculture in other centers of irrigation civilization. Twined weaving has an equally wide distribution. Ceramics probably originated one or more times in the New World, but no one knows where. The heddle loom also has an undetermined origin.

That the various elements making up the earliest farm culture of the Andes were derived from other areas need not involve us in intricate problems of diffusion. Their functional integration in the local way of life and their role in the subsequent development of irrigation states are the same whether they were invented locally, borrowed from other parts of America, or imported from Asia. The general pattern of the Incipient Farming culture is one of a folk society, a fairly stable though small village. In the Virú Valley, the three villages of this period showed a very small population as compared with later eras (see page 90). The villages were probably structured along kinship lines and were politically independent. They had some form of shamanistic religion, and the beginning of a village cult is suggested by the ceremonial chamber at Aspero. There is no evidence in this era of the economic, ceremonial, or political integration of several villages in a larger sociocultural system.

4. THE FORMATIVE ERA: EMERGENCE OF THEOCRATIC STATES

The Era of Incipient Farming terminated with the establishment of the stable farming folk community and the introduction of many, though not all, of the important productive processes and manufacturing techniques. The Formative Era witnessed the emergence of local, theocratic states, which were supported by irrigation and integrated by a temple cult. The principal features of this culture are found not only throughout a large part of northern Peru—Ancón, Supe,[4] Chavín de Huántar—but also in Meso-America and North America. By all indications, it was a nonmilitaristic, highly religious culture, and Bennett therefore designates it a period of "cultists." Cults, however, have to have the support of a local population, and there is no doubt that the priests who supervised the ritual at the mounds and temples also exercised considerable social control over the communities scattered around them.

In describing the development of the Andean state in this and subsequent sections, we shall lean heavily upon the evidence from the Virú Valley in northern Peru. The entire prehistory of this valley was studied just after World War II by a joint expedition of some seven North American and Peruvian institutions, and it is now known in greater detail perhaps than any other comparable locality in the world. We have not only detailed information on the succession of farm practices, ceramic types, house forms, weaving, metallurgy, mounds, and other material remains ranging from the lowest pre-Ceramic levels of Cerro Prieto and the nearby Huaca Prieta sites to the time of the Spanish Conquest, but the studies of Gordon Willey,[5] upon which we draw heavily, have disclosed the settlement patterns developed at each period.

The Formative Era culture is concentrated on the central and north Peruvian coast. One of the most impressive sites, Chavín de Huántar, however, is in the north highlands. The seeming absence of Formative remains in southern Peru and Bolivia is perhaps principally due to our ignorance of them, for these areas are very incompletely known.

Agriculture was substantially improved during the Formative Era through the beginnings of irrigation and the addition of maize, peanuts, warty squash, beans, avocados, pacae, and possibly manioc or yuca to the list of crops. These species are all native to America. Each irrigation system covered only a small portion of a valley and entailed cooperation between only a few communities. Sea foods have always been used on the Peruvian coast, and the large shell middens attest their importance during this era.

In the Virú Valley, the settlements increased in number—there are seven known Formative villages as against three sites datable to Incipient Agriculture—but they are not much larger. Each village consisted of a cluster of single-room house dwellings. The house walls were built of stone, stone and adobe, or conical adobes and were surmounted by a thatched roof. The more imposing structures are temples, which probably served the people of several communities. Temples are distinguishable by their greater size, their masonry or adobe wall construction, and their multiple rooms, platforms, steps, clay columns, and painted, carved, or incised walls. The temple or "castillo" at Chavín de Huántar in the highlands is a truly impressive edifice. Its base is some 250 feet square, and its exterior is built of terraces and sloping walls to a height sufficient to afford three interior stories. It is honey-combed with rooms as large as 12 to 14 feet square and with ramps, stairs, passageways, and airshafts.

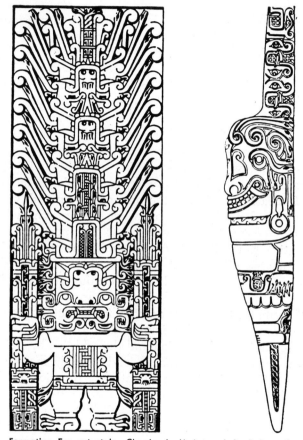

Formative Era art style: Chavín de Huántar. Left: Raimondi stela. (After Julio Tello, "Wira Kocha," in Inca, vol. 1, 1923.) Right: Lanzon. (After Samuel K. Lothrop, "Gold and Silver from Southern Peru and Bolivia," Journal of the Royal Anthropological Institute, vol. 62, 1937.)

Wall exteriors are constructed of dressed masonry and ornamented with carved stone heads. The castillo is but one of a group of structures which were obviously planned and required vast labor.

The Formative Era religion is based on the worship of a feline god, perhaps the puma, which constitutes the principal art motif of the culture, being found in temple decoration, carved stone, pottery, and goldwork. The feline deity is sometimes portrayed anthropomorphically; a human face may have feline traits, and one molded pot shows a face one half of which is human, the other half catlike. Symbols indicating a condor, a serpent, or a fish may be added to the feline deity. The exterior of the Chavín castillo bears carved stone heads representing old men, a motif also found in ceramics.

The social function of the Formative Era religion is not entirely clear. The occurrence of the feline motif on household objects as well as in temple art suggests that the deities did not pertain solely to priestly ceremonies but were part of everyday worship. The temples, however, clearly indicate some kind of public ceremonialism, which was of a higher order than any village cults and which united people of a fairly large region. Each temple served several communities. The Chavín castillo served an extensive territory. The widespread sameness of god concepts does not mean, however, that all of north Peru was unified politically under a single religious organization.

Bennett suggests that the Chavín temple was less a headquarters of religiopolitical organization than a center which drew persons on periodic pilgrimages from far and wide. There must have been some political cohesion, however, among the people worshiping even at the largest temples, for the structures were built by special artisans and run by a priesthood, both of which had to be supported. Moreover, many of the cultural works, such as objects of gold or carved stone and probably some of the finer textiles and ceramics, were produced for the temple. These religious centers, in other words, had to have an economic basis firmly supported by the rural population and controlled by a special managerial class. It is inconceivable that all the specialization implied in the cult religion could have been sustained on a purely voluntary basis.

It would perhaps not be rash to guess that the practical interests of an agrarian population in the annual rhythm of farming and in the crucially important matter of irrigation water would find some expression in religious concepts and ceremonial practice. The basic religions of the early irrigation civilizations of the world grew out of the supernaturalism connected with the agricultural calendar and the cycles of water supply.

The Formative Era seems to have been a time of general peace in contrast to later periods, which present considerable evidence of militarism. It is necessary, however, to distinguish skirmishes executed as raids or personal vengeance from national warfare. Many primitive bands and villages fought for glory, revenge, or for supernatural reasons, such as dream fulfillment. Organized warfare, wherein individuals submit to an authority which has the power to make war and conclude peace, is generally a characteristic of a true state. States may wage war in order to take captives and to acquire tribute or territory. The Formative Era cultures lack forts, which are an important feature of the later warring states, but the village sites yield a considerable number of weapons—bows, clubs, daggers, lances, and spear throwers or atlatls. These may not all have been used in the hunt, and it is possible that there were intervillage fights despite the absence of economic or political motives for true warfare. The capture of sacrificial victims may have been the purpose of raids at this time.

Considerable technical progress during the Formative Era is shown by both domestic artifacts and cult goods. The common folk attained a high degree of competence in ceramics, which they modeled or molded expertly into various forms but never painted. With simple but vigorous realism, they reproduced human and feline heads, human figures—a Cupisnique pot is in the form of a mother nursing a child—plants and animals, and even houses. The pots were baked in a reducing kiln, which produced a very dark grayish or brownish color. Characteristic ornamentation includes a stirrup-shaped spout and surface designs which show either the feline motif or geometric figures outlined by relief or incision, with small punches, scratches, or stamped marks filling the enclosed areas to provide a contrast between polished and roughened portions of the design.

The Formative Era population made revolutionary progress in the production of textiles in that they acquired the true loom with heddles, a device which permits the employment of an infinitely faster and more efficient technique than finger twining. Their fabrics were not finely woven and ornamented, like those of later periods, but they were made by a number of techniques—plain weaving, brocade, gauze, tapestry—and some were decorated with the feline or condor motif. They also made feather headdresses and capes, which were perhaps ceremonial gear.

Another basic invention of the Formative Era is metallurgy. The people knew how to work gold and possibly silver into wrist and ear ornaments and other objects. They used thin sheets of gold which they wrought by hammering, embossing, welding, soldering, and annealing. In spite of the use of heat in metal smithing, they apparently knew nothing of smelting.

There were skilled stone carvers during this period, but their work was generally done in a kind of low relief and resembles metalwork and stucco. True sculpture in the round, or statuary, is rare.

The standard of living of the common people was improved by the introduction of a number of new household goods which facilitated daily chores. Stone mortars and pestles were used for grinding foods, and stone bowls and boxes as well as pots and baskets served as containers. Sewing was done with bone awls and needles. Clothing as such was limited to breechclouts, belts, and headgear, but personal adornment was very elaborate. The body was painted, probably by means of special stamps, the ears were ornamented with plugs and pendants, and various kinds of necklaces, combs, bracelets, and finger rings were worn. The ornaments were made of gold, stone, bone, shell, and semiprecious stones, most of them wrought in somewhat realistic forms. In addition, skulls were artificially deformed. The degree of personal vanity is further attested by the general use of pyrite and jet mirrors, some of them convex.

Despite the evidence of a class-structured society that must have been part of the theocratic state, status differences seem to have been much less marked in this than in subsequent eras. Luxury goods, including goldwork, fine ceramics, and articles of personal adornment, are found not only in the temples but in village sites. Nor are there such clear-cut status burials—special graves prepared for overlords containing an abundance of precious goods—as characterized later eras. Graves are fairly simple pits, except at Cupisnique, where a chamber and shaft were used, and they contain ordinary objects as grave offerings as well as objects decorated with deity figures. The Formative Era, in other words, was not a time of extreme specialization in either production or status. Every household had some skill in the principal crafts and was privileged to make and use the products.

5. REGIONAL DIFFERENTIATION OF LOCAL THEOCRATIC STATES

The cultures of this era might justifiably be included with the Formative Era, for states were not yet highly evolved and there was much progress in productive technology. The cultures, however, do not continue the previous tradition in all respects. The temples of the feline deity and the widespread art styles were abandoned. In each of some half dozen major regions of the Central Andes there emerged distinctive traditions whose attainments, though inferior to those of the subsequent Era of Regional Florescence, established the technical and aesthetic foundations of the latter. The cultural continuity in each region between the present era and the following one is, in fact, so great that the eras might well be grouped together. Since the actual flowering of the trends, however, could not take place without well-developed states, it is best to treat this separately, as a time when the foundations of the states were laid.

The break in cultural continuity which initiates this era is less marked in fundamental features than in stylistic ones. Technological accomplishments of the Formative Era were retained, and new inventions were ordinarily diffused to all the regions. Domestic architecture, cooking pots, farm practices, weaving, and other features carry over from the

Formative Era. New inventions, such as the firing of pots in the open to produce an orange-red ware and the ornamentation of pots with white paint or with "negative" designs—a method of decoration in which the ornamental pattern, when coated with some such substance as wax to resist the paint which is then applied, becomes the unpainted portion of the pot—are shared by many of the regional cultures and are called "horizon styles." Regional differences consist partly of artistic styles and of details of form and construction. They also consist partly of local interest in ceramics in the north, in textiles in the south. Such differences indicate a growing localism, a somewhat less slavish borrowing than during the Formative Era.

On the basis of stylistic features, six regional subcultures are distinguished: (1) Salinar in the Chicama Valley and Puerto Moorin in the Virú Valley of the north coast of Peru; (2) Huaraz and Chavín de Huántar in the north highlands; (3) Chancay at Cerro de Trinidad, Baños de Boza, and other sites of the central coast; (4) possibly Chanapata, a pre-Inca style of uncertain date in the central highlands; (5) Carvernas at Paracas and Ocucaje on the south coast; (6) Chiripa in the Bolivian highlands south of Lake Titicaca.

The basic techniques of food production were well established during the Era of Regional Development, although they were later employed on a much vaster scale. The coastal people built irrigation works principally in the narrow, upper portions of the valleys, and the highlanders of Chiripa and Chanapata constructed stone-faced agricultural terraces. Agriculture became more diversified through the introduction of the frijoles or kidney bean, canahua, pepino, and quinoa, the last a grain which became the staple of the highlands. Hoes were used to cultivate the land.

The people also had greater skill in food preparation. Dried meat is known to the modern Indians as "charqui," a word which the Spaniards carried to North America, where it became "jerky," or jerked meat. Fruits and vegetables were seemingly fermented to make an alcoholic beverage which is known today as chicha and which was the only intoxicating beverage of native South America. (Aboriginal America never learned to distill liquors.) Coca was used and possibly cultivated. The leaf of this plant is chewed, today usually with lime or ashes, so that the narcotic effects of its cocaine are enhanced. The guinea pig, a common household pet and food of the modern Indians, was probably domesticated at this time.

Man's much improved control of nature during this era permitted a rapid expansion of population. In the Virú Valley, the Salinar period has eighty-nine sites and an estimated total population of 5,000 persons as compared with seven settlements and perhaps 500 persons during the preceding Ancón-Cupisnique period. Settlements consist of groups of two to ten houses built on stone platforms. Each house is about 6 by 9 or 10 feet square and built of adobe walls with a single-slope, thatched roof supported by beams. These small, folk communities could not have averaged more than 50 persons each, and very likely each comprised an extended family.

In some cases, each community had its own temple; in others, one temple served several villages, which were built near temple mounds. One of the typical mounds is a rectangular, flat-topped, earthen structure some 95 by 135 feet at the base and 22 to 25 feet high.

The Salinar people made warfare a state matter, if we assume that certain hilltop forts belong to this period, and they possessed the weapons typical of later Andean peoples—spears, spear throwers, slings, and bolas.

While the north Peruvian communities were being drawn together to form small states which served the supracommunity functions of controlling irrigation, carrying out the worship of the temple cult, and perhaps fighting wars, southern Peru seems to have lagged somewhat in its political development. The people of Cavernas and Chiripa lived in small villages of semisubterranean lodges. The Chiripa houses were quite large and had closetlike storage niches all around the inside. Possible differentiation of social status in the Cavernas culture is shown in the burials. In soft stone, the people hollowed an underground chamber which was connected with a still lower vault where several burials were placed. Perhaps these were family vaults, but the individual "mummy" bundles—these were bodies which were wrapped in many yards of cloth and desiccated but not embalmed—disclose some differences in personal riches. Later Peruvian communities worshiped their principal ancestors and accorded them special elaborate burial in the family plot. Perhaps lineage heads were attributed special power at this time.

There is little in the way of art symbolism to suggest what the god concepts of this period may have been. Some pots from Cavernas, however, preserve the feline motif, while others show a human face with "tear streaks" extending down each cheek from the eye. Tear streaks are very characteristic of the art of Tiahuanaco, the first of the Pan-Peruvian empires, and though Cavernas and Tiahuanaco are otherwise stylistically different, it would seem proper to designate these Cavernas faces the "weeping god."

The manufacturing processes of the Era of Developmental Regional States include few important new inventions. Products of the era differ from Formative goods in their local stylistic distinctiveness. This is particularly true of pottery. The people of Salinar continued in the Cupisnique tradition of modeling jars in many realistic shapes, but they now added white paint to the surface decoration and made some jars with a small figure perched on top and connected with the spout by a strap of clay. Chancay, on the other hand, did more painting than modeling, while Cavernas typically made incised designs and put paint of several colors in the lines.

The south coast was distinctive in its emphasis on weaving. While the Salinar people wove only of cotton, the Cavernas population began also to employ wool, maguey fiber, and human hair. Their textiles, too, were outstanding for the fineness of their gauzes, brocades, single-faced weft patterns, embroidery, and painted cloth.

Metallurgy is the one industry that shows steady progress throughout the prehistory of the Andes. Chiripa and Cavernas made objects of pure copper; Chancay and Salinar used a gold-copper alloy. Gilding, engraving, and casting, while possibly introduced at this time, were certainly known in the following Gallinazo and Mochica periods.

The lives of the common people were enriched not only by the better ceramics, textiles, and metal objects but by new household utensils. For containers they employed pots, baskets, stone bowls, skin bags, and pyrograved calabashes. For cutting, they used bone knives, stone and bone scrapers, and bone chisels. Thanks perhaps to the comparative ease of weaving on the heddle loom, they paid more attention to clothing and less to bodily adornment. On the north coast, knee-length skirts and varied headgear became the style, while Cavernas adopted shirts, shawls, breechclouts, belts, turbans, and headbands. Both practiced skull deformation.

This era provides the earliest evidence of the use of musical instruments: clay Panpipes and five-hole flutes.

6. REGIONAL FLORESCENT STATES: PRIESTS, WARRIORS, AND ARTISANS

Local states attained such maturity between about 200 b.c. and a.d. 450 that there can be no question that they had embryonic form during the previous era. Based on a dense population, they now became strongly structured along occupational and class lines. Their internal stability is attested by the flowering of the material arts, which were now well established and paid off in the finest products ever made in the Central Andes—products which equal and in some respects surpass the best of ancient Meso-America, China, and the Near East. This material florescence resulted less from technological progress—the basic techniques had already been introduced—than from the opportunity afforded specialists and the stimulus of demands to produce for the state. The finest goods were destined for the upper class of warrior-priests, and they must be regarded as national cultural products, that is, as cultural attainments contingent upon the newly established state patterns, in contrast to the simpler goods, the household utensils and other objects, that were made for domestic consumption by the common folk.

The social, political, and religious patterns that mark a fully established state are clearly disclosed by several kinds of evidence. What cannot be confidently inferred from the temples and palaces, the status burials, the forts, the irrigation systems, and the settlement pattern is strikingly and convincingly illustrated in Mochica and Nazca ceramic and textile designs. The modeled life forms and the meticulously painted pictures on pots are veritable source books of contemporary ethnology, showing not only realistic forms but whole compositions depicting subsistence activities, warfare, ceremonialism, lords and underlings, domestic affairs, and even human sexual activities. Many archaeologists, among them the Peruvian Larco Hoyle, whose collection of Florescent ceramics is unsurpassed, have drawn upon ceramic art to reconstruct the native culture. As yet, however, this source of information has hardly been scratched. If the thousands of Mochica and Nazca pots in museums were systematically studied, the ethnography of these cultures would be surprisingly complete.

Regionalism during this era was manifested largely in emphasis and stylistic patterning. Probably most of the basic inventions were diffused throughout Peru, and the ceramic technique of negative painting on pottery, a "horizon style," was widely used. Even such widespread motifs as the feline, snake, sea otter, and ray fish appear in the different local styles.

As each regional style is a continuation of what was begun in the developmental era, the major divisions of the Central Andes are about the same as before. There is one difference, however. In several regions, somewhat distinctive ceramic styles coexisted independently. Thus the Mochica style invaded certain valleys which had the Gallinazo culture, and the two survived side by side. Similarly, the Interlocking and early Lima ceramic styles both occurred on the central coast and Pucara and early Tiahuanaco in the south highlands. These associated traditions probably signify minor population movements. That ceramic styles and other cultural features could remain intact despite close association with somewhat alien styles attests the vitality of each tradition; or it might indicate that the makers of the two styles were segregated in social isolation as different classes, such as conquerors and conquered.

Food production in the Central Andes reached its peak of efficiency during this era. The people brought a large portion of the arable or irrigable land under cultivation. In order to make maximum use of the water supply, they constructed huge systems of canals and ditches that not only served entire valleys but in some cases carried water over earthen aqueducts to several adjoining valleys, and they terraced mountainsides thousands of feet high to provide additional land. A canal in the Chicama Valley is 75 miles long, and an aqueduct which crosses the valley at Ascope consists of an earthwork four-fifths of a mile long and 50 feet high. The agricultural terraces no less than the waterworks evidence prodigious labor. On the gentle slopes the terraces are broad and low, but on the steeper pitches they may be 20 feet high and only 6 feet wide. It would take several years of labor for one man to terrace enough land to support himself. Such seemingly uneconomical construction can only be explained by a combination of considerable leisure time and a crucial shortage of land that could be reached by water. Most of the land must have been very productive, for it was still new, neither leached of its minerals nor rendered infertile by accumulation of alkalines from prolonged irrigation. To increase the fertility of the soil, the Indians made trips off the coast in balsa rafts constructed of reed bundles to fetch back guano from islands where hundreds of thousands of birds had nested for untold generations.

A considerable number of domesticated plants was added to the already long list of Andean crops, and varieties became more specially adapted to the different altitudes and climates. Since the interest in plant domestication had been firmly established, the Andean Indians now experimented with scores of species, many of which proved to be of little value. Table 1 lists only the more important species of plant domesticates. Some of these, together with others not listed, attained only minor importance and a very limited distribution. A complete list of varieties would number well in the hundreds. The world's debt to this untiring experimentation is quite obvious.

The new crops of the Era of Regional Florescence complete the inventory of basic foods that were to support the Central Andes until the Spanish Conquest. Potatoes of the kind we call white potatoes, along with quinoa and special varieties of maize, became high-altitude staples. Peanuts, pumpkins, beans, maize, and sweet potatoes were the principal lowland crops. Other domesticates, which are not widely known outside the Andes and semitropical America, include such vegetables as mashuas, ullucos, jíquimas, yacones, and lupines and such fruits as pacaes, tumbos, tunas, guanábanas or soursops, granadillas, cherimoyas, papayas, and pineapples. Only the last two are familiar to most North Americans.

The Central Andean people were primarily horticulturists. They failed to develop a herding economy, not for want of skill or effort, but because of the absence of native species suitable for domestication. They nevertheless made full use of what was at hand, and during the Florescent Era they pastured large herds of llamas and probably alpacas, while around their houses they kept guinea pigs and dogs. The herds were important not only as a source of meat and wool but as adjuncts to transportation. A llama can carry only about a hundred pounds, but this was a substantial help in a country where there was considerable exchange of produce between the specialized regions.

Wild food resources were not neglected. Ocean-going balsas carried fishermen outfitted with nets, fishhooks, and harpoons. A new weapon, the blowgun, came into use for hunting birds. Hunters are depicted in ceramic paintings taking deer with nets and traps. Apparently pumas, monkeys, bears, and foxes also were hunted.

The population approached its maximum density during this era. The Virú Valley probably had some 25,000 persons, a number that at most was only slightly surpassed in the subsequent Tiahuanaco period and may not have been as high. This growth, however, was brought about more by increase in community size than in number of communities, a factor which remained about the same. There were some 100 communities, each consisting of forty to fifty rooms, which indicates a population of 100 or more. The villages, however, were by no means uniform. A Gallinazo site in the valley is built on six flat mounds. The largest mound, about 600 by 1,300 feet in ground plan and 15 feet high, had several thousand houses, each about 30 feet square.

Throughout northern and central coastal Peru, state planning, control of constructional efforts, and regimentation of mass labor are seen in the numerous gigantic public projects such as mounds, temples, palaces, and forts. These, like the irrigation systems, clearly indicate managerial control and sociopolitical integration of large populations, although it is impossible to delineate state borders at this time. When a valley was served by a single irrigation system and had its main points of entry protected by forts, it can be fairly inferred that it constituted a political unit. Some states, however, may have embraced more than one valley, while others may have been limited to portions of larger valleys.

One of the outstanding public constructions of this era is the cluster of temple mounds at Moche, near Trujillo, which must have been the religious and administrative center of an exceptionally large state. The main edifice, the Huaca del Sol or "Sacred Place of the Sun," consists of a platform about 750 by 450 feet at the base and 60 feet high. It is surmounted by a stepped pyramid 340 feet square and 75 feet high, built of adobe columns which are filled in with rectangular adobes. This device of using columns as part of the fill is found elsewhere, but columns were also used as independent architectural units.

A second major construction at Moche is the Huaca de la Luna, or "Sacred Place of the Moon," a platform about 260 by 195 feet and 75 feet high. Other, almost equally impressive platforms and pyramidal mounds occur elsewhere on the north coast, and some of them surmount natural hills. They were typically constructed of individual, rectangular mold-made adobes and decorated with frescoes and cutout relief designs. Some of these were undoubtedly built during several periods and reveal

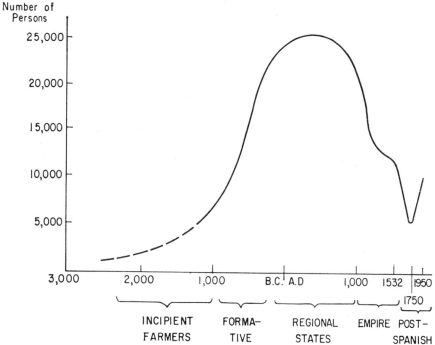

Population change in the Central Andes exemplified by the Virú Valley, northern Peru. (This is an interpretation of the data of Gordon R. Willey, "Prehistoric Settlement Patterns in the Virú Valley, Peru," Bureau of American Ethnology Bulletin 155, 1953.) The curve is a guess based upon the number and size of settlements and the assumption that there was one person per acre of cultivated land. The relative figures at different periods are more signifi- cant than the absolute figures. A very small population of preagricultural people began to increase slowly after crops were introduced, and the curve climbs rapidly during the Formative Era and Early Florescence of States. The local decline, which began a little before the Era of Cyclical Conquests or Empires, probably represents a removal of part of the local population to near-by urban centers, which were now developing, and not a decrease in Andean population. The sharp post-Spanish drop, however, is probably the result of the over-all decrease of Indians at this time as well as local loss of land formerly used for subsistence crops.

the increasing concentration of political and religious power. Lesser temple mounds are interspersed among the communities.

Some of the large mounds on the central coast, such as those at Pachacamac and Cajamarquilla, although still used in later periods, were probably begun during or before this era. Several-storied temples in the north highlands perhaps also are religious centers belonging to the Recuay culture.

Large-scale building, especially the erection of massive mounds of adobe, was not characteristic of the southern highlands. The religious center at Pucara is an example of architectural planning in masonry construction rather than of mass effort in creating artificial hills. A court some 45 feet square is surrounded on three sides by stone-walled compartments, each of which opens on the court and contains a slab altar. Below the court are two masonry-lined burial vaults. Pucara religious concepts are suggested by some statues showing the weeping god carrying a human trophy head, but many stelae are decorated with purely geometric designs.

The evidence of militarism parallels that of economic and religious organization in its sociological implications. Forts, or castillos, some of them perhaps also serving as palaces and temples, were built at strategic points to protect the valleys and provide places of refuge in times of siege. Clearly, a pattern of state warfare had replaced any earlier, simpler patterns of individual raids for war honors or loot. Ceramic paintings show uniformed warriors equipped with shields, helmets, metal-headed maces, spears, spear throwers, and semicircular knives. The same weapons have been found in archaeological sites. Preceded by scouts, accompanied by trumpeters blowing conch shells and leading war dogs on leashes, armies moved into battle. Victors returned bearing loot and leading naked prisoners by ropes. The prisoners were brought to kneel before the lords. Some paintings show victims being toppled from peaks in sacrifice to mountain deities.

Although territorial conquest of neighboring states may not have been a motivation for warfare, the religious demand for sacrificial victims and for human trophies—heads and perhaps other parts of the body—is obvious in the paintings. Capture of loot seems to have been another purpose. Thus, once the culture became functionally dependent upon warfare, the militaristic pattern would become self-perpetuating. Moreover, it would spread. Neighboring states would fight first in self-defense and later acquire the full complex. Although this kind of warfare was later abandoned in the Central Andes, it survived in full force among the Circum-Caribbean chiefdoms at the Spanish Conquest.

The functions of the war lords and the high priests of the Regional Florescent culture were evidently combined in the same persons, for status burials show that prominent men were interred with weapons as well as with ceremonial gear. A lavish burial found by W. D. Strong in the Virú Valley was evidently that of the supreme ruler himself.[6] Moreover, the foremost deity is frequently represented in realistic art as both civil ruler and military chief.

The politicoreligious pattern of the north coast is obviously one of strong regimentation of the population by their priest-warrior rulers. In time this strong rule developed into territorial conquest, and although briefly interrupted by the Tiahuanaco Empire, it led in later periods to the domination of the entire north coast by the Chimu Kingdom and

a

b

Mochica culture depicted on ceramic paintings. (a) A god fishing. (b) Anthropomorphic fish demon. (From Rafael Larco Hoyle, **Handbook**, vol. 2.)

to the growth of large cities. By contrast, the states of the south coast seem to have centered around a cult of the dead. This suggests that personal ties within the state were somewhat more important than among the northerly societies dominated by priest-warriors. Public works are not lacking in the south, but the efforts of surplus production seem to have been directed largely toward the manufacture of exceptionally fine textiles that were made principally as burial wrappings for the dead.

The Mochica state was internally structured along lines of status and occupational specialization. The class of warrior-priests had superior

Pottery paintings representing Mochica culture. (a) Battle of warriors using helmets, maces, and shields. (b) Victorious warriors with nude captives and loot. (c) Ritual sacrifice of human beings: naked captives are thrown from mountain cliffs, where the mountain spirit is represented by a rainbow (?) deity. (From Rafael Larco Hoyle, **Handbook**, vol. 2.)

status, as is shown not only by their elaborate burials but by pictorial representations. Elaborately attired dignitaries are seated on stools or raised platforms sheltered from the sun, while lesser persons kneel in obeisance before them, their heads lowered and their hands clasped. The lords are carried on litters by pairs of runners or towed on balsa rafts by swimmers.

These rulers led the armies, supervised ceremonies, and hunted and fished for recreation. They were unrelenting in their demands for obedience and punished offenders by amputating their lips, noses, and feet,

Whistling jars are an example of early Peruvian inventiveness. When these double jars are tilted, the water running back and forth forces air through the head-like spout to cause a whistle. (Courtesy of the American Museum of Natural History.)

and even by skinning their faces and by having them stoned to death in public. Frequent pictorial representations of the supreme god, a feline being, give further evidence of the respect accorded his warrior-priest representative on earth. The god is accompanied by various anthropomorphic animal attendants: a lizard is his servant, a dog his faithful friend, a cormorant his fishing assistant, an owl his medicine man, a falcon his shield-bearer, and a marine eagle his conveyor of sacrificial blood.

The state superstructure must have consisted of a large pyramid of nobles topped by the supreme ruler, the representative or incarnation of the god. This structure rested upon a vast number of specialists of lesser status. The servants of the lords included messengers, attendants, healers, and litter bearers. There were many minor state functionaries, such as architects, war captains, and lesser priests. There were also artisans, who specialized in ceramics, weaving, metallurgy, or carving. And there were doctors, musicians, and dancers.

The basic population were the principal producers. They not only tilled the soil; they furnished manpower for the construction of state irrigation works, temples, and forts. They probably also served as soldiers, in which capacity they are portrayed with the shield, mace, and spear. Possibly as successful warriors they could acquire special status.

Whether there was a still lower class of slaves and war captives is not known. Many captives became sacrificial victims, but it is possible that some were spared to perform menial chores. Naked litter bearers, for example, may have been captives.

The religious conceptions upon which the Mochica state cult were based reflect a very keen awareness of nature. As in the Asiatic Shinto religion and other forms of nature worship, all living things of the land and sea, as well as natural features such as mountains, were deified. The supreme deity is represented as a wrinkle faced old man with fangs and catlike whiskers. Like the Chavín feline god, he appeared in both human and animal form. He was involved in all aspects of life, for he is shown as the recipient of sacrificial victims, as a farmer shelling maize, as fisherman, doctor, hunter, and musician. He intervened to ensure victory in war, and he aided human fecundity. He sometimes took the form of various animals; or he fought the animal demons which infested the world, such as vampires, crabs, fish, sea demons, and various dragonlike spirits. These various representations disclose a general belief that all of nature was filled with spirits which, like human beings, were engaged in a great struggle with one another.

But this deep religious interest in nature also involved agriculture. A special zoomorphic deity, who presided over agricultural scenes in association with the supreme god, had a frog's body and a feline nose and legs. Manioc and lima beans grew from his body. Many pictures also show anthropomorphic vegetables and fruits.

Mochica religion entailed considerable public ceremonialism, as is expectable. Pictures show dancers clad in feather capes, masks, and other special attire performing under the direction of priests to the accompaniment of drums, tambourines, flutes, clay and reed Panpipes, gongs, rattles, shell trumpets, and both straight and coiled clay trumpets.

The prominence of the feline deity together with evidence of conquest in some pictures suggests that the Mochica states represent a resurgence of the older Chavín-Cupisnique concepts. It is, of course, difficult to distinguish state from community and household religion in archaeological evidence. The feline deity, however, is clearly the state god. Lesser and more localized deities and spirits probably predominated in local worship. Finally, shamanistic practices and ritual observances at crucial points in the life cycle survived at the family and individual level.

Pictures show shamans, or medicine men, both male and female, seated beside prostrate patients, chanting, praying, shaking gourd or pottery rattles, massaging the patient, and sucking out the disease-causing object. These activities are like primitive shamanistic practices

Early Peruvian musical instruments. The Panpipes (center and blown by figure lower left) are among many culture elements which might have been introduced to Peru across the Pacific. (Courtesy of American Museum of Natural History.)

the world over. The doctors also administered herbs. Women are shown attended by midwives delivering children. Death observances were probably family affairs, but considerable pains were taken to equip the deceased with food, clothing, and other goods. Mochica, however, provides no evidence that the deceased became major state deities in a cult of the dead.

The socioreligious pattern at Nazca and Paracas Necropolis on the south coast was very different from that of the Mochica state. The area is more arid, and the population was probably much sparser. Whether these facts account for the backward south-coast state organization is not clear. In any event, these southern people were contented to construct simple houses, generally semisubterranean, of hand-made adobes (Nazca villages have not been found) and to avoid major efforts at building mounds, temples, palaces, and forts. Their productive energy

Mummy bundle. This complex wrapping of an early Peruvian from Trujillo exemplifies the importance accorded ancestors. (Courtesy of American Museum of Natural History.)

was converted into the more tedious business of weaving. The mass output of textiles, which far exceeded everyday needs, itself revealed a basic socioreligious pattern.

The Nazca and Necropolis people were predominantly interested in their dead. The inhabitants of the north coast provided fairly lavish burials and grave goods, and they even held dances in which performers imitated skeletons, but they did not dedicate so much effort to their deceased as the south-coast people. The latter eviscerated each corpse, then probably desiccated it, and finally wrapped it in many yards of cloth. Shrouds may be nearly 50 feet long, and many mummy bundles are wound into balls measuring as much as 5 feet in diameter. Some deceased received more care than others, but they were probably lineage heads rather than members of a priestly class. The art motifs disclose less of major deities than in the north, although ceramic and textile designs show a human being with a staff and a masked anthropomorphic feline.

Marginal as the south coast was in sociopolitical development, it had attained some war patterns, for trophy heads are frequently represented on pots and textiles. Warfare could easily have been carried on to achieve individual status and obtain trophies without the additional purpose of conquest and tribute. This is one of many instances in which traits of warfare spread to simpler cultures and were readapted to the local pattern.

As a very large proportion of the artifacts from the Era of Regional Florescence come from graves, for which they were probably specially made, knowledge of the common household goods of that period is incomplete. In general, however, it appears that the household culture was carried over from the preceding era with comparatively little change. The greatest changes were in burial objects and goods produced for the state, and these differ less in technical features than in style and in the care devoted to their manufacture.

Ceramics were now produced with the utmost skill. Modeling continued in vogue, especially on the north coast, where it was used to produce a great variety of life forms. The north-coast predisposition for speed-up processes is shown in the manufacture of most of these pots in molds, but painted ornamentation was now applied with great skill on a white background. Nazca in the south excelled in its polychrome decoration, as many as eleven colors sometimes being employed on a single vessel, but its designs, while executed with consummate skill, were generally limited to stylized plant, animal, and human forms. North-coast art, on the other hand, was quite uninhibited in its pictorial representations, which show whole scenes in great detail and range over all subjects from the activities of the very gods themselves to the simple doings of human beings, birds, fishes, and animals.

Ceramic styles of the other regions of the Central Andes are distinguishable by vessel shapes, decorative techniques, and design motifs. None, however, are so indicative of sociological patterns and motivations as the Mochica ceramics and the Nazca textiles.

The excellence of weaving has already been mentioned in connection with the Nazca culture, which surpassed any other region in the range of materials, number of techniques, fineness of weave, and quality of decoration employed in this craft. These people used the wool of llamas, alpacas, and probably wild vicuñas of the highland along with cotton to make embroidered cloth, brocades, gauze, lace, double cloth, tapestry, and warp- and weft-striped cloth. They were also skilled in braiding. Their textiles were characteristically ornamented with polychrome designs, and a single fabric has shown as many as seven basic colors in 190 hues.

Not all textiles, even among the Nazca and Paracas peoples, were destined for mummy wrappings. They were used extensively for clothing, a need that was much greater in the chilly highlands than on the comparatively warm coast. The basic Central Andean dress now consisted of breechclouts and belts, shirts with a neck slit, wrap-around skirts, robes, and headgear. In addition to these articles, however, a vast variety of special adornment indicating status and profession was worn. Some of these were of featherwork and others of precious metals. Earplugs, nose plugs, and lip plugs came into common use and possibly were status badges.

Metalwork was more common than before, especially in the Mochica area, and objects were made of gold, silver, and copper and various alloys of these metals. Metals were still used predominantly for ornaments and ceremonial objects, but the Mochica made some spear points, axheads, and digging-stick points of copper. Copper objects were sometimes cast.

Workmanship of a quality comparable to that in metallurgy, weaving, and ceramics is also shown in the handling of other materials, such as carving bone tubes, inlaying shell mosaics, and sculpturing and carving stone.

The people of the Florescent Era differed from one another and from the people of a comparable stage of cultural development in other irrigation centers in their special emphasis. They were essentially craftsmen— artists, ceramicists, weavers, and builders. Central Andean culture during this and subsequent eras lacked the intellectual attainments of other centers. It should be noted, however, that wide experimentation in ideas had brought them very near to some of the basic accomplishments of other irrigation cultures at a similar stage of development.

Another basic accomplishment, which was given up before it became fully developed, was perhaps writing. According to Larco Hoyle, beans marked in kidney-shaped areas with straight, curved, broken, and parallel lines, points, circles, crosses, and other figures were ideographic symbols.[7] Many beans bear the same designs. Pictures on pots and textiles show runners carrying such beans in bags and traveling on roads. These "messengers" were symbolized by anthropomorphic deer, falcons, hummingbirds, dragonflies, and centipedes. Foxes, viscachas, and felines were, according to Larco Hoyle, "interpreters" and "scribes."

A very different explanation is that some of the beans were counters in a dice game. One ceramic decoration shows men who appear to be casting stick-dice while they hold some beans in their hands and other beans lie on small sand mounds. Some authorities have agreed with Larco Hoyle that there is a striking similarity between the ovoid shape of the beans and the glyphs used in Mayan writing. Moreover, it should be noted that both the beans and the glyphs appear at the same stage of cultural development. Whatever kind of symbolism the beans represented, it was soon lost. The Inca had no form of writing, pictorial, ideographic, or phonetic.

During this same era, the Maya developed their basic calendar, which reckoned time by very detailed counts of days, months, and years that were recorded in glyphs. Certainly the Central Andean people were no less alive to the need for exact knowledge of the annual rhythm of nature which controlled their agriculture, but they recorded no known calendrical reckonings. Certain textiles of the period, which show a complex sequence and rhythm of design elements, have been claimed as calendars, but this is the merest conjecture. The Inca reckoned seasons within each year, but their records or counts of successive years were not comparable in accuracy to those of the Maya. The Andes also lacked any advanced knowledge of mathematics, which is the expectable concomitant of long calendrical computations. The knotted strings, or quipus, by which numerical counts were kept and perhaps simple calculations were made do not appear until the Tiahuanaco period.

As physicians and surgeons, however, the Central Andean people were outstanding. In addition to their shamanistic practices, they were accomplished herbalists. As surgeons, they not only were skilled in setting bones and making amputations, but they practiced trephining (or trepanning) on an extensive scale. In this operation, a section of the skull, often several inches in diameter, is removed. The Peruvians are famous for the large percentage of recoveries from this difficult operation. Just why trephining was so common is unclear. Perhaps the warriors received an unusual number of bashed heads; or perhaps, holding the widespread theory that disease was caused by some object having intruded itself into the body, they undertook to cure headaches in this way.

7. CYCLICAL CONQUESTS: PREHISTORIC EMPIRES

A state functions in two capacities: first, it is an integrating and coordinating agency that serves the needs of its people; second, it is a consuming institution that demands goods and services from the people. In the first capacity, it arranges that a certain portion of the effort of its component communities and classes be channeled into projects that are beneficial to everyone. An irrigation state plans, creates, and manages waterworks that increase the yield of farm land, and it brings new land under cultivation. In order to do this, however, it must devise a political organization and a power structure. In a prescientific era, it may back its power with supernaturalism, that is, with a state church or cult; and it may have to employ military force if the groups that it seeks to bring into cooperation resist rational or supernatural appeals.

Once state political, religious, and military institutions are created, they exist of their own right and for their own sake as well as to serve the public. Special classes of people—lords, priests, soldiers, or bureaucrats, as the case may be—become identified with state institutions and functions and have to be supported by the public. In the irrigation civilizations of the north coast of Peru, the warrior-priests were, in effect, the state.

So long as an economy is expanding through improved technology and the exploitation of new and abundant resources, the state may demand a constantly increasing amount of productive output without endangering itself. During the Era of Regional Florescence, as we have seen, the state exacted ever larger portions of national productive effort, as is witnessed by the construction of larger and larger mounds, temples, palaces, and forts and the manufacture of mounting quantities of ceremonial and luxury goods. When technological progress ceases and new resources are not available to support larger numbers of specialists, demands upon the society cannot be augmented indefinitely. Apparently, however, no state has ever been content to live within its own productive capacity, to remain in a condition of economic and cultural equilibrium or *status quo*. When the state rulers have finally exacted all that the local traffic will bear, their only recourse is to acquire a portion of the output of other states. A predatory primitive society may carry out sporadic raids against its neighbors and bring home the loot. More developed states, such as those of the Central Andes, however, insist upon continued and assured access to their neighbors as tribute-paying vassals, or they expand their own political structure and incorporate their neighbors into a multistate empire.

An empire by this definition is a group of states—size is less important than the nature of the structure—which have been forcibly subjugated by a single, more powerful state in order that a portion of their produce may be appropriated to the institutions of the dominant state, that is, to the classes which in effect are the state. The empire may increase the security of its people through socialistic measures, as the Inca did, but its principal reason for being is to control and appropriate production. This is an economic definition of empire, but it is required by the facts. It is doubtful whether history discloses any true empires that were built primarily to impose their religion on alien peoples or to afford an outlet to militarism for its own sake.

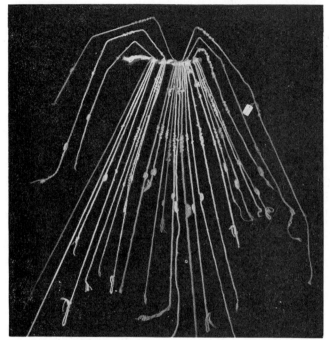

Peruvian quipu, or knotted-string account based on decimal system. Each knot near the end of a string counts one, next higher count ten, and those farther up count one hundred. Introduced probably in the Tiahuanaco period of the Era of Cyclical Conquests, these were used by the Inca to record population, crops, and other matters of state interest. (Courtesy of the American Museum of Natural History.)

In the early irrigation civilizations, independent states were qualitatively different from empires. Whereas the state existed in an expanding economy and primarily served public interest, the empire was a phenomenon of a rather frozen economy. While it endeavored to increase production and may have brought a slight population increase, expansion was reaching its limits. In time, the standard of living of the general population was lowered through greater demands for goods and services. The native empire had then to develop a strong political and legal system to control its people. Centralization of administrative, military, and religious controls led to large centers of population concentration or cities.

Imperial warfare was carried on primarily for conquest. Inca warfare contrasted with that of the Regional Florescent cultures in that captive taking to supply the temple with sacrificial victims was given up. It also contrasted with that of the Circum Caribbean peoples in that the latter, who evidently resembled the Regional Florescent cultures in their military patterns, not only took prisoners but allowed individual soldiers an opportunity to improve their social status. The custom of building walled cities instead of relying on hilltop forts as refuges also shows a change in warfare. Service in the army is but one of the many services required by the empire of the common man, whose inability to achieve upward social mobility is a characteristic of imperial society. As population pressures increased, class distinctions became frozen. Military, political, and religious statuses became fixed in a complex, hereditary hierarchy. Conquered states were not dissolved; they were fitted into the imperial hierarchy under the overlordship of their conquerors. Manufactured products also reflect imperial social regimentation. Local styles and a fairly free and vigorous art gave way to forms and designs which, though technically excellent, were standardized and mass-produced.

This analysis of empires may be stated differently by saying that an empire represents a level of sociocultural integration that is higher and qualitatively different from the state level, just as the latter is different from the community level. An empire, therefore, can be viewed in terms of at least three different levels of internal integration. The folk communities form the lowest or basic level. They carry on the primary functions of producing goods for their own consumption, procreating and rearing children, and living day by day in the context of local social and religious life. The archaeological evidence already presented shows that domestic house types, utensils, shamanism, and family organization changed comparatively little during the long sequence of prehistoric periods. The multicommunity, theocratic state represents the second level. The state developed wholly new forms of religion, political and economic organization, and militarism. The folk of the local communities contributed goods and services to the state, participated in the ceremonialism, and probably profited by the trade which followed local specialization. But their community activities were very similar to those of independent folk villages. The empire, an amalgamation of states, constitutes the third level. It is like an additional layer of culture superimposed upon the other two layers. The states were not destroyed; their institutions and leaders were incorporated into the larger hierarchy.

It is admittedly difficult to recognize the patterns of empire and the processes of their formation with certainty in archaeological data. We know, however, that the Inca had built a tremendous empire by the time of the Spanish Conquest, and there must have been some point at which the conditions leading to empire appeared. The end of the Era of Regional Florescence seems to be this point.

During the Era of Regional Florescence, the states developed internally. Production was expanding, population increased, more and more individuals became specialists, and the socio-politico-religious structure became well defined. The technical and aesthetic achievements of the era were direct responses to the stimulus of state elaboration.

Toward the end of the Era of Regional Florescence, the conditions of imperialism were beginning to appear. Irrigation agriculture had been brought near maximum productiveness in most regions, the basic technologies were fully established, and the population had expanded close to its limits. A very large proportion of the productive effort was being devoted to state institutions. Militarism was strongly developed, and while it served religion through supplying sacrificial victims, it had also become an implement of imperialism.

As Bennett and Bird interpret the archaeological data, the Mochica had already occupied five of the major north-coast valleys; the Lambayeque, still farther north, were spreading their influence to neighboring regions; the Recuay and Cajamarca cultures of the north highland were expanding their territories even as far as the coast; and the central coastal valleys were united stylistically, if not politically. "This widespread expansion resulted in considerable conflict and confusion. In some regions, the irrigation systems seem to have broken down and the populations diminished and scattered. In fact, the peoples of the central Andes apparently became engaged in serious internecine warfare."[8]

Changes in the Virú Valley during the Tiahuanaco period are illustrative of those which occurred widely throughout Peru under the domination of an empire. There are about a hundred communities of this period, but the total population is little, if any, larger than previously. The difference lies in a tendency of some of the population to concentrate in planned centers. Such sites often consist of walled compounds, the houses being laid out in rows. The larger sites, or cities, have mounds and temples inside the walls.

The Virú Valley people had probably already been members of a state which included neighboring valleys. It was part of the Mochica-culture area, which had distinctive types and styles of materials and included a number of states. During the Tiahuanaco period, however, a new culture abruptly appeared. It is found not only in the Virú Valley and the Mochica area but throughout most of Peru, where it partly replaced local styles. The Tiahuanaco culture is characterized mainly by an art style, by certain religious motifs, and by a considerable number of distinctive cultural objects.

How can we account for these sudden innovations? The Tiahuanaco culture certainly consisted in part of new religious concepts and practices. For this reason, some authorities are disposed to regard it as primarily a cult movement, which somehow caught on and was readily adopted throughout the country. They consider it comparable to the Formative period cult with its feline god, which made the Central Andes fairly homogeneous in ceremonial manifestations but failed to unite it politically. That Tiahuanaco influences brought a new cult cannot be doubted, but its comparability to the Chavín-Cupisnique-Ancón religion is very questionable.

The religious pattern of the Formative Era was introduced to people who had previously had no state level of religious organization. Pre-Formative ceremonialism was limited to a simple complex involving community shrines. Village acceptance of the Formative Era mounds, temples, and feline deity met with no opposition from an established state or cult religion. The readiness with which the ceremonialism was accepted is indicated by the spread of mounds, temples, and even the rather distinctive style of pottery through Meso-America northward into the Mississippi Valley. The Tiahuanaco cult, on the other hand, confronted firmly entrenched local state cults or religions in every valley. These local religions, moreover, were strongly integrated with state structure. Local societies would not be likely to acknowledge the supremacy of new gods and to adopt new forms of worship merely because these had become fashionable among their neighbors or because they were advocated by some proselytizing priests.

The fundamental conditions of empire formation were present when the Tiahuanaco period started, and the most convincing explanation for the spread of this culture is that it was imposed upon Peru by a military conquest. If the Tiahuanaco Empire seems large, we have only to remember that the Inca Empire was much larger, extending some 2,000 miles along the Andes, and that it was built up in less than a hundred years. We cannot prove, of course, that the area affected by the Tiahuanaco culture was an empire, but there is no equally good explanation why so many regions rather suddenly abandoned local practices nor why, after a fairly short period, the Tiahuanaco features themselves were given up and the local customs resumed. The fact that symbols of local regions were revived after a short time strongly suggests that the local religions had been forcibly suppressed.

The Tiahuanaco culture took form in the southern Andean highlands, although it is not certain that this region is the center of dispersal for the culture or the seat of its empire. The site of Tiahuanaco, which lies in the Altiplano some 12,000 feet above sea level 12 miles south of Lake Titicaca in Bolivia, however, contains what is considered a "pure" Tiahuanaco culture, a culture that developed locally and was not mixed with features derived from other regional cultures. Therefore, presumably, it shows in unadulterated form the elements which characterize this culture.

The site covers a large area and contains a tremendous number of platforms, courts, mounds, stone structures, and carved stones which probably date from several periods. The "classical" complex is represented by a group of four major structural units consisting of courts, stairways, gates, and buildings. These are notable both for the architectural skill evidenced in large-scale planning and for the vast regimentation of sheer manpower involved in construction. Several features are diagnostic of Tiahuanaco architecture. Many of the stones, some of which weigh up to 100 tons, have been transported more than 3 miles from the quarry. Prior to construction, the stones were wrought into rectangular forms with complicated angles, yet they were somehow fitted together and joined by copper cramps. Some of the construction was monolithic. In a number of cases, a huge gateway or a gateway and stairs were carved from a single stone. What amounted almost to a compulsion for stonecutting led these builders to carve out stone seats and other forms even in solid rock.

The major construction at Tiahuanaco was erected around a low natural hill that was shaped into a faced mound, some 700 feet square and 50 feet high, surmounted by house sites and a reservoir. Perhaps this served as a fortress. Another structure is a rectangular platform about 450 feet square, faced with large vertical slabs between which are smaller stones. An inner court, 190 by 130 feet, was entered by a megalithic stairway. This contains stone statues and the famous monolithic gateway, the "Gateway of the Sun." This last is a single huge rectangular piece of stone, 10 feet tall, carved with human, condor, and sun symbols.

Construction similar to that at the site of Tiahuanaco has been found elsewhere in Peru, but a more widespread diagnostic of the period is the stone carving. Carved forms include statues, friezes on gateways and buildings, and human and animal heads attached to buildings by tenons. Human statues are squarish, rigid figures of standing men with their hands on their bellies. The identifying stylistic features of the flat carvings were also represented on ceramics and textile designs. The eyes are shown with one or two tear streaks. This "weeping god," who first appeared in the Regional Developmental Era in a different style, is very characteristic of the Tiahuanaco culture. In full face, the eyebrows meet to form a T with the nose. Front views depict human beings with a staff in each hand. Side views show men wearing a puma or condor mask and often running with a cape flying out behind. Designs characteristically have appendages, which end in puma, condor, or fish heads. Geometric designs include rectilinear, stepped elements.

Ceramics, which are made in a number of distinctive forms, bear similar decorations in polychrome on a red background. The design is outlined in one or two colors. Textiles have not been found at Tiahuanaco, but they are represented in the dress of the carved figures and show the same designs as these figures. Tie dyeing, the tying of portions of cloth so that dye will not penetrate, and ikat, the tie dyeing of individual threads, were processes introduced at this time.

The Tiahuanaco culture attained a very wide distribution, although it did not equal the Inca. It spread to Cochabamba in eastern Bolivia, Arequipa in southern Peru, Calama in northern Chile, and all of Peru except Huamachuco and Cajamarca in the north highlands and Lambayeque and Piura on the north coast. The center from which this cultural and political conquest emanated is not known. Tiahuanaco is an impressive site, but it was not necessarily the capital of the empire. The highlands have been so incompletely explored that every few years major spectacular ruins are discovered, after which comes the exacting work of examining them scientifically so as to ascertain their chronological and cultural position.

The center of the empire, however, was certainly in the highlands, which were more deeply affected by the Tiahuanaco culture than the coast; for it is there that the full complex of structural remains as well as ceramic and textile styles are found. Wari, in the central highlands, has large pillars, statues, dressed stone tombs, and other lithic features. The coastal sites, on the other hand, show Tiahuanaco influence more in the ornamentation of ceramics, textiles, and other goods than in major constructions. Evidently the conquerors had not had time to build in their own style on the coast and used existing mounds and temples. It should be noted, however, that the highland had always built more with stone and the coast with adobe. Each material requires special constructional methods.

A. L. Kroeber pointed out many years ago that the major cultural impulses in Peruvian development seemed to emanate from the highlands. It is certainly true that all the Pan-Peruvian cultures are most strongly represented in the highlands. The Formative Era Chavín culture, though found on the coast, had its most impressive site in the north highland. Tiahuanaco was of highland origin and fades somewhat on the coast. The Inca were also of highland origin.

It is probable that geographical factors account for the wide spread of culture in the highlands. It is a fairly continuously settled country, whose major deep valleys run north and south and are not a barrier to communication. Culture can spread rapidly throughout this area, except in the extreme south, where deserts are encountered. The coast, on the other hand, is completely arid and uninhabitable except where rivers reach the sea. The oasislike valleys had easier communication with the interior highland than with one another.

The Tiahuanaco culture undoubtedly reached all parts of the coast from the interior. As the empire did not endure more than 200 years, its failure to introduce architectural styles to the coast may mean that there was insufficient time. The Tiahuanaco conquest, however, probably also encountered rather serious resistance, for the isolation of the north coast valleys from one another had begun to break down during the Regional Florescent Era, when coastwise roads and seacoast navigation put the small valleys in touch with one another and furthered political amalgamation of this region.

The Tiahuanaco conquest by no means gave complete cultural unity to the Central Andes. The north coast not only preserved its local architecture and some of its art styles, but it improved its metallurgy through using copper-arsenic alloys and silver plating. The north highlands continued to construct temples or to use older temples in the general architectural tradition of the castillos of the Formative Era Chavín culture, and it buried its dead in stone grave boxes. The south coast practiced urn burial, manufactured silver-copper alloys, and maintained its excellence in textile manufacture. The central highlands were distinguished by their two-color negative-painted pots. None of these regional characteristics is found at the classical site of Tiahuanaco.

Toward the end of the Tiahuanaco period, a new style of painting ceramics in black, white, and red attained a minor vogue throughout the empire, but it was not accompanied by other cultural features of significance.

The rise and fall of empires is the inexorable result of cultural forces and not the unpredictable consequence of military encounters, political maneuvers, and other factors which depend fortuitously upon individual decisions. The conditions and processes which led to the formation of the Tiahuanaco Empire also contained the seeds of its destruction and of the rise of another empire.

An empire as conceived here is a device for concentrating goods and services in the hands of a ruling hierarchy. It regiments and organizes production, but the ancient irrigation empires had little scope for expanding production. When population pressure relative to a fixed amount of production becomes serious and the standard of living of the common man has decreased to the point of threatening his survival, the political and economic patterns of empire can no longer be supported. Local revolts overthrow alien cults and rulers, despite every effort to maintain order through armed force. In the ensuing chaos, it is probable that irrigation works are not kept up, production drops off, and famine decimates the population. There is an interim of dark ages. Local sovereigns finally return to power, irrigation works are repaired, local religious cults are resurrected, and there follows a period of regional states, or lesser empires, before one or another of these gains supremacy in the constant struggle for power. China and the Near East both endured some 2,000 years of cyclical conquests—periods of warring states followed by imperial growth—after their florescent ages. The Central Andes had reached the peak of its second empire, that of the Inca, when the Spaniards arrived.

The rise and fall of empires entailed cultural changes only to a minor extent. Essentially, the cycles represented social change within the framework of a fairly fixed cultural pattern and complex. The basic technologies and productive processes of the Central Andes were unaltered after the Era of Regional Florescence. During the Era of Conquests, each peak of empire brought a florescence of cultural features associated with the imperial institutions. While Inca architecture, religious concepts, and art styles differed from those of Tiahuanaco, both empires made outstanding achievements. But considerable state culture survived the Tiahuanaco Empire and reinstated itself when the empire fell. The folk or community culture survived all these changes comparatively intact; in fact, it lasted well into the Spanish period in spite of national or imperial institutions introduced from the Old World.

At the dissolution of the Tiahuanaco Empire, the Central Andes became divided again into a large number of local or regional states. These were apparently not so small as the states of the Regional Florescent Era, and the cultural remains do not show a resumption of the pure local styles of the earlier era. Rather vigorous and large states grew up in the different regions, and each developed new styles which were fusions of several earlier styles, including features of Tiahuanaco.

As these local states were later incorporated in the Inca Empire, the names of some of them, though by no means all, were preserved and have come down to us through the Spanish chroniclers. Each of these so-called "kingdoms" dominated several neighboring valleys on the coast. In the north, where the rivers are larger and more closely spaced and the population was denser, political amalgamation was more advanced. The most powerful state in the far north was the Chimu Kingdom, which had its great capital at Chanchan. Cuismancu dominated several valleys on the central coast. South of it was Chuquimancu, while still farther south the coast valleys from Chincha to Nazca were under the Chincha kingdom. Highland kingdoms are less well known, but Tiahuanaco in the south continued to be a substantial state, though no longer an empire. During this period the Inca, though probably a small state, had a very undistinguished culture.

The most impressive and best-known example of these states is the Chimu Kingdom. After the period of unrest following the collapse of the Tiahuanaco Empire, the irrigation systems were restored and the

Air view of the great Chimu city, Chanchan. Though cross-cut by modern highways, the native rectangular city plan is evident. (Courtesy of the American Museum of Natural History.)

population recovered its numbers, probably to nearly its former peak. The settlement pattern, however, is marked by a sharp tendency to concentration in urban centers, a trend that had begun in the previous era. Chanchan, the great Chimu capital in the Moche Valley, covers some 11 square miles and had a population of several hundred thousand persons. In the Virú Valley, which was now part of the Chimu Kingdom, the population declined sharply, evidently having been drained off to Chanchan. There were about forty communities during the Chimu period compared to one hundred during the Tiahuanaco period.

Chanchan is one of the most imposing and carefully planned cities ever built in the New World. It consists of ten major units, all of them walled. Each unit contains blocks of adjoining, gabled houses, which are surrounded by walls 30 feet high and probably represent ultimate social divisions, perhaps extended families or kin groups. The divisions include not only dwellings but reservoirs, gardens, cemeteries, pyramids, temples, roads, courts, stairways, and other structures.

Chanchan is clearly a major political and ceremonial center, and it is a true city, for a vast population of common people lived there. The tendency for the population to concentrate in fewer and larger settlements and for these sites to be protected by high enclosing walls is

Pelican design in adobe (mud) on a wall at Quinta Esmeralda. (Courtesy of the American Museum of Natural History.)

marked everywhere. Even the smaller communities in such rural areas as the Virú Valley were built within compounds. The older defense pattern of hilltop forts, or castillos, placed at strategic points and serving as refuges evidently left the common people too exposed to attack. Virtually everyone on the coast now lived in the protecting confines of a walled village, town, or city, where they were not only safer but could be administered more closely.

The Chanchan pattern is characteristic of the coast, but it is not so developed in the highland, where somewhat dispersed settlements continued throughout Andean history. Probably one reason for this difference is that the coastal farm lands and population were much more concentrated within the narrow irrigation limits of its valleys, whereas the highland people were more or less scattered through the mountains, valleys, and altiplano. The grouping of house clusters within the coastal compounds, however, suggests that the basic Andean social unit, the extended family, which had formed the core of the folk community, was not destroyed by the new settlement pattern; it was merely relocated.

Productive processes during this period show improvement only in metallurgy. The most notable achievement is the discovery of true bronze, an alloy of 10 per cent tin and 90 per cent copper, which was made possible by the rich tin deposits in Bolivia. The people now definitely knew how to smelt ore, and they added the processes of inlay and *mise en couleur* to their older metallurgical techniques. The products consisted largely of objects of personal adornment—beads, headpieces, pendants, earrings, and other ornaments—and dishes of gold, silver, copper, bronze, and various alloys of these metals. Bronze was not now nor was it ever sufficiently abundant to revolutionize the basic productive processes. The common people benefited by it only in being able to make digging-stick tips, knives, and needles of bronze. Probably a greater quantity of bronze went to the army, which used it for club heads and daggers.

Textile and ceramic arts felt the effects of mass production and standardization. Stylized birds, fishes, and geometric figures are found on pots and fabrics. Similar motifs were carved out and painted on adobe walls of the great buildings. While pottery molds were used earlier in the Mochica period mainly for luxury and ritual vessels, the coastal Tiahuanaco culture employed them extensively for domestic ware, and, by Chimu times at least 90 per cent of all pottery was mold-made.

Featherwork was developed with considerable vigor during this period, and like the other finer cultural products, it was probably utilized by the ruling classes.

8. FOUNDING THE INCA EMPIRE

The Inca conquest, which was the most tremendous political event in the history of native America, was the last episode in the aboriginal development of the Central Andes. We shall describe this conquest in the present section, leaving an account of Inca culture to the following section. Native Inca culture is fairly well known ethnographically through written documents of the Conquest period, and it will serve to complete the history of native development while providing a background to the acculturational changes that occurred during the Spanish period. A good deal less is known of the antecedents of the Inca Empire than might be expected of a people with such military and political genius. For all their developed technology and organizational skills, the

Inca had no written records whatever, and they were surprisingly deficient in a sense of history for such a developed society. The past was preserved largely through narrative poems and genealogies of ruling families, but the latter are far less complete than those of many societies that are much more primitive, for example, the Polynesians. Oral traditions recount only thirteen Inca rulers in the line of succession. The last seven of these are substantial and probable individuals, who carried out the imperial conquest. The preceding six were undoubtedly actual men, but little is known of them or their times, and the first barely emerges from the legendary past, when the traditions of the affairs of men reveal myth patterns rather than historical events. Therefore, while the Inca conquest is known in broad outline, the pre-Spanish picture of the Inca and of the Central Andes must be reconstructed through inference.

As we have seen, the Central Andes of pre-Inca times was divided into a number of local states and small empires or "kingdoms." The total number of independent political units is not known, but a clue to the cultural and linguistic heterogeneity of the country is afforded by the Inca custom of incorporating distinctive territorial units into their empire as administrative provinces. Most of the provinces probably had their own language or dialect, and many had distinguishing cultural features. Though not necessarily independent at the time of the Inca conquest, the provinces had very likely been separate states at some earlier period, perhaps during the Era of Regional Florescence. John Rowe lists forty-eight Inca administrative provinces[9] in the Peruvian-Bolivian highlands and thirty-eight on the Peruvian coast. In Ecuador and northern Chile, where the conquest was latest and the native cultures and languages survived longest, there were perhaps thirty more.

When first identified archaeologically during the early part of the Era of Cyclical Conquests, the Inca were merely one of many south highland states. They comprised a group of eleven ayllus, perhaps lineages, living in the vicinity of Cuzco. Inca genealogies begin with some accuracy with the rule of Manco Capac, about A.D. 1200. The following list is based on rather carefully preserved genealogies of the different lineages making up what became the Inca royal family.

1. Manco Capac	9. Pachacuti Inca, 1463–1471
2. Sinchi Roca	10. Topa Inca Yupanqui, 1471–
3. Lloque Yupanqui	1493
4. Mayta Capac	11. Huayna Capac, 1493–1527
5. Capac Yupanqui	12. Huáscar, 1527–1532
6. Inca Roca	13. Atahualpa, 1527–1532
7. Yahuar Huacac	(Spanish Conquest)
8. Viracocha Inca, 1438–1463	

All of these rulers were considered to be divine, for their ancestry was traced to the sun god. Manco Capac, who first emerges from the origin myths as an actual person, was supposed to have turned into a stone, which became a highly sacred object. The preserved bodies of the subsequent rulers were venerated.

Until the reign of Pachacuti, which began in 1463, no real conquest was undertaken. Towns had raided one another and imposed tribute when possible, but they were not consolidated politically. During the time of Viracocha, however, the Inca of Cuzco dominated the people of their immediate vicinity. Meanwhile, strong states had arisen on all sides of Cuzco and were contending for power. Through Pachacuti's adroit political manipulations and his creation of a strong army, the Inca acquired the balance of power among these states.

After consolidating his power in the Cajamarca region and the Titicaca Basin (see page 115), Pachacuti, assisted by his able son, Topa Inca Yupanqui, extended the conquest through the highland north to Quito, now the capital of Ecuador, and on to the Ecuadorian coast. Topa Inca then moved down the coast and successfully attacked the powerful Chimu Kingdom from the north. After this, he conquered the south coast from Nazca to Mala. Topa Inca, succeeding to power in 1471, made forays against the Wachipeiri (Huachipairi) and Masco, tropical-forest Indians of the upper Madre de Dios River in Bolivia, but had to turn back to put down a rebellion in the Titicaca Basin. He then carried the conquest across the Atacama Desert southward to the Maule River in Chile, beyond which lived the Araucanian Indians. The Araucanians, though not yet on the threshold of state organization, were unrelenting warriors. Their formerly independent villages united in the face of invasion and repelled all comers, including the Spaniards, who drove them southward but never really defeated them. The Inca hold on the Araucanians was insecure and brief. Topa Inca's conquest subdued the highland peoples of northwest Argentina as far as Tucumán, but stopped short of the primitive Gran Chaco.

Huayna Capac succeeded his father, Topa Inca, in 1493, and by 1525 he had completed and consolidated the empire throughout Peru and Ecuador as well as in the southern Andes. Expeditions to the east failed, and the Tupian-speaking Chiriguano, tropical-forest-village people of Bolivia, even made forays against the empire.

At Huayna Capac's death in 1527, his two sons, Atahualpa, who was administering the northern provinces from Quito, and Huáscar, who was duly installed as emperor at Cuzco, engaged in bitter rivalry for power until 1532. Atahualpa defeated his brother just as Pizarro arrived with his small band of Spaniards.

The story of Pizarro's bold march to Cajamarca, his treacherous seizure

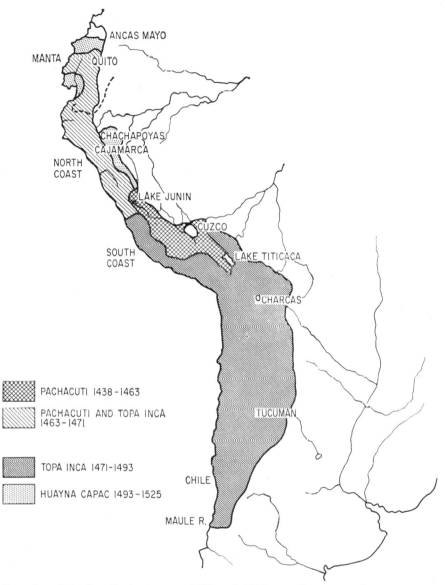

ANCAS MAYO

MANTA QUITO

CHACHAPOYAS
CAJAMARCA

NORTH
COAST

LAKE JUNIN

CUZCO

SOUTH
COAST   LAKE TITICACA

CHARCAS

PACHACUTI 1438-1463

PACHACUTI AND TOPA INCA
1463-1471

TUCUMAN

TOPA INCA 1471-1493

HUAYNA CAPAC 1493-1525

CHILE

MAULE R.

Expansion of the Inca Empire between 1438 and 1525, according to oral history and archaeology. (From John H. Rowe, **Handbook,** vol. 2.)

of Atahualpa, and thereby his control of the empire has often been told. Why a handful of Spaniards could seize an empire of at least 3,500,000 persons can be understood only in the light of the highly centralized and personalized Inca political structure, which will be explained in the following chapter.

The Inca conquest of the Central Andes cannot be understood in military and political terms alone. Its success was conditioned by local cultures and environments. The empire first incorporated the central highland states that were culturally most like the Inca, and next the peoples of north Peru and highland Ecuador, stopping at the tropical forests to the north and east. Next it was pushed across the deserts of south Peru, Bolivia, and northwest Argentina. Finally, it added bits of the eastern Peruvian highlands and the Ecuadorian coast. Thus, by the time the Spaniards arrived, it had incorporated virtually all the people who had had a state organization and a culture like that of the Central Andes. It stopped in the north where the great mass of the Andes begins to break up into separate blocks in Colombia, in the east where the highlands drop abruptly into the rain forests of the Amazon Basin, in the southeast at the arid Gran Chaco, and in the south where the grasslands and forests of Chile begin. Possibly the empire could have been extended farther north into Colombia, but the conquest failed completely in the east and south. The Inca could not conquer even the primitive Arawakan and Panoan villages in the Montaña just a few miles east of Cuzco, their capital.

The eastern and southern boundaries of the empire were in a sense environmentally determined. The whole Inca subsistence pattern and the sociopolitical structure were highly adapted to an irrigation area and could not be supported in a tropical rain forest like that of the Amazon Basin, in a steppe country like the Gran Chaco, or a mediterranean climate like that of Chile. But the failure of conquest involves more than the possibility of establishing a Central Andean type of subsistence in these areas. It was also caused by the incompatibility of the sociopolitical structure of the people of these areas for incorporation in an empire. A population of sedentary, agrarian folk communities, which has already adjusted itself to state institutions, can readily accept a higher sovereignty; for it is accustomed to state control and a change of authority does not deeply affect the folk level of its culture. Loyal and obedient to its own rulers, it will fight against invasion, but once defeated it can easily accept an imperial regime. It is the rulers rather than the commoners who have lost. Acceptance of a new religious cult and payment of tribute to new rulers does not disrupt community life. Moreover, the large and fixed communities make the population readily susceptible to tight controls.

A society organized on a village basis, without any higher authority, cannot be fitted into the structure of an empire. Obligations to state religious and political institutions are foreign to anything in their culture. When defeated at arms, the warriors simply fade back into a more inaccessible part of their territory, moving their villages with them. Complete subjugation would require tremendous garrisons and constant warfare, and village societies do not produce enough goods to justify such effort.

When viewed in terms of the kinds of societies they attacked, the successes and failures of the Inca conquest are easier to understand. In slightly less than a hundred years, the Inca subjugated an area extending some 2,000 miles from north to south, but they failed completely to incorporate people less than 50 miles to their east. They succeeded where the population had been accustomed to some form of state control, probably since the Formative Era, and where an empire had previously been imposed during the Tiahuanaco period. The allegiance of the basic population was primarily to their local communities, and so long as these communities were not disrupted higher levels of social control did not matter too much. The Spaniards represented a later change of sovereignty, and they too found conquest easy. The Inca failed to conquer tribal societies which did not understand that military defeat meant imposition of a higher sovereignty and payment of tribute and whose sparse population and shifting settlements could not be pinned down for administrative and exploitative purposes.

The success of the Inca conquest was not without its difficulties, which were overcome with superb generalship and statesmanship. When possible, conquest was undertaken peaceably through persuasion or through playing off local rulers against their enemies. In warfare, the Inca armies were augmented by those of allies and subjugated states. As the empire grew, disaffected peoples were bodily moved amongst pacified and loyal populations, and rivals were used to control one another. So far as possible, the state rulers were incorporated in the empire as local administrators, which left them with status and wealth, though no longer with independent power. The Inca conquest was cultural as well as political, for Quechua, the Inca language, the Inca cult of the sun, and Inca customs were imposed upon the provinces. This acculturation was furthered by moving Inca colonists into many regions. Finally, the empire was strengthened by a very thorough regimentation of all classes of people.

There is no doubt that the Inca showed genius in building their empire, but they should not be accredited too much originality. We must remember that the history of the conquest comes from the Inca themselves, who naturally recount it in glowing terms. Actually, the pattern of conquest had been laid much earlier: the Chimu, among others, had achieved a substantial empire before the Inca expansion. The Inca learned much from the Chimu and these other people.

NOTES

1. *A Reappraisal of Peruvian Archaeology,* Society for American Archaeology, "Memoirs," vol. 13, no. 4, part 2, 1948. The articles in this Memoir evidence somewhat different conceptual bases for characterizing prehistoric periods.
2. See, for example, Louis Stumer, "Informe Preliminar Sobre el Recorrido del Valle de Cañete realizado como parte del proyecto arqueologico de la costa peruana," mimeographed, no date. Edward P. Lanning, "Ceramica antigua de la costa peruana: nuevos descubrimientos," mimeographed, no date. Federico Engel, "Tejidos y cesteria de la agricultura incipiente en la costa peruana," mimeographed, no date.
3. For very recent information on this era, see Engel, *op. cit.* Also, *Early Sites on the Peruvian Coast,* Southwest Journal of Anthropology, vol. 13, pp. 54–68, 1957.
4. Gordon R. Willey and John M. Corbett, *Early Ancón and Early Supe Culture: Chavín Horizon Sites of the Central Peruvian Coast,* Columbia Studies in Archeology and Ethnology, vol. 3, Columbia University Press, New York, 1954.
5. Gordon R. Willey, *Settlement Patterns in the Virú Valley,* Bureau of American Ethnology Bulletin 155, 1953.
6. William Duncan Strong, *Cultural Stratigraphy in the Virú Valley, Northern Peru: The Formative and Florescent Epochs,* Columbia Studies in Archeology and Ethnology, vol. 4, Columbia University Press, New York, 1952.
7. Rafael Larco Hoyle in *Handbook,* vol. 2.
8. Wendell C. Bennett and Junius B. Bird, *Andean Culture History,* American Museum of Natural History, Handbook Series, no. 15, 1949, p. 182.
9. John Rowe in *Handbook,* vol. 2.

▶ five

NATIVE CENTRAL ANDEAN
CULTURE OF THE
HISTORIC ERA

1. THE ABORIGINAL INCA EMPIRE[1]

Although the Spaniards reached Peru in 1532 at the very peak of the
Inca Empire, they left no complete, eyewitness descriptions of its culture. A great deal of native Andean culture survived for a long time, and
in the highlands there are considerable remains today. But the culture
that survived longest was on the lower levels of organization, especially
the community level. Imperial Inca institutions—the temple, government, military, and economic patterns—were promptly abolished by the
Spaniards, who substituted their own colonial institutions. The Neo-Inca
state attempted to revive and perpetuate aboriginal imperial institutions
for a hundred years or so, but these were a far cry from the native empire. Our sources deal largely with imperial institutions and say little
of community culture, but no general account even of the empire was
written while it was still flourishing.

General descriptions of the Inca culture date from thirty to one
hundred years after the Spanish Conquest, and most of them had to
draw upon a variety of minor contemporary sources, such as official reports and censuses, Indian testimony, and the like. Considerable credence
has been given the accounts of Garcilaso de la Vega because it was
felt that somehow his royal blood, which was derived from an Inca
princess by a Spanish soldier, qualified him to speak. Garcilaso, who

wrote his "Royal Commentaries" after retiring to Europe in 1560, was, however, thoroughly prejudiced in depicting the empire as a highly benevolent, socialistic state despotism. Pedro de Cieza de León, whose *Crónica del Peru,* written in 1551, was based on his own firsthand observations as a soldier, was in a position to record crucial features of Inca culture, but his work is inadequate in many ways.

The best general works are largely secondary compilations of early primary sources: the Jesuit Bernabé Cobo, who wrote in about 1653;

Megalithic wall of the fortress at Sacsahuaman showing nicely fitted stones of many tons brought from miles away. (Courtesy of the American Museum of Natural History.)

Oviedo and Las Casas, who synthesized materials while residing in Europe; and others. Meanwhile, the primary sources themselves, some of them still unpublished, are the best. Among the more important collections of these sources, which have been widely utilized, are the *Informaciones,* which consist of reports prepared for Francisco de Toledo, Viceroy of Peru, and the collection of reports to the king of Spain, known as *Relaciones geográficas de Indias,* published by Marcos Jiménez de la Espada. Strongly partisan as many of these are, it is possible to reconstruct from them the clear outlines of the Inca Empire.

There are many recent descriptions of the Inca Empire, but John Rowe's in the *Handbook,* which utilizes both primary and secondary sources, is undoubtedly the best.

The sources leave no doubt that the Inca Empire was one of the most highly regimented societies the world has known, but, as we have shown, this is expectable in view of the conditions which led to empire formation.

The native population of the Central Andes at the coming of the Spaniards has been estimated at between 3,000,000 and 12,000,000 persons. We have accepted 3,500,000 for Peru and Bolivia and about 600,000 more for Ecuador and other parts of the empire as conservative and consistent with estimates for other parts of the New World. The total was almost certainly no greater than at the close of the Era of Regional Florescence, and it may have been smaller. The greater nucleation of the population into urban centers left some areas partly depopulated. The demographic trend, however, cannot be fully known until more detailed archaeological investigations have been made of settlements and population.

Written documents on the Inca support the inference from archaeological data that no fundamental improvement had occurred in productive patterns. All of the plants listed in Table 1 were in production, many of them having become specialized in scores of varieties adapted to the different climates. The highlands were able to produce so many varieties of potatoes, ullucos, oca, quinoa, and other specialized crops that the population was spread quite continuously over great portions of the Altiplano that lay 12,000 feet or more above sea level. In fact, some species were cultivated up to 14,000 feet. The people of the lower valleys utilized not only all level land but terraced up entire mountainsides and brought water to them by means of canals extending back many miles into the mountains. In some places slopes of 45 degrees or more are terraced for a thousand feet above the valley floor and for a score of miles along the mountains. Lands were fertilized with llama and human manure in the interior and bird guano on the coast. This farming was as intensive as any in the New World; in fact, it has been estimated that the Inca could support a family on one-half acre whereas Meso-America needed at least one acre. There is, however, some evidence that in the older irrigation areas alkalinization and leaching had already depleted the soil and reduced the cultivable area.

Farm work was carried out by the rural population according to a ritual calendar which followed the rhythm of the seasons and was directed by state supervisors. Both sexes tilled the fields, but the heavier jobs fell to men, who broke the soil with digging sticks provided with footrests and sometimes shod with metal, and cultivated it with hoes.

The highly efficient subsistence basis of the Central Andes supported a large nonfarming population, which was divided into status and occupational groups. In a developmental sense, the empire was structured on three levels of sociocultural organization, or patterns, which had emerged successively during its history: first, the community or folk patterns; next, the state, which had imposed its institutions on the communities; finally, the empire, which overlaid the states. The imperial institutions included the government, which was controlled by the Inca royal family and their descendants; the Temple of the Sun, which had been the Inca state religion and was made the official imperial cult; an economy in which the empire controlled all goods and services; and the army, which supported the other institutions. Under the empire, local state institutions were preserved so far as possible. Former state rulers were frequently made provincial administrators, and local temples were allowed to function provided they were subordinate to the Sun Temple. Community patterns were by no means seriously disrupted by the empire. The common people had to contribute goods and services to the empire, acknowledge the supremacy of the sun cult, and submit to military draft, but their previous relationship to the local states had entailed similar obligations. The empire demands were more exacting and the controls were stringent, but qualitatively the effects upon the commoners were not very different from those of the states.

Inca plowing festival. The foot plow was pushed into the earth by means of a cross stick on the plow handle. (After Guaman Poma.)

In a sociological sense, the emposition of an empire on the Central Andes merely strengthened the two-class system that had already emerged in many regions. The fundamental division had been an upper and a lower class, rulers and commoners. The Inca incorporated the state ruling classes into a more elaborate hierarchy of authority and social status, but the basic twofold division remained.

Imperial economic institutions. The principal function of the empire was to control the goods and services of the common people. To this end, the entire productive apparatus was owned and controlled by the government. There was no private property, no currency, and no possibility of capital accumulation. All land was held by the government and allotted according to imperial needs. All labor could be commandeered and its output channeled to governmental ends. For this reason, the economic basis of the noble class represented imperial sufferance—

rewards for services rendered—and the role of the commoners was that of producers of goods and services. There was no place in this system for free enterprise or accumulation of wealth. Local barter consisted merely of exchange of family surplus, and it was not a mechanism for the distribution of specialized products in a true market economy. No man was able to amass productive capital, for it was owned by the government, nor to accumulate concentrated wealth, for there was no currency. Precious metals were not only denied the common man, but their flow through the empire was strictly controlled.

This extreme economic power of the empire was made possible by the dependence of the society upon water, which, of necessity, was state regulated. The very existence of a large and diversified population of soldiers, priests, artisans, and administrators depended in the final analysis upon maximum utilization of water resources. With the empire in control of the waterworks but at the same time dedicated to extraction of increasing amounts of produce from a society which has reached the limit of water resources, governmental control of all productive activities was inevitable.

All land was held in title by the Inca emperor and assigned to the people for cultivation. Assignment followed a fundamental threefold division between temple, state, and commoners, the size of each part depending upon various factors. Temple lands supported all religious institutions, and they were subdivided so that not only the national Sun Temple but lesser, local temples and shrines received enough food to maintain their priests and other personnel. These lands were divided into plots which were assigned to individual families of commoners for cultivation. The family head, assisted by his wife and children, worked the temple plot until it was finished. After this, the family began work on a government plot which had been assigned it. These tasks were performed under close supervision. When work on the imperial plots was finished, the family was at liberty to cultivate its own fields, which also were allotted it by the government, the size depending upon the number of persons in the family and other needs. Agricultural work came before all else, and if a man had to be absent, for example, at war, his fellow villagers cultivated his plots for him.

The needs of each family were thus reckoned very carefully by state officials. In addition, the sick, crippled, widowed, aged, and needy and the victims of famine in any region of crop failure were provisioned from public granaries, where the crops from government lands were stored. Government control also facilitated the movement of crops between areas of specialized production, so that the people consumed a much greater variety of foods than they produced.

This great concern of the government that all the people should be amply cared for has been cited to prove the essential benevolence and socialism of the Inca Empire. It must be remembered, however, that absolute power rested with the emperor and that provision of minimal food requirements for his subjects did not necessarily mean that the commoners had a high standard of living. The expropriation of the entire produce of two parts—though not necessarily two-thirds—of the land for church and state consumption must have cut down the commoner's land considerably. Only very efficient land use could have supported so large a superstructure of nonproducers. The crucial factors in total food production were land and water, not manpower. The emperor had labor to spare, and it is recorded that Huayna Capac ordered a huge hill moved from one place to another solely to keep his people occupied. But a country rich in manpower and limited in resources faces dangers. That the Inca should have terraced vast mountainsides, which in any other country would have been considered hopelessly submarginal as farm lands, demonstrates that tremendous effort was made to use the last drop of water. No doubt the average member of Inca society was fairly well fed in 1532, but there had been a time during the Tiahuanaco period when population evidently outran production. If Inca land use had reached its maximum, as seems to have been the case, the government could assign surplus labor to state projects, but there would come a time when the state could not feed everyone.

As among most primitive tribes, Inca women were the carriers of wood, although the llama was a beast of burden. (After Guaman Poma.)

The herding economy of the Inca, although important in certain respects, was a somewhat minor accessory to food production. The Andean peoples were predominantly vegetarians, except on the coast, where they took abundant fish. Llamas and alpacas were more valuable for their wool and for their use in transportation and as sacrificial animals than for food. Pastures, like croplands, were divided into three parts for the state, temple, and commoners. Temple herds supplied temple needs, especially llamas for sacrifice and divination. State animals provided wool, which was stored and distributed among all people. Commoners were limited to ten animals each, while nobles received a number determined by their status. Every farmer had many tame guinea pigs around his house, but these animals did not supply much meat. In parts of the empire, the Muscovy duck was semidomesticated.

A very important social aspect of the agricultural labor of the commoners was the mutual help rendered by villagers. This is a worldwide feature of folk societies which are not yet part of a system of private ownership, cash-crop production, and wage labor, and it still survives in parts of the Andes and elsewhere in South America. It is not only an efficient means of accomplishing the more onerous farm jobs, such as planting and harvesting, and other tasks, like house building, but it is a powerful social integrating factor in the community, for it provides a measure of economic insurance. Feasting, drinking, and visiting make the work enjoyable as well as profitable.

In addition to cultivating the lands of the state and temple, the common people were subject to draft on state projects, an obligation known as mita. The mita assignments included post service on the roads, personal service for the nobles—the rate of one servant for every ten men ruled by the noble is a remarkable consumption of man-hours in this work—the army, the mines, and construction of irrigation works, roads, bridges, temples, palaces, and other public edifices. Sacsahuaman, the Inca fortress above the capital, Cuzco, is said to have employed 30,000 men at one time. The basis for furnishing these labor drafts was a decimal system. Calls for labor were distributed among the chiefs of tens, fifties, hundreds, and so forth so that each district supplied a proportionate share. Several exempt districts supplied specialists: litter bearers, court dancers, carvers of ceremonial firewood, and the like.

In addition to production and mita labor for the imperial institutions, there was a large number of specialists, such as architects, weavers, metallurgists, ceramicists, and others who had to be supported by the state stores.

Imperial political institutions. The imperial political institutions consisted of the great hierarchy of officials and bureaucrats who controlled the economic system, the temples, and the army. Members of the Inca royal family held the top positions in all these activities, and they were subordinate to the emperor, who was thought to be the direct descendant of the sun and reigned as a god on earth.

The emperor theoretically had absolute power and divine right. His status was so exalted, in fact, that only his full sister was qualified to be his wife. The principal administrators under the emperor were his own descendants and members of the eleven royal ayllus, probably lineages, of Cuzco. Where possible, heads of conquered states were retained as provincial administrators, but in many cases local political development had not produced competent men and certain posts were filled on the basis of ability. The political structure, however, inevitably led to hereditary status, and the Inca evidently modeled a great deal of their administration on the Chimu Kingdom, where strong hereditary classes had probably existed since the Era of Regional Florescence. To ensure the loyalty of local rulers, their children were educated in Cuzco and returned to their provinces. A distinction was made, however, between members of the royal ayllus, the "Incas," and local rulers, the curacas or "Incas by Privilege."

For administrative purposes, the Inca divided the empire into four quarters and each quarter into provinces; these divisions corresponded in some measure with earlier states and cultural subgroups. Each province had an administrative capital, some of which were newly built according to plan. Government architects made relief maps of the terrain to determine the best location, then had government buildings erected in the Inca style of architecture. These were a special type of city or urban center, for they consisted of a nucleus of stone buildings for the nobles, priests, and their assistants, laid out in squares separated by narrow streets and plazas. In native times, Greater Cuzco may have included 200,000 persons, but it consisted of rather scattered, small outlying villages. Inca towns were not fortified, and as in the Era of Regional Development, refuge in time of war was found in heavily walled hilltop forts. Sacsahuaman, overlooking Cuzco, was the fort for residents of the capital. By contrast, states on the north coast compressed homes and government buildings within walled cities, perhaps because the population was concentrated in the valleys and planners wished to avoid building on level farm land.

The Inca emperor is transported in a litter, a nearly worldwide symbol of high status. (After Guaman Poma.)

The provinces were divided into moieties, which were dual political divisions and not in any sense exogamous marriage groups. The moiety pattern was evidently taken from the grouping of the eleven Inca ayllus of Cuzco into an upper and a lower moiety, though some of the regions may have had a similar native division. Sometimes, however, the grouping was threefold. The moieties were made up of ayllus, a term used not only for the royal lineages but also for the local communities. Many of the ayllus scattered throughout the countryside were small farm villages, but others were resettled away from their hilltop forts and closer to their fields, and in some instances several ayllus were grouped in single towns. It is probable, however, that the ayllu retained its identity after resettlement. Even on the north coast, where urbanization drew many communities into walled cities, the ayllus were evidently allotted separate areas within the great compounds.

The administrative structure was adjusted to the territorial divisions. The prefects of quarters and the provincial governors were of the Inca royal lineages. Below them were the hereditary heads of divisions of 10,000, 5,000, 1,000 and 100 men. In addition to grouping common men in this decimal hierarchy, persons were classified into twelve age groups, each theoretically capable of certain chores. Records of men, produce, and other things were kept on quipus, which are groups of strings knotted for tally, based on a decimal system. Quipu censuses were constantly fed up to higher officials, who summarized them and passed them on to the emperor.

In the course of empire building, the Inca incorporated newly conquered peoples by a process of colonization known as mitimaes. A mitima, or colony, of recalcitrant people was bodily moved to a pacified area, and an older group which understood and accepted the Inca system was moved into their place. Although native dress, gods, and other features were generally preserved among the mitimaes, the procedure had a powerful effect in leveling cultural differences, for the Inca language and many practices were widely spread by this cultural transplantation.

Obedience of whole populations to Inca edicts was enforced by military measures. Obedience of individuals was assured by civil and religious means. Trials were conducted by officials in the presence of witnesses. Crimes included everything from laziness, theft, and minor misdemeanors to homicide. While all these were considered to constitute disobedience to the emperor, the most serious were those against the property and personnel of the empire, and they were generally punished by death. In so highly ritualized a society as the Inca, breach of religious taboos or sin was not sharply distinguished from crime. A well-developed system of confession to priests thus constituted a religious means of enforcing obedience to imperial institutions. Penances followed by a ritual bath were required after confessions. Although confessions and penance are Catholic practices there is no question that they are aboriginal in the Andes. It is a functional response to the fact that religion became an imperial institution, inseparable from secular power.

In their ethical connotations the religions of states and empires contrast with those of most simpler nomadic or village people. The latter typically emphasize individual or family welfare in shamanistic curing, birth, puberty, and death rites, magic, and sorcery. It is rare that such religions also impose moral codes that prescribe the individual's behavior toward his society.

Proper functioning of the imperial institutions required adequate means of communication, which was a major problem in so large and diversified an area. The need was met by a system of excellent roads and imperial runners. Two principal roads traversing the length of the empire, one in the highland and the other on the coast, were connected by shorter roads. In the valleys, the roads were shaded, fenced highways 12 to 15 feet wide; in the deserts they were marked lanes; and in the highlands they were graded paths that were terraced along cliffs, often hewn from stone and even tunneled if necessary. They crossed gorges on suspension bridges as much as 200 feet long. Crews kept the roads in repair. Relay runners stationed at huts built at intervals along the roads carried messages to the capital. They could cover 150 miles a day. They traveled entirely on foot, for the llama is a poor mount. The messages consisted of quipus accompanied by verbal instructions.

In addition to facilitating the imperial intelligence service, the roads served other functions of empire. They were routes of travel for the army, which could draw provisions from storehouses built at intervals along the way. They were lines of transport for the incessant flow of government goods carried by human beings and llamas from one region to another. And they were highways along which the emperor and other officials could be borne rapidly in litters on tours of inspection.

Sea communications were less adequately developed. On the south coast and on Lake Titicaca, reed-bundle rafts were the only watercraft. On the north coast, however, where balsa wood could be obtained from the tropical-rain forests of southern Ecuador, large log sailing rafts capable of carrying a considerable cargo were used in coastwise transportation.

Imperial religious institutions. The imperial religious structure paralleled the political structure quite closely. Supernatural beings and the priests who served them formed an elaborate hierarchy, but apparently only the lower ranks were hereditary. Kirchhoff explains this as the result of a former struggle between the priests and civil authorities, wherein the former, under the leadership of one of the royal lineages, nearly won control of the state. The higher ranks of the clergy were elected by a convocation of priests, but the emperor's brother nonetheless always held the highest office as head of the entire priesthood.

The priests wielded great power in everyday affairs. They not only controlled the common man and even nobles through confessions, penances, and fear of supernatural punishment, but, in their capacity as diviners, they influenced political decisions and, as ceremonial leaders, they played an important part in the agricultural cycle around which ritual was built. The priesthood was stratified on the basis of function. Top-ranking priests were in charge of the major temples and ceremonies. Below them were the seers and confessors, who probably also served as ritual leaders in the lesser temples. Finally, there were the menial workers in the temples, drawn from the commoners. Within these ranks there was probably also some specialization. Eunuchs were in charge of the chosen women of the temples, whom they served as confessors and they headed special convents of nuns.

In the hierarchy of supernatural beings, the Inca deities ranked above the local, state gods. These Inca deities had been only local gods of the predynastic ayllus of Cuzco. After the conquest, the empire required only that they be acknowledged as superior to the local gods. Lest there be any uncertainty about this, the images of state gods were taken as hostages to Cuzco. Divided loyalty to supernatural beings was a genuine threat to the empire. Pachacamac, the central-coast supreme deity, was a serious competitor to the Inca sun god for some time. Apart from their legitimate fears as to the provinces' spiritual allegiance, however, the Inca justified their conquest, especially its later phases, as a crusade to bring the Andean people the benefit of their superior religion.

In the deistic hierarchy of the empire, Viracocha, who has been described as a bearded, white man, was the supreme being, the creator of other gods, men, and animals, and the giver of culture to mankind. After finishing his work, he departed across the sea, leaving the other gods to manage the world. When the Spaniards first arrived, the Indians thought that Viracocha had returned. Foremost among the other gods was the sun, protector of crops and the direct ancestor of the emperors. Thunder, the weather god, who was represented as a man with a war club and sling, was the sender of rain. The moon was the wife of the sun god and regulator of the ritual calendar. The Inca and their local predecessors conceived all aspects of nature to be charged with supernatural power and to affect human destiny. Various stars, animals of the land, air, and sea, mountaintops, caves, springs, and lakes were deified, some attaining major importance as local gods. Hundreds of particular places and objects such as piles of stones and bodies of ancestors became huacas, or shrines. The gamut of supernatural beings ran from the imperial gods down to village shrines and household amulets and images.

Although the principal temples have been called sun temples, they were used in the ritual of all the imperial gods. Ceremonialism was devoted to agricultural success and health, and it was all a single fabric. The temple was not a place of public worship and ritual but the repository of the images of the different gods and the residence of the priests and virgins of the sun, the chosen women of highest status. The principal temples were in the charge of priests of the royal blood and were served by equally noble virgins, or nuns, dedicated to them. Lesser temples were run by lower-ranking priests and chosen women, who were from the commoners and might become concubines of nobles. At the village level, shrines of local interest were cared for by commoners. Priests at all levels served several different functions: they supervised ceremonials, made sacrifices, prayed, divined, heard confessions, and healed.

Under the Inca Empire, llamas instead of human beings were used for blood sacrifice. A man slaughters a llama, tearing out its heart, while an attendant receives the blood in a bowl. (After Guaman Poma.)

Great public ceremonials were held in the open plaza and were scheduled more or less according to the agricultural calendar, although special rites might be held in time of crisis. The ceremonies were strictly standardized and included considerable recurrent ritual detail: prayers; blood sacrifice; offerings of coca, shells, gold, silver, and other precious goods; aspersions; ritual continence; dancing; recitations and dramatization; drinking of beer, or chicha; and other features. It is noteworthy that llamas and guinea pigs, instead of human beings, were ordinarily used for blood sacrifice. Human beings were sacrificed only at times of crisis. Most of the scheduled ceremonies simultaneously served several purposes; initiating royal youths into manhood, bringing rain, furthering the growth and maturity of crops, and exorcising sickness.

Divination was a vital function of Inca religion, for it was used to determine the outcome of major decisions, choose between heirs, determine the truth of confessions, diagnose illness, find lost property, and other purposes. For more serious matters, special practitioners propitiated the supernatural beings by means of fire, food, coca, and sacrifices of children, llamas, and precious metals. Lesser oracles simply conjured up the spirits, evidently as shamans call upon their spirit-helpers in simpler religions, and asked them questions. Much divination, however, was based on magic rather than consultation of spirits. Priests and other persons could prognosticate by consulting the lung of a sacrificed guinea pig, llama, or bird, by casting maize grains, beans, pebbles, and the like into piles, or by observing the movements of birds and animals. The interpretation of omens was a highly developed system.

Although religious ceremonials and other ritual observances were designed in part to ensure good health, the greater part of curing seems

llama sacrifice continues today among the Uro-Chipaya in the remote portions of the Andes. It is accompanied by libations and offerings of coca. (Photo by Alfred Métraux, courtesy of University of California.)

to have been done by a class of genuine shamans, who were very similar to those found among tribal societies throughout the world. Disease was believed to be caused by the anger of supernatural beings, by sorcery, by evil forces in certain springs or wind, and by loss of one's soul in fright. It was manifested by the presence of a foreign object in the body or by general symptoms of malign influences.

The shamans were usually also diviners, and they operated on a principle very different from the priests'. Whereas the latter mediated between man and the deities, using prayer, sacrifice, and other ritual forms in supplication, the shaman had direct control over a spirit-helper, which had come to him in a vision and given him supernatural power and instructions. To cure sickness, the shaman removed the disease-causing object, recovered the patient's lost soul, or counteracted the malign influences in ways that would be familiar to most primitive peoples; but he also used Andean ritual elements, such as sacrifices, offerings, and others. It is possible, of course, that some individuals functioned both as priests and shamans, although conceptually the two roles are distinct. Although shamanism is part of the old folk culture, its basic practices were applied to nobles and commoners alike when they became ill.

Imperial military institutions. The militaristic patterns of the Inca differed from those of the Regional Florescent states in their purpose, furthering political domination and economic vassalage of tributary states. The Inca army was created by a draft levied on all provinces that could be trusted, and it was commanded by members of the royal family. Inca militarism did not allow volunteer soldiers to capture slaves for their own households and thus raise their status, as was customary among the Circum-Caribbean chiefdoms. Individual soldiers of the Inca army might be honored and even granted certain privileges, but the fate of subjugated populations and all loot was decided solely by imperial administrators.

The patterns of empire also precluded the use of militarism as an adjunct to religion through providing sacrificial victims. During a long period following the Formative Era in Andean prehistory, war captives had become sacrificial victims in a rather bloody cult, and trophies of heads, arms, and whole bodies were used ceremonially. This cult survived among the Circum-Caribbean peoples, while trophy-head taking had spread to a number of tropical-forest farm villages. Such human sacrifice depended upon a supply of victims from enemy states. The situation was different when all states were incorporated in a single political and religious structure, and there were no enemy groups. Animals were routinely sacrificed, instead of human beings, and the few human sacrifices deemed necessary were provided from the general population. Human trophies, however, were still sometimes taken in battle—skulls to be made into cups, whole skins stuffed with ash and straw, flutes made of arm and leg bones, drumheads of skin, and necklaces of teeth—but these were war trophies, not religious articles.

Social structure. The Inca Empire, like any modern state or nation, was made up of different sociocultural segments, that is, regional and social classes of people, whose ways of life or subcultures were distinctive in various respects. The distinctiveness of the local states or provinces had been very marked before the Inca conquest, but was rapidly leveled by imperial policies. The differences both in status and in cultural behavior between the social classes, however, were greatly enhanced by the imperial institutions. Subcultural differences between classes, in fact, became much greater than those between regions.

Inca society must be regarded as a two-class system from the point of view of status and authority, despite a complex system of ranks among the ruling groups and of occupational distinctions among some of the lower classes. The upper class, or nobles, were the rulers and represented the imperial institutions. The lower class, or commoners, who constituted by far the greatest proportion of society, were the producers. Cultural distinctions followed class lines. The culture of the nobles developed from their identification with the imperial institutions. That of the commoners was a carry-over from much earlier folk communities, whose subcultures were modified first by state governments and later by the empire but were by no means destroyed. It is possible that there was a third subcultural group—perhaps an intermediate class—consisting of the artisans, servants, and other specialists who had left their communities to serve the nobles, but little is recorded about this class. These two or three classes, though differentiated culturally, were functionally interdependent through reciprocal duties and obligations.

The nobles. The upper-class culture was fairly uniform despite the many statuses within it. The nobles made up a pyramid of power with the Inca emperor at the apex, the members of the royal Inca ayllus or lineages directly under him, and the Inca by Privilege and other officials under them. Members of this class were civil administrators, priests, and generals. Their duties were to make the empire function smoothly and to ensure that the commoners received just treatment and fulfilled their obligations. The nobles were exempt from agricultural labor but received foods, services, and large amounts of luxury goods, enjoyed differential treatment according to their status, and participated in many activities denied the common folk. Their way of life, in fact, constituted a somewhat distinctive subculture.

Noble children were born into homes of luxury. Their parents lived in large houses, which, among the upper strata, can be called palaces. These homes were equipped with fine textiles, dishes of gold and silver, and exquisite pottery and were attended by servants, furnished in a number depending upon their master's status. Nobles ate rare foods brought by runners from the coast or from the tropical interior. Unlike common children, who worked at special chores at an early age, noble youths received special schooling to train them for their adult responsibilities as priests, soldiers, and administrators. When their education was complete, these young men were ceremonially inducted into the status of manhood through certain tests. These were part of the national public rites held under the charge of the priests. Young noble women were generally educated in convents, after which they became wives or perhaps entered the higher ranks of nuns, or chosen women.

Noble men were privileged to take several wives, and unlike the commoners, who married endogamously within the village, their principal wives normally came from other localities. This practice was probably a function of the growing importance of lineages with hereditary status among the nobles: for lineage exogamy combined with class endogamy would frequently require marriage outside the community. And it served to link the communities and provinces through kinship. Additional women were probably concubines rather than wives. Taken from the commoners, they were an economic asset because of their capacity to perform useful labor. The Inca emperor himself married a full sister, on the theory that no one else was equally exalted, and some members of the royal lineages might marry a half sister for the same reason.

In every aspect of their lives, the nobles were distinguished from the common people by pomp and privilege. Dressed in the finest cloth of alpaca and vicuña wool and adorned with gold and silver ornaments and various insignia of status, such as large, cylindrical earplugs—whence their common designation orejones, or "large ears"—they sat upon carved wooden stools to receive lesser persons and traveled in litters, while their subjects bowed in obeisance to them. They sojourned to the highlands to hunt deer and other game in great drives on royal preserves. At death, a noble was buried with his wives and retainers, who were made drunk and then strangled. The grave was also filled with luxury goods. The noble's body, and often that of his wife also, especially if she were his sister or a member of the royalty, was mummified and placed in a temple or special shrine, whence it was taken out, along with the images of the gods, for display during public ceremonies.

The way of life, or subculture, of the noble class depended entirely upon privileges made possible by the political power structure. Nobles owned no property in a modern sense and had no independent power. The lands and herds allotted them, the services rendered them by the commoners, the symbols and benefits of authority and rank, and even the palaces in which they lived all depended in quantity and quality upon their status and were awarded in return for complete fealty to the emperor. For any lapse of obedience to the divine ruler, nobles were punished as surely and severely as commoners.

Among the nobles as among the commoners, membership in patrilineal

the sick, and at birth, naming, marriage, and death. The community had many local huacas, or sacred places and objects. The lineages were strongly tied to their village through the local burial ground, where their sacred ancestors lay. Within the lineage, each household had its special shrine and each individual a guardian spirit.

In addition to these community bonds, the common folk met their own simple needs in ways that long antedated the Inca. They tilled and harvested the fields allotted them and tended their llamas. The construction of their dwellings was not very different from that of previous eras. A house consisted of a single small, dark, rectangular room with walls of stone or stone and adobe and usually a gabled, thatched roof. Where the Inca had resettled the local population, dwellings were built in clusters, probably one for each lineage, which in turn were grouped within walled compounds. Some of the more ambitiously planned centers are Machu Picchu and Ollantaytambo. But the family-unit dwelling in these planned settlements was no more luxurious than elsewhere.

Household utensils and furniture were simple and scanty. People cooked on a low, clay stove in plain pottery jars. Kitchenware included dishes, pitchers, semicircular bronze and copper knives, a stone slab and rock for grinding food, mortars and pestles, and wooden cups and ladles. The commoners slept either on the floor or on a kind of frame bed, and they always sat upon the floor, for stools were reserved for the nobles.

All the people of the Andes dressed alike in garments made of finely woven but untailored cloth. The fashion for men called for a breechclout and a sleeveless tunic made of a rectangular cloth with a head slit in the center and the sides sewn together. Women wore ankle-length skirts wrapped around the body under the arms and held in place with pins over the shoulders. Both sexes wore woven mantles and sandals made of hide. As buttons were not known, large-headed metal pins were used to secure the garments. Little is known of the distinguishing characteristics of the commoners' clothing, except that the materials were homespun. Use of vicuña wool by commoners was forbidden, and the commoners' llama-wool cloth, although probably fairly well woven, did not compare in fineness with that made for the nobles. The nobles could be further distinguished by their gold and silver ornaments, which were denied commoners, and by their insignia of status.

Household utensils and clothes, together with farm tools, looms, and other basic necessities, constitute the fairly meager inventory of domestic goods in a culture so well known for its superlative national products. The great public edifices and works—the palaces, temples, forts, and roads—were vastly more magnificent than the commoners' huts and local shrines, whether the comparison is based on man-hours of construction, cubic content, ornateness, or any other measure. The very small extent to which the commoner was a genuine consumer of the national products of his culture is not generally recognized. The common people stood outside these national cultural products; they were spectators rather than participants, producers rather than consumers.

There was another group of persons that cannot be clearly fixed in the sociocultural scheme of things for want of adequate data. The commoners who worked on projects—who met their mita requirements—ordinarily were away from home only temporarily. But there were large numbers of specialists who apparently remained permanently in government work, rendering services to nobles of both the civil and religious branches of the empire. Some of these, who are known as yanaconas, served in such capacities as bodyguards, administrators of lands, engineers, architects, and the like. Although such persons lived fairly comfortably and on terms of intimacy with their lords, they have sometimes been called slaves, for they might be drawn from war prisoners, commoners, or the sons of yanaconas; some of them were evidently sons of nobles. Other specialists included artisans, who worked in metals, textiles, wood, stone, ceramics, and the like. Apparently many of these were relieved of other obligations so that they could devote full time to their crafts, and they often left their communities to live and work on the job. Architects and master masons, for example, had full-time employment. In like manner, the chosen women of the lower orders were selected peasant girls, who lived at the temples, weaving textiles for the priests and idols. Some of them went on to become concubines of the nobles, and others were virgins who became nuns in convents.

It would be incorrect to designate any of these groups as slaves. Although subject to their master's authority, they could not be bought, sold, or traded as in chattel slavery. The empire, in fact, had no logical place for slaves. The mass of its population was at the disposal of the nobles, and there was no necessity for a status group lower than the commoners. Captive populations were incorporated into the two-class system, but they were not enslaved in any real sense. The various specialized occupational groups, therefore, must be regarded as commoners, who rendered special forms of service and in doing so were removed from their communities and placed in a more intimate relationship to their masters.

Technological and intellectual achievements. There is little to add to what has already been said concerning Central Andean technological development during the Inca period and previous periods. Irrigation farming, as we have seen, had reached its limits of productivity. Transportational devices were notable for the work put into roads, but no improvement was made over human carriers and pack llamas. The wheel was never invented.

Inca architecture is remarkable for the labor it represents but not for use of advanced architectural principles. Stones weighing many tons were hauled on rollers perhaps 10 miles from the quarries by sheer manpower, using only bronze and wooden levers. They were put in place by use of ramps. Some stones were polygonal, or many-sided, and others were rectangular, but all were fitted with extraordinary precision. What every writer has said of this masonry is literally true: "one cannot fit the blade of a knife between the stones." The stones were worked with stone hammers and bronze chisels and polished with sand. But construction was done without the true arch, and only limited use was made of the corbeled arch and column. Interior rooms were narrow, and two- or three-storied structures were not very common. Roofs were thatched.

Certain stylistic features distinguish the Inca palaces, temples, storehouses, forts, baths, and tombs, whether the buildings were made of stone or adobe: sunken joints between the stones, protuberances on the stones made originally to aid in transportation, trapezoidal niches and doors, and, perhaps most characteristic of all, rows of adjoining niches in walls.

Weaving in the Inca period showed no technological improvement, but it employed every available kind of fiber: cotton and llama wool for coarser fabrics, alpaca for finer weaves, vicuña for exceptionally soft and fine textiles, and even bat and viscacha hair. Thread was spun by hand, for mechanical spinning wheels were unknown. The belt loom, which was invented in Mochica times, was the most common type. The warp was wrapped around two parallel bars, one of which was tied to a post, while the other was fastened to a strap encircling the weaver's waist. To tighten the warp threads, the weaver leaned back. Belt looms and horizontal looms—which are horizontal frames around which the warp is wrapped—seem to have been used for warp-faced plain or striped cloth made for the commoners. Horizontal and vertical looms, or upright frames, were characteristic of the southern highland. Vertical looms were used to make the more elaborate polychrome tapestries. Some of these have as many as 250 warps per inch, and one specimen has 327 warps and 500 wefts. These looms fell into disuse after the Spanish Conquest. In addition to tapestry, the best textiles included feathered and gold-bangled cloth.

Ceramics of the Inca period are notable only for the widespread manufacture of rather standardized and probably mass-produced polychrome wares of excellent quality. An interesting feature of the pots is that they were often decorated with many stylized realistic designs, including flowers, insects, people, llamas, pumas, and serpents—the last two were also carved on public buildings—which, however, had no place in religious symbolism.

Metallurgical processes probably did not advance during the Inca period. Mines were owned by the government and worked by commoners on the principle of the mita. Copper was available to everyone, but use of gold and silver was a privilege granted by the emperor to certain nobles. Platinum was mined in Ecuador, and tin obtained in Bolivia was alloyed with copper to form bronze. Lead furnished inlays for woods; mercury and arsenic were used in alloys. Ores were smelted

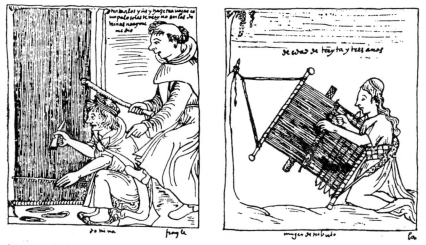

Inca weaving on the vertical loom (left) and belt loom (right), both early prehistoric methods. (After Guaman Poma.)

high in the mountains, where the wind furnished the blast for the furnaces. Other metallurgical processes included casting, hammering, repoussé, incrustation, inlay, soldering, riveting, and cloisonné. The precious metals and copper were used for ornaments, but copper and bronze were made into axes, chisels, knives, crowbars, bolas weights, war-club heads, mirrors, tweezers, needles, scales, and bells.

Iron was not known, but it is interesting to speculate whether its discovery would have initiated an entirely new cultural era as it did in the Old World. V. Gordon Childe has shown that the ancient civilizations of the Near East entered a new era after iron became generally available because it provided abundant tools for everyday purposes and led to increased manufacturing, commerce in small goods, coinage, and finally a totally new urban and commercial pattern. It is difficult to see how this course could have been followed in the Central Andes because the ultimate resource was water, which could not have been increased in the slightest by iron tools. Manufacturing would undoubtedly have been facilitated by using primary tools of hard metal, instead of bone, wood, stone and other materials, but any increase of production would certainly have been channeled to the upper classes without any fundamental change of economic institutions. A pattern of manufacturing, markets and commerce, coinage, and accumulation of capital could hardly have been initiated until the control of the food supply was wrested from the state.

A discussion of Inca inventions and achievements would not be complete without mention of some things they lacked. We have previously called attention to the absence of wheeled vehicles, the potter's wheel, the mechanical or foot-operated loom, the true arch, iron, draft animals, writing, developed mathematics, the zero, and distillation of liquors. Other lacks included glazed pottery, porcelain, glass, true knitting, planked boats, and tanning of leather. None of these is explainable by any inherent difficulties, except that iron was precluded by the absence of ores and planked boats by the absence of timbers. The remainder are simply unexplained gaps in the inventory of a culture which perhaps stressed effort—both in attention to detail and quantity of labor—over thoughtfulness regarding fundamental improvement.

Recreational activities. The picture of Central Andean life so far presented has been one of rather serious preoccupation with producing great quantities of goods. All productive occupations, however, had a certain festive element in that some form of ritual and, frequently, major ceremonies were involved. Planting, mining, temple building, and the like were ceremonial occasions, and even birth, puberty, and death entailed ritual. There were other activities, however, of an essentially recreational nature, and probably the commoners as well as the nobles participated in them to some extent.

The Indians of the Central Andes and their immediate neighbors were similar to most North American Indians and unlike other South American Indians in that they played a number of dice games with pottery pieces, sticks, stones, beans, and the like and that they gambled in these and other games. Why this close parallel to North America should have been restricted to the Andes is an unexplained fact. In addition to games of chance, the Inca had various athletic contests and games of skill.

Music was not wanting in the Inca Empire, although little is known about it except the instruments used. The majority of the musical instruments, however, served imperial rather than private purposes. Two-headed skin drums, conch-shell trumpets, and bone flutes accompanied soldiers into battle, and tambourines, bells, and rattles furnished rhythm for temple music.

Dancing was a common feature of ceremonials, and it often was somewhat imitative, the performers wearing costumes and masks appropriate to the theme.

The music, dance, and songs of the ceremonies all formed a kind of pageantry, and definite literary patterns had developed in connection with the prayers and hymns, but the Inca seem also to have had some secular literature and drama. Narrative poems, though including much mythology, also recounted actual historical events. Whether there were genuine plays apart from the dramatic episodes of religious ceremonials is questionable. The much-discussed play "Ollanta" may be a native secular drama, but some authorities ascribe it a post-Spanish date. The failure of early observers to record texts or to give adequate detail on these native oral renditions leaves us very little evidence on which to judge Inca literature. One form of literature, however, which is still practiced to some degree, is the lyric poem, which commonly had a love theme.

Whatever pleasure these recreational features of native culture afforded the common man, his main solace was drinking chicha, the native beer. Chicha could be made of practically any vegetable or fruit, though corn was preferred, by mixing a mash, spitting some chewed corn into it, and allowing it to ferment. The Indians might drink chicha at any time, but they were expected to become ritually drunk to the point of unconsciousness at certain stages of the ceremonies. Chicha is still the common drink of the Andean Indians, especially at fiestas. The amount of fighting that accompanies drunkenness today suggests that the Inca knew well what they were doing in providing for the ceremonial release of aggressions, of which their subjects undoubtedly had plenty.

Whereas chicha was the poor man's solace, coca, the plant from which cocaine is derived, was used only by nobles and priests. Coca, however, was largely a ritual plant, used for offerings and in divination. After the Spanish Conquest, the prohibition on general use of coca was lifted, and soon this potent drug was considered an everyday necessity. Every highland Indian today carries a bag of coca leaves and lime, which he chews together to narcotize the effects of altitude, fatigue, and undernourishment as he goes about his work. He keeps a quid always in his mouth. The history of coca is rather similar to that of tobacco, which, though used sparingly in the Andes, was common in other parts of South America. Aboriginally used principally, though not exclusively, to induce religious excitation, tobacco is now also becoming an everyday habit.

2. THE SPANISH MILITARY CONQUEST

The initial conquest of Peru was one of the quickest in history, although forty years elapsed before organized native resistance was finally quelled. In 1532, Pizarro landed with a small armed and mounted force on the coast. Regarded with considerable awe as supernatural beings, the Spaniards made their way peacefully to Cajamarca in the highlands, where they were received by the emperor, Atahualpa, who was surrounded by his army. Secure in their own strength, the Inca could not conceive that the Spaniards would attempt a coup. When the latter treacherously seized the emperor in the midst of peaceful discussions, the Indians dared do nothing for fear their divine ruler would be slain. Ransoms of incredible amounts of gold did not bring about Atahualpa's release nor prevent his death. With Atahualpa's demise, the state was decapitated and the Indians helpless; for the Inca's greatest political weakness was the absolute authority of their emperor together with lack of a clear rule of succession. After Atahualpa's death it was three years before the Inca recovered sufficiently to stage a general rebellion under Manco Inca. By this time the Spaniards were too firmly entrenched and the uprising was suppressed.

Despite Pizarro's coup, the Spaniards did not at once dominate the entire Inca Empire. Their reinforcements came from Spain to the coast, which was the first part of Peru to be subjugated completely. Meanwhile, a considerable portion of the native population withdrew to the less accessible interior portions of eastern Peru and Bolivia, where they founded a Neo-Inca Empire that survived for forty years. This empire, as Kubler has shown, was in many ways more acculturated than the pacified populations directly under Spanish control. It sought to preserve the native pattern, but could not do this for several reasons. First, its population was necessarily very mobile. Second, it was essentially militaristic and utilized all its energies for survival. The agrarian basis was weakened, the production of luxury goods largely abandoned, and the social stratification leveled owing to the exigencies of a military camp. Even the military tactics were borrowed from the Europeans. Third, having lost much of its productive basis while the population it had to support was augmented by refugees, it was forced to carry on predatory warfare and contraband trade with the Spaniards in order to maintain its economy. Finally, the Catholic Church, while making no great effort at this time to missionize the pacified Indians, devoted much attention to the new empire.

The final destruction of the Neo-Inca Empire in 1572 marked the end of the Conquest. Later rebellions were usually symptoms of local discontent with the established Spanish system, not attempts to recreate native patterns. Widespread rebellions at the end of the eighteenth century, while revealing a smoldering nostalgia for aboriginal culture among the curacas, or leaders, had the practical purpose of capturing rather than overthrowing Spanish institutions. Several nativistic movements originating in the eastern Andes were minor and short-lived efforts of messianic leaders to throw off the Spanish yoke, but acculturation had already gone far beyond the possibility of reconstituting native patterns.

3. CULTURAL EFFECTS OF SPANISH INSTITUTIONS

Conflict of empires. After the Conquest, Spanish institutions deeply affected Inca culture. But the changes in native life were not the simple result of the Indians' adoption of the customs and behavior of their new masters. The Central Andes came under a new set of imperial institutions that were completely and fundamentally different from those of the Inca. Hispanic patterns not only replaced native patterns at the apex of the social and cultural pyramid, but owing to the policies of land use, tribute, and forced labor employed by the new economy and new concepts of land ownership, government, and religion, native community and family life were affected. But aboriginal folk or community culture was not destroyed. It was modified by the demands of the new imperial structure rather than through face-to-face contact of Spaniards and Indians. Except for the native upper class, servants, and artisans, the Indians were exploited at first through "indirect rule," the encomienda. It was not until much later that the rural native population became so thoroughly a part of the new state structure and had had sustained and intimate contacts with Spaniards that they lost native customs and attitudes and became thoroughly Hispanicized, acculturated, or assimilated on a community and family level.

The assimilation of the Indians was most rapid on the coast, but it was accelerated everywhere after the early nineteenth-century revolutions launched the American republics on independent courses and allowed modernization or "Westernization" to undermine the feudal colonial institutions. Despite these trends, nearly 50 per cent of the population of the Central Andes is classified as "Indian" today, and most of these are in the highlands.

Because the initial factors in change were on the state or imperial level, we shall compare salient features of the Inca and Spanish empires before examining their effects upon the basic rural population.

The Inca and Spanish empires were alike in having an agrarian basis, a two-class structure, a powerful monarch, and a national religion, but they differed profoundly in their economic foundations. The Inca Empire was an amalgamation of irrigation states, and its source of power was its efficient management of waterworks, its army, and its Sun Temple, or state religion. The emperor did not so much exact tribute from his subjects as he controlled the labor which produced all goods. The Spanish nation was welded of small feudal states, and authority was based not on control of irrigation but on private rights to land use. It was a preindustrial, Iron Age culture, which produced and exchanged enough commodities to require a monetary standard. Its economy permitted capital accumulation, and its land had to yield specialized cash commodities to produce a money income.

Modern descendants of the Inca in Cuzco. (Courtesy of Abraham E. Guillém.)

In the Spanish feudal agrarian estate, the landlord's status and power were based on his *de facto* ownership or control of the land, not upon usufruct granted by the sovereign, although lands might be expropriated and reassigned if the sovereign had sufficient military power. The agrarian estate consisted of an upper class of landlords and retainers and a lower class of peasants, each distinguished by a very different standard of living and way of life, or subculture. The peasants of the agrarian estates were largely self-sufficient; they grew their own foods and produced most of the simple goods required in their domestic life. The landlords, however, maintained a standard of living that required the products of specialists. As the Industrial Revolution in Europe produced

Modern Peru is largely mestizo. This man not only has European dress but whiskers which prove strong Spanish admixture in his near-beardless Indian ancestry. (Courtesy of Abraham E. Guillém.)

greater quantities and varieties of manufactured goods, the Spanish noblemen came to demand these goods. Land-bound, the Spaniards would not abandon an agrarian way of life for an industrial and commercial economy. The Moors and the Jews had partly met the Spaniards' needs for manufactured goods by serving as merchants and artisans. But, as their production and trade expanded and as investment capital in nonagrarian enterprises began to accumulate, there was danger that these new middle classes of bankers, businessmen, and manufacturers would enter as a wedge between the two basic rural classes and destroy the power structure. The countries of north Europe were already experiencing the upheavals of the Industrial Revolution, which unseated

This woman shows European influence, especially in her finely woven, so-called Panama hat. (Courtesy of Abraham E. Guillém.)

the aristocracy, gave the moneyed groups considerable power, and destroyed the authority of the Catholic Church. The Catholic Church, which sanctioned the two-class agrarian society, helped the state meet this threat by condemning and persecuting the Jews and Moors as heretics and, finally, expelling them from Spain. But the need for luxury goods and manufactures grew, and New World gold offered a means of paying for them.

This brief mention of these Spanish goals and institutions explains the nature of colonization and the policies devised for ruling the native populations. The Spanish colonial goals did not envisage occupation of the land by middle- or lower-class families, like the Anglo-American settlers, who would build permanent colonies and produce cash crops for trade in a world market. Spanish colonialism was initially dedicated to extraction of commodities needed at home, and the greatest need was gold with which to buy manufactured goods. Trade of other products within the empire was strictly controlled, and the colonies were permitted to sell crops, hides, and other goods only at a few designated ports. It was not until the eighteenth century, when the enticements of growing markets outside the empire brought the pressure of colonial resentment to the danger point, that Spain relaxed her strangle hold on colonial trade. By this time it was too late. A series of revolutions dissolved the empire and relegated Spain to a position among the lesser nations.

In her conquest of the Central Andes, Spain's basic economic motivations were so different from those of the Inca that she could not appropriate the latter's institutions to her own needs. Moreover, Spain began her colonial expansion in the early sixteenth century without a blueprint for empire. *Ad hoc* solutions for dealing with masses of native peoples had to be made while resistance was being overpowered by armed force. The improvisations of the period of conquest became future trends, but the different periods are marked by distinctive socioeconomic, political, and religious configurations. In each period, also, the acculturation of the various segments of native population followed different courses. In addition, there were conflicts between the crown and colonial encomenderos and landlords, and competition between Spanish secular and religious authorities. It is not yet possible to delineate the subcultures of all the components of Central Andean society during each period, nor to grasp all the cultural processes that operated. This is a subject which has fallen between anthropology, history, and the other social sciences and been largely ignored by all. Thanks to the brilliant analysis of Kubler, however, the significant acculturational periods have been roughed out and many insights into the processes have been suggested.

Economic institutions. The economic objectives of the Spanish Empire could not be achieved either by transferring the patterns of land use directly from Spain to the Andes or by merely appropriating the Inca institutions. In the Central Andes, the Spaniards found a very dense and stable native population which could not be replaced by Spanish lower-class settlers and whose native productive patterns and social arrangements did not lend themselves to direct incorporation into Spanish agrarian feudal estates. Before Spain could fully exploit the wealth of the Andes it was necessary to convert land use to the production of things wanted by the Spaniards and to devise means of mobilizing native labor to this end. The solutions improvised during the sixteenth century had to be changed repeatedly.

Inca agriculture, though highly adapted to native needs, was by no means satisfactory to the Spaniards, who required certain foods and

Wheat, introduced by Europeans, is a major highland crop but may still be winnowed by hand. (Courtesy of Abraham E. Guillém.)

domesticated animals not found in the American economy. The conversion of large portions of land from subsistence crops to production of commodities demanded by the Spaniards created a food crisis and gave the Indians few compensating advantages. Where the Indians were unwilling or unable to make this change, they often lost their lands. Some lands were devoted entirely to the production of crops that were used solely for tribute. Grapes, for example, were grown in large portions of the southern valleys and highlands to satisfy the Spaniards' demand for wine. Viniculture would not have been adopted voluntarily by the

Quechua, for they preferred chicha, their native drink. Wheat, which was grown in quantity on the Altiplano, was also consumed largely by the Spaniards, since the Indians preferred quinoa and potatoes. Livestock removed tremendous amounts of land from crop production. Horses and cattle not only required much more pasture than had been available for llamas and alpacas, but they needed feed crops, such as alfalfa. They had some value to the Indians, however, for they served as draft animals and yielded meat, hides, and other products.

The balance was not entirely on the debit side. Sugar cane was eagerly adopted by the Indians because it filled a need that was not met by any native crop, and onions and garlic became popular condiments which had no native equivalents. Sheep, goats, and pigs supplied many products while interfering comparatively little with food crops. Certain fruits, too, such as apples, peaches, apricots, citrus fruits, and plums, were welcome, although native fruits were numerous and the European species required land that could ill be spared. Chickens, on the other hand, provided a means of paying tribute that did not interfere with basic crops.

In general, these European crops and animals were accepted, not because the Indians wanted or needed them but because the Spanish tastes and habits required them. The net result was a very serious curtailment of the amount of land devoted to producing native foods, and this was unquestionably a major factor in the decline of the native population from 3,500,000—or possibly 6,000,000—to 1,500,000 persons in forty years. The farm communities were unable to support all their members, and those who did not die or move eastward to cast their lot with the Neo-Inca Empire became migrant laborers.

In nonagricultural production, the change that made the greatest difference to the Indians was the tremendous increase in mining. Whereas the Inca had carefully prorated the commoner's obligations to mine and perform other services for the state through the mita system and had cared for his family during the short time he was away from home, the Spaniards' insatiable desire for gold tore thousands of families from their communities, leaving them impoverished and culturally and socially disorganized. Similarly, the drafting of personal servants by individual Spaniards soon created an excessively large class of yanaconas, who lost their ties with their native communities.

The drastic and rather disastrous Spanish policies during the early phases of colonial administration must be understood as the result of the combination of land shortage and an abundant supply of labor. The conquistadors' objective was to exploit the country's wealth, especially the gold, and their key problem was to mobilize the manpower. Since the native lands were held in the name of the crown, and were not at first granted to individuals, the Indians theoretically retained the right to use and remain on this property. But the surplus population of the local communities just described was a potential source of labor. To appropriate this labor, the Spaniards had recourse to three principal measures. First, a form of tribute was exacted through a system of indirect rule, known as the encomienda. Second, the native type of draft labor, or mita, was employed. Third, the native pattern of yanaconas, or personal servants, was expanded and modified.

The encomienda was designed primarily to exploit the basic agrarian populations while not molesting them or changing their native ways. An encomienda consisted of a grant to an individual Spaniard, the encomendero, of the rights to the products of the labor of a certain group of Indians, who were known as a repartimiento. The privilege of exacting tribute carried the obligation of caring for the Indians' spiritual welfare, but it did not permit direct use of the land or interference in native affairs. Since enforcement of the tribute obligations was in the hands of native rulers, or curacas, the encomienda was theoretically a form of indirect rule, not unlike that which has been found widely useful in early colonial times and under similar conditions among peoples in other parts of the world. While preserving their native culture, it skimmed their wealth for the white man.

In practice, the abuses of the encomienda were quite disastrous to the native communities, for the demands for tribute in gold and in farm produce of the kinds previously mentioned were so great as to curtail production of subsistence crops to the danger point. The demands were the more onerous because an enlarged native administrative hierarchy had to be supported and because communal grazing lands that formerly had been set aside for the use of all persons were pre-empted for the enormous herds of livestock of the Spaniards.

The encomienda did not provide a permanent solution for exploiting Indian labor, for there was a constant splitting and reassignment of repartimientos, even though the number of encomenderos decreased. Moreover, an encomienda was normally granted for only two or three generations and then reverted to the crown. The abuses of the encomienda were so great that at the turn of the seventeenth century a system of direct administration by crown representatives, or corregidores, was inaugurated. These men were charged with collecting tribute and ensuring justice, but as it turned out, their corruptness was more damaging than the previous system.

The pressures of European tribute together with the complications of Spanish law, which were incomprehensible to the Indians, led to the progressive alienation of land. Land loss has been the key factor in Indian acculturation to the present day, and it is because the process went fastest on the coast that the Indians of this area are most completely assimilated to Western culture.

The mobilization of native labor through the mita far surpassed the Inca use of this system. It has been estimated that one-fifth of all the men in certain areas were impressed into public jobs. At first restricted to public works, mita labor came to be used for mining, textile manufacturing, and other industries. By far the most important of these was mining, and labor drafts were levied regardless of the ability of a province to deliver. Sick, impoverished, and often unable to return to their villages after their work in the mines, Indians died, became migratory workers, or found new homes. Whole provinces became seriously depopulated. Under the Inca, the mita laborer on state projects was compensated through provision for his family in his absence. Under the Spaniards, he was paid partly in cash, but he was by no means a wage laborer free to sell his services to the highest bidder. It is symptomatic of the excess of manpower that it was not until 1720 that a decree allowing voluntary labor was promulgated, and even then it was not enforced. The Spaniards did not have to bid for labor. Their land use and tribute policies automatically created a vast homeless population that was so near starvation that it could not choose its employment.

Most payments to mita laborers were made in goods, often useless things, sold at inflated values and recorded in complicated books which the Indians could not comprehend. The Indians' confusion and perpetual indebtedness are by no means unique to the Andes. More often than not, primitive people have been introduced to a monetary, commercial system through its more mysterious procedures of credit grants and advances of goods for services rendered before they become really acquainted with the symbolic values represented by hard cash. The agent may be the trader, the company store, or, as in Peru, the corregidor.

By the third method of mobilizing the labor force for Spanish purposes, individual Spaniards took former yanaconas—servants, artisans, and other specialists formerly assigned to the native nobles—into their service. The restrictions on the encomienda against interfering with native life were evaded by enticing the yanaconas, as well as rural Indians, to enter domestic employment through offering various favors and advantages as members of the European communities, such as exemption from tribute and mita service. This class supplied the Spaniards with their household servants and attendants, and, prior to the rise of artisans skilled in the production of Spanish goods, they apparently met the many needs of the various crafts and building trades. Toward the end of the sixteenth century, however, they became excessively numerous and began to augment the national labor pool. Crown decrees thereupon limited their number and fixed their relationship to their

Spanish masters quite precisely. The restrictions in effect converted them into mitayos, workers on the mita.

Religious institutions. The very close functional association of church and state among both the Inca and the Spaniards meant that the latter had to root out native belief and practice at all points where they sanctioned socioeconomic institutions contrary to those of Spain. Although the military conquest of the Inca was completed in 1572, the socioreligious conquest required nearly a century longer. Full-scale efforts to stamp out native belief began only about the turn of the seventeenth century.

Religious conversion was intended to eradicate all native religion, but in practice the greatest effort was made and success achieved at those levels which mattered most to the Spaniards. The cults of the sun god, Pachacamac, and the other major deities, and the temples, ritual, and other appurtenances of native state religion were completely suppressed. The curates found, however, that there was an almost unlimited number of lesser nature gods, sacred places, and objects (huacas) which received veneration, while magic, shamanism, and birth and death rites were rife in the villages. Concession was made to this folk religion on the principle that, since it was merely "superstition," which did not involve any belief in a "divine essence" in the ritual objects, it could be tolerated, whereas state religion was heresy or idolatry and must be abandoned. To the extent that every farm village was integrated to the colony as a producer of tribute and provider of mita and yanacona labor, controls were maintained by the clergy, as well as by secular administrators. The coercive power of impressive ceremonialism, payment of tithes, confessions, and primary devotion to the Christian God were necessary to mobilize and channel productive effort in the proper direction.

The features of native religion that survived were predominantly on the household and individual level, and as such they did not compete with the Catholic Church. These features not only persist today among the Indians, but many whites, who have been in close association with the Indians, have acquired certain of the "superstitions."

Since native community-level religion was not in conflict with Christianity, the latter was introduced to the villages alongside the former. It imposed an additional economic burden, however, in that tithings, support of the priests, the construction and maintenance of churches, and other obligations were required of the people. On the other hand, Catholicism became an important integrating factor on the community level. The great churches, burdensome as they were economically, were matters of pride and intervillage rivalry. A calendar of religious festivals involving about one-fourth of the days of the year afforded recreation. These ceremonials, moreover, were not merely mass demonstrations under the priests, but were opportunities for religious organizations known as cofradías, or sodalities, to function. These were religious brotherhoods, which rotated the obligation to organize and finance the festivals on various saint's days. The members, though hard pressed economically, received great prestige for their efforts. The importance of the cofradías and festivals to the modern Indian "corporate peasant" villages is discussed in Chapter Five, section 5.

Sociocultural patterns. The Spanish imperial institutions affected all segments of the Central Andean society, though in different ways, but only certain segments had sustained personal relations with the Spaniards, especially in the early colonial period. The native upper classes and their servants, the yanaconas, were most rapidly assimilated to Spanish culture, while the agrarian population was least assimilated, in spite of being changed in certain ways. The result was a mixed cultural structure: a society whose upper class had a European upper-class culture and whose lower class consisted of two sociocultural types, an Indian agrarian folk culture and a Spanish proletariat culture.

The culture of the Spanish ruling classes in the early years of the empire was brought directly from Spain. It was probably not uniform, for it consisted of crown appointees of various kinds, churchmen, impoverished noblemen and various riffraff seeking fortunes, and others representing different regional, status, and occupational groups of Spain and other countries. Their subcultures were not greatly different, however, and they all held superordinate positions respecting the Indians. They ranged in authority from the viceroy on down, and they included religious officials and encomenderos of different statuses. Their way of life included European tastes in food, drink, clothing, housing, and the like, a strongly patrilineal family and double standards, ritual kinship or the compadrazgo (parent-godparent relationship), and strong Catholicism. The adoption of these traits was to become the mark of the mestizo as against the Indian. The Spanish upper classes, however, were not immune to Quechua influence. They adopted not only many of the native foods but other material features that were useful in the Andes, and where contact has been continuous, they have even picked up considerable folk belief.

The native nobles, or curacas, first entered European ranks through their role as administrators of encomiendas in the system of indirect rule. Assigned to collect tribute from repartimientos, they retained upper-class rank and were closely associated with the Spaniards. Some were formally indoctrinated in Spanish schools.

The culture of the yanaconas, or the yanaconate, would merit special study, for, seemingly, it became the nucleus of a mobile labor force at a very early time. As servants in the Spanish households, the yanaconas learned fast enough what was expected of them and were quick to adopt Spanish customs appropriate to their situation. In time, however, Spanish towns—as contrasted with the native villages—began to spring up and became centers of trade and manufacture. The manufactures employed such Old World technology as the potter's wheel, the foot-powered loom, and other means of mass production. Classes of weavers, tile makers, carpenters, potters, and dozens of other specialists developed.

The cultural behavior of the artisans, servants, and other workers became thoroughly Hispanicized and resembled that of similar occupational and social groups elsewhere. At the present time, these towns are important acculturating centers, to which Indians come from their native villages. Here, they learn a trade, become familiar with the commercial system, improve their Spanish, adopt white dress, food habits, and other modes of behavior, and finally drift on to other parts of Peru as members of the national laboring class. At this point, assimilation to national culture is complete, and although a person may be wholly Indian in race, he has lost his native culture and is no longer classed as an Indian.

Where Spaniards acquired the land of many of the native communities, they established haciendas, or farms, devoted to cash crops. The hacendado, or owner, employed Indians whose native community functions were soon lost, leaving little native culture except that which functioned on a family or individual level.

Where the native communities remained independent and retained their lands, the folk culture survived fairly well in spite of these disturbing influences. Local customs in respect to land use, property, community shrines and veneration of ancestors, family patterns and marriage types, and home manufacture of clothes, pots, houses, and other minimal necessities have persisted to the present day. The villages are linked to the larger society or outside world through production of cash crops, and can now be described as peasant communities.

The modern peasant communities, hacienda workers, and other groups of native people are described more fully in section 5 of the present chapter. Meanwhile, we give a short summary of the four principal periods of post-Spanish acculturation proposed by George Kubler.[2] These represent culminations in the change brought about by the forces previously discussed.

4. PERIODS OF POST-SPANISH ACCULTURATION

Protocolonial Quechua, ca. 1532–1572. This period was marked by armed conflict between the Spaniards and Inca and by substitution of

Spanish imperial institutions for those of the Inca. The Indians who were brought under Spanish military and political control at the outset were rapidly acculturated in some of the ways previously mentioned. The native nobles were incorporated into the colonial hierarchy and were quickly assimilated. Spanish crops and livestock were forced upon the Quechua villages through tribute demands by means of the encomienda. Many Indians had to leave their farms because subsistence crops were reduced. Together with the yanaconas, they began to form the colonial proletariat. Sociocultural statuses and roles were not yet stabilized, for there was much shifting and jockeying for position in the flux which characterized the change-over from Inca to Spanish institutions.

Political subjugation of all of the Quechua was completed when the Neo-Inca Empire was conquered in 1572. Henceforth, Spanish institutions spread throughout the Central Andes.

Early colonial, ca. 1572–1650. The Spanish institutions now became effectively geared to wholesale exploitation of the Quechua. El Dorado, the wealth in gold, which had been the principal Spanish objective, was realized when Indians were drafted en masse for mita labor in the mines. This enormous manpower, together with European mining technology, produced great quantities of gold, which flowed back to Spain.

Life in the Quechua village, meanwhile, changed in several respects. First, a policy of resettlement of the people into fewer, larger, and more strategically placed towns weakened their local political structure. Many of the villages were moved from their ancient sites near their huacas and ancestral cemeteries to points intermediate between the mountain pastures and valley croplands. Second, the encomienda, which was becoming much like a system of slavery, was replaced in part by crown control of the Indians through corregidors. This change saved the Indian community, but it imposed stricter administrative controls on it. Third, extensive missionization introduced a functioning Catholicism as the religious integrating factor of community life, although it did not abolish family and household levels of native religious belief and practice.

Mature colonial Quechua, ca. 1650–1750. There were about one hundred years of comparative stability within the patterns previously established. No drastically new imperial policies disturbed the adjustments that had been made, although economic patterns moved gradually toward production of special cash products and purchase of manufactured goods. In part, this economic shift was a means by which the Quechua sought to meet their economic obligations; for they were now committed to mita labor, tribute, support of their curates, tithes, and many other expenditures. In part, it was probably also a response to the increasing commercialism of the times, to the partial dependence of the more acculturated villages on trade goods and the consequent need for cash.

Specialized local crafts and industries were established as communal projects to pay off the levies imposed on the villages.

Despite the drift toward a commercial economy and despite continued loss of lands, most Quechua communities continued to function as before. We have little detail on the folk culture, but it appears that not only native farm methods in the production of subsistence crops but dress, houses, household goods, social structure, marriage, and folk religion survived fairly intact, while the new religious brotherhoods, or cofradías, and the ceremonies contributed social cohesion. Administration, however, was taken over largely by the corregidors, and the powers of the village headmen were seriously curtailed.

Late colonial, ca. 1750–1821. The increasing burden on the Quechua villagers and the corruption of the corregidors led to general unrest and a rebellion under Tupac Amaru by the end of the eighteenth century. Leadership was assumed by the wealthy curacas, whose purpose seemed to be compounded of several motives. Primarily they desired to control the colony, but they also evidently had a certain humanitarian concern for the Indians that was stimulated by enlightened eighteenth-century political thinking. They made considerable symbolic use of the native Inca achievements, however, and these no doubt served as a rallying point for themselves as well as an appeal to the Indians. But the real purpose was to control the Spanish institutions independently of the colonial administrators, not to return to an Inca type of empire. No outstanding cultural change occurred during this period except that mining declined considerably and the labor pool may have decreased.

Republican Quechua. The revolution of the colonies and the establishment of independent republics made no great difference to the Quechua at first. The Indians had been closer to the crown and church than to the local landlords, for the former, despite corruption of local representatives, had endeavored to protect them. The republic continued to collect tribute until 1895, and the mita was continued under the name of faena. An attempt was made to individualize land holdings by law, but its disruptive effects were immediately recognized and it was dropped.

The most profound changes in native life were brought about through the indirect effects of economic factors rather than through state intervention. Freed from the restrictive policies of the Spanish Empire, the Andean nations were at liberty to engage in unrestricted trade. Mining had declined to the point where its yields under colonial technology were relatively unimportant, and it did not revive until foreign capital and modern methods were introduced. Agricultural wealth steadily increased, however, when landlords were free to produce for a world market. The stimulus of unrestricted trade led to the rapid growth of huge estates, called haciendas or latifundia, devoted to the production of specialized export crops. The processes which had previously contributed to loss of Indian lands were augmented by the competitive advantages of the large hacienda over the small holding. The attractiveness of money returns also led many Indian villages to grow cash crops. This quickly brought about individualization of land holdings, but as the small farmer could not compete with the hacienda or plantation, he was forced to sell out to it.

5. THE CENTRAL ANDEAN INDIANS TODAY

The modern "Indian"

The 1950 census reported that Peru had a population of over 8 million persons of whom 46 per cent were Indian, and Bolivia about 4 million persons of whom 52 per cent were Indian. By this reckoning, the Central Andes had between 5 and 6 million Indians, a number equal to the more conservative estimates of the aboriginal population. But the censuses are based on cultural rather than biological or racial characteristics. A person who wears sandals, lives in a mud-walled, thatch-covered house, believes in a "pagan" religion, and has certain other simple cultural features is classed as an "Indian." One who wears shoes, eats bread, has a tile-roofed house, practices Christianity, and exhibits other features of Hispanic culture is "mestizo," or, if he has light skin or is a near-white descendant of well-to-do criollos, he is "white."

The designation of a person as white has traditionally signified that he has characteristics of the Spanish upper class: ideals of gracious living, warm hospitality, and interest in spiritual and intellectual rather than material things. These are characteristics of the old class of landed gentry, and they are not necessarily found—in fact, they cannot well be maintained—among the lower classes of landless laborers. Present-century influences of world industrialization and urbanization, however, are creating new middle classes of professionals and businessmen, skilled laborers, and government officials who, in time, will probably be increasingly accepted as white. Skin color is not without importance in the Central Andes, but it is far less an obstacle to sociocultural mobility than in North America.

While the categories "Indian" and "mestizo" are cultural rather than biological, they have little significance in culture change. As the preceding chapter has shown, Indians began to acquire special roles and statuses within the Spanish colonies and later within the republics. They became peasant farmers, hacienda workers, artisans, and laborers, according to their special place in the larger society. These are new

The tile-roofed house and Spanish dress mark acculturation in the highlands at Ayacucho, Peru. (Courtesy of Abraham E. Guillém.)

Spanish colonial balconies at Ica on the coast. (Courtesy of Abraham E. Guillém.)

subcultural types, which gradually evolved over the centuries. They have lost their distinctive aboriginal patterns yet have not been assimilated in the typical white, or upper-class, Hispanic patterns. In the following pages we shall describe these modern types and the factors which brought them into existence.

Indians on the coast. Owing to water-borne contacts with the outside world, to commercial crop production, and to urbanization, the aboriginal features of the coastal population have almost entirely disappeared. Although largely Indian in race, the lower classes of the coastal communities now work on modernized plantations, on public works, and in the cities. Some coastal people of Indian ancestry have acquired an education and achieved success in the professions.

One of the few coastal communities which the Peruvians consider "Indian" is Moche,[3] a community which differs from its neighbors not so much in retention of a pre-Columbian culture as in such sixteenth-century Spanish features as witchcraft, ritual, and household characteristics. These small farmers contrast sharply with the workers on the large, mechanized, monocrop plantations around them. Since, however, they are producing cash crops in the competitive market, they are rapidly losing their lands to their powerful neighbors. With the loss of land, the people are becoming assimilated in the various national occupational groups, and the community is losing its identity.

Meanwhile, the excess Indian population of the highlands has been overflowing in increasing numbers to the lower valleys and the coast. On the coastal farms, which grow sugar and cotton, workers were typically paid in cash or goods, regardless of crop yield, rather than in a share of the harvest, as in traditional highland haciendas. They have a rather impersonal relationship to the managerial staff, a pattern which in part has been introduced along with foreign capital.

The recent migrants from the highland, however, are somewhat reluctant to enter into the wage-labor system of the coast. In order to recruit these men as workers, the system of enganche has been developed. Enganche is a collective contract whereby several workers agree to perform a specified task and are given an advance on their wages. While some highlanders voluntarily come down to the coast, it is common for a contratista or an official of a coastal farm to visit the sierra in search of laborers. Once obligated to the farm through a loan which can be repaid only with difficulty, the workers find themselves required to renew their contracts for many years. In the end, they become permanent workers on a particular farm or migratory laborers who move from one farm to another.

While the subculture of these coastal farm workers has never been studied, there is no question that, fundamentally, it resembles that of other members of the laboring proletariat and differs greatly from that of the highland peasant communities or hacienda workers.

The highlands. The basic population of the highland is strongly Indian in several respects. The Quechua and Aymara languages are still spoken, and many persons including whites are bilingual, speaking Spanish and

Reed or "balsa" raft used by the Uru of highland Bolivia is found in the treeless Central Andes. (Photo by Alfred Métraux, courtesy of the University of California.)

an Indian language. Much aboriginal culture survives in family life, for example, one-family, sod or stone huts, domestic manufacture such as pots and llama-wool ponchos, farm implements, dress, family structure, religious elements, Panpipes, and many others. None of the highland people, however, are truly Indian in the aboriginal sense. They not only acquired many sixteenth-century Spanish features, such as oxen, plows, religious brotherhoods, a long series of church festivals, and new crops and animals, but, more importantly, their whole pattern of life has been modified by their relationship to the larger world of commerce. Many Indians have become assimilated as skilled and unskilled workers in the highland towns. Far more have come to constitute two principal subcultural types of rural people: hacienda workers and peasant farmers.

The highland hacienda. During the colonial period, when the Spaniards in the New World were permitted little access to world markets,

The modern Aymara Indians use the llama as a beast of burden. (Courtesy of Marion Tschopik.)

agricultural production was largely for local consumption. Cultivation of the fields was done with oxen and plows, and crops were processed by simple machines powered by animals or human beings. During the last half century, these inefficient methods have been superseded on the coast by the latest in modern technology. In the highlands, however, the older kind of production is still carried on, for labor is cheap, the market is local, and transportation is extremely difficult.

The typical productive arrangement of Spanish owners in the highlands is the hacienda. The hacienda land was expropriated from the Indians through various means over past centuries. The hacienda labor is drawn from the Indian population whose lands are insufficient to support them. Lacking alternative ways of making a living and unwilling to migrate to the coast, these Indians are not free to choose hacienda employment as a coastal laborer may take or leave a wage job. Instead, they enter into various contractual arrangements which they cannot really avoid and which tend to bind them to the land and to require labor service beyond mere cultivation of the fields. They may work as laborers, tenant farmers, or sharecroppers. But in all cases their lack of alternatives, together with constant indebtedness to the hacendado, or owner, compels them to renew their contracts annually.

Chipaya houses of adobe blocks in highland Bolivia. (Photo by Alfred Métraux, courtesy of the University of California.)

The subculture of the hacienda workers has never been thoroughly studied. It appears, however, that these families lose contact with their natal communities and develop a way of life and cultural values quite foreign to the Indian peasants of the highlands.

The highland peasant community. Highland Indians retain their own lands only in limited areas. They live in what may be called peasant communities, each of which is, in effect, an Indian reservation, for it is fairly isolated, autonomous, and cut off from intimate contact with the larger society.

These communities have been called "corporate" or "closed" because they are not only largely self-sufficient and self-contained but highly integrated and their members are suspicious of the outside world.[4] In these respects, they differ from the "open" peasants of Brazil and Paraguay, who move freely about the country, take up new land, make new alliances, and rarely form a stable community. The corporate or closed peasant appears in areas of land shortage, where the best lands have been taken by haciendas and the surplus population in the community must find employment elsewhere. The open peasant appears in areas of abundant land, where expanding families send out their sons to prepare new fields for cultivation.

The Andean highland peasant communities are by no means aboriginal Indian in culture, although they retain many native culture elements. Most importantly, they engage in some degree of commercial crop production, which today is fundamental in transforming their whole way of life. Although not wholly isolated, these communities have been penetrated less by national law, economic dependency, and outside cultural influences than mestizo or white communities. Since these communities possess only limited land, the overflow population is forced to work on the highland haciendas, in the mines, and in the few towns, or else go to the coast. Tschopik's study[5] of the central highlands has shown how Indians who could not support themselves in their hamlets first drifted into Sicaya, a center of commerce and transportation, where they began their orientation to the larger society and national values. They became accustomed to wage labor and cash transactions, they began to comprehend national institutions, and they began to participate in modern life. From Sicaya, they went on to the coast or elsewhere and were absorbed in the national labor proletariat.

Most of the highland peasant communities owe their origin to the policies of the crown officials (corregimientos) and to resettlement (reducción) early in the sixteenth century, when the Spanish king attempted to break the power of the large colonial landowners. Much land was set aside for the Indians as communal property (ejidos), but, in order to facilitate administration and to bring the Indians to their lands, many native settlements were amalgamated. Until the close of the last century, however, onerous burdens were imposed upon these peasant communities. The Indians were required to provide corvée labor to build roads, irrigation systems, and other public works, and, until 1895, the highlands provided one-sixth of the national income. Today, owing especially to the growth of national concern for the Indians—a concern that reflects the spirit of indígenismo, or the Indianist movement, throughout the Americas—burdens have been lightened and restrictions lifted.

These modern peasant communities are not necessarily compact settlements. In some cases, especially in the very high altitudes, where tillage is less productive than herding, houses are scattered, each family living next to its fields or pastures. In other cases, the settlement is typically Spanish in having a central plaza surrounded by church and public buildings, and, beyond the plaza, barrios, or wards, of houses. The streets are narrow and crooked, and the houses are small, thatch-roofed, and sparsely furnished.

The peasant community generally consists of several extended patri-lineal families which are related to one another through marriage. The in-group feeling is so strong that the people fear and are suspicious of other Indians as well as whites, and consequently there is a strong

Church at Cajamarca, highland Peru. (Courtesy of Abraham E. Guillém.)

preference for marriage within the community. An outsider who marries into the community may become a target of witchcraft. This endogamy serves not only to enhance the solidarity of intermarried families but to prevent alienation of land.

Today, the highland communities retain a marginal economy, and their primary need is to produce their own food, despite partial de-pendence upon cash products. They contrast sharply with the large coastal plantations in their use of simple, unmechanized techniques. Most of them use native digging sticks rather than draft animals to culti-vate the land. Even where use of draft animals would increase produc-tivity, the Indians lack the meager capital needed to invest in them. The more affluent peasants who possess oxen employ them to plow and thresh grain in ways known from early colonial years. Where irrigation is employed, it is on a small scale and the ditches are hand-dug. The highlands never needed and could not profitably utilize vast irrigation systems like those constructed by the Inca in the middle and lower valleys. Nonetheless, these people, faced with land shortage, extract the maximum produce possible according to their special needs and by the methods available to them.

Preparation of the fields is laborious and time-consuming. Turning the soil, sowing, and harvesting are generally done in aine, a system of

The highland market at Ayacucho shows Spanish dress, sheep, and pigs. (Courtesy of Abraham E. Guillém.)

reciprocal labor whereby an individual repays the assistance received from neighbors on a man-for-man, day-for-day basis. Every member of the community belongs to a voluntary work party geared to the aine system. Preparation of a field is customarily done by a team of three persons, two of whom dig up the soil while the third, usually a woman or boy, turns the clods to the left and right to form a furrow. In sowing, one person makes holes with a digging stick, another plants, and a third spreads fertilizer. Harvesting involves an even more complex arrangement. All field labor is characteristically a system of reciprocal exchange in the aine pattern.

Community lands are divided into a number of large sections, some of which lie in the level pampas, while others are on the less favorable hillsides. Ideally, each family holds plots in several sections and farms fields of varying quality, which are planted in different crops. The rotation of crops is practiced everywhere. It generally involves a three-year cycle of potatoes, oca, and barley, followed by a three-year period of rest, during which other fields are cultivated. The hillsides, however, are usually planted in potatoes for one year, after which they lie fallow for five to ten years, when they are given over to pasture.

Maize, which has spread throughout the world to an incredible number of climates, may be grown in the Andes up to 11,000 feet, although it is more productive in the lower valleys, where a number of other semitropical and tropical crops are also raised. Quinoa and other high-altitude grains are produced only in relatively small amounts and mostly in southern Peru. These varied crops are exchanged in local markets, where they are either bartered for other foods or sold in small amounts for cash.

Today, with the penetration of national legal concepts as well as other influences to the peasant communities, in theory, nearly all arable land is individually owned. The changing economy has brought traditional usage respecting land ownership into conflict with modern national law, but the latter is gaining acceptance. The commons, or ejidos, are now limited largely to pasture land, but even this is constantly being converted into farm plots in order to accommodate the increasing population. Every year, however, the farm plots are reallocated in the pre-planting season in an official ceremony over which the governor of the district presides. While the governor's role is perfunctory, since he merely reaffirms existing boundaries, the ceremony is attended by considerable pomp and fanfare. Before the official reaffirmation no one is permitted to begin plowing, and violations are penalized by fines.

The conflict between national law and traditional usage concerning land tenure is seen in the bitter disputes between community members when the remarking of field boundaries may benefit one party by even an infinitesimal shift of boundary markers. Some persons resort to sorcery, the traditional means of maintaining their rights. Others resort to litigation in national courts.

This conflict between the traditional and the new concept of land tenure and validation is being resolved more and more in favor of the latter. Increasingly, individual ownership is recognized and fought for; and the concept of individual land ownership as against community solidarity is disrupting the extended families within the community and the community itself. Even women are now claiming ownership of particular plots of ground and are asking national courts to adjudicate their claims.

Two potent factors furthered this trend: overpopulation and participation in a cash economy. Excess population puts individual families into competition with one another for the limited lands, whether these are to be used for subsistence or cash crops. Production of cash crops intensifies competition, for cash can be used to purchase manufactured goods which benefit the individual or his family. Once the individual has learned to depend upon these goods, he is reluctant to give up the right to land which enables him to buy them.

The belt loom has survived from the earliest prehistoric periods of Peru. (Courtesy of Abraham E. Guillém.)

There are no adequate statistics on acreage yields in the highland communities, but all indications are that production is insufficient to support the growing population. Bernard Mishkin[6] states that in Kauri, near Cuzco, only about 20 per cent of the families produce a marketable surplus, while half the community grows barely enough on which to subsist. The remaining 30 per cent raises too little to meet its needs and is forced to seek employment elsewhere.

The highland people supplement their small incomes from the land through the manufacture and sale of native wares. The most important home industries are weaving, cordage, and hats. Textiles are woven of llama, alpaca, vicuña, and sheep wool. Several types of loom are used, and a wide variety of designs are produced. The manufacture of baskets,

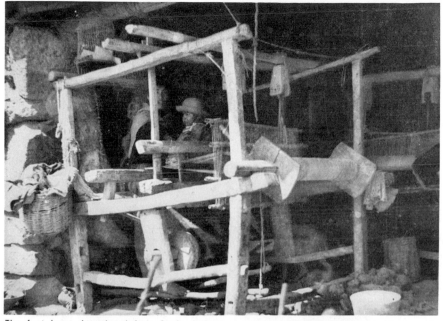

The foot loom, introduced from Spain and powered by the feet, is meeting modern needs for mass production and labor saving in the Andes. (Courtesy of Abraham E. Guillém.)

Image of "Christ of the Earthquake," Cuzco, Peru. (Courtesy of Abraham E. Guillém.)

carved wood objects, clay tiles and bricks, gourds, gold, silver, and copper ornaments, and numerous other products are subsidiary industries. Most of these goods are produced for native consumption and are bartered or sold in highland markets. Many items, however, find

Devil dancer carrying whip in highland Peruvian festival. (Courtesy of Sol Miller.)

their way to tourist centers and receive nationwide and even international distribution. Recently, artisans from the highlands have been producing their wares in lowland towns and urban centers primarily for the tourist trade. The vast majority of highlanders who migrate to the lowland towns and farms, however, go to find employment as unskilled laborers.

Inequalities in landholding have developed within communities as a result of inheritance and the sales which follow individual ownership of fields. This in turn has weakened the aine system, since large land-holders require more assistance than they are prepared to exchange in the traditional method. They prefer to pay for all or much of the labor they receive in cash or produce. The factors of kinship and common

Survival of aboriginal religion: offerings of magical substances to the deities and spirits in the Andean highlands. (Photo by Alfred Métraux, courtesy of the University of California.)

residence which determined the composition of aine work groups are becoming nonfunctional. Individualization of land tenure and breakdown of the reciprocal labor groups are part of a series of modifications which are weakening the corporate solidarity of the peasant communities.

The formal political structure of the highland communities has its roots in the colonial period, when the Spaniards organized municipal governments throughout Peru. The village head is an alcalde, who is subordinate to the district governor and who, together with his assistants, is elected by the community elders.

The principal requirement for political office is full participation in community religious rituals that were introduced by the missionaries. One achieves community respect and prominence through accepting a series of religious obligations (cargos) which require the outlay of considerable time and money. A man may expect financial assistance from

Two-man band with trumpet, whistle, and drum at Cajamarca, Peru. (Courtesy of Abraham E. Guillém.)

friends, relatives, and members of his religious brotherhood (cofradía), but he is obligated to reciprocate this assistance when any of them undertakes a cargo.

Contemporary Quechua religion is a tangle of Catholic and pagan beliefs, which entail ritual celebrations geared to a church calendar. Religion is integrally part of the political, social, and economic life of the community and has only a tenuous connection with the Catholic Church. Nearly all communities have land set aside for the support of religious ceremonies, but population pressure has been so great in some instances that this land has been divided into individual holdings for the support of new families.

Religious duties are far more important than political office. A man may decline election to the alcaldeship of his community, but he would not shirk his religious obligations, even though they constitute the avenue to political office. In many communities, moreover, the alcalde is under the thumb of the district governor and the position has lost the respect of the people. But this has not nullified the political force of religion. As Mishkin observed, there develops a *sub rosa* political leadership, headed by community elders who are frequently sorcerers and curers. These are the genuine leaders of the community, to whom people turn when the occasion demands. Politicoreligious authority in the corporate community is strictly local. There are no intervillage political ties.

Basic to the corporateness of community organization is the solidarity of the extended family, which functions as a socioeconomic unit, operates in the religious sphere, and is the mainstay of the labor-exchange system. The extended family occupies a household or compound and is governed by the paterfamilias. With the decline of community solidarity and the growth of individualism, the nuclear family has attained greater importance.

NOTES

1. Information on the aboriginal Inca Empire is drawn largely from John Rowe's article in the *Handbook of South American Indians*, vol. 2. Rowe combined a very thorough study of early Spanish sources with considerable archaeological information. Current research in Peru will probably deepen our understandings of the Inca Empire, and it will certainly contribute greatly to knowledge of the subcultures and processes of change among the contemporary people.
2. George Kubler, *Handbook*, vol. 2.
3. John Gillin, *Moche: A Peruvian Coastal Community*, Smithsonian Institution, Institute of Social Anthropology Publication 3, 1947.
4. Eric Wolf, "Types of Latin American Peasantry: A Preliminary Discussion," *American Anthropologist*, vol. 57, pp. 452–471, 1955.
5. Harry Tschopik, Jr., *Highland Communities of Central Peru: A Regional Survey*, Smithsonian Institution, Institute of Social Anthropology Publication 5, 1947.
6. Bernard Mishkin, *Handbook*, vol. 2.

► six

CHIEFDOMS OF THE CIRCUM-CARIBBEAN AREA AND EASTERN BOLIVIA

1. GENERAL FEATURES AND VARIETIES OF CHIEFDOMS

A number of small multicommunity societies, which have been designated "states," "chiefdoms," "federations," "realms," and "kingdoms," existed at the time of the Spanish Conquest in somewhat scattered localities in the northern Andes, Central America, parts of Venezuela, the Greater Antilles, and portions of eastern Bolivia. These societies varied considerably, as the many terms applied to them may suggest, but all were distinguished from the riverine horticultural villages of the tropical forests by some kind of class structure, state gods, persons who functioned as priests, and organization of several communities into small states.

The *Handbook* category of "Circum-Caribbean" peoples, which was based upon Kirchhoff's suggestions,[1] was the first rough distinction to be made between the people of the Central Andes and those of the northern Andes, Central America and the Greater Antilles, and between these latter areas and the tropical-forest riverine villages. Oberg[2] later proposed that the Circum-Caribbean peoples be divided into at least two principal subtypes: first, the "Politically Organized Chiefdoms," as exemplified by the Calamari, Quimbaya, Tolú, Cenú, and Mompox of northern Colombia and the Arawak of the Greater Antilles; and, second,

174

the "Feudal Type State," of which the Nicarao of Nicaragua and Chibcha, or Muisca, of Colombia are outstanding examples. Kroeber, in the *Handbook*,[3] described the Chibcha as a "realm."

It will be obvious that many of the chiefdoms described in these chapters deviate greatly from the typical pattern. Their classification as chiefdoms, however, does not mean that a wide variety of societies are artificially subsumed under an "ideal" but unreal type. Since we are more interested in the causes or processes that bring about culture types than in external characteristics, chiefdoms represent an interaction of surplus production, population density, and religious and military activities. In some cases, all of these factors combine in full force to create strong chiefdoms like that of the Chibcha, or Muisca. In others, as among the Aruacay and Palenque of eastern Venezuela, the priest-temple-idol complex was entirely absent and the war patterns created only weak chiefdoms. It might well be argued that such people should be classed as typical forest villagers. To do so, however, would be to lose sight of the forces that tended to cause intervillage federation and internal social stratification. The principal basis for distinguishing subtypes of chiefdoms, therefore, is whether military and religious patterns of different kinds were effective rather than the degree to which these patterns brought about characteristics of chiefdoms.

Oberg's distinctions stimulate further examination and classification of the societies considered in this section. We use Oberg's term "chiefdoms" to designate a generic type which includes not only the people classed in the *Handbook* as "Circum-Caribbean" but also certain societies of southern Colombia, Ecuador, and eastern Bolivia. Although the former were designated "Andean" in the *Handbook* and the latter "Sub-Andean," both have the general features of chiefdoms. We use the term "chiefdom" with some misgivings, however, owing to the wide range of meaning in scientific literature ascribed "chief" and to the highly varied use of the term in popular history and fiction; yet there are no better alternatives. The early Spanish writers called the rulers of these states or federations "kings," "lords," and "caciques," the last being best translated as "chiefs." "King" and "lord," however, imply too much power and organization. While "chief" usually denotes the leader of a band or village, we extend its meaning to designate leadership of several communities which we call "chiefdoms."

No societies of South America were so kaleidoscopically varied culturally as the chiefdoms; for they shared elements with the Central Andes, the tropical forests, and Meso-America, and these were combined in innumerable ways. Division of these people into culture areas characterized by lists of elements or traits is rather futile, for the choice between large and small divisions poses the impossible difficulty of determining "how different is different." For this reason, none of the area subdivisions proposed by different authors are the same.

Another difficulty in classifying the cultures in this area is that many of the living Indians have a tropical-forest type of culture even though complex archaeological remains are found in their territories. A clue to the discrepancy between prehistory and history was first provided by Lothrop. During the 1930s, Lothrop excavated a site near Coclé, Panama, where he found cemeteries of "lords" whose wives or retainers had been buried with them.[4] The cemeteries contained great riches in mortuary offerings of exquisitely wrought gold, precious stones, ceramics, and other objects wholly unlike anything made by the modern Cuna Indians of this region. Lothrop then examined the early Spanish descriptions of Panama (see Chapter Seven, section 6) and found that at the time of the Spanish Conquest the Indians of Coclé were organized in small states or chiefdoms, had a strongly class-structured society, and possessed outstanding skill in manufacturing luxury goods such as those he found in the graves.

It became clear that the Cuna Indians,[5] who are the modern descendants of the Indians buried at Coclé, had been so broken by the Spanish Conquest that their native chiefdoms were destroyed, their social classes eliminated, and their skills in producing art goods in textiles, ceramics, and metallurgy were lost. What remained was a primitive society much like that of the Amazonian Indians. That is, the Cuna retained the simple features of their native village life but lost the institutions and skills associated with chiefdoms and social classes.

This dramatic illustration of culture change—and in this case it was deculturation, or loss of important features—underlined the importance of delving into early Spanish sources in order to find out how four centuries under the rule of Europeans had affected the Indians. In the 1940s, Paul Kirchhoff and Gregorio Hernández de Alba, after reviewing the old documents, suggested that many native societies of Ecuador, Colombia, and Venezuela had had a fairly rigid class structure and produced outstanding art goods, even though their modern descendants had been pushed into less desirable regions and either have lost their native state characteristics or have been absorbed into the national peasant population. Kirchhoff proposed the term Circum-Caribbean for the area.[6]

Although chiefdoms were once widely distributed within the Circum-Caribbean area, they cannot account for all the elaborate archaeological remains found there. Some of these remains seem to date back well into prehistoric times, when cultures different from those of the historic people existed.

The present broad category of chiefdoms serves to distinguish a culture type characterized by small, class-structured states from the lineages and bands of nomadic hunters and gatherers, the independent villages of the tropical-forest riverine and coastal people, and the irrigation states and empires of the Central Andes. The local differences between the chiefdoms represent an interaction of two factors. First, food production in the extremely varied environments afforded differing amounts of surplus and consequently permitted specialization, class formation, and state development in different degrees. Second, not only were different cultural features borrowed from other areas, but they were locally patterned in different ways.

Despite the considerable range of differences, there were two general subtypes of chiefdoms, which are distinguishable primarily by the nature of warfare and its relationship to religion and social structure. The first, which may be designated militaristic chiefdoms, were found in the northern Andes of Ecuador and Colombia and among many of the Indians of Central America. Although the component villages of these chiefdoms were more or less self-sufficient in food production and religious worship, they united under a supreme chief to conquer lands, exact tribute from the people, and take captives. But they warred for far more than glory or tribute. Warfare was crucial to religion in supplying human victims for blood sacrifice in temple rites, and for cannibalism. It was also an essential factor in achieving social status, since the individual warrior gained prestige by displaying human trophies —parts of the bodies of his victims—and by adding captives to his household. The gory religious nature of this warfare was very similar to that among the Aztec of Mexico.

The second type of chiefdom, which we call theocratic, was found in the Greater Antilles, Venezuela, and eastern Bolivia. These chiefdoms were less warlike than those of the northern Andes. Although the Venezuelan Caracas, Palenque, Caquetio, Jirajara, and others were fairly bellicose, human sacrifice had minor religious importance and religion was otherwise quite separate from warfare. In fact, the aboriginal purpose of warfare is far from clear. The display of human trophies was rare, but cannibalism was practiced among the Carib of the Venezuelan coast. The religious chiefdoms also differed from the militaristic chiefdoms in that elements diffused from the Andes diminished in number in eastern Bolivia and Venezuela and became even fewer in the Antilles.

While the religious chiefdoms differed from one another because the nature of religion in the three areas where these chiefdoms occur was unlike in certain formal features, the function of religion in integrating local communities was rather similar in all. Among the Antillean Arawak, there was a hierarchy of personal guardian spirits that ranged from those of the common people through those of village leaders to those of the heads of chiefdoms. The last were state deities, and ceremonial ball courts seem to have served a religious purpose in connection with these chiefdoms. Among some of the Venezuelan chiefdoms, there were traces of a priest-temple-idol complex, but the full cult was reported nowhere. In eastern Bolivia, where public ritual resembled a kind of glorified men's society ceremony not unlike that of Amazonia, it evidently brought men of several villages into association. In all of these cases religion served community and state purposes, and it required the services of specialists who held superior status in the class structure.

While the development of these different kinds of chiefdoms must be explained partly by culture history, since crucial features were borrowed from neighboring people or areas, the types are not merely assemblages or agglomerations of culture elements which they happened to borrow. Moreover, the chiefdoms do not represent a developmental stage in any large scheme of South American culture history. They do not necessarily exemplify an early phase of cultural development in the Central Andes or a potential development of the tropical-forest farmers or of the food hunters and gatherers. The chiefdoms differed from the tropical-forest farmers and the hunters and gatherers in that they were based on surplus production which permitted social differentiation. They shared many features with the peoples of the tropical forests, such as house and village type and community life, and yet they resembled the Andean and Meso-American "high cultures" in certain religious and military patterns and in many architectural features and manufactures that served state purposes. To understand why these chiefdoms developed, it is more important to know how these features interacted in each locality to form total cultures than to trace the origin and diffusion of each element or complex of elements.

2. ENVIRONMENT AND PRODUCTION IN RELATION TO TYPES OF CHIEFDOMS

Environment and culture

Each chiefdom occupied a rather small area, which was often an enclave among coastal horticultural villages. Some even adjoined hunting-and-gathering nomads. The cultural diversity of the chiefdoms paralleled the environmental diversity, and it contrasted sharply with the cultural and environmental uniformity of the Central Andes. The Central Andes consists of a broad, high, unbroken mountain massif which runs from northern Peru to northern Chile. It is differentiated principally between the cold puna of the northern and central highlands and the complete desert of the coast, which sweeps up and over the highland in the southern Andes of Bolivia and northern Chile.

In Ecuador, the Andes narrow and become lower than in Peru, while the coast broadens and changes abruptly from virtually rainless desert to steaming tropical rain forests. An overlay of Central Andean culture specific to the Inca period was introduced to highland Ecuador by the Inca conquest. In addition to military and political domination, the Ecuadorians, especially of the highlands, received a knowledge of bronze, llamas, ceramic styles, and many other particulars from the Inca. Neither highland nor coastal Ecuador, however, evolved native states or empires as large or as completely organized as those which were based upon irrigation in the Central Andes.

In Colombia, the Andes split into two main ranges: the Cordillera Occidental, or western range, and the Cordillera Oriental, or eastern range, which extends into Venezuela south of Lake Maracaibo and on northeast to the gulf coast. These ranges are separated by large, low river valleys, parts of which are covered with rain forests in which palms are dominant. These forests could be cultivated only by means of slash-and-burn farming, and, like the Amazon-Guiana rain forests, most of them did not support chiefdoms or states. Western Colombia, especially the valley of the Atrato River, which drains northward to the Gulf of Darien at Panama, is so rainy and disease-ridden as to be almost unin habitable. The tropical-rain-forest lowlands around Lake Maracaibo also supported only a horticultural-village type of culture; for example, that of the Motilones, who have persistently avoided direct contact with whites.

Chiefdoms, however, developed not only in the Colombian and Venezuelan highlands but also in those portions of the river valleys and north-coast lowlands that are dominated by savanna or scrub steppe. Highland chiefdoms are typified by the Chibcha, or Muisca, of Colombia and the Timoteans of Venezuela, and archaeological remains suggest that similar societies once flourished in the Santa Marta Mountains of northern Colombia. Lowland chiefdoms were found among the Cenú, Mompox, Cumanagoto, and others.

Chiefdoms occurred still farther north in Central America, where the mountain ranges are not massive and few rise above the rain forests. While it is difficult to relate culture and environment in this area, owing to our very scant knowledge of the former in both prehistoric and historic times, it seems certain that two factors stimulated cultural development beyond the seeming environmental limitations imposed by the swamps in the unhealthy lowlands and the prevalent rain forests on the mountains. First, Central America had been an avenue of cultural exchange between North and South America for several thousand years. It acquired subsistence techniques, knowledge of manufactures, and sociocultural patterns from both continents. Second, coastal resources supplemented farming among some groups such as the Cuna of Panama. Some Central American Indians, however, never developed chiefdoms, and all chiefdoms disintegrated shortly after the Spanish Conquest.

The Greater Antilles are fairly similar to Central America in environment. The islands are dominated by tropical rain forests, except in savanna areas of rain shadow, and they have mountainous interiors and coastal plains. In contrast to Central America, however, this area was negligible as a route of diffusion for culture between North and South America. Moreover, it has little game and its coastal fisheries are comparatively unimportant. Nevertheless, food production, which included some irrigation farming, supported a dense population and small states. It is noteworthy that, as Rouse points out,[7] archaeology shows that the settlements of the Arawak, in contrast to the villages of their tropical-forest-type predecessors, were located more in the highlands than on the coastal plain.

The absence of chiefdoms in the Lesser Antilles is less a question of favorable environment than of a late but rapid and extremely aggressive prehistoric invasion by the warlike Carib villagers.

There is not, of course, a one-to-one relationship between culture and environment in the diversified areas of the chiefdoms, but there is a fairly clear broad correlation. First, this type of culture occurred predominantly, though not exclusively, in regions that did not depend primarily upon irrigation nor face the extreme difficulties of slash-and-burn farming. Such areas were found principally in the mountains and in the lowland savannas. Second, the instances wherein chiefdoms developed in rain forests were fairly restricted and seemingly represent exceptional effectiveness in utilizing resources, owing to diffused techniques and socioeconomic organization.

Subsistence patterns

The chiefdoms were based upon intensive farming, which ordinarily relegated hunting, fishing, and the gathering of wild foods to a role that was less important than among the tropical-forest Indians. Farming, in fact, was so important among these people that it had become the principal task of men, which contrasts with its place in the tropical forests, where men cleared the plots of trees and then left cultivation to women while they hunted and fished.

Cultivation was best carried on in the highlands and the semiarid, brush-covered lowlands, where the difficulties of clearing rain forests were less than in the lowlands and where the fields could be fairly permanent. In many places, mountainsides were terraced to facilitate cultivation. Since rainfall was fairly adequate, terracing did not necessarily imply irrigation, but irrigation was practiced by a number of groups, including the Cañar of Ecuador, the Chibcha of Colombia, the Timoteans (who also built storage tanks), the Cumanagoto of Venezuela, and the Island Arawak. This spotty distribution of irrigation probably correlates in part with sharp local or microgeographical differences in rainfall. Within this highly diversified area, there may be profound difference in precipitation within a few miles, as in Puerto Rico, where the north coast receives about 80 inches of rain a year and the south coast, 40 miles away, is in the rain shadow of the mountains and receives only 10 inches.

The considerable range of altitude in many parts of the Circum-Caribbean area permitted considerable crop diversity. The number of species and varieties did not equal that of the Central Andes, but it far surpassed that of most tropical-forest peoples. Moreover, it provided not only a more abundant diet but a better balance of proteins and carbohydrates than could be produced in the tropical forests. Since the native people seem constantly to have been experimenting with new species and varieties, their total inventory of domesticates was probably larger than our records show.

In the lowlands and middle altitudes of the northern Andes, the Indians grew sweet potatoes, maize, yuca or sweet manioc, beans, peanuts, and such fruits as pineapples, avocados, papayas, custard apples (*Annona squamosa*), cherimoyas (*Annona cherimola*), and capuli (*Physalis peruviana*). In the middle altitudes, between 5,000 and 8,000 feet, they also grew maize, arracacha (*Arracacia esculenta*), quinoa, achira (*Canna edulis*), and auyama (*Cucurbita verrucosa*); and in the highlands, above 8,000 feet, potatoes, quinoa, ullucos (*Ullucus tuberosus*), and cubios (*Tropaeolum tuberosum*).

Most of these crops were grown also in Central America and Venezuela (Table 1), but the Antillean Arawak cultivated fewer crops. Coconuts are reported throughout the Circum-Caribbean area, but since they are Old World, arguments have been advanced that in America they were (1) brought by prehistoric migrations from the Pacific, (2) carried by ocean currents from the Pacific, or (3) introduced since the Spanish Conquest. Bitter manioc, the all-important staple of the tropical forests of the Amazon and the Guianas, seems to have been aboriginal in Venezuela. While there is some question when it spread to the Island Arawak and to Central America, it is very probable that the Antilles received it in pre-Columbian times, especially since paraphernalia of the kind used for processing it have been found in aboriginal sites.

Crop productivity varied regionally, and it was reflected in population density. In highland Ecuador, there are paramo grasslands instead of cool savannas as in the Central Andean puna, but eastern Ecuador has montaña rain forests like those on the eastern slope of the Central Andes. The Pasto, Cara, Cañar, Panzaleo, Puruhá, Palta, and others lived in the intermont basins and depended primarily upon potatoes, maize, beans, and quinoa. The Puruhá were especially intensive agriculturalists, and their area was among the most densely populated in Ecuador.

The Indians of highland Ecuador also cultivated cotton, maguey, and cabuya for their fibers, which they wove into fine fabrics and traded to coastal people for salt. The Cañar, who occupied a vast area in southern Ecuador, resembled their Peruvian neighbors in that they practiced irrigation to an unusual extent and, in fact, cultivated more land than their modern descendants. The Palta, although apparently late prehistoric arrivals in the Ecuadorian highlands from the Montaña to the east, adopted the local crop inventory from neighboring groups.

In northern Colombia, the rainy mountain slopes and some of the river valleys also permitted agriculture sufficient to support chiefdoms. The Cenú, Calamari, Mompox, Yapel, and other people of the northern Colombian lowlands were all intensive agriculturalists. Their staple crops were maize and sweet manioc, supplemented by sweet potatoes, beans, and various fruits. Most of these groups also hunted and fished along the rivers, and like the tropical-forest Indians, they preserved meat by smoking it on a babracot, or grill, made of sticks. Surplus production supported not only specialists within each state but also specialization and trade in products and manufactures between localities.

In the Cordillera Oriental and Venezuelan Andes, the Timoteans, Lache, Chitarera, Chaké, and others were sedentary farmers, but their techniques varied locally from the simple slash-and-burn practices of the Chaké to the advanced terracing and irrigation systems of the Timoteans. All had some form of irrigation, however, and even the Chaké ran simple ditches through their temporary fields. The Spanish conquistadors were greatly impressed by the economic and social development in Venezuela —the agricultural surpluses, the size of the towns, some of which had as many as 800 stone-walled houses, the roadways, and the ample storage facilities. In portions of lowland Venezuela, some people, such as the Jirajara and Caquetio, irrigated large manioc and maize plantations, and the Cumanagoto irrigated plantations of cacao, a crop of Meso-American origin. The Indians of western, lowland Venezuela carried on less intensive agriculture. The Palenque, Cumanagoto, Chaima, and Aruacay supplemented their agricultural harvests to a great extent with ocean and river resources which they exploited rather fully.

In the Greater Antilles, farming, although predominantly of the slash-and-burn type, yielded two crops a year of such plants as matured rapidly. The Indians fertilized their crops with urine and potash and in some cases irrigated extensively. The more important crops included several varieties of beans, sweet manioc, maize, sweet potatoes, peppers, gourds, and various fruits.

The Mojo, Bauré, Manasí, and Paunaca of the eastern Bolivian lowlands and the nearby Paressí of Mato Grosso were efficient food producers, even though semimigratory horticulturalists and nomadic groups lived adjoining and interspersed among them. On their farms in the savannas they raised squash, maize, sweet manioc, sweet potatoes, gourds, beans, peanuts, tobacco, cotton, and many other domesticated plants. The Mojo plantations were especially large.

Domesticated animals were less important to the chiefdoms than to the Central Andean people since the former lacked alpacas and only Ecuador had llamas. The vicuña, which is not a genuine domesticate, was not found north of Peru. Guinea pigs, although small and exceedingly bony, were bred in some quantity in the northern Andes and contributed considerably to the meat diet. Two other domesticated species had a fairly wide distribution: the Muscovy duck, which was kept as a semidomesticate by most of the chiefdoms, and a mute dog, which was fattened for eating by the Circum-Caribbean people. Domesticated turkeys, probably of Mexican origin, were found among scattered groups, especially in Central America. Apiculture was carried on in Venezuela and eastern Bolivia. While Mexico was a center of bee domestication, it is not certain that all of these cases of apiculture can be traced historically to that area.

While we have no information concerning the quantity these domesticated animals contributed to diet, it is probable that most chiefdoms obtained their meat proteins principally from wild game and fish. Hunting, although relatively less important than in the tropical forests or the southern plains and savannas of Paraguay and Argentina, was carried on in all the chiefdoms. These predominantly rainy, forested, and mountainous regions offered deer, rabbits, birds, wild guinea pigs, peccaries, and other small mammals and rodents. The people killed them by means of spears, slings, and clubs. The bow and arrow seems to have been introduced fairly recently, in some areas within historic times.

In many areas, fish provided a much more important supplement to the predominantly vegetable diet than game. In Eastern Bolivia, fish stranded in pools when the annual floods receded were taken in great quantity. In Colombia, the Gorrón built special ponds in which they raised fish for trade with other groups. The coastal people of northern Venezuela, especially the Quiriquire, were excellent seamen, who fished the rivers and coasts. The Antillean Arawak did not neglect fishing, but they lived away from the coast and depended primarily upon plant cultivation. Similarly, in Central America, fishing had negligible importance not only to the highland people, whose small rivers understandably afforded few fish, but even to such lowland groups as the Sumo, Mosquito, and others.

It is probable that the relative unimportance of fish was less a matter of cultural emphasis upon other foods than of the scarcity of sea foods in their environments. Much of the coast line drops off sharply to extreme depths, as in the Antilles and the Caribbean coast of Panama and northern Colombia, and lacks banks or shoals where fish occur in quantity. The occurrence of abundant maritime fish resources closely corresponds to continental shelves such as those off the Pacific coast of Colombia and Central America and the northern coast of Nicaragua. In addition, mangrove swamps occupy much of the coast and preclude important utilization of shellfish resources.[8]

These people also used wild plants, including not only edible fruits but species that provided fibers for making baskets, mats, sandals, and bark cloth.

Another natural resource of great importance was salt. Throughout native America, the importance of salt had a fairly direct relationship to subsistence upon cultivated plants rather than animal foods, and it was a major trade item and often a ceremonial item among the chiefdoms, as in the Central Andes. This importance was undoubtedly related to biological need or desire among plant eaters rather than hunters. In many localities salt deposits were a valued possession.

Population and settlements

Chapter Three has dealt with the question of population and settlements in general terms. Food productivity among the chiefdoms permitted a population density much greater than that of the nomadic hunters and gatherers and tropical-forest farmers but less than that of the Central Andes. The clustering of this population in settlements, however, depended upon additional factors.

In the highlands of Ecuador and Colombia, where large-scale irrigation was neither needed nor possible, the administrative functions were less important than in the Central Andes and did not require large urban centers. Although warfare was a constant threat, the population tended to be dispersed and towns were small. The people lived in scattered houses of stone or wattle and daub, and in times of war, they gathered in special forts or redoubts.

In some of the forested lowlands, however, the people found protection by living in palisaded villages, where they built pole-and-thatch houses. Maximum village sizes range from 1,000 to 3,000 persons. In Central America and the Greater Antilles, early Spanish chroniclers described well-ordered towns which exceeded 1,000 persons. Rouse[9] ascribes to some of the Greater Antillean towns as many as 3,000 inhabitants. An unusual feature of these Antillean villages is a ball court or dance plaza which may have had a ceremonial purpose.

In eastern Bolivia, the chiefdoms also had large and permanent communities. The Mojo villages, for example, were reported by the early Spanish writers to have consisted of as many as 400 houses, which probably means at least 2,000 persons.

Transportation

Throughout the regions of chiefdoms, well-developed transportational facilities provided ready communication between the different villages. In the northern Andes, Central America, and Venezuela, roadways ran through mountains and plains, and they frequently crossed gorges by means of suspension bridges similar to those of the Central Andes. While beasts of burden were unknown, these highways facilitated movement of goods and soldiers. In eastern Bolivia, causeways bordered by canals crossed the swampy savannas and permitted transportation both on foot and by canoe. The Mojo and Paressí villages were especially well interlinked by roads. In the coastal areas of Central America, northern Venezuela, and the Antilles, canoe transportation contributed also to the linking of communities.

3. KINDS OF SOCIAL AND POLITICAL STRUCTURES

Introduction

We have seen that potential surplus production together with a dense population provided a basis for formation of large communities, development of classes of specialists, and growth of multicommunity states or chiefdoms. The actual conversion of "adequate" food production and leisure time into production of surplus foods that supported classes of specialists who were relieved of food production was brought about principally by diffused patterns of warfare and religion. Diffusion also explains the differences between the northern Andean and Central American subtype and the Antillean–Venezuelan–eastern Bolivia subtypes.

The importance of specific diffused factors that might crystallize social classes is strongly indicated by its absence among the Araucanians of central Chile. Although the population density of the Araucanians was about as great as that of the northern Andes and therefore suggests about equal productive efficiency, the Araucanians never received the military and religious patterns that led to state formation among the chiefdoms. This is understandable when one considers that the extreme deserts of the southern Peruvian coast and northern Chile reduced the population density of the Atacameño and Diaguita to about the same as that of the nomadic hunters and gatherers and limited their communities to single lineages which were no larger than those of the nomads. While these people received many culture elements from the Central Andes, their nearly waterless deserts did not permit surplus production and state formation. Some features of Central Andean craft production had filtered through this sparsely inhabited area and reached the Araucanians, but the temple-idol cult and wars for conquest, tribute, or religious purposes, which characterized the Andean states, failed to cross the deserts. The Inca conquest of Chile imposed an imperial superstructure upon the northern Araucanians which lasted very briefly and did not permanently affect the native socioeconomic groups.

The chiefdoms resulted from the combination of potential surplus production with factors that amalgamated individual villages into larger units requiring social, military, and political controls of much wider and greater power than anything known among the Araucanians or the tropical-forest villages. Social differentiation and stratification and the importance of the military and temple cult were proportionate to the size of these chiefdoms. While the general pattern of chiefdoms conformed to the type previously described, there were many local variations such as realms or small kingdoms created by military conquest, federations resulting from agreement to cooperate (but no doubt stimulated both by the threat of force and by the lure of gain from joint warfare), and predominantly theocratic chiefdoms, where a temple-idol cult or hierarchy of priest-chiefs constituted the principal attraction to the member villages.

Class structure

A community which consists of a single lineage cannot well be divided into social classes, especially into hereditary classes. A lineage consisting of a number of nuclear families related through either male or female descent may be divided into sex, occupational, and age groups, but it would be impossible to preserve close relationships among all members of the extended family if some members held hereditary privilege.

The chiefdoms were characteristically differentiated into social classes. Several factors underlay this class structure. First, support or partial support of special classes of rulers, "lords," warriors, and probably artisans was made possible by surplus production. Second, villages far exceeded the size of single lineages and could therefore be crosscut by nonkinship groups. Third, the special functions of administration, religious leadership, and warfare, whether achieved or hereditary, brought about class differentiation.

While the functions of the classes among the chiefdoms are not always described clearly, some idea of their nature is indicated by the usual designations: "chiefs" or "caciques," "nobles" or "lords," "commoners," and "slaves." The chiefs were rulers and were accorded various kinds of obeisance by their followers. The lords were lesser rulers of villages or territories within the chiefdoms, successful warriors, and religious functionaries. The commoners were, as the name implies, the basic farming people, although they may have been internally differentiated. The designation "slave" is unclear, for these chiefdoms certainly did not have chattel slaves. Possibly it refers to the female captives who were concubines and perhaps drudge workers. But there is little evidence that male and female slaves begat a permanent slave class, for male captives seem usually to have been killed in the blood sacrifice.

This fourfold social stratification was not equally represented in all chiefdoms. Smaller chiefdoms, such as those of certain Ecuadorian and Colombian Indians, had attenuated classes. Although these Indians had fairly strong chieftainship and intergroup federation in time of warfare, there is little evidence that classes were well developed or hereditary. Since the capture of men for religious sacrifices, for human trophies, and for cannibalism was common, it is likely that military prowess was an avenue to higher social position. Moreover, successful warriors gained prestige by incorporating female captives into their households.

Social position was hereditary only in the more organized chiefdoms; and among some chiefdoms of the Circum-Caribbean area, there was a hierarchical arrangement of greater and lesser rulers. In Chibcha society, the gradation of rulers perhaps corresponded in part to larger and smaller political provinces. A similar but less elaborate hierarchy also occurred among the Páez, Moguex, Puruhá, and Cañar in the northern Andes, the Lile, Quimbaya, and their neighbors, the Ancerma and other peoples of the Cauca-Atrato region, most of the groups of the north Colombian lowlands, the peoples of northern Venezuela, the Antillean Arawak, the Talamancan groups and peoples west of the Panama Canal, and the ancient Paressí of the Mato Grosso.

Chiefs exercised considerable authority in all these societies and could muster large fighting forces in time of war and collect tribute for their maintenance. The chief's house served as a rallying point for the villagers and often as a repository for special idols in societies where temples were not constructed. Chiefs were accorded the privilege of having many wives, even in societies in which polygyny was not frequent. They also wore especially fine garments and jewelry, sat in state upon carved wooden stools, and among some groups were carried in gold-covered litters and granted great respect. At death, their wives, retainers, and precious goods which were attributes of chiefly office, were interred with them. A spectacular instance of this practice is the protohistoric Cuna chiefs' burials exhumed by Lothrop in Panama.

Among a few northern Andean chiefdoms, such as the Chibcha, chiefs tended to preserve the purity of their family line through marriage to their sisters or their sisters' daughters, a practice similar to the marriage of the Inca emperor to his sister. This custom was probably also practiced by nobles, whose status was strongly fixed by heredity.

Next in importance to chiefs were the nobles. Some of these were close relatives of the chief, while others obtained high social position through military exploits or through their priestly function.

Since many of the commoners were related to chiefs and nobles and since acquisition of wealth or military prestige provided for some upward mobility, the gulf between the nobility and the commoners was neither very great nor fixed. Among nearly all groups, commoners contributed to the support of the higher classes, either through direct payment of tribute or through economic services. Such was the case, for instance, among the Cara, where the chief apportioned the communal land; the Lile, whose chiefs and nobles received tribute; the Arma, whose common folk built their chief's house, worked his fields, paid him tribute in gold, and provided him many wives; the Chibcha, whose chiefs were supported by taxes; the Antillean Arawak, whose chiefs controlled surplus production and could requisition crops; and the Manasí, who built their chief's house and worked his special fields. In other instances, such as some of the peoples of the Cordillera Oriental and the Venezuelan Andes, chiefs and nobles held a relatively weak position and apparently received little obligatory support for the common class.

The role and status of the so-called slaves is obscure. It might be expected that, at a certain point in political and economic development, war captives would be kept as economic assets. It seems, however, that most male captives were doomed to ceremonial sacrifice, while females were perhaps more important in lending prestige to their captors as concubines than as producers.

Warfare

The origin of the closely related patterns of warfare, human sacrifice, and a temple-idol cult in the northern Andes and Central America may have some antiquity. While this pattern resembles that of the Aztec, which was remarkable for its bloody features, it differs fundamentally from that of the Inca Empire, where llamas and guinea pigs had been substituted for human beings in most blood sacrifice. After the establishment of the empire, sacrificial victims could be captured from enemy people only in small numbers and on the remote frontier. Moreover, Inca militarism was designed principally to conquer, regiment, and exploit populations. Closer parallels to northern Andean warfare are suggested in earlier Andean periods, for example, the Nazca culture, whose ceramic and textile designs clearly depict human sacrifice and human trophies.

While the inter-American Formative Era seems to have been one of peace, or at least one in which populations were expanding into new lands and did not need to carry out wars of conquest, capture of sacrificial victims may have begun at this time. Interstate raids could well have spread by a chain reaction into more remote areas. In fact, warfare to take human trophies and cannibalistic victims spread widely in the tropical forests, where both territorial conquest and exaction of tribute were impossible, owing to lack of surplus production of the varied foods needed for adequate diet. When warfare later contributed to empire formation in both Meso-America and the Central Andes, the new motive of economic conquest may also have been introduced to the Circum-Caribbean peoples, who now had a potential surplus production.

Among the northern Andean and Central American chiefdoms, warfare served several functions. First, it supplied the state temple cult with victims for the blood sacrifice which was demanded by the gods. Second, it afforded individual warriors an opportunity to gain status through the display, often in their homes, of such human trophies of their victims as heads, teeth, and even stuffed whole skins. Third, it was believed in many cases that the warriors acquired some kind of supernatural power in cannibalistic rites. Fourth, warfare enabled men to add captive women to their households as concubines and probably as food producers, thus enhancing their economic and social status. Fifth, needs for defense required fortification and in the forested areas led to nucleated, palisaded villages.

Underlying the status functions of warfare was a social mobility not found in the Central Andes. Under the Inca, armies consisted of conscript soldiers who fought for imperial purposes of conquest and who had limited opportunity to improve their own status. Upward mobility among the chiefdoms, however, was a matter of degree, which depended partly upon the size and organization of the chiefdoms. The very large and highly regimented population of the Chibcha, or Muisca, chiefdom somewhat approached the Inca in the hereditary nature of its classes. Among other groups, class was based somewhat more upon achievement than heredity, and warfare seems to have been carried on far more to capture victims for cannibalism and human trophies than for economic purposes. Thus, the Lile and Gorrón of the upper Cauca River in Colombia had only small, weak federations, yet they continually fought the Arma, Carrapa, Pozo, Picara, and others to their east to take human trophies and victims for blood sacrifice and cannibalism. Among some of these people, the importance of human beings as an essential food seems to have equaled their importance as ritual victims. The Picara went so far as to fatten those who would be eaten; and the nearby tropical-forest enclave of Guayupé and Sae made human beings a major food item.

War tactics throughout the northern Andes were based upon the use of what the Spanish conquerors described as "large armies." While both the size and organization were obviously exaggerated, the warriors clearly had some degree of order and unity of purpose. Constant allusion in the northern Andes and in eastern Venezuela to women who not only accompanied the warriors to care for them but frequently also fought, offers a subject for speculation. The chroniclers may have accurately described what they saw, or they may have merely passed on some legend comparable to that of the powerful women Amazons. Possibly there was some connection between these alleged female warriors and transvestitism, which was also frequently mentioned.

The warriors usually fought with spears and shields in the northern Andes, but the bow was sometimes used in Central America, and it was the typical weapon in Venezuela, where arrows were often poisoned. In the dispersed settlements of the highlands, protection was often found in hilltop redoubts. In the forested, lowland areas, villages were tightly palisaded. The Antiochians, who lived in pile dwellings between the Cauca and Atrato Rivers, poured boiling water down on their attackers.

Details of warfare among the Central American peoples are few, spotty, and late. The Mosquito fighting forces were ranked in military orders and wore distinguishing insignia. Cannibalism and the taking of slaves were two motives for warfare. A similar pattern seems to have been characteristic of Nicaraguan groups who were continually at war and who were ranked and organized into regular military units. Fights over boundaries and capture of sacrificial victims were said to have been the major causes of warfare. The peoples of the Talamanca group and the Canal Zone were also highly warlike, as were the Cuna who later allied themselves with both the British and the French and took many Indian captives for the slave trade.

While many of the Venezuelan people carried on considerable warfare with organized armies and while most of them palisaded their villages against attack, blood sacrifice of human beings played a negligible role. The Antillean Arawak were on the whole rather peaceful. They fought defensively against the marauding Carib, but they seem not to have palisaded their villages. The chiefdoms of eastern Bolivia engaged in some warfare in aboriginal times, and they palisaded their villages, but they did not sacrifice or eat their victims. The purpose of their wars is not clear, for information pertains to the period after Spanish settlement, when these Indians captured slaves from neighboring people for sale to the settlers. This seemingly led to their retaining both male and female captives within their own societies, where a servile class had begun to develop.

Religious patterns

Three rather different patterns of religion were found among the chiefdoms. In the northern Andes, Central America, and Venezuela, the pattern in its most developed form resembled that of Meso-America and the Central Andes. State and community deities were represented by idols which were kept in special temples and worshiped in public cere-monialism presided over by a class of hereditary priests or by shamans who served as priests. The religion of the Antillean Awarak was con-ceptually very different in that a hierarchy of deities paralleled the hierarchy of chiefs. Every person had a guardian spirit, but the power of the spirits increased with the person's status, and the chiefs' spirits were the tribal gods. The third pattern, found in eastern Bolivia, repre-sented a development of the tropical-forest-type men's society and men's house into a state religion that functioned much like a temple cult.

The priest-temple-idol complex in the northern Andes and Central America varied locally. Some societies had large temples which housed idols of the gods, and they supported a hereditary class of priests. Others lacked special temples and kept the idols or god symbols in the chief's house. In many instances, a shaman rather than true priest conducted the ceremonies. Moreover, the deities were approached in some cases as oracles rather than in public ceremonialism for supplication.

It is necessary at this point to distinguish the terms "priest" and "shaman," which denote persons whose functions are logically quite different, even though, in fact, they may overlap. The religious leaders of the Central Andes, for example, were typically priests because they were a hereditary class of men who conducted public ritual in supplica-tion of state gods for state purposes. By contrast, the shaman, who is found typically among the more primitive peoples organized on a lineage or village basis, is primarily a doctor or curer of diseases, whose power is derived from a supernatural helper, and he may also be a sorcerer or magician. The shaman acquires his ability to cure sickness and to work magic through dreams or visionary experiences in which spirits become his own permanent helpers. Characteristically, he assists indi-viduals rather than whole societies.

In many societies it is believed that a shaman's ancestors or ghosts become his supernatural helpers, and in this sense shamanism may be hereditary. But this slight tendency to specialization and a hereditary role could not establish a class of shamans in the absence of surplus production. Among many of the riverine horticultural people of the tropical forests, the shaman took charge of the few village ceremonies which had a community purpose, such as promoting crop growth or warding off illness. In officiating over these group ceremonies, he served as priest rather than as shaman, for he did not necessarily call upon his own spirit-helpers to achieve community purposes. The shaman also often wielded more secular power in the village than the nominal chief, because the people feared his power to work black magic.

Among the chiefdoms, however, the shaman often filled the dual role of doctor-magician and priest. These societies had community and state deities, and they held public and private ceremonies to supplicate them. In the societies which lacked a genuine priesthood, the shaman apparently not only presided over public ritual for the gods but entered the inner sanctum and met the gods face to face.

The pattern of the priestly role of the shaman varied locally. In some cases, the shaman asked questions of supernatural beings and communicated their answers to the people, an oracular function. In some cases he seems to have dealt with his own spirit-helpers as if they were village or tribal deities. In other cases, he confronted state gods over which he had no control and which he approached in the role of a priest.

The priest-temple-idol cult attained its most complete expression among such people as the Chibcha, Ancerma, Nutibara, Caramanta, and Fincenú. Many of the northern Colombian temples were large and erected on mounds, thus forming a link in the almost continuous distribution of temple mounds from the Mississippi Valley to the Central Andes. The great temple of the Fincenú could hold a hundred persons. The Ancerma, Caramanta, and Nutibara temples housed village gods represented by idols that were painted and decorated with gold leaf. In Central America, the Bribri and Güetar clearly had a class of hereditary priests, although construction of temples is in doubt.

Elsewhere, the pattern was much more attenuated. The Pasto of Ecuador kept idols of clay, stone, and wood in their homes, and their shaman filled all priestly functions. The Lenca in recent times performed agricultural ceremonies and made pilgrimages to sacred places on hilltops.

The early deculturation of many of these people, especially in Central America, leaves the nature of native religion in doubt and raises danger of misinterpretation. There has, for example, been some disposition recently among archaeologists to speculate that large prehistoric religious centers in Central America and elsewhere were objects of pilgrimages. While this would be difficult to disprove, it should be noted that it would have been decidedly rash for a pilgrim to enter the territory of an enemy state that would like nothing better than to capture him as a sacrificial victim. The recent Lenca pilgrimages to their shrines may be no more than a lingering attachment of a deculturated and dispersed people to their former great ceremonial centers.

In Central America, the fullest development of the priest-temple-idol complex was found among the Nahuatl- and Chorotegan-speaking people who had migrated southward from Mexico in prehistoric times. They waged war to supply victims for cannibalistic ceremonies, and they had a class of priests who performed harvest ceremonies and rituals of birth and death.

In the Cordillera Oriental and Venezuelan Andes, such people as the Lache, Timoteans, and Chitarera kept idols in special temples. Timotean idols were made of clay, wood, stone, and cotton thread. Only the priest-shaman had access to the temples. A somewhat different combination of features occurred among the Jirajara and Caquetio of northwestern Venezuela. Each community had a temple where shaman-priests officiated, but idols were kept in individual houses. These people were exceptional in their sacrifice of human beings to the sun in order to obtain rain. Still farther east, the Palenque, Maracapana, Cumanagoto, and Aruacay did not construct temples, and the shaman, who was often also the village chief, functioned as an oracle in communicating with the gods on behalf of the populace.

The religious organization of the Antillean Arawak was functionally similar to the priest-temple-idol complex, although somewhat distinctive in form. The chief was the main religious functionary, there being no separate order of priests. The guardian spirit concept combined with fetish worship involved a hierarchy of idols called zemis. Individuals kept their zemis in their houses and supplicated them with food and various other offerings. The zemis of chiefs had greater power and more public significance than those of the commoners, while that of the main chief was supreme.

Among the chiefdoms of eastern Bolivia, the temple cult was represented in different ways. In Paressí villages, the men's house, which served as the temple and the repository for sacred trumpets, was dedicated to the serpent god. The Mojo had a shrine for jaguar trophies, where special offerings were made by the shaman-priests. Among the Bauré and Manasí, a class of hereditary priests dealt with village gods, but other evidence of a temple-idol complex is unclear.

The diversity in conceptualization of deities and the variety of their material symbols was very great. In highland Ecuador, for example, the Cara revered sacred mountaintops as their ancestors, and the Puruhá sacrificed human beings to two volcanoes which they believed to be their forebears. Deification of mountains, lakes, and the like was very characteristic of the Central Andes. The Jirajara and Caquetio sacrificed to the sun, the Cuna and Lenca worshiped the sun, and the Catio revered celestial beings.

The Fincenú revered zoomorphic idols of which the jaguar was most important, and the Mojo had a special jaguar cult. These are probably special cases wherein this animal, which is widely feared and attributed supernatural power throughout South America, became the focal point of religious organization.

Very different conceptually were the Arawakan zemis of the Antilles and the serpent spirits of the men's cult in eastern Bolivia.

4. TECHNOLOGY, MANUFACTURES, AND CONSTRUCTIONS

The number of technical processes in ceramics, weaving, metallurgy, and the like related directly to surplus production and specialization. The riverine and coastal tropical-forest farm villages had more processes and products than the nomadic hunters and gatherers, and the chiefdoms had more than the tropical-forest people but less than the Central Andes. The gradation of technical achievement closely paralleled population density, village size, class specialization, and the variety and number of all material products. For example, as Willey has shown in his general fourfold classification of South American pottery,[10] the nomads either made no pots or else produced only a "crude" or "simple" type. A somewhat better or "controlled" type occurred among some of the tropical-forest people but was best developed in the Circum-Caribbean area, where its local variations correlated to a high degree with productive efficiency and population stability. The "advanced" type was largely limited to the Central Andes.

The South America culture types, however, differed not only in their number of techniques but in the diligence with which they were applied. The difference was partly a question of time and effort. The many-colored vessels of the Central Andes, for example, required far more time than the two- or three-colored northern Andean pots, although they involved much the same techniques. Similarly, the finely woven textiles of the former area demanded infinitely more care and effort than coarser textiles woven with the same methods.

A further difference in manufacturing was in the nature and purpose of the products. The best weaving, metal objects, pots, precious stones, and stone carvings were for religious, state, or upper class consumption in contrast to the products of the tropical-forest people, who devoted their skills largely to manufacturing goods for their own, everyday domestic use.

Pottery

The ceramics of the chiefdoms utilized all the technical features of the Central Andes but with less freedom, variety, and aesthetic achievement. Some of the best pottery was made in the northern Andes, and expectably it was most similar to that of Peru because of diffusion from the latter. The considerable range of vessel forms included tripod bowls, pedestal-base forms, compoteras, double vessels, stirrup-spout jars, and whistling jars, the last three especially linking Ecuador with the Central Andes. In the northern Andes, there were also clay seats, ocarinas, whistles, spindle whorls, stamps, and figurines. But molded and modeled forms were restricted in form as compared with those of Peru. Many of these vessel forms, including tripods and effigies, and other pottery objects such as stamps, figurines, whistles, incense burners, drums, rattles, and spindle whorls were made also in Central America. In the West Indies, however, there were far fewer forms.

Vessel ornamentation included both plastic treatment and painting. Among the former were incisions, punctation, appliqué, and adorno or stuck-on decoration. These occurred in the northern Andes and in Central America, but again were more limited in the Antilles. Vessels were painted largely in geometric designs with two and three colors in the northern Andes but usually with only two in the Antilles. In the Central Andes, polychromes were far more characteristic and employed as many as eleven different colors on a single vessel. Another common type of decoration, called negative decoration, consisted of designs painted in reverse, in a manner similar to batik or resist dyeing.

While northern Andean pottery in general was what Willey called "controlled," the Cuna remains at the site of Coclé, Panama, represented an "advanced" ware. These vessels were made in a variety of shapes, including effigies, and were beautifully painted in three- and four-colored zoomorphic and geometric designs.

Weaving and clothing

Although all these peoples made woven goods, the quality and the extent to which they were used for clothing varied regionally. In the highland areas of Ecuador, Colombia, Venezuela, and Central America, people wore fuller clothing than in the lowlands. Such clothing may have been a response to the cooler climate of the highlands, but Central Andean influence was no doubt a contributing factor.

Except for those parts of Ecuador and the southern Andes where llamas were present in the pre-Inca period, woolen garments could be obtained only by trade, and the distribution of woolen cloth was very similar to that of herding peoples. Cotton textiles, however, were manufactured in all chiefdoms. A few groups such as the Pasto, Lile, Gorrón, and Arma made bark cloth. There was also widespread use of wild fibers for bags, cordage, sandals, nets, and so forth.

Throughout the highland and temperate parts of Ecuador and Colombia the people wove cotton blankets, capes, sleeveless tunics, belts, wrap-arounds, and breechclouts. The Quillacinga sewed men's garments, a practice which is unique for the region. Many of these people, such as the Chibcha, decorated their cloth with painted-on or printed rather than woven designs. This feature is also found in the Montaña of eastern Peru and contrasts with the Central Andean woven-in decoration.

Weaving on a two-bar loom was rather highly developed in Central America, where domesticated cotton was made into mantles. Considerable use was also made of bark cloth, which, to judge by archaeological finds of stone bark-beaters, appears to have been a very old technique in the region.

In northern Venezuela, weaving was less developed and employed a wild cotton. The Antillean Arawak probably did not use the heddle loom and may, in fact, have done no weaving. Their bags, hammocks, and other objects made of cotton and wild fibers were evidently netted, possibly twined.

The Mojo, Paressí, Bauré, and Manasí of eastern Bolivia made fine cloth on the so-called "Arawak loom," in which the warp is wrapped around two horizontal bars set in a vertical frame. While the Arawak may have been instrumental in spreading this type of loom, there is no proof that they invented it. (Its designation as "Arawak" came about through the accident of its use by Arawak of Guiana where Roth[11] made a detailed study of weaving. Characteristic dress in eastern Bolivia included the cushma, or long shirt, which was made either of cotton or bark cloth.) The Manasí were reported to be especially skillful weavers.

Metals and precious stones

The number of metals and metallurgical processes employed in the chiefdoms decreased in rather direct proportion to distance from the Central Andes. We do not intend to imply where metallurgy developed or how it diffused, for these are peripheral considerations. However, the latter area extracted about a dozen metals, many of them through smelting the ores, it alloyed them in various ways, and it employed a large number of techniques to manufacture the final product. By contrast, Ecuador and Colombia extracted only gold, silver, copper, and platinum, principally through placer mining in rivers. Root[12] questions whether the northern Andes really knew how to smelt copper ores. While cold hammering was widely used in this area for shaping gold, silver, and platinum, more difficult techniques were also employed by some groups; for example, alloying gold and copper to form a lustrous metal called tumbaga, molding, casting (including cire-perdue, or lost-wax), and gilding. The last was accomplished by application of acid to a gold-copper alloy so that the surface copper was dissolved away and the remaining gold film could be burnished to make the object look like solid gold.

Central America, Venezuela, and the Greater Antilles probably extracted only gold, which was the metal most readily found and worked by primitive techniques and which, for the same reasons, was the earliest metal used in the Central Andes. Objects of copper and tumbaga have been found in these areas, but they were probably trade items in Central America and Venezuela and certainly were in the Antilles. The eastern Bolivian people extracted no metals, although they received some metal objects in aboriginal times through trade from the Andes and later learned simple metalworking techniques from the Spanish missionaries.

While use of metals was discovered in an unknown area in the Formative Era, the knowledge of more complicated techniques diffused little beyond the Central Andes, although knowledge of working copper, in addition to gold, developed also in Meso-America. In addition to diffused knowledge, however, environmental resources played a role. The Central Andes seem to have been much richer in metals, and owing to the absence of dense forest cover as well as to the very magnitude of the mountains, which expose many geological strata, these metals were easier to find. Moreover, tin, which must be alloyed with copper to form bronze, the only hard metal in native America suitable for weapons and tools, occurs in great abundance in Bolivia, which is today one of the world's principal sources of tin. We can suppose, therefore, that American bronze was first developed in the area.

Since the comparatively soft, yet lustrous metals used by most of the chiefdoms had little utility as weapons or tools, they were generally made into articles of personal adornment, effigies, idols, vessels or containers, decoration for litters, warriors' paraphernalia, and other objects affording a veneer of splendor. It seems probable that these metals, which clearly required enormous expenditure of time by miners and artisans, were dedicated principally to the upper classes whose status they validated and that they were used to make idols and other accouterments of the deities which constituted the center of state religion. Among the objects of personal adornment made of metal were gold labrets or lip plugs, pendants, nose plugs, necklaces, chest plates, crowns, masks, and beads.

The extent of the local production and use of gold had a very direct bearing upon the Spaniards' conquest and subjugation of American

Indians. The Conquest was first concentrated on Peru, owing to the vast quantity of gold that Pizarro obtained from the Inca. The Spaniards became interested a little later in the northern Andes, where native temples and burial sites were fairly rich in this treasure. According to a very early saying of the Spanish colonialists of Cartagena, in Colombia, "Misfortune to Peru if they discover Cenú," which meant Darien, or Cinú. In the course of time, the Spaniards did discover the gold at Cenú and all other parts of the northern Andes. The items of personal adornment, the religious figures, and the objects put into graves were largely melted down and shipped to the crown's treasury in Spain. A few gold objects in original form, however, have been recovered from time to time in the Caribbean Islands and Florida, where Spanish galleons went ashore. But much more importantly, metal objects of native craftsmanship are still recovered in the northern Andes; and today, the Colombian El Museo del Banco Nacional de Oro is collecting such objects, many of which it has reproduced in beautiful photographs, some in color, that give an excellent idea of the skill of the native goldsmiths. Other excellent illustrations of American metalwork may be seen in Lothrop's monograph describing the protohistoric Cuna site at Coclé.[13]

The northern Andes were exceptional in their work in precious and semiprecious stones, especially in emeralds which were found in Colombia. The Cuna, too, were outstanding lapidaries as well as ceramicists and metalworkers, as the finds at Coclé indicate.

Various places along the Caribbean Coast afforded rather rich pearl fisheries, of which the Indians took advantage. Mother-of-pearl was also used, and some of the canoes of the Caribbean coast were not only richly carved but inlaid with mother-of-pearl.

Engineering works

Engineering works, such as roads, bridges, and aqueducts, were constructed by most of the chiefdoms, while the Antillean Arawak and Lenca of Central America also made ball courts. A ball game much like hockey was fairly widespread in northern South America and it was played on an open field. The Antillean Arawak and Lenca, like the Meso-Americans, made sunken courts and possibly used a ball of rubber or other latex that would bounce. These courts, which are known from archaeological excavations, required a fairly large and controlled labor force rather than special skills.

Roads were found among all chiefdoms and served to connect villages with one another and with their surrounding fields. Many of these roadways were straight and wide, especially in the lowlands, where there were fewer obstructions and engineering problems. In the more rugged topography of highland Ecuador and Colombia, liana bridges were built across deep gorges. The Pasto, Quillacinga, and Coaiquer built wooden bridges suspended by vines, while the Páez and Moguex constructed bridges of lianas and bamboo.

Irrigation aqueducts of some complexity were built, especially in the highland areas of Ecuador and Colombia. In eastern Bolivia, canals bordered the roadways that linked various villages and served as waterways for canoes in the harvest season, when crops were carried back to the villages. In Colombia, Cauca Valley groups such as the Aburra, Nutibara, and Urezo built aqueducts alongside straight, wide roadways that crossed their fields. Fairly large irrigation systems were also constructed by certain northern Venezuelan peoples, for example, the Cumanagoto, who watered orchards of fruit trees. The Antillean Arawak also practiced irrigation.

Weapons

The bow was either absent or recently acquired in most of the highland parts of Ecuador, Colombia, Venezuela, and Central America. In these regions, the spear which was sometimes thrown by means of the spear thrower, or atlatl, together with the club and the sling comprised the characteristic weapons for both hunting and warfare. In addition to these weapons, the lowland peoples also used long chonta-palm lances and painted shields made of wood or jaguar skin. Copper and bronze weapons have been found in Ecuador, but bronze is largely of the Inca period. Blowguns that shot pellets were used in Central America, but the blowgun with poisoned dart was common in Ecuador and Colombia, and darts reached Central America in late prehistoric or early historic times.

5. CULTURAL-ECOLOGICAL ADAPTATIONS OF THE CHIEFDOMS

The chiefdoms and states, like the other cultural types in South America, represented special ways in which people were organized to achieve cultural objectives in particular environments. The objective of the nomadic hunters and gatherers, representing one extreme, was largely physical survival; and nearly every aspect of the culture of these nomads was in some way affected by the incessant need to find food. At the other extreme, the Central Andean theocratic states and militaristic empires had a complex of culturally developed objectives rather than bare survival goals, since a large portion of the population was relieved entirely of food production. And yet the general character of these objectives was ultimately determined by the nature of food production. The creation and expansion of irrigation systems required managerial controls that were fundamental to the growth and structure of this particular kind of state.

The chiefdoms lay between these extremes in several respects. The nomads invented little of technological importance, having borrowed most of their culture elements from other peoples. After the Formative Era, the Central Andes, on the other hand, were more richly inventive than other areas and contributed innumerable features to other South American Indians. The chiefdoms were largely recipients of traits from the Central Andes and Meso-America in later times, but contributed some features themselves. The nature of their sociocultural organization was determined less by simple biological requirements than among the nomads and less by an internally developed socioeconomic organization than among the Central Andean people.

The principal factors that brought about the chiefdoms were: first, a considerable variety of farm crops, which afforded a balanced diet; second, an abundance of these crops, supplemented by ocean and river products, which yielded sufficient surplus to release civil, military, religious, and craft specialists from the tasks of food getting; third, permanency of cultivated fields and communities; fourth, population density adequate to permit large, multilineage villages; fifth, state institutions, such as a temple-idol cult, warfare for conquest and sacrificial victims, and particular kinds of class specialization, which amalgamated several communities. These state institutions were largely borrowed from neighboring areas, but they acquired distinctive patterns, owing to the local requirements in production.

In terms of culture content, the chiefdoms resemble both the high civilizations of Meso-America and the Central Andes and the riverine villages of the tropical forests. But the resemblances are of different orders. The chiefdoms are like Meso-America and the Central Andes largely in such state institutions as gods, temples, priests, and warfare for conquest and tribute and in such related features as class structure and the production of aesthetic goods—fine weaving, ceramics, metal objects, precious stones, and monumental architecture—for state purposes. They resembled the tropical-forest people in domestic and village features: house types, mortars, hammocks, cooking pots, wooden stools, palisaded villages, shamanism, and village chiefs.

NOTES

1. Paul Kirchhoff, *Handbook*, vol. 4.
2. Kalervo Oberg, "Types of Social Structure among the Lowland Tribes of Central and South America," *American Anthropologist*, vol. 57, no. 3, part 1, pp. 472–488, 1957.
3. Alfred L. Kroeber, *Handbook*, vol. 2.

4. Samuel Kirkland Lothrop, *Coclé: An Archaeological Study of Central Panama,* Memoirs, Peabody Museum of Archaeology and Ethnology, Harvard University, vol. 7, Cambridge, 1937.
5. David Stout, *Handbook,* vol. 4.
6. Paul Kirchhoff and Gregorio Hernández de Alba, *Handbook,* vol. 4.
7. Irving Rouse, "Settlement Patterns in the Caribbean Area," in Gordon R. Willey (ed.), *Prehistoric Settlement Patterns in the New World,* Viking Fund Publications in Anthropology, no. 23, pp. 165–172, 1956.
8. Food and Agricultural Organization, United Nations, vol. 6, no. 5, pp. 162–163, 1953.
9. Rouse, *op. cit.*
10. Gordon R. Willey, *Handbook,* vol. 5.
11. Walter Edmund Roth, *An Introductory Study of the Arts, Crafts, and Customs of the Guiana Indians,* Thirty-eighth Annual Report of the Bureau of American Ethnology, 1916–1917.
12. William C. Root, *Handbook,* vol. 5.
13. Lothrop, *op. cit.*

seven

WARRING CHIEFDOMS
OF THE NORTHERN ANDES
AND CENTRAL AMERICA

In Ecuador, Colombia, and Central America, the chiefdoms are designated "militaristic" because warfare was extremely important and served many purposes. It was the means of conquest and extraction of tribute, it provided religion with sacrificial victims, and it enabled the common man to improve his status. Not all these functions of warfare were shared by the chiefdoms of Venezuela and the Greater Antilles or eastern Bolivia. The chiefdoms of Ecuador, Colombia, and Central America were also distinctive in features borrowed from Meso-America and the Central Andes, for they were on the route of diffusion between Middle America and South America.

Throughout most of this area, the native cultures were destroyed and the Indians absorbed into the basic farming and laboring elements of the colonies within a hundred years or so of the Conquest. The early Spanish chroniclers were not especially interested in describing native life, and their accounts must be judged by the writers' own stake in the Conquest: by whether, as conquistadors seeking gold, they exaggerated the numbers, organization, and power of the native armies facing them; whether, as missionaries, they deplored without understanding the beliefs and practices of those they considered idolaters and infidels, and whether, in judging native religion by their own concepts, they did not badly describe it; and whether, as crown administrators, they did not misrepre-

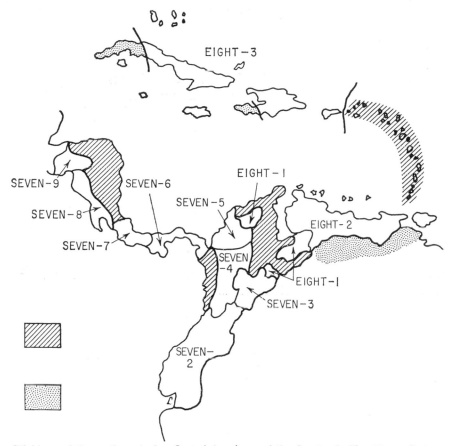

Chiefdoms of the northern Andes, Central America, and the Greater Antilles. The spelled-out and arabic numerals correspond to the chapters and sections in the text. The heavy lines delineate the chiefdoms; the lighter lines, the regional variations of chiefdoms. Within and adjoining the areas of chiefdoms were areas of nomadic hunters and gatherers, which are stippled, and of tropical-forest village farmers, which are diagonally hatched.

Seven. The chiefdoms of the northern Andes and Central America.

    2. Ecuador and southern Colombia

    3. The Chibcha proper or Muisca

    4. Western Colombia

    5. North Colombia lowlands

    6. The Cuna and their neighbors of Panama

    7. The Southern Caribbean lowlands

    8. The Meso-Americans

    9. The Lenca

Eight. The chiefdoms of northern Venezuela and the Greater Antilles.

    1. The Cordillera Oriental and Venezuelan Andes

    2. Northern Venezuela

    3. The Arawak of the Greater Antilles

sent both native life and the colonists' activities in order to justify the crown in demanding a larger share of the new wealth.

We deal in these chapters with the highlands and west coast of Ecuador and Colombia and with northern Colombia. The eastern portions of these countries were inhabited by tropical-forest village people. Central America may be defined for present purposes as the area extending northwest from Panama to approximately the Ulua River in Honduras. This river marked the Maya frontier, a rather sharp boundary beyond which were the great Meso-America cultures of Honduras, Yucatán, Guatemala, and highland Mexico.

While Central America, like Colombia and Ecuador, was culturally diversified, having enclaves of tropical-forest farmers among the chiefdoms, it was culturally affiliated more with South America than with Meso-America. The Chibchan languages of most of the Indians were derived from South America and so were most cultural features. The principal exception is a number of enclaves of Nahuatl-speaking groups, most of them probably late prehistoric migrants from the north who retained a distinctive Mexican culture.

1. PREHISTORY

Knowledge of the prehistoric development of these chiefdoms is limited by two difficulties not encountered in the Central Andes. First, very little archaeological research has been carried out in the northern Andes and Central America. Second, the nature of the materials poses great difficulties. A stratigraphic sequence in Peru often contains evidence of one or more widespread cultures or "horizons," such as the Chavín-Cupisnique, Tiahuanaco, or Inca. Objects found in the ground above or below these widespread cultures can be given relative dates. For example, since Tiahuanaco objects are about the same age wherever found, materials lying stratigraphically under them must be pre-Tiahuanaco wherever they are found, even though they may differ locally, while objects found above them are post-Tiahuanaco.

The situation is different in most of the northern Andes and Central America, where each locality seems to have had its own distinctive sequence of styles and cultures through all periods. These areas had fewer widespread horizons which permit cross dating of the localities. This is not to say that many culture elements did not attain a wide distribution. Stoneworking, deep pit and shaft-and-vault burials, stone statues with the "alter-ego" motif, negative-painted ceramics, bark cloth, temple mounds, and other features occurred among many groups. The difficulty is that each locality made these things in its own way. Distinctive stylization, which is a strong indication that people were in close contact and shared a common tradition, was, with certain exceptions, never widespread. This is especially true of those motifs which have religious or other state significance. The implication is, therefore, that most organized states which might impose their styles on local regions were not territorially extensive. Exceptions to this generalization are mentioned subsequently. Historic evidence leads to the same conclusion: few of the chiefdoms observed by the Spanish conquerors were large territorially.

There is, however, some evidence that a culture having some features of the Formative Era culture of the Central Andes had an inter-American distribution which extended to Meso-America and perhaps beyond into North America. In the Guayas Basin of coastal Ecuador, Evans, Meggers, and Estrada[1] have established that certain ceramic features of the local Chorrera and Tejar periods have pottery similar to that found in Formative Era sites in the Central Andes and Meso-America and that several ceramic details, such as "napkin-ring" earplugs and bowl forms, are more nearly like those of Meso-America. In the absence of structural features, such as mounds, settlements, temples, and the like, it is impossible to know whether the pottery styles were actually associated with state formation. Since, however, a similar ceramic style

Stone statue from San Agustín, Colombia, representing a very early, perhaps Formative Era art style. (After Samuel K. Lothrop, "Gold and Silver from Southern Peru and Bolivia," Journal of the Royal Anthropological Institute, vol. 67, 1937.)

is found with incipient states in the Central Andes and Meso-America, the same may be true in Ecuador.

Cultures represented at San Agustín, Tierradentro, Quimbaya, and other sites in Colombia, although not dated with certainty, seem not to have been the products of the historic people. The chronicles of the contemporary Spanish observers show that neither the Andaquí of the region of San Agustín, the Páez of Tierradentro, the Popayanese, nor the present Indians of Santa Marta had any idea who built the archaeological remains in their territories. Whether these belong to a Formative Era is controversial.

To judge by the prehistoric distribution of basic cultural features, the Formative Era was a time when newly developing plant domesticates and farm techniques were increasing farm productivity, when population was expanding, when communities began to consist of houses dispersed around religious centers, and when peace prevailed. Religious centers and other state features were even established in some tropical-forest areas east of the Andes and in Central America, where warfare subsequently destroyed them. The Formative-period culture had the following features: religious mounds, altars, idols, offertories, and shrines; persons who exercised priestly functions and tended to form a special class; elaborate ritual burial of leaders or upper-class people; celestial, animal, and place deities; a managerial control, probably by priests, of the labor needed to construct religious edifices and other public works; loom weaving of domesticated cotton; use of tie dyeing on textiles; painting, negative painting, incising, and plastic treatment of pottery; featherwork and feather mosaics; goldworking; metates; coiled and possibly woven baskets; cloth garments; sandals; and bark cloth.

It is possible that human sacrifice, cannibalism, human trophies, fortification, village palisades, and other elements of the war pattern known in historic times were part of the hypothetical Formative culture. More likely, intervillage or interstate raids to take human sacrificial victims were relatively unimportant, and group contacts were peaceful, permitting free interchange of cultural inventions.

If the northern Andean and Central American chiefdoms followed the apparent developmental pattern of the Central Andes and Meso-America, warfare that served the religious demand for human victims was later than the Formative period. By the time of the Spanish Conquest, however, this kind of warfare was fully established among the chiefdoms, and it wrought several changes in them. It led to nucleation and palisading of settlements in the forest areas, it provided opportunity for a class of warriors to achieve status, and it may have added some kind of servile class to the societies. It made settlements in certain of the tropical-forest areas vulnerable, and it certainly contributed to their destruction or abandonment.

The ultimate origin of all these widely distributed features cannot be determined, for some are found in early sites and some are known only through ethnographic data.

At Santa Marta, large villages constructed of stone were unearthed. The large stone burial chambers, monolithic carved monuments, and what appear to be both burial and temple mounds made of earth resemble structures in the Central Andes.

San Agustín, a very early prehistoric site in Colombia, is strikingly similar to early sites in the northern highlands of Peru, especially in its carved stone statues, structures of dressed stone, the style of stone carving, and subterranean box-type grave chambers. Construction at San Agustín clearly necessitated regimented or controlled labor; for example, in handling the stone slabs of 10 by 14 feet which were used to roof the temples.

At Quimbaya, the modeled pots resemble those at Mochica in Peru, while the double-spouted jars are much like those at Nazca.

At Tairona in Colombia, there are ruins of large concentrated villages. These are constructed mainly of stone and comprise religious edifices and dwellings. One site includes terraced platform dwellings, burial mounds in which the sepulchers are lined with stone slabs, large rectangular ceremonial courts, long slab stairways and wide roads within the village, stone-slab bridges, and stone-lined reservoirs. The population at San Agustín seems to have been dispersed around a religious center in contrast to the nucleated villages of Tairona. The site at Tierradentro is similar in general aspects to San Agustín.

Archaeology in Nicaragua, Honduras, and Costa Rica has provided little knowledge of prehistoric dates or developmental sequences, and it leaves in doubt the relation of the archaeological finds to the historic people described by the Spaniards.

On the northeast coastal region of Honduras, house mounds and temple mounds, canals, stone-paved roads, and stone monuments are found, although most of the native people at the Spanish Conquest had a tropical-forest village culture rather than chiefdoms. The site of Travesia in northwest Honduras consists of terraces, temples, stairways, altars, and ceremonial courts, which suggest technological skills and a level of socioreligious and political control similar to that of the northern Andes of Colombia. Whether, like the materials at Coclé, these were prehistoric

Guayas, Ecuador

Coast	Basin		Peru	Era
Manteño (Huancavilca)	Milagro Quevedo	(Cayapa-Colorado)	Inca Chimu	Integration (militaristic empire)
Guangala	Tejar		Recuay Salinar	Regional Developmental (regional differentiation and florescence of states)
Chorrera Valdivia	Chorrera		Chavín Guañape	Formative (Formative: emergence of theocratic states)

or protohistoric remains of recent chiefdoms or whether they are very much older is not known.

Recent research of Estrada, Evans, and Meggers extends the major prehistoric culture sequences of Peru into the Guayas Basin and coast of Ecuador. The chart on page 207 is summarized from Estrada[2] but includes our terms in parentheses, as well as Estrada's, for the developmental eras.

The Huancavilca, who left the numerous Manteño sites, were, according to the early chronicles, apparently a very warlike people who practiced sacrifice of human beings and excised their hearts, displayed human trophies, and worshiped serpent idols in temples. They were expert navigators in balsa and log rafts, and it is not unlikely that they participated in coastal commerce between Central America and northern Peru. It is interesting in this connection that the Yurumango, who speak a language of the North American Hokan family, live on the southern coast of Colombia.

Because few of the Circum-Caribbean people are known in great detail and because there was great local cultural variation, it is impossible to present any as typical. Instead, we offer a series of sketches which illustrate the principal regional variations.

2. ECUADOR AND SOUTHERN COLOMBIA: OUTPOSTS OF THE INCA EMPIRE

The peoples of highland Ecuador and southern Colombia constituted a somewhat distinctive division because of their environmental similarity to the Central Andes and because their culture was influenced by Peru, especially when they were brought under the Inca Empire.

This division had considerable linguistic diversity before the Inca conquest. Although most of the languages belonged to the Macro-Chibchan family, some were Andean-Equatorial. The imposition of Quechua, the Inca imperial language, produced bilingualism but did not eliminate all the native tongues. The best-known highland groups from north to south were: the Coconuco, Pijao, Páez, Puruhá, Cañar, and Palta. These were subdivided into dialectic and probably political divisions, but the number is not known in each case. The coastal Indians, exposed to the ocean-borne Spanish invasion, rapidly disappeared as cultural entities, and their population was decimated. Here, as in other lowland, tropical-forest areas, the Spaniards imported Negro slaves to meet their labor needs.

The comparatively dense, sedentary population of highland Colombia and Ecuador was typically dispersed in small villages of single-family dwellings constructed of wattle-and-daub walls with thatched roofs, although Oviedo mentions a town of 400 houses on the north coast of Ecuador. The nature of the community or state which united the scattered residents, however, varied. Among the Popayanense, a large temple within a fortified village was the rallying point of many families. In other cases, the house of a chief or shaman containing the state idols was the center of religious activities.

The territorial extent of these chiefdoms is difficult to estimate. While the Manteño sites are widely distributed, this Huancavilca culture is associated "with a number of tribes." In any event, none of the chiefdoms compared territorially to the Inca Empire.

Economic cooperation was much less important to sociopolitical development than in the Central Andes. As a rule, each family cultivated its own lands, men doing the heavy work of clearing the land and breaking the clods of earth. Cooperation was informal and voluntary, and it took the form of exchange labor, called minga, or mingaco, wherein groups of neighbors went from the property of one to another to do certain jobs. Collective work under a centralized control was apparently found where irrigation was carried out, but we do not know how this work was managed or who participated in it.

Religion and warfare were far more important than economic activities in welding local communities into chiefdoms. While most villages were fairly autonomous in times of peace, they readily joined forces in time of warfare. The ruling classes, therefore, were war leaders.

The purposes of warfare were primarily to obtain human victims for blood sacrifice and cannibalism. Such economic goals as territorial conquest and exaction of tribute, however, were also prominent. Among most of these chiefdoms, trophies were made of the sacrificial victims. For example, enemies' skulls were displayed on long poles in villages, human teeth were strung for necklaces, and whole skins of the enemy were filled with ashes or used as drumheads. The Moguex and Páez cut off an enemy's penis and exhibited it on the road in order to shame the foe. The Pijao and Popayanense ate their victims in order to acquire valor, and the Pijao seem truly to have relished human flesh as a food.

Warfare was carried on with considerable éclat, ostentation, and organization. Ordered formations of painted and ornamented warriors commonly attacked at dawn in surprise raids. Songs, yells, trumpet blasts, and drums stimulated the attackers and intimidated the defenders. Women commonly accompanied their men in battle and carried their weapons. Among some groups, women fought alongside the men. Spears, slings, and pikes were the usual weapons.

Religion was also important in furthering political integration of the chiefdoms, although it varied locally in many features. All groups had what may be called a priest-temple-idol cult, but the nature of the idols, the priests, and the temples differed considerably. Idols of wood and stone were universal. The Popayanense also made golden idols, while the Pijao had stone idols with three heads, six arms, and six legs. Some groups placed their idols in sanctums within specially constructed temples, while others kept them in private dwellings.

In some cases, priests constituted a hereditary class and were distinct from shamans. More often, the same person filled both roles. Among the Pasto and Popayanense, priests communicated with the gods and mediated between them and the people. The Puruhá had no priestly class as such, although they sacrificed human beings to their gods. Shamans functioned as intermediaries between gods and the people and held public oracular sessions and officiated at the maize harvest ceremony. Shamans, both male and female, played an important role among the Pijao, where they served as priests and prognosticated matters of future interest to the local group. In addition, they cured illness in the characteristic manner of shamans elsewhere.

Conceptualization of supernatural beings resembled that of the Central Andes in that natural phenomena, such as sun, moon, stars, planets, mountains, and other natural objects were deified in a hierarchical pantheon. Most Ecuadorian people believed that their ancestors originated from mountains and other natural objects. The widespread practice of mummifying the bodies of deceased chiefs and giving them luxurious burial is a form of deification also found in the Andes.

While group ceremonies were primarily concerned with public purposes, such as crop growth, epidemics, and public safety, and involved dancing and drinking, some were *rites de passage* held at "life crises." The Páez and Moguex held a public rite at a girl's puberty, ceremonial dances at the death of an infant, and in post-Conquest times, religious festivals at baptismals, weddings, and periods of communal labor (minga). Prayer was always offered the dead for permission to dance.

The Manta and Huancavilca of the Ecuadorian coast shared some of these highland features. The Manta worshiped the sun, moon, trees, stones, and sea, they built temples to house idols which took the forms of sharks and snakes, and they sacrificed animals and human beings to the gods. They decapitated captives of both sexes and stuffed their skins with straw or ashes. Their priests consulted oracles. The Huancavilca believed that human hearts became divine and that human sacrifice cured disease.

In Ecuador and southern Colombia, religion seems to have welded the households into villages, while warfare brought about intervillage federations, alliances, or chiefdoms and was, therefore, more fundamental to social and political status and to power structure.

There is no direct evidence of the kinship composition of the dispersed villages. Nuclear families, however, traced relationship to one another through the female line in contrast to the predominance of male lineages of the Central Andes.

While the Spanish chronicles are inaccurate and exaggerate in describing the authority of these different kinds of chiefs, their frequent accounts

Popaynán pottery figurine, Colombia. Warrior seated on bench, probably indicating military status. (After Wendell C. Bennett, "Archeological Regions of Colombia," Yale University Publications in Anthropology, no. 30, 1944.)

of the pomp and splendor—matters that were observable, though not fully understood, and viewed from a European feudal point of view—leave no doubt that there was a superior class of chiefs whose high status was shown in many ways. The chief's house generally served as the focal point of village life, and the chief held a position of power and prestige in the community and the allied group of communities. Among the Cara, he administered communal land and was considered to be the bravest and most industrious person among them. Everywhere, chiefs were distinguished by their ornate dress and large houses, their gold jewelry, elaborate adornments of featherwork and other aesthetic symbols of prestige, and the ornately carved wooden stools upon which they alone might sit. In Ecuador, possession of multiple wives or concubines was their special privilege. At death, chiefs were usually given special burial wherein their status in the afterworld was insured by interring with them their wives, jewels, and other adjuncts of superiority.

It seems fairly clear that the chiefs of communities and federations held permanent status through inheritance. The position, however, seems to have passed from father to son—that is, patrilineally—among the Cara, Panzaleo, Puruhá, and Cañari, but matrilineally, or from a man to his sister's son, among the Páez and Moguex. It was even recorded that the last had chieftainesses.

3. THE CHIBCHA, OR MUISCA: THE GREATEST CHIEFDOM

Chibchan dialects were spoken throughout Colombia, most of Central America, and much of Ecuador, but these dialects were mutually unintelligible, and the societies had neither over-all political unity nor cultural similarity. The Chibcha proper, or Muisca, from whom this widespread language stock was named, lived in the Cordillera Oriental east of the upper Magdalena River in east-central Colombia at altitudes varying between 4,000 and 10,000 feet. Bogotá, the capital of modern Colombia, was the Chibcha capital. At the time of Spanish contact, the Chibcha were estimated at about 300,000 persons, the greatest density and the most populous state between Peru and the Valley of Mexico. Even though, as has been contended, the early Spaniards greatly overrated the Chibcha, their realm or kingdom was undoubtedly larger and closer knit than the other chiefdoms.

Although the Chibcha were separated from Mexico by all of Central America, where population movement at least in the later prehistoric eras was predominantly from south to north, they had a number of features more characteristic of Mexico than the Central Andes: markets, possible use of money, human sacrifice to the sun and excision of the victim's heart, and sacrifice of a victim who was tied to a pole. These and other features found among the chiefdoms may have survived from an early era of inter-American culture exchange. On the other hand, they could have spread southward despite northward migrations; for culture diffusion is often more rapid than population movement.

Subsistence. The Chibcha were intensive agriculturalists and farmed the temperate, fertile highland valleys. They grew maize, white potatoes, quinoa, sweet manioc, sweet potatoes, beans, squash, tomatoes, ají, coca, and tobacco. They obtained fruits in trade from the tropical lowlands and salt from salinas, or salt flats.

The protein content of Chibchan diet must have been low, since few fish were available and deer, although plentiful, might not be killed by common people. Small game such as rabbits and guinea pigs formed the principal meat supply.

Local specialization in food, crafts, and mineral production formed a basis for extensive and regular trade. Markets were held every four days in some settlements to exchange food, cotton, salt, and precious stones and metals. The Chibcha also traded outside their domain with people such as the Muzo and the Panche. This commerce was stimulated by the Chibchan demand for gold, which was lacking in their area but which their nobles required for burial goods, offerings, and display. It is possible that counters of cast gold served as a standard of exchange ' or money, and there are even indications of a rude credit system.

Settlements. Houses were generally constructed with wattle-and-daub walls and thatched roofs. The sparse furniture included utensils for preparing food and platform beds. Ordinary people squatted on the ground, but persons of rank were provided carved stools.

It is said that there were forty-two different settlements in the five major political groupings in Chibcha territory. These settlements were said to be "large" and palisaded, and certain ones were designated as regional capitals. Village size, however, is in doubt. A concentration of all 300,000 Chibcha in forty-two towns gives the improbable average of more than 7,100 persons each. A large portion of the population was undoubtedly dispersed over the countryside.

Sociopolitical organization. At the time of the Spanish Conquest the Chibcha chiefdom or realm was divided into five large territorial or statelike political divisions, each ruled by a powerful leader of great prestige. The largest state, Zipa, or Bogotá, consisted of six subdivisions, each under the leadership of a lesser chief who was confirmed by the supreme ruler. These component divisions or states were somewhat unstable, for local chiefs contended for power with their overlords and a powerful chief might invade and subjugate a neighboring territory and exact tribute as long as he could dominate it. The situation is reminiscent of that which obtained in the Valley of Mexico at a time when political states were so loosely integrated that hostilities marked the jockeying for power within the group. It probably also exemplifies the situation within most of the chiefdoms.

The rulers of the Chibchan political subdivisions were accorded a respect by their vassals comparable in kind, if not in degree, with that given the Inca nobility. They traveled in gold-covered litters, preceded by attendants who strewed the road with flowers. They lived in wooden "palaces" which were connected by roadways to the temples. They enjoyed the luxury of special royal baths. A subject was forbidden to look his ruler directly in the face and had to approach him with face averted, bowing deeply. The status of chiefs and nobles was ensured in the afterworld by providing them special burial in which wives and retainers, stupefied by drugs, were interred with them. These many special privileges were maintained by a system of taxation paid by the commoners in cloth and other produce and in labor.

The commoners, or basic farmers and producers, seem to have been patrilineal. At least, the kin group which occupied and used the land was patrilineally organized, and movable personal property was inherited patrilineally. But within the priesthood and the ruling group, inheritance was somewhat mixed. Succession to office was matrilineal, passing from a man to his sister's oldest son, whereas inheritance of personal property was patrilineal, passing from a man to his own son. Polygyny was more characteristic of, but not restricted to, the ruling and priestly classes. Whereas a member of the latter might have one hundred wives, a commoner had no more than two or three.

An heir to a high administrative position underwent a period of six year's training, similar to that required for entry into the priesthood. The training prescribed sexual abstinence, dietary taboos, and confinement in a temple during the entire period. In one instance it is reported that upon assuming office a neophyte, lavishly covered with gold dust, went out on a lake in a raft. This is reminiscent of the Inca custom wherein the emperor, sheathed in gold, stood on a mountainside in early morning so that the reflection of the sun's rays made him shine with dazzling brilliance.

Warfare. The Chibcha carried on two somewhat different kinds of warfare. First, they raided such tropical-forest village neighbors as the Muzo and Panche, to take human trophies. But they had no more success in conquering the tropical-forest peoples than the Inca had in subjugating the Peruvian Montaña. Second, they fought political wars among themselves. Like the Peruvian Indians, the Chibcha fought with lances, spears and spear throwers, slings, two-handed clubs, and wooden shields but used no bows.

Despite the scale of their political organization, the Chibcha were easily conquered by a very small number of Spanish troops. The unstable alliance of their political divisions prevented their offering a solid front against the invader, and each division fought separately in defense of its own territory. They engaged in no large battles and their main armies were easily routed by the Spanish cavalry, although survivors continued guerrilla warfare for a brief time in the forests and swamps, where horses could not operate. The Chibcha were effectively subdued in less than a year, and the people divided into repartimientos and distributed to the conquistadors in encomienda. Minor rebellions occurred until 1541, but the Chibcha were rapidly acculturated under the impact of colonialism and lost their identity.

Religion and ceremonialism. Chibcha temples, like ordinary dwellings, were built of wattle-and-daub walls and thatched roofs, but they were of great size and many were protected by a palisade. Each political division had its own hierarchy of priests who constituted a hereditary class and ranked as nobles. These men were clearly distinguished from shamans. A priest inherited his office matrilineally from his mother's brother, but he had first to prepare himself for twelve years. When ready, he was invested by the ruler and presented with insignia of office, such as a special robe and a calabash to hold coca. Thereafter, he lived in or near the temple with his fellow priests and practiced abstinence, fasting, bloodletting, and perpetual penance. At public ceremonials the priests interceded for the public good in such matters as drought. They dealt with private individuals and imposed dietary and behavioral strictures upon them. This practice resembles the Inca confessionals and imposition of penance. The priests also served as oracles. A person wishing questions answered gave the priests gold as an offering to the deity and gold and woven mantles in payment for their own services.

In addition to the major state temples and idols, there were many shrines dedicated to the mountains, lakes, and rivers which the people believed to be holy places. These too received offerings of gold.

Ceremonial patterns included offerings, public rites, pilgrimages, and human sacrifice. Gold and cotton cloth were offered to certain deities, especially in temples that were frequented by nobles, rulers, traders, and goldsmiths. In certain other temples, pregnant women came to make offerings. Offerings were placed in special containers which were secretly buried when they became full.

There is little evidence of a fixed calendar of public ceremonies, but a maize-harvest festival involving masked processions to the temples and a New Year's ceremony were annual events. At New Year, each household burned its refuse and threw out its hearth ashes. Pilgrimages, some of which lasted twenty days, were made to Lake Guatavita and other places. At Lake Guatavita, the pilgrims consumed large quantities of intoxicating chicha and concluded their worship with a night-long ceremony.

Human beings were sacrificed to the sun, usually in a special temple. Sacrificial victims were obtained not only from war captives and slaves but also from small children bought by traders from non-Chibcha tribes.

The children were reared in temples and were considered sacred. All but those who had failed to remain sexually continent were taken at puberty to the Temple of the Sun, where they were cut open and their hearts and bowels were removed and their heads cut off. Captive children of the enemy were also sacrificed in the Sun Temple, after which their blood was sprinkled on the floor and posts and their bodies left in the mountains for the sun. In order to appease the sun during droughts, priests sacrificed children on mountaintops and annointed the rocks that faced east with the blood.

Removal of the victim's heart resembles Aztec custom. Hurling spears into a man bound to a post also has a Mexican parallel. In this case, the victim was a slave whose blood was caught by priests and whose body was later buried in the mountains. Another kind of sacrifice occurred when live girls were pounded up with houseposts to ensure the solidity of the house and the well-being of the inhabitants. Parrots were also sacrificed, first being taught to speak, then killed and their heads preserved.

Shamans were distinct from priests and served individual persons rather than the community or state. They cured illness, partly by means of remedies which they sold. They interpreted dreams, and they forecast the future. They put themselves in a state of trance by drinking infusions of datura, tobacco juice, and other herbs.

4. WESTERN COLOMBIA: AN AREA OF LOCAL VARIATIONS

The habitat of the chiefdoms in western Colombia is topographically diversified, consisting of mountainous terrain, intermont plains, deep gorges, and narrow valleys formed by the many tributaries of the Cauca, Atrato, and Magdalena Rivers. Typical of tropical latitudes, the flora, fauna, and agricultural possibilities vary with altitude. The chiefdoms were generally found in the more temperate portions of this area, including the scrub steppe portions of the valleys and the paramo grasslands of the mountains.

The people of this region were first encountered by Europeans at the beginning of the sixteenth century, when the Spanish conquistadors made a number of inroads into Tierradentro in search of precious metals. The population must have been fairly great, for it was written that "in more than 30 leagues of road there is someone every step of the way." Colonial policy brought rapid depopulation and deculturation of most of the native groups. Fifty years after the arrival of the Spaniards, the Indian population had been largely replaced in the areas of intensive mining by imported Negro slaves.

The chiefdoms of this area were distributed in several groups which will be described separately—the upper Cauca River, the Cauca–Atrato River area, and the region east of the Cauca River. Among all of these, human sacrifice and cannibalism were strongly developed, and a priest-temple-idol cult was generally present. Political divisions of the chief-doms were based upon territorial units. Since six divisions are mentioned several times, it is possible that this was some arbitrary pattern, although the Ancerma had eight divisions.

The upper Cauca River

North of the Popayanense, near the headwaters of the Cauca River, lived several societies, the most important of which were the Chibchan-speaking Lile and the Gorrón. The Lile, Gorrón, and their neighbors may be classed as chiefdoms more because early accounts show a strong sociopolitical organization, which was supported to some extent by warfare, than because religion had an important integrating function.

The societies practiced intensive cultivation of maize, manioc, and a great number of tropical fruits, although they used only simple digging sticks. Their extensive use of fruits was made possible by the low altitude of their habitat. The Gorrón were also commercial fishermen, who traded their product to Spaniards and Indians as distant as the province of Cali. They constructed artificial fish ponds which yielded large amounts of fish that were collected each summer when the ponds dried up. Both the Lile and the Gorrón hunted forest animals such as deer and birds.

The Lile and Gorrón lived in large and well-made houses which were furnished with special benches or tables on which to display the trophy corpses taken in war. Houses were closely grouped in large villages, which were sometimes palisaded.

There is some evidence that the Lile were divided into six territorial political divisions, each under a local chief but all federated under a paramount chieftain. The aristocratic class, which included the chiefs and other prominent persons, received tribute from the commoners, enjoyed the privilege of polygyny, wore golden plates and other ornaments of gold, and at death were given special burial. A chief took his niece, or occasionally his own sister, as principal wife, a practice which would perpetuate a small ruling group. Chieftainship passed to the oldest son of the principal wife.

After the Spanish Conquest, chiefs provided the Spaniards with Indian labor on a contractual basis.

Warfare. The Lile and Gorrón were extremely warlike and fought frequently with their neighbors. Even the women accompanied men into battle, carrying arms, fighting, and taking human trophies. The principal weapons were lances, wooden swordlike clubs (macanas), and painted wooden shields.

The principal purpose of war was to obtain human trophies. The victors flayed their victims' skins and stuffed them with ashes or straw, modeled wax on the skulls to restore lifelike features, and after reassembling the head and body, set them in places of honor on special benches and tables within their households. They even stuffed the entrails and festooned them inside the house over the door, and exhibited the hands and feet. Often, after flaying a victim, the victors ritually ate his flesh in a house specially built for this purpose. In one village, the Spaniards found a hut containing a "great quantity" of skulls, bones, and other human remains.

Since the Lile and Gorrón lacked a priest-temple-idol cult, it is clear that people were welded together in chiefdoms through warfare and not religion. Shamans performed all religious functions. They communicated with their own spirit-helpers to cure sickness, they carried out divination, and they practiced witchcraft. These services were rendered for individuals rather than for villages or states.

Public ceremonialism was minimal or absent, except that the Lile had an annual mourning ceremony which involved the people of two communities, who were led by their respective chiefs. But this ceremony was as potentially divisive as integrative. Activities began with a general feast, but they culminated in a ritual battle of spear throwing. Although participants defended themselves with shields, many people were wounded and some were killed. While it was said that this ceremony did not cause hostility between the two groups, it obviously did not contribute to solidarity.

Chiefdoms east of the Cauca River

The Arma, Carrapa, Paucura, Picara, Pozo, and Quimbaya, who lived immediately east of the Cauca River, had a fairly dense native population, which was organized in the general pattern of northern Andean chiefdoms.

These people cultivated maize, beans, and sweet manioc, along with a number of tropical fruits, cotton, and coca. They also collected many wild foods and hunted some small game, but did little fishing except, perhaps, on the Cauca River and other large streams.

Pozo villages were surrounded by cane palisades and encompassed watchtowers and sacrificial platforms. Arma villages consisted of houses which were divided into compartments and arranged in streets separated by bamboo palisades and surrounding a sacrificial platform. The Arma also built large roads extending as far as the province of Cenufaná.

The Quimbaya constituted a federation of six subgroups, each with its own chief and headed by a paramount chieftain. The chiefs of the Quimbaya and their neighbors exercised authority in times of peace as well as war and received special treatment from their subjects. The followers of an Arma chief built his house, worked his fields, paid him tribute in gold, and provided him many wives. Pozo and Arma chiefs painted their bodies with many colors and wore gold labrets. A Quimbaya chief was cremated at death and his ashes buried deeply in a gold urn, while his subjects ceremonially wept, drank chicha, and sang. Sometimes, however, he received direct burial, accompanied by wives and retainers who had been stupefied with drugs.

Succession to office was kept within a small group of relatives through the marriage of a chief to his sister or niece, who became his principal wife. While inheritance seems to have been patrilineal throughout the region, the principal wife of a chief who died without sons inherited his rank and wealth and passed them on at her death to the chief's sister's son. In the case of brother-sister marriage, the chief's sister's son was, of course, his own son.

Like their neighbors of the upper Cauca River region, all these groups were very warlike. The Arma even fought among themselves. Weapons were like those of the other Cauca River peoples, except that the Arma also used a kind of gold armor, whence their name. The Quimbaya wore gold helmets and carried shields made of their own hair. The Arma, Carrapa, and Pozo followed war banners made of woven cotton decorated with figures of gold.

Trophy taking and cannibalism were the major objectives of warfare. The Arma, Paucura, and the Picara kept their captives in special enclosures to fatten them for cannibalistic ceremonies. Although endocannibalism—eating members of one's own group—is reported by one chronicler, it seems improbable. The Indians dismembered their victims with flint knives and displayed their skins, skulls, and bones inside their houses and on bamboo poles outside.

The Quimbaya made offerings of maize and daily sacrificed human victims in large temples. The Arma, Picara, and Paucura also made periodic human sacrifices to their gods. Before going to war, the Pozo made sacrifices to gods who were represented by carved and painted wooden idols having human skulls with features modeled in wax. The Carrapa had no temples, but they worshiped the sun and believed that this god would appear before them if they made prayerful offerings when sick.

The Cauca–Atrato River region

This temperate and mountainous region lies north of Gorrón territory and west of the Cauca River peoples just described. It extends between the Cauca and Atrato Rivers down to the province of Darien and the Caribbean coast, where the country becomes tropical lowland. Some of the better-known groups who lived there were the Toro, Quinchía, Zopia, Caramanta, Buritica, Antiochia (Antioquia), Evéjico, and Catío. They shared a similar culture, which differed little from those peoples living to the east and south of the Cauca River, and they spoke dialects related to the Chocó language.

These peoples raised many food plants: maize, beans, sweet manioc, sweet potatoes, guayavas, avocados, quinces, guamas, soursop, palms, and other fruits, cotton, coca, ají, and a palmito from which they made a beverage and a kind of bread. Their meat was obtained from iguanas, turtles, deer, peccaries, tapirs, opossums, rabbits, and many other smaller animals and birds which they hunted with spears and bows and arrows. Fishing does not seem to have been of importance.

Dwelling types varied somewhat and reflect the different effects of warfare. Houses were usually of pole-and-thatch construction and were grouped in palisaded villages. Pile dwellings were common, however, and the Toro built their houses in trees for defense. Antiochian houses accommodated more than 200 people and were reached by ladders. Catío houses were built high on poles and fortified by thick palisades which had loopholes for shooting arrows and were protected by dead-falls. Antiochian villages were large and divided into barrios, whereas the Toro lacked villages and lived widely dispersed.

Chiefdoms consisted of a number of subdivisions, each headed by a local chief but all federated under a paramount chief. The Ancerma had eight such subdivisions. While the Nutibara and Abibe were distinct political entities, their chiefs were brothers and the former controlled the latter.

A chief enjoyed special privileges. He was carried in a gold-plated litter, had a large polygynous household, wore robes decorated with gold leaf and other forms of luxurious dress, allowed his fingernails to grow long, and painted his face with distinctive marks. He had multiple wives (among the Catío, as many as twenty) and received gifts of gold from his followers. At death, his body was preserved through desiccation over a fire and deeply interred on a hillside or under the house accompanied by food, ornaments, wives, and weapons. Among the Nore, the chief was wrapped in blankets and buried in a mound along with ornaments, weapons, and live women and slaves. Afterwards the people ceremonially wept for several days and cut the hair of the chief's closest wives.

Inheritance of wealth and rank passed through the paternal line, but among the Ancerma a daughter might inherit in default of a son and among the Zopia and Nutibara an older sister's son might be the heir.

War captives constituted the lowest class. They served as drudge laborers, they were traded, they were eaten in cannibalistic rites, and they were often buried with a chief. The Nore and Gauca married war captives, but later sacrificed and ate their offspring in cannibalistic feasts. Slaves and gold were the main items of trade among these Cauca-Atrato groups.

Trophy taking, cannibalism, and capture of human beings for trade were the main motives for the intense warfare found in this region when the Spaniards arrived. Spears, bows, slings, and clubs were the most common weapons. The Antiochia threw boiling water down upon attacking forces from their pile houses, and the Evéjico and Catío placed pitfalls on the approaches to their villages. The Catío are said to have hired other Indians as mercenaries to fight the Antiochia, and they had hilltop forts to ward off attacks.

Nearly all of these Indians displayed human trophies over their house doors. Among the Ancerma, these trophies included skulls which were painted red, arms and legs, and skins which were stuffed with ashes and placed on cane poles in the center of their villages.

Cannibalism was largely ritual. The Ancerma, for example, ate their victims in order to acquire superior powers. The Caramanta and Antiochia, however, bought captives from the Ancerma to be eaten as staple food, and the latter illuminated their gold mines with torches of human fat.

The Ancerma, Caramanta, Nutibara, and others built special temples on hilltops. Among the Ancerma, only chiefs and priests and two virgins had access to the temple. These Indians worshiped a principal god, Xixarama, and his children whom they supplicated to bring water for the crops.

Worship of gods and idols took many forms. The Caramanta kept idols of wood and gold either in their dwellings or in special places outside their houses. They also had special temples, where they made ritual sacrifices to ensure favorable weather for their crops. The Nutibara supplicated a jaguar idol by placing gold offerings in its temple. The Evéjico lacked idols, but had priests who supplicated the gods. Among the Antiochians, old men communicated with the major deity.

5. NORTH COLOMBIAN LOWLANDS: FURTHER VARIATIONS

The lowlands of northern Colombia, especially the Cauca Valley and the country to the northwest of it, are predominantly scrub steppe, while the Magdalena Valley is rain forest. The best-known chiefdoms of this area were the Calamari, Turbaco, Urabá, Cenú (Fincenú, Pancenú, and Cenufaná), Mompox, Yapel, and Utibara. Most of these spoke languages related to Chocoan. The Tairona, Cágaba, and Arhuaco to the northeast were societies of the simpler village type. These chiefdoms all disappeared early in the colonial period, and the Spaniards compensated for the declining Indian labor force by importing Negro slaves.

The people of these lowlands were intensive farmers of maize, sweet manioc, beans, and sweet potatoes, grew an abundance of fruits, including plantains, pineapples, and guavas, and raised cotton for the manufacture of textiles. The Spanish chronicles comment on the large size of Tolú fields and the full stores of Cenú maize. Agriculture was supplemented by hunting and fishing. Game included rabbits, guinea pigs, iguanas, caymans, peccaries, turtles, turkeys, and other birds. The Urabá captured and fattened young peccaries for food, but these animals were not truly domesticated. The babracot, a kind of wooden grill, was used to cook food and to smoke and preserve meat. Salt and aji were the principal condiments, and they were important trade items.

There was considerable trade in other products, especially between the coast and the interior. The excellent gold objects manufactured by the Fincenú were in wide demand. Coastal groups, such as the Calamari, Tolú, and Urabá, exchanged textiles, canoes, hammocks, and dried fish with inland peoples for gold. The Tamalameque held markets which stimulated intergroup trading relations. Canoe travel on the rivers and gulf cost helped maintain this network of trade. The Cenú traveled downstream in balsa canoes, which, being easily made, they abandoned.

Large palisaded villages of pole-and-thatch houses were characteristic of the region. The Turbaco built beehive-shaped houses of pole-and-mud walls and thatched roofs. Mompox and Tamalameque villages along the Magdalena River were orderly arranged in plazas, streets, and barrios.

The ample size and permanency of these villages are indicated by certain features which caught the attention of the early chroniclers. For example, the female chieftain of the Cenufaná had a court composed of twenty houses which were surrounded by several large storehouses. Other structures of note are the deep-shaft burial mounds of the Urabá which were lined with stone slabs and reached by a stone stairway; the wells dug by the Calamari; and liana bridges 700 feet long built by the Mompox. The building and maintenance of these structures required a considerable labor force and managerial controls.

This area had political federations of local groups whose chiefs were under a regional headman. It is noteworthy that the chieftainship of various subgroups within a federation was in the hands of siblings or closely related, consanguineal kinsmen. This is reminiscent of the dynastic arrangments found among other Colombian peoples to the south, wherein rules of marriage and succession tended to keep chieftainship within a family group.

While women were important in the ruling class among all Colombian chiefdoms, the Fincenú were actually ruled by a woman, whose husband was accorded greater respect than the chiefs of the Cenú subgroups. The chieftainess had a retinue of female servants who catered to her and carried her on their backs when she traveled. Some of these servants were stupefied and buried with her at death. In the other chiefdoms, women received gold in tribute from their people and were transported in gold-adorned litters.

Polygyny was principally the prerogative of chiefs and wealthy men, although commoners sometimes had several wives, especially if they could support them. In view of the matriarchal tendency to descent among rulers, however, these "wives" were more likely concubines. Among the Urabá, a wealthy man took his sister's daughter as his principal wife and bequeathed his wealth to her first son.

Among the Calamari there was a special class of male inverts who went from village to village selling their sexual services. There were also women prostitutes.

War patterns were quite similar to those of the tribes to the south in the Cauca-Atrato region, and trophy taking and possibly cannibalism were the primary motives for hostilities. Military federations were formed under powerful leaders. Attacks were accompanied by great shouting and trumpet blasts. The individual usually had considerable freedom in battle, but the Tolú fought in orderly formations directed by commanders. Cenú chiefs were carried into battle on gold-hung litters ahead of the troops. Among some groups, virgin girls went into battle to fight as well as to bear weapons for the men. They were entitled to participate on an equal footing with male warriors in the drunken revelries which followed hostilities.

Although the Cenufaná ate their captives, cannibalism among the other chiefdoms is in doubt. The Urabá were said to cook their own dead over babracots and eat them. While funerary cannibalism was practiced in the northwest Amazon, it is unexpected here.

A priest-temple-idol complex was fully developed among the Calamari, Cenú, Cenufaná, Fincenú, and Urabá. The Fincenú temple was 100 yards long, accommodated about a thousand people, and was the repository for twenty-four large wooden idols which were covered with gold leaf and crowned with tiaras. In front of each idol were receptacles for public offerings. Temple guards prevented ordinary people from entering the inner sanctum while the priests were communicating with the gods. Graves of important persons were arranged around the temple and marked by a mound or a tree from which hung a special gold bell.

The religious leaders, like the political rulers, had hereditary positions.

6. THE CUNA AND THEIR NEIGHBORS:
EXEMPLIFICATION OF HISTORIC DECULTURATION

Most of present-day Panama was occupied by small chiefdoms, the best known of which are the Cuna or Cuna-Cueva, a Chibchan-speaking people whose habitat was the comparatively low central region east and west of the Canal. A similar culture was shared by several groups speaking varied but unknown languages immediately to their west, and probably also by a few people still farther west whose very identity is unknown.

The Cuna and their immediate neighbors are of special interest for several reasons. Their aboriginal culture is comparatively well known thanks to Lothrop's excavation of late prehistoric sites in the Coclé region and his collation of Spanish accounts of the sixteenth century.[3] These data disclose a strong class system, multivillage political integration based primarily upon warfare, and exceptionally fine products in metallurgy, ceramics, and carved teeth, bone, shell and precious and semiprecious stones.

The present-day Cuna, who are known through the field research of Stout,[4] contrast with their pre-Columbian forebears in certain crucial ways. Although they retain much aboriginal culture in their family and village life, all features connected with the chiefdoms have disappeared. Moreover, they are slowly being affected by influences from the modern, outside economic and political world. Cuna change since the sixteenth century thus represents the processes of deculturation, or culture loss, as well as acculturation, or culture change.

While the archaeology of Coclé is unquestionably representative of native Cuna culture, we cannot be sure that Lothrop's principal site, Sitio Conte, or other sites in the region were definitely Cuna sites. West of Sitio Conte, both the archaeology and the ethnology are little known. Fragments of evidence, however, suggest a diminution of features typical of chiefdoms toward the west and an increase of features characteristic of the tropical-forest villages. This diminution apparently continued into the southern Caribbean lowlands to the north (section 7 of the present chapter), while only a tropical-forest village type of culture was found in the northern Caribbean lowlands (Chapter Twelve, section 12).

The aboriginal Cuna and their neighbors

Maps of the Spanish conquistadors place the Cuna and their neighbors in an area of some 7,500 square miles of fertile land which was divided among at least three principal chiefs and fifty-three lesser chiefs.

While slash-and-burn farming was employed, the men preparing the fields and the women cultivating them, hints of larger-scale, more permanent farming are contained in the statements that one chief owned a plantation of more than a hundred acres and that "the fields [of another] extended for above six leagues [and] were all full of Maiz, like corn-fields." The Cuna also relied heavily upon fish, which they took with bows and arrows and nets, and upon game. The Spaniards expressed considerable satisfaction with the variety and quantity of the cuisine.

Local specialization in production led to extensive commerce not only within the area but possibly with peoples as distant as the Aztec of Mexico and the Inca of Peru. Goods were transported on land by slaves and along the coasts in large dugout canoes, which possibly had cotton sails. The principal commercial products were salt, maize, mantles, ham-mocks, thread, raw cotton, salted fish, gold, and slaves.

The boundaries of the chiefdoms were constantly shifting as intergroup warfare, intrigue, and marriage brought the hegemony of one or another chief over his neighbors. Three principal chiefs were listed by the con-quistadors, although there were no doubt others in the area. These were Parita, who was ascribed control of an area which extended about one hundred miles, mostly along the Pacific Coast; Escoria, who defeated Parita and married his daughter; and Nata, about whom more particulars are known.

Nata's main town in 1527 had forty-five to fifty houses, with a total population of only about 250 persons if each house sheltered a nuclear family. The surrounding country was said to be densely settled, but under Nata and his ten subchiefs there were only 1,500 persons, an aver-age of 150 persons per subchief. The size of this chiefdom was rather insignificant compared with the Inca or even the Chibcha realm. None-theless, class distinctions were strong and the authority and status of the main chiefs very great. The latter had despotic power and could impose torture and the death penalty for civil crimes such as theft or rape. They lived luxuriously with many wives and retainers, among whom were slaves. When traveling, they were carried in hammocks. They wore head, nose, ear, neck, and breast ornaments delicately wrought in gold. Many of these ornaments were decorated with their marks or insignia, and they placed these same marks on their property and tattooed them on their slaves.

At death, the body of a great chief was desiccated (an Andean cus-tom), then buried in a special grave, like those at Sitio Conte. The chief's corpse was accompanied by the bodies of wives and retainers who had been poisoned or stupefied, and it was provided with bowls of food, ornaments, and other gear for the afterworld. Lothrop found as many as twenty-one skeletons with that of the chief in a single grave, and he cites Oviedo that the victims might number forty or fifty.

Chieftainship was inherited patrilineally. Upon installation in office,

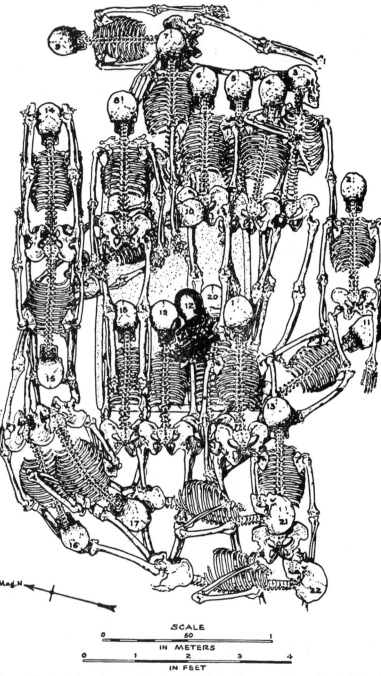

Suttee-like burial at late prehistoric Sitio Conte, Panama. A warrior is interred with wives, retainers, and burial goods. (After Samuel K. Lothrop, "Cocié," Memoirs of the Peabody Museum, Harvard University, vol. 7, 1937.)

the new chief's genealogy was recited as affirmation of his status, and the status of his relationship with his neighbors was announced. In view of intergroup warfare, marriage, and intrigue, this statement was no doubt very important in clarifying how obligations and authority among chiefs stood at the moment. The installation was completed with music and ceremonies.

The role and status of the subchiefs were like those of the main chiefs, but they had less wealth, ostentation, and power. Moreover, a certain mobility within this class was possible, since these men were primarily war captains who had been rewarded with gifts of land, women, and slaves for their exploits and for their wounds. Even when a lesser chief inherited his title, he had first to prove his military prowess.

There was undoubtedly a class of commoners, although the sources paid little attention to it. If each of Nata's subchiefs controlled only 150 persons, including wives and slaves, the number of nobles and commoners cannot have been great.

Slaves seem to have been war captives who served the chiefs. Among them was a special class of homosexual male slaves who did women's work.

The principal purpose of warfare in the Coclé region was to conquer lands and people and to acquire prestige. While cannibalism is doubtful, male enemies were killed in order that the sun god might "drink" their blood. The slayer of twenty enemies received a special title. Military operations were carried out only after consulting a shaman. Intrigue and espionage were as important as battles, wherein warriors were armored with quilted garments and used atlatls to hurl their spears. (Bows and arrows were reserved for hunting.) Defense was provided by palisades.

Sitio Conte contained a stone-paved edifice which apparently served both as a religious center and as the chief's domicile. The same man, according to Spanish chronicles, performed as priest in community ceremonies, as prophet, and as shaman in healing and working magic. Among the practices in physical therapy that were employed were the use of herbs and enemas, and bloodletting by means of a venesection bow. Major gods included the sun and moon, but the greater chiefs were also deified in that their bodies were desiccated after death and received elaborate ceremonial burial.

The modern Cuna

A few years ago, the Cuna on the island of San Blas were publicized as "white Indians." Actually, the people in question are an unfortunate, somewhat ostracized group of albinos who comprise less than 1 per cent of the population.

The truly interesting features of the modern Cuna are: first, the loss of state institutions—the hereditary social classes, the chiefdoms, the war-

Gold pendants from Sitio Conte burials, Panama. (a) Monkey; (b) crocodile; (c) woman. (After Samuel K. Lothrop, "Coclé," Memoirs of the Peabody Museum, Harvard University, vol. 7, 1937.)

fare, the human sacrifice to the sun, and such associated features as suttee burial and the production of fine objects in metal (gold and tumbaga), in emerald, quartz, and other stones, and in four-color ceramics, textiles, and other arts—while village culture has survived; and second, the recent influences of the outside world upon the Cuna. Even though the people live in comparative isolation, they depend somewhat upon outside trade for such goods as manufactured cloth, metal tools and other hardware, and even chicha jars. Moreover, local contact with Europeans and African slaves has directly introduced alien features, while the many Cuna who have served as seamen on ocean-going freighters must have picked up foreign customs during their experiences.

The modern Cuna are village farmers, but men now devote themselves entirely to cultivation, whereas formerly they left much of it to the women. In addition to their native crops, the Cuna grow such Old World plants as bananas, plantains, rice, coconuts, coffee, and citrus fruits, some of these for sale. The Cuna have also adopted pigs and chickens but raise them primarily for trade. While we know little of the productive and commercial arrangements, the Cuna now clearly have a peasant economy. They utilize marginal lands, having lost their better lands to Europeans, and they engage in small-scale production of trade commodities as supplements to subsistence crops. But they continue to use primitive slash-and-burn, digging-stick methods, and they hunt and fish. In fishing they employ such native techniques as nets, spears, bows and arrows, weirs, and harpoons, and they use decoys to catch sea turtles in nets.

The Cuna still use the long, narrow native type of dugout canoe for river travel, but the insular Cuna now build a larger canoe with a sail for ocean voyages. Goods are carried on land in large baskets supported either by tumpline or the coolie yoke, both aboriginal methods.

Today the Cuna live in villages of thatched houses arranged in streets. Among the eastern groups some houses are raised on piles. As in native times, hammocks and wooden seats are the principal furnishings.

Since the late nineteenth century, European dress has all but replaced native clothing, although some nose rings, ear pendants, necklaces, and featherwork are still seen, and feathered headgear is worn by ceremonial leaders.

The former system of social classes—major chiefs, lesser chiefs, commoners, and slaves—has been replaced by two loosely defined classes based on wealth. Political power now rests with elected village chiefs and their subordinates. Election of officers seems not to fit the native pattern and may be a recent innovation. There are, however, reports of a similar practice among people of the Conquest period to the west and northwest. The chief presides over village meetings and performs a ritual chant which recounts mythological and semihistorical events. Two political parties crosscut Cuna society, and are found most strongly developed in the San Blas area.

Marriage is predominantly monogamous today, although polygyny is permitted. Since postmarital residence is matrilocal, households consist of several matrilineally related families. The senior male heads the household and has authority over his sons-in-law and grandsons-in-law, while his principal wife outranks the other wives. At death, the household leader is succeeded by his oldest son-in-law.

The Cuna today have no trace of a priest-temple-idol cult, and the sun, to whom human beings were formerly sacrificed, is no longer considered a deity. The principal god and his wife seem clearly to reflect Christian teaching and possibly African belief. The more important aspects of modern religion are animistic and shamanistic, both no doubt in the native tradition. The loss of one's soul is considered the main cause of illness, and it is cured by shamans. Shamans are classified into three types according to their specialties. The largest group comprises men and women who have learned special chants and medicinal lore and whose function is primarily to cure sickness. While practicing they use fetishes, hold staffs of office, burn paper and bean pods, and use mnemonic pictographs to help recall their chants.

The second type of shaman is less numerous than the first and consists of persons who specialize in curing whole villages during times of epidemic illness. They perform an eight-day ceremony during which they use braziers, long cigars (aboriginal cigars were 2 feet long, and a single cigar served a whole community in a festival), and fetishes. The third group consists of persons who are born to the role but who must undergo extensive training. This type has close rapport with evil spirits and is adept at foretelling the future, recovering lost or stolen objects, and diagnosing illness. Fetishes are vitally important to them in maintaining connection with the spirit world.

Another survival of native ceremonialism is seen in the elaborate puberty ceremonies for girls. First, the girl is confined, doused with water, given a haircut, and painted black. A year later, she makes her debut at a chicha-drinking ceremony in which chanting, cigar-smoking, and burning cacao beans are the main features.

People of western Panama

Between the Coclé area and the Guaymí Indians of extreme western Panama lived several groups whose language and identity are unknown. This area was quickly depopulated after the Spanish Conquest, and many Guaymí were moved into it. Any aborigines who survive today are mixed with other groups.

Early Spanish chronicles mention slash-and-burn farming, fishing, and hunting much like that of the Coclé area. They also indicate that basketry, weaving, and wood carving were well developed but that goldwork, while excellent, lacked many of the Coclé techniques.

The principal evidence of chiefdoms is social classes similar to those of the Coclé. Supreme chiefs had despotic power and received many privileges and honors. They dwelt in large, many-room houses and were surrounded by their numerous wives, retainers or slaves, and "nobles" or lesser chiefs. They wore special dress, particularly long cotton cloaks, and gold ornaments. Each had his own emblem, which, like the property marks of the Cuna, he tattooed on his followers.

We do not know the territorial extent of these chiefdoms, but compact, palisaded villages of 1,500 persons are reported.

Lesser chiefs attained their rank through warfare as well as through inheritance. They seem often to have been village chiefs who were under the principal chief. They differed from their overlords in that they had less property, fewer wives, retainers, feather ornaments, nose plugs, pendants, and other objects of gold and precious stones.

Commoners performed the economic labors which supported the upper classes, but they had some potential upward mobility in that they could marry into chiefs' families or gain rank through war exploits. Slaves were prisoners of war. The brands or tattoos put on their faces were evidence of their low social position as well as marks of ownership.

Warfare was a means of taking slaves and was therefore crucial to the sociopolitical pattern. There is no information, however, as to whether it also served religion. Each town maintained a standing army, which fought with bows and arrows.

The Spanish chroniclers give no clear idea of religion and ceremonialism. A number of apparently highly symbolic objects have been uncovered by archaeological research which possibly indicate that religious development was advanced. While a rubber ball game was widespread in South America, this game was played ceremonially in a special court in Meso-America. Somewhat similar courts have been found in this region and in the Greater Antilles, and they undoubtedly served a community religious purpose.

7. THE SOUTHERN CARIBBEAN LOWLANDS: IN THE ROUTE OF DIFFUSION

The Chibchan-speaking Guaymí, Bribri, Cabecar, Changuena, Güetar, Rama, and others form a group of peoples who lived principally in the Caribbean lowlands of western Panama and Costa Rica. The Guaymí were the largest group and are best known, owing to the ethnographic research of Pinart in the last century and of Johnson in the present century.

Fragmentary information about the culture of these peoples at the time of the Spanish Conquest indicates that the Guaymí, the Talamanca group, and the Güetar had chiefdoms, but a number of characteristics distinguish them from the Indians of the Coclé region of Panama: clan organization, a boys' puberty ceremony, burial customs, and stylistic features of ceramics and art objects.

This area contains archaeological remains of fairly advanced cultures, but it is impossible at present to relate most of them to the historic people. Some remains may date back to the inter-American Formative Era. Others may tentatively be related to the historic Chibchan-speaking people who arrived in relatively recent times from the South American continent. For example, the excellent prehistoric cast-gold objects are probably Chibchan. Lothrop believes that the deep-pit burials in the province of Chiriquí, in what may have been Güetar territory, are of Chibchan origin and perhaps predate the Spanish Conquest by only two hundred years, even though these burials, the stone stools or metates, and the pottery are easily distinguished from Coclé objects.

Elsewhere archaeology has yielded stone statues including those with the alter-ego motif (a main figure with a lesser figure riding its shoulders, a type which has inter-American distribution), and those of the Chac-Mool style (a recumbent figure which has a bowl carved into its belly and is probably of Meso-American origin). There are also many locally distinctive styles of pottery, metates, stone stools, and other objects of unknown origin.

The aboriginal culture

The native Guaymí, Talamancan, and Güetar chiefdoms were consolidated primarily by warfare which was carried on to obtain sacrificial victims, slaves, territory, and other economic benefits. These military units were temporarily strengthened by their resistance to the Spaniards. The social structure of these chiefdoms, however, seems to have represented a blend of kinship and class institutions. The Güetar were ascribed three classes: nobles, who wore gold ornaments and carried staffs; commoners; and slaves, the last being female war captives. But the Bribri and perhaps the others were basically organized in exogamous, matrilineal moieties— dual groupings—which were subdivided into clans. Since inherited class status is somewhat incompatible with kinship status, it is significant that war chiefs achieved rather than inherited their rank. Among the Bribri, Cabecar, and Terraba, these chiefs were usually elected and "exercised absolute power over the tribe," even though they "belonged to a special class and were frequently given special burials."[5]

The social role of religion is far from clear. The Bribri had a formal priesthood consisting of their own people but presided over by a person chosen from the Cabecar. The Güetar also had an organized priesthood which sacrificed human beings at every moon and at burial feasts. Patterns of shamanism, however, resembled those of Panama.

The aboriginal people of this area may be considered transitional between a simple kin-based clan and village organization, like that of the tropical forests described in Chapters Eleven and Twelve, and fully developed chiefdoms, even though their territory has archaeological materials more characteristically associated with the latter.

The modern culture

The contemporary people of the southern Caribbean lowlands differ from their predecessors largely in their loss of state institutions and in changes induced by their increasing dependence upon an outside economy and by their acquisition of European features.

Today, they have added such Old World plants as rice, peas, and plantains to the aboriginal crops but nonetheless depend less upon farming and more upon hunting than formerly. Whereas native farming afforded some surplus, land shortage today leaves many workers landless and impoverished. Each family owns several plots which are rotated so that some lie always fallow. Among the Guaymí, men clear new land by the slash-and-burn method, and then celebrate the preparation of the fields in a simple ceremony which excludes women. After this, women plant and cultivate. In all other groups, men do the planting. The Bribri formerly used outdoor granaries, but today they store food on a small scale in house lofts and bins.

Since aboriginal times there has been a steady trade between the savannas and the tropical forests in regional specialties, especially in salt. The modern Indians, although on the fringe of a money economy, still engage in extensive bartering.

The introduction of cattle and horses in 1900 was a potent factor in stimulating culture change. It became necessary to fence farm lands against the animals. New regulations governing ranges, inheritance, and cattle theft had to be devised by the tribal councils. Since cattle herding takes men away from agricultural activities for part of the year and leaves more farm work for the women, agricultural production has decreased; and yet cattle are so high-priced that they are seldom killed for meat. Meanwhile, livestock has brought in a new status system based on wealth. In addition, land is now owned by individual families and is a source of wealth and prestige.

The Indians continue to hunt with the traditional techniques: stalking, ambushing, and using dogs, traps, bows and arrows, and in the forests, a blowgun that shoots a pellet. They fish with hooks, spears, arrows, weirs, and when fish are especially abundant, by hand.

Transportation today is often by pack animal, although some persons continue to use baskets supported by a tumpline. Lowland and coastal peoples use substantial dugout canoes, sometimes equipped with sails.

Aboriginal manufacturing techniques have declined in the wake of sociocultural and economic readjustments brought on by the Conquest. Today pottery specialists are rare, and spinning and cloth weaving have tended to die out as European textiles and other wares are becoming available.

Villages at the time of the Conquest typically consisted of a group of large dwellings surrounded by a palisade, although Guatuso houses were widely scattered. Modern communities are small, and resemble those of the tropical-forest farm villages.

Contemporary social structure shows the effects of economic changes. The enhanced importance of the individual, or nuclear, family in owning property and producing wealth has weakened the extended kin groups or clans as well as the former hereditary classes. Although descent is matrilineal, property tends to be inherited patrilineally. Polygyny, how-ever, is still practiced.

Chiefs today are titular leaders who have considerable prestige and some authority. Bribri chiefs continue to exercise some control over the Terraba and the Cabecar, but their authority is now backed by the Costa Rican government. While some groups have moved away from the growing Panamanian towns, those who remain are coming under the jurisdiction of Panamanian law.

8. THE MESO-AMERICANS: NORTHERN INFLUENCE

It is not surprising that many cultural features characteristic of Meso-America rather than of South America found their way into Central America. But the history of these features is complex, and they were transmitted in different ways. Many individual elements were spread by diffusion from one group to another, some reaching South America. Domesticated turkeys, ball courts, cacao, commerce and money, markets, ritual incense, the game of voladores, jade working, steam bathing, tongue piercing, and apiculture are ethnographic examples, while Nicoya-type pottery and Chac-Mool stone statues are archaeological illustrations.

Although these and other traits diffused southward to Chibchan-speaking people, there were also migrations which took Nahuatl-speaking groups from Meso-America into Central America, where they formed cultural enclaves. Johnson[6] postulates four migrations. The first brought several enclaves of Macro-Otomanguean–speaking Chorotega to Central

America. The second brought the Maribio or Subtiaba. The third and fourth were rather continuous and involved Nahuatl peoples whose language belonged to the Uto-Aztecan branch of the widespread North American Azteco-Tanoan family. These migrations began in the twelfth century and were probably stimulated by the general unrest and revolutions in Mexico, which saw the Chichimecs enter the Valley of Mexico and the Toltec invade Yucatán. The Nicarao were the first Nahuatl people to reach Nicaragua. Later came the Nahuatlato, Begace, and others. Migration of Aztec colonists and traders known as the Desaguadero and Sigua lasted until the sixteenth century and reached widely scattered areas. These last were, in a way, pioneers of the expanding Aztec Empire, whose growth was halted by Cortez.

In Central America, these migrations created a series of dislocations of native peoples and caused culture contacts that undoubtedly had far-reaching effects. It is impossible to appraise their influence, however, since nearly all information about them comes from the Chorotega and Nicarao, who have been in the area so long that their Meso-American culture has been greatly modified, and from the Nahuatl, who have become mestizoized and have lost their identity. Early sources, moreover, usually do not distinguish these groups and refer broadly to all of them as "Nicaraguans."

The Nicaraguans used slash-and-burn farming to grow many crops, of which maize, cacao, and tobacco were the most important. Wild game and fish, although important for their proteins, were secondary to farming.

Of settlement patterns we know only that streets of houses were clustered around pole-and-thatch "palaces" and temples, which were erected on low earth mounds and scattered throughout the countryside. The central importance of the mounds and temples was related to a strong status system which was based upon three classes but took two somewhat contrasting forms: the hereditary, or autocratic, and the democratic.

Most groups seem to have had the first type, that is, hereditary classes which included chiefs and priests, commoners, and slaves. There was some social mobility, however, in that a person might improve his status through acquiring wealth; but the priests were in a class by themselves. Even the Nicarao, who represent the first type, had a "hereditary-elective" cacique (chief), or head of state, whose actions had to be approved by a council of elders who were elected for a term of four moons. The council also appointed officials who were paid in cacao, maize, and mantles.

In the democratic type, probably exemplified by the Chorotega, the elected council chose the supreme leader, whose principal function was commander in chief in warfare. This elective pattern recalls that of the northern Caribbean lowlands, the Bribri, Cabecar, and Terraba of the southern Caribbean lowlands, and the present-day Cuna. There is no doubt that it was aboriginal among the Meso-American enclaves, for the Spaniards abolished it and created a feudallike system by dividing the Indians into repartimientos under caciques whom they appointed and could control.

The basis of both types of chiefdoms was intensive warfare which was carried on by trained and organized companies. The purpose of warfare was not only to capture victims for religious sacrifice and cannibalism but to gain economic ends. While human sacrifice and cannibalism were carried to extremes in Colombia, the practices somewhat faded out in Central America only to be emphasized again in the Meso-America division. Here, as among the Aztec, human sacrifice was the key practice in many ceremonies of the various religious cults. But cannibalism involved a genuine taste for human flesh and the rearing of captives for gastronomic purposes which resembled that of the Pijao, Antiochia, and others of Colombia. Warfare had an economic purpose and was said to concern boundary disputes. This seems to imply property rights in land, which are probably related to a pattern of commerce based on money, a pattern not found in the Andes.

While there is usually some question whether Indian markets in Latin America are of aboriginal or Spanish origin, especially where money is used, the Nicaraguan markets and media of exchange were undoubtedly aboriginal. Why this pattern developed invites speculation. A partial answer is that the idea of money and, more specifically, the use of cacao beans, maize, and cotton cloth as money were introduced from Mexico. One may also surmise that markets flourished only with difficulty in autocratic chiefdoms where the principal chiefs controlled wealth, even though the Chibcha markets do not support this speculation. Perhaps a democratic sociopolitical system was favorable to, if not a precondition of, markets. Why these markets were run by women and boys, while men had to stay away from them, presents another problem that cannot now be answered.

Despite the meagerness of information concerning the Nicaraguans, certain broad interpretations of what is known are suggested. These people brought a Meso-America pattern into an area where a tropical-forest culture had been overlaid and partly repatterned by northern Andean features. They retained a strong priesthood, human sacrifice, a ceremonial calendar, markets, money, commerce, and elective officials, but apparently lost stone architecture, roads, canals, writing, and other features associated with the powerful states of Mexico. They retained, however, some culture elements not dependent upon the environment or the larger culture patterns, for example: ritual perforation of the tongue with thorns, the game of voladores (swinging from poles attached to a rope), and Nicoya-style polychrome pottery.

9. THE LENCA

The Lenca are the northernmost of the Indians whose culture was somewhat South American in character but whose language is Chibchan, of South American origin.

Aboriginal Lenca culture is virtually unknown, except through hints seen in the contemporary culture. This culture, investigated by Doris Stone,[7] is gradually undergoing mestizoization and local differentiation, and almost every township is developing some distinctive, modern characteristics. The Lenca, like other Central American Indians, have lost all state institutions since Conquest times and have only a village culture. Today, their settlements are laid out according to a Spanish plan. They consist of small adobe houses which surround a plaza containing the Catholic church and commercial buildings.

Slash-and-burn farming still prevails, and maize is the staple, although many European crops have been adopted. The Lenca have a few cattle, horses, goats, and sheep. They gather many wild plants, especially palm hearts and sprouts, and they hunt, often with the assistance of dogs. While fishing is unimportant, communal parties drug fish under the direction of the village head, who apportions the catch among the households. Women are banned from this activity.

Native manufacturing declined in the wake of the Spanish Conquest, although today there is some specialization in basketmaking in various villages. Weaving and cordage industries have died out, and pottery making has deteriorated.

Formerly, each village was an autonomous and endogamous unit whose chief and council controlled the land. The council was composed of the chief, a "curandero" (a curer, probably a shaman), a "priest-soothsayer," and a number of village elders. Intercommunity problems were settled either by negotiations between councils or by warfare.

Today, caciques still inherit their office in some towns. Most villages constitute a corporate, land-owning group, whose headmen allot land to individuals. In some instances, where land is worked communally, the chief distributes the produce among the people but keeps the surplus for trading, which he controls.

The aboriginal class system is defunct today, although there is loose stratification into an upper and a lower group. The chief, his family, and the village elders comprise the upper class, while laborers make up the lower.

The Lenca marry early in life, husbands being fourteen to eighteen years old and wives twelve to fourteen. The marriage is usually arranged by the parents and generally begins with a trial period during which the young couple become accustomed to each other. This period ends either with separation or celebration of a permanent marriage. During the first year or two after marriage, the young couple lives with the girl's parents. Polygyny is still prevalent in Lenca society, and it is not uncommon for a family head to have three wives.

The Lenca are nominally Catholic, but through this veneer extrude vestiges of aboriginal features, such as a reverent attitude toward the sun and belief that certain mountaintops are sacred. The highland Lenca make a pilgrimage each April to the hills of Lake Yojoa. Pre-Columbian copper bells have been found in a cave in these hills, suggesting that the cave was used for ceremonial purposes in ancient times. Planting and harvesting follow a rough ceremonial agricultural calendar of aboriginal origin, and socioreligious festivals combine native and European features: consumption of much chicha, burning of straw crosses in the fields or bonfires alongside the fields at harvest time, and offerings of copal incense to the four directions. The Lenca justify drunkenness by saying that it purifies the soul for planting the fields, but they insist on sexual abstinence at the same time. Because women are believed to endanger the crops by their impurity, only men may enter the fields. This belief creates little difficulty since men are the principal farmers.

Shamans serve principally as curers, when they use both supernatural and herbal remedies, but they also make sacrifices of copal or chickens at hilltop shrines. Formerly, they also foretold the future.

NOTES

1. Clifford Evans and Betty J. Meggers, "Formative Period Cultures in the Guayas Basin, Coastal Ecuador," *American Antiquity*, vol. 22, pp. 235–247, 1957. Clifford Evans and Betty J. Meggers, "Preliminary Report on Archeological Investigations in the Guayas Basin, Ecuador," *Cuadernos de historia y arqueología*, Año IV, vol. 55, no. 12, 1954. Emilio Estrada, *Valdivia: Un Sitio arqueológico Formativo en la costa de la provincia del Guayas, Ecuador,* Publicacíon del Museo Víctor Emilio Estrada, no. 1, [Ecuador] 1956.
2. Emilio Estrada, *Ultimas Civilizaciones Pre-Históricas de la Cuenca del Río Guayas,* Publicación del Museo Víctor Emilio Estrada, no. 2, [Ecuador] 1957. Emilio Estrada, *Los Huancavilcas: Ultimas Civilizaciones pre-históricas de la costa del Guayas,* Publicación del Museo Víctor Emilio Estrada, no. 3, [Ecuador] 1957.
3. Samuel K. Lothrop, "Coclé, an archaeological study of Central Panama. Part I. Historical background. Excavations at Sitio Conte. Artifacts and ornaments," *Memoirs,* Peabody Museum of Archaeology and Ethnology, Harvard University, vol. 7, Cambridge, 1937.
4. David Stout, *Handbook,* vol. 4.
5. Frederick Johnson, *Handbook,* vol. 4.
6. *Ibid.*
7. Doris Stone, *Handbook,* vol. 4.

▶ eight

THEOCRATIC CHIEFDOMS
OF VENEZUELA AND
THE GREATER ANTILLES

1. THE CORDILLERA ORIENTAL AND VENEZUELAN ANDES: INTERMEDIATE TYPES OF CHIEFDOMS

Native chiefdoms were found in much of Venezuela north of the Orinoco River, although enclaves of tropical-forest farmers occupied some of the lowlands adjoining Lake Maracaibo and nomadic hunters and gatherers lived along the Orinoco River on the southern borders of the chiefdoms. The distribution of the chiefdoms began immediately northeast of the Chibcha or Muisca of Colombia and, although broken by tropical-forest villages, followed the Cordillera Oriental of the Andes to the northeast, where it splits into two branches, one extending west of Lake Maracaibo and the other northeast to the Caribbean coast.

The best-known chiefdoms were found in the highlands among the Lache and Chitarera northeast of the Muisca, the Arhuaco of the Sierra Nevada de Santa Marta, and the Timotean-speaking peoples of the Venezuelan Andes. The lowland Corbago also had characteristics of chiefdoms.

Owing to very fragmentary knowledge of aboriginal culture and to different levels of sociocultural development within very small areas, it is difficult to classify many of the Indian societies. Some, like the northern Andean and Central American people, may have lost features characteristic of chiefdoms so soon after the Spanish Conquest that they were not recorded, but it is more likely that such people as the Tairona,

239

the Motilones to the west and southwest of Lake Maracaibo, and others between the Lache and Chitarera and the Timoteans were aboriginally tropical-forest villagers. The Chaké and their neighbors who occupied a large area of lowlands southwest of Lake Maracaibo between the two branches of the Andes were certainly of the village type.

Since the Venezuelan Andean chiefdoms were more kaleidoscopically varied than the Colombian chiefdoms, a classification based upon culture elements and culture areas would be impossibly complicated. The present chapter is concerned only with the chiefdoms of the Lache, Chitarera, Corbago, and Timoteans, about whom the Spaniards recorded some information.

Intensive farming among these groups was evidenced by use of irrigation and an impressive list of crops. The Timoteans had permanent and often terraced fields, stone-walled irrigation ditches 2 to 3 rods wide, cut through hills and rocks, and storage tanks. The Chitarera were called "Pueblo de los Silos" because of their underground bins for storing maize. They grew at least thirty different crops, which included both lowland and highland species.

Settlements were large and permanent. One Lache town was said to have 800 stone-walled houses, and a Corbago settlement to be of equal size. Towns of the Venezuelan Andes impressed the Spaniards because of their size, orderly arrangement, and central temple. Jamú settlements were divided into quarters and ornamented with flowering trees, fruit trees, and aviaries. But not all towns were so large. Chitarera villages had only twenty houses.

Causeways have been found in the plains south of the Venezuelan area, but these were probably built by a much earlier people.

The settlements or towns of these people were probably consolidated into chiefdoms more through religion than warfare or commerce. While the Indians were warlike, especially after the Spaniards entered their territory, there is little evidence that they took captives, practiced ritual human sacrifice (except that the Jamú sacrificed children to a water god), and cannibalism, or displayed human trophies. There was commerce in salt and jurao (a sodium carbonate from lakes used as a salt substitute), and thread and shell disks were used as money. There are no clear reports of commercial markets or warfare for conquest.

Religion took several forms. Among the Lache, it centered in a temple, the "House of the Sun," which faced east over the plains so that the sun reflected from gold objects placed outside it. It contained beads, shells and chests of gold, and served as a religious center and burial place.

The Indians of the Venezuelan Andes worshiped idols of thread, clay, wood, and stone in the town temple, but they also performed rites in the mountains and at lakes to the supreme being. Offerings included deer antlers and bones, cotton thread and cloth, beads, green stones, salt, cacao, incense, and sacrificed deer. The most famous temple was at Icaque, and it was the goal of pilgrims from far and wide. Its inner sanctum was entered only by priests, who communicated with the gods to inquire about the future.

Evidence bearing directly on the question of social classes is entirely absent. A strong managerial control may be inferred from the extent of irrigation works, while a powerful priesthood is implied by the temples, although little is recorded of either priests or shamans. Special status may be inferred from archaeological finds in the Venezuelan Andes of special stone tombs which contained seated or squatting burials.

A good many Andean elements were known to these people: certain food crops, irrigation, liana bridges, full-length cotton garments, coca, sun worship, and others. There is no mention of metallurgy, but a few gold objects were traded. In studying element distributions, however, it is not sufficient to note that areas did or did not share certain features. Ceramics in this area, for example, were painted in no more than two colors, whereas in the northern Andes three or four colors and in the Central Andes as many as eleven were used. Moreover, the Chitarera were named from their extensive use of calabash rather than pottery containers.

2. NORTHERN VENEZUELA: PREDOMINANTLY THEOCRATIC CHIEFDOMS

Chiefdoms occurred in northern Venezuela where the extension of the Andes becomes a lower and more broken range which runs east and west near the Caribbean coast. The better known of these are the Jirajara and their neighbors the Gayón, Coyón, Cuiba, and others and, adjoining them on the north, the Arawakan-speaking Caquetio. The Caquetio occupied both shores of the Gulf of Venezuela, the great expanse of Caribbean Sea frontage as far east as Lake Valencia and the Caracas River, and some of the Leeward Islands. Eastward from the Caracas River to the Delta of the Orinoco were a number of peoples, mostly Carib-speaking: the Quiriquire, Tacarigua, Teque, Toromaina, Tumuza, Chaima, Palenque, Cumanagoto, and Aruacay. All had characteristics of chiefdoms, although the western, central, and eastern portions of this region differed in certain particulars.

Almost all of these peoples were vanquished by the Spaniards early in the colonial period, and the area greatly depopulated. The surviving Indians retreated into the forests, where they were soon deculturated to an unstratified, simple village or folk level of society. The chroniclers, however, generally reported dense populations, cultivation of many crops, large towns, and political federations.

Subsistence. In western Venezuela, the Jirajara and Caquetio had plantations of manioc, maize, and sweet potatoes, and the Jirajara of the highlands irrigated their fields by artificial ditches which tapped mountain streams. These Indians also collected wild cactus fruits and agave leaves to supplement their harvests. Their basic fare was maize soup seasoned with ají. They hunted deer, tapirs, and smaller game with bows and arrows and fire surrounds. The Quiriquire depended more upon fish, which they drugged with barbasco.

The Caraca, Teque, Toromaina, and others farmed many crops but depended more upon meats than their western neighbors. They took anteaters, deer, peccaries, rabbits, tapirs, many birds, and lobsters. They raised mute dogs and kept domesticated bees in calabash hives. They stored considerable surpluses of dried meat and other food for use in time of war and general scarcity.

In the east, among the Palenque, Cumanagoto, Chaima, Aruacay, and others, bitter manioc was the staple food. The Cumanagoto had large orchards of coca bushes, arranged in even rows and watered by irrigation canals. Slash-and-burn agriculture was common, but the Aruacay cultivated low fields that were periodically enriched by the silt carried by the overflowing Orinoco.

When harvests were poor the Indians collected wild roots and fruits and gathered oysters. They relied considerably upon the rich game resources: tapirs, deer, peccaries, porcupines, anteaters, rabbits, rats, mice, tortoises, iguanas, and many other small animals and birds. They used bows and arrows to hunt large game and nets and snares for birds and small game. In the llanos, as many as four hundred hunters might assemble to surround game with fire. Fish were even more important than game, and were taken in the rivers, lakes, and sea by means of arrows, pronged spears, harpoons, baskets, traps, and nets or by a semicircle of swimmers who drove them onto the beach. At night fish were attracted to canoes by torches. Surplus foods were preserved by smoking, salting, or cooking and pounding into a paste or powder.

Considerable trade was carried on by northern Venezuelan peoples, who used dugouts on the larger rivers and the coastal waters. The Quiriquire traded fish and maize to the Curarigua, Jirajara, and Nirgua for gold. Inland traders exchanged maize, slaves, and other goods with the coastal Chiribichi and Cumaná in return for fish, coca, and salt. The Curiana bartered gold for pearls obtained from a distant coastal region.

Settlements. The people around Lake Maracaibo built pile dwellings offshore to protect themselves against enemies, to escape the myriad mosquitoes that infest the hot interior, and to have access to fish and shellfish. In villages built on the land away from the lake, houses were arranged in rows facing each other along wide streets. Jirajara and

Caquetio houses were clustered in small groups near the cultivated fields in order to guard the crops against marauding animals. Roads connected villages and ran out to the surrounding fields.

The central region is reported to have had palisaded villages which were defended by a special leader who was appointed by the chief and who delegated a body of men for village defense.

Palenque and Pariagoto towns had two or three rings of palisades made of tree trunks that often took root and grew. The trunks were tightly bound with lianas, but had loopholes for shooting arrows. One such town was said to have been laid out in streets and plazas, among which were several storehouses and the cacique's harem of two hundred wives, while outside the village were additional storehouses for food, maize, and pineapple chicha.

Post-Conquest change in settlements is seen in the case of the Aruacay, whose villages were small in the seventeenth century but in the sixteenth century had as many as two hundred large houses.

Sociopolitical organization. The Jirajara constituted a chiefdom of several semiautonomous subgroups (Nirgua, Cuiba, Curarigua, Coyón), each under a local chief, who recognized the over-all leadership of a war chief. Similarly, the Caquetio were divided into a number of subgroups which recognized the authority of a paramount chief. The latter was accorded deferential treatment, such as being carried in a special hammock, and he was thought to have power to bring fertility to the crops. He received special treatment at death, but unlike the suttee burials of the northern Andes, this consisted of desiccating his body and eventually powdering the bones and drinking them mixed with masato.

An elaborate political structure is ascribed the Caquetio. In addition to the over-all chief and the lesser chieftains, there was a class of nobles consisting of distinguished warriors and a class of wealthy men whose status seems to have been hereditary. Some class fluidity is indicated, however, in that success in warfare led to accession to the nobility.

In the north-central coastal region, the Toromaina, Teque, Arvaco, and Meregoto also formed federations of local groups under the leadership of a paramount chief. While their federations were strengthened during the middle of the sixteenth century by resistance to the Spaniards, a tendency toward federation, at least in time of war, was aboriginal. Among the Caraca, whose subdivisions federated for military action, warriors formed a special class within which their rank was indicated by tattooed insignia. Among the Maracapana, the chief had power of life and death over his military appointees as well as over poachers caught on reserves set aside for him.

In addition to the classes of chiefs, warrior-nobles, and commoners, there were slaves who consisted of captive children whose lives had

been spared. They held the lowest socioeconomic status and were probably the property of chiefs and nobles, who might transfer them to
their friends as gifts or barter them in the market.

Among the Aruacay, Piritú, and Palenque of eastern Venezuela, age
as well as heredity was the basis of status. Old men were so greatly
respected that younger men did not sit in their presence, and they often
formed a council having judicial powers. The Piritú had hereditary chiefs
whose office passed in the patrilineal line to the oldest son, but among
the Paria the paramount chief and five subchiefs were elected each year.
The Aruacay paramount chief, who seems to have worn a beard as a
badge of office, ruled over nine subchiefs, each of whom was in charge
of a barrio in the large town.

Great pomp surrounded leading chieftains. They were carried in litters,
which were sometimes carved and embellished with gold plates. The
chief of one Palenque group delivered his decrees from an artificial
mound within his palisaded stronghold, which commoners were forbidden to enter. His harem of two hundred women was guarded by
eunuchs.

A chief's power was very great in matters of group interest, and he
had power of life and death over those who broke rules such as fishing
without his permission. Individual or interfamily disputes, however, were
often resolved by blood revenge by the families concerned. A chief's
power depended somewhat upon the size of his polygynous household,
his wealth in gold and canoes, his ability to recount noble deeds of his
people, and his magical powers. It was also enhanced if the chief also
served as shaman.

Special treatment was accorded nobles at death. The Chiribichi desiccated the bodies of nobles and hung them in the house, the skull being
given to the man's principal wife. The bodies of common people were
roasted so that the fat could be collected and drunk with beer when
they were buried.

The warlike Jirajara dominated Lake Maracaibo in their swift canoes,
fighting with bows and poisoned arrows and with clubs. They and the
Caquetio sacrificed human beings who were, presumably, war captives.
The Jirajara resisted the Spaniards until they were forcibly subjugated
in 1614 and, along with many other peoples, incorporated into the system
of encomienda. Some groups, like the Caquetio, however, retreated to
the forested region of the interior.

In central Venezuela, intensive native warfare was reported by the
Spaniards, and it is indicated by the palisaded villages. War objectives
other than taking slaves are not recorded. Only the Maracapana practiced
cannibalism, eating the viscera of executed enemy chiefs, but other
groups sometimes took body parts as trophies. Confederacies were solidi-

fied by the Spanish invasion, but were finally broken late in the sixteenth century.

The Spanish chroniclers left the purpose of warfare unclear, although they described its external features. Warfare was carried on in eastern Venezuela and Trinidad among the Cumaná, Piritú, Chiribichi, Cumanagoto, and Palenque, where the erection of palisades, the posting of night vigils, and the maintenance of arsenals attest its importance. Some cannibalism was reported, but it was a minor war objective. It was said that the chief of a Palenque village kept an arsenal of bows and arrows for 10,000 men and had a patrol of 600 men constantly on duty. The Cumaná and Piritú formed temporary military alliances. In preparing for hostilities, people drank a brew of tobacco and coca in order to foresee the outcome of battle. Women participated in warfare and were said to have handled bows and arrows as well as men. A ranking within the warrior class is suggested, since the more important Aruacay men wore puma- or bearskins, and those of Trinidad, gold breastplates.

Religion and shamanism. Features of a priest-temple-idol cult occurred in northwestern Venezuela, especially among the Jirajara and Caquetio, but the full complex was not reported anywhere. The Caquetio had community temples but kept idols in individual households, while chiefs shared religious power with shamans. The latter officiated as priests in offering sacrifices to the principal gods, the sun and moon, and serving as oracles in foretelling future events and predicting the results of warfare through communicating with the gods. In addition to these public functions, the priest-shamans cured sickness in individuals and practiced divination. The Jirajara and Caquetio as well as certain Carib in Venezuela practiced human sacrifice—the source of the victims is unknown—and offered the blood to the sun god. The Caraca sacrificed to their gods before going to war and fasted for a whole day.

Among the easternmost groups of Venezuela, where chieftainship and prestige based on age and election seemed to be competing with inherited status, there was no trace of the priest-temple-idol complex, although this complex was present among the adjoining hunting-and-gathering Warrau of the Orinoco Delta. The sun and moon were the major deities, and lunar eclipses and thunder and lightning were believed caused by the sun's anger. Each year, the people ceremonially ate roasted deer, and in another rite dancers carried wooden effigies of fish. The purpose of these acts is not known, but offerings of first fruits, fresh fish, pearls, coral, and other objects were no doubt fertility rites.

As in tropical-forest villages, shamans were often village headmen owing to their supernatural power. They were trained during two years of confinement and then became members of the shamans' fraternity, living apart and holding their own ceremonies. They could become werejaguars, and they caused sickness, but they cured illness by removing the malignant object or spirit from the patient's body. They also served as seers, calling upon their spirit-helpers to foretell harvests, eclipses, and other matters of community interest.

3. THE ANTILLEAN ARAWAK: HIERARCHIES OF DEITIES AND MEN

Three cultural types are represented in the Antillean Islands: the hunting-and-gathering Ciboney, the tropical-forest horiticultural Carib villages, and the Arawakan chiefdoms. At the time of the Spanish Conquest, the bulk of the population of the Greater Antilles consisted of the Taino Arawak, who lived in large permanent villages, carried on intensive agriculture, in some cases irrigated, and had a hierarchy of social classes and powerful chiefs based upon a parallel heirarchy of spirits, or zemis. The Arawakan groups occupied most of the Greater Antilles—Cuba, the Bahamas, Jamaica, Hispaniola (now the Dominican Republic and Haiti), Puerto Rico, and the Virgin Islands—but there were enclaves of Guanahatabey, or Ciboney, on western Cuba and southern Haiti (Chapter Fourteen, section 14). The Lesser Antilles were occupied by Caribs (Chapter Twelve, section 2), who are presumed to have driven out a former Arawakan population about a century before the arrival of the Spaniards, but enclaves of Arawak remained in the Barbados and Tobago. Trinidad, although an island, belongs culturally with the chiefdoms of the Venezuelan mainland.

Fairly extensive archaeological work has been done in the Caribbean Islands, especially in the Greater Antilles. Rouse[1] has tentatively reconstructed the prehistory of the region in three major periods. It is fairly certain that the Guanahatabey, or Ciboney, reached the Antilles before the Arawak arrived in the area and inhabited at least part of the larger islands. Their origin is unknown, although some scholars believe they migrated from Florida. Next came the Arawak, who largely displaced the comparatively primitive Guanahatabey. The Arawak were in turn driven from most of the Lesser Antilles and from parts of the other islands by the unrelenting attacks of the Carib, who were the last to appear in the insular area. It seems certain that the Arawak reached the Greater Antilles from the mainland of South America. While Cuba is near Yucatán and the Arawak have in common with Meso-America the ceremonial ball game and court, their culture and language relate to South America. Moreover, the inhabitants of westernmost Cuba nearest to Yucatán were the hunting-and-gathering Guanahatabey.

The native population of the Arawak had a density equal to that of the northern Andes, and there were many large settlements, some of which had 3,000 persons. Owing to the early Spanish settlement of the islands and the establishment of repartimientos, the Indians suffered rapid population decline. Forced to work in the gold mines, many lost their lives. This gave rise to the leyenda negra, or black legend, of the Spaniards who opposed the policy in the area, and it was said that the Indians had become extinct within one or two generations. While there was undoubtedly a sharp population decline, it is not true that the Indians became extinct. It is more important that the chiefdoms quickly disintegrated and that the surviving Indians were either absorbed into Spanish life or fled to the mountains and later mixed with Negro slaves. The encomienda, or indirect rule designed to exact tribute, could not operate in an area which offered little surplus gold, the Spaniards' principal objective, or other produce desired by Spain. Today, only slight vestiges of Indian culture survive in a few isolated islands.

Prehistoric circular stone object from Puerto Rico, sometimes called a "collar" or "yoke" but possibly used as a belt in ceremonial ball games. (After J. Walter Fewkes, "A Prehistoric Island Culture Area of America," Bureau of American Ethnology Annual Report 34, 1922.)

Subsistence. The Taino Arawak, though practicing slash-and-burn cultivation probably raised two crops of certain plants each year. They fertilized the manioc and maize fields with both urine and wood ash, and in the southwestern part of Haiti they operated extensive irrigation systems. Bitter manioc was probably, but not certainly, introduced after the Spanish Conquest. Just as on the continent, it was made into a pulp on scraping boards, the poison removed by means of a press (tipiti), and the flour cooked on a clay platter to make beijú cakes. Maize was relatively important as a staple, while potatoes, arrowroots, beans, peppers, avocados, papayas, and coconuts and peanuts are also reported to have been pre-Spanish. The modern people of Puerto Rico grew a considerable number of other tropical fruits and root crops which early Spanish sources strongly suggest to have been aboriginal.

Hunting was unimportant since the Antilles lack the mammals of the continent, but a rodent (agouti), birds, reptiles, worms, spiders, and insects went into the ever-simmering pepperpot which was so characteristic of Arawak and tropical-forest people of northern South America.

Iguanas and a certain variety of agouti were special delicacies reserved for chiefs. No domesticated animals were used for meat, but the Arawak raised mute dogs and hunting birds.

Fish were relatively scarce owing to the absence of continental shelves, but some were taken by hooks and lines, nets of cotton thread weighted with stone sinkers, drugs, multipronged spears, and weirs, while crabs and shellfish were gathered on the beach. Storage pens were built for fish and turtles.

Settlements. Owing to the importance of farming as well as the danger of Carib attack, people lived away from the shore. Houses were probably somewhat dispersed, and settlements varied from single dwellings holding several families to towns having as many as 1,000 houses and a population of 3,000 as in Haiti. Each village had one or more ball courts, which were often stone-slabbed and adjoined the chief's house. Outside the village stood the chief's storehouses and his temple, where he kept his zemis, or spirit images.

Sociopolitical organization. The island of Hispaniola was divided into six chiefdoms, of which five were Taino and one Ciguayo. If the aboriginal population was 100,000, the average chiefdom had some 16,500 persons. In Puerto Rico, which is presumed to have had 50,000 inhabitants and eighteen chiefdoms, the average is about 2,800 persons. In Hispaniola, each district or chiefdom was governed by a supreme chief and was subdivided into as many as thirty smaller territories, each with a subchief. This would give an average of 500 to 600 persons per territory. If the territories consisted of as many as seventy to eighty villages, each under a headman, the villages must have been very small. No doubt only larger districts were divided into so many villages, for the village chief was accredited considerable dignity. He organized the daily work of his people and had despotic power over them. He determined the distribution of surplus goods, officiated as host to visiting dignitaries, managed intervillage affairs, and led fiestas, singing, and dancing. The chiefs of territories had power over many villages, while the paramount chief controlled all the lesser chiefs of his district. The chiefs received no tribute but had power to requisition surplus crops and men for military undertakings. They judged crimes and dealt out punishment, often death sentences. Chiefs had many prerogatives such as use of special houses, five titles by which they were addressed, unusually large canoes or litters in which they traveled, and special food, dress, and ornamentation.

Chieftainship was inherited matrilineally by the oldest son of the chief's oldest sister. In the absence of heirs in the female line, the chief was succeeded by his own son or female relatives. If there were no suitable heirs, however, the successor was chosen by the people.

Just beneath chiefs in rank were the "nobles" (mitayos), who assisted the chiefs in the management of the daily routine of the villages and who attended war councils. To judge by the Andean meaning of mitayo, these men were probably privileged servants rather than genuine nobles.

Commoners, who performed most of the work, and slaves, who assisted them, comprised the other two social classes. Chiefs lived with their wives and children in a large, rectangular, gable-roofed, single-room, pole-and-thatch house, but several families of commoners occupied a single smaller, round, conical-roofed house. Household furniture consisted of platform beds and carved wooden or stone stools for chiefs and nobles and hammocks for commoners. Equipment included gourd containers, hunting and fishing gear, storage places, and cooking utensils.

The social classes tended to be endogamous. Despite matrilineal inheritance, postmarital residence seems to have been patrilocal. Polygyny prevailed and was not confined to the upper classes, except in so far as wealth determined the number of wives a man could support.

Bride price was paid to the father of the woman, or else bride service was given before the marriage. Chiefs paid the price in strings of stone beads and plates of tumbaga (a copper-gold alloy acquired in trade) over a period of a month, after which the marriage was celebrated.

Economic organization was little developed. The chiefs controlled economic surplus through management of distribution of goods rather than through tribute. Despite this control, there was much trade, even in the absence of markets, between districts and islands. Manioc, pepper, stools, wooden bowls, pottery, gold, and carved stone were exchanged. Gonave Island specialized in woodwork, Hispaniola in gold production. Objects of tumbaga, or guanín (an alloy of gold and copper but perhaps other metals), silver, and gold came from the mainland.

Warfare. The Ciguayo were the most warlike of the Haitian Arawaks, but the Taino were relatively peaceful among themselves and with their neighbors on other islands. Wars generally resulted from disputes over territorial rights or refusal to pay the bride price. Among commoners, blood revenge for murder, but not tribal warfare, resulted in feuds.

During hostilities nobles acted as bodyguards for chiefs. All men took part in the fighting and, before engaging in hostilities, painted their bodies red, put on miniature stone zemis (images of guardian spirits), and danced. Part of a warrior's training was to practice dodging missiles. An attacking force attempted to ambush or surprise the enemy. Spears and spear throwers, javelins, clubs, and stones were the most common weapons. Bows and poisoned arrows were used by the Ciguayo and the Taino nobles.

Neither the Carib nor the Spaniards had much difficulty in defeating Arawakan troops.

Religion and shamanism. The religion of the Taino Arawak was based upon the concept that the control of nature spirits and ancestors gave a person supernatural power of different kinds and degrees. The spirits were represented by idols of wood, bone, cotton, clay, and gold, all called zemis. A person might have one to ten or more zemis. Commoners housed their zemis in their own dwellings, while chiefs kept theirs in special temples outside the village. Zemis were also placed in sacred caves, their representations were carved on rocks in the form of petroglyphs, and their symbols were painted on the owner's body, carved in jewelry, and used to decorate utensils. Zemis usually took the form of

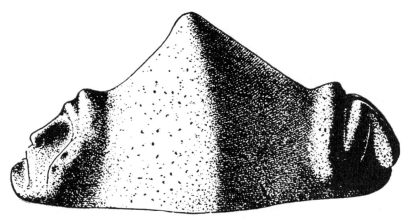

Three-pointed stone object, Puerto Rico, possibly representing a zemi or deity. (After Fewkes, 1922.)

grotesque anthropomorphic figures with exaggerated sex organs, but there were many animal forms. The bones of ancestors also became zemis. Most zemis were manufactured according to supernatural dictates and were representations of the dramatis personae of dreams and visions.

Since a chief's zemi was regarded as the most powerful of all and was given festivals by the chief's followers, his authority and the power of his zemi were closely related. In order to acquire power from his zemi, the chief inhaled snuff, which induced visions that revealed the zemi's will. Each person extolled the power of his zemi, but since zemis could be stolen or transferred, some were obviously considered more powerful than others. Each zemi had a name and a particular history which its owner sang. There was specialization in the powers of zemis, such as control of weather, crops, hunting, childbirth, and so forth.

A shaman's power also came from his zemis, but otherwise he cured in such typical ways as sucking the disease-causing "object" from the patient. An unsuccessful shaman was beaten, but not killed, by the family of a person who died under his treatment. His recovery was attributed to the power of his zemi, which turned into a snake and licked his wounds. While chiefs and their assistants had supernatural power and were sometimes shamans, this was not necessarily the case.

Offerings made annually to the chief's zemis in a postharvest ceremony in which the whole village participated was a major manifestation of group religion. The people entered the village temple while the chief beat a large drum at its entrance. The chief's attendants then dressed the zemis in ceremonial costume, and the people vomited to purify themselves. (The ritual emetic was also used by the Indians of the southeastern United States.) Inside the temple, the people handed bread to the attendants, who presented it to the zemis. They then danced, sang, and praised the chief's zemis. At the end of the ceremony, the attendants gave pieces of manioc bread to the family heads, who kept them until the next annual ceremony.

While Antillean Arawak societies were clearly classifiable as chiefdoms, the importance of the parallel hierarchy of chiefs and zemis together with the negligible role of warfare is found nowhere else. The idea of temples and of idols or effigies of supernatural beings may have reached the Antilles from continental South America, but conceptually the zemis are more like glorified guardian spirits than the kinds of deities usually associated with temples.

Other continental traits diminished in the Greater Antilles. Clothing was restricted to genital coverings and aprons. Ornaments were not numerous. Metallurgy consisted only of placer mining and cold-hammering of gold. Canoes were large but lacked sails. The Taino wove blankets, but they netted or twined rather than wove cotton for cloth and hammocks, and they apparently lacked knowledge of bark cloth. Their pottery, stonework, and woodwork were unexceptional in variety or aesthetic features. And yet, owing to farm surplus, the Antillean Arawak were able to develop essentially theocratic chiefdoms and hereditary social classes to a degree unknown to most of their far-flung linguistic kinsmen on the continent.

NOTES

1. Irving Rouse, *Handbook*, vol. 4.

nine

CHIEFDOMS OF EASTERN BOLIVIA: TROPICAL- FOREST CHIEFDOMS

1. GENERAL FEATURES

There were several groups of Indians between the Bolivian highlands, the Guaporé River, and the Xaray marshes of the upper Paraguay River to the east whose culture consisted of a combination of elements derived from the tropical forests and from the Central Andes but whose economic, social, political, and religious patterns resembled those of the chiefdoms of the Circum-Caribbean area more than those of their immediate neighbors. These people have been designated "Sub-Andean." The presence of chiefdoms in eastern Bolivia is attributable to a high subsistence level, which permitted the development of dense populations, large communities, and some social and economic specialization.

The better known of these Indians are the Mojo, Bauré, Paressí, and Manasí, but the little-known Xaray apparently also belonged to the type. The first three spoke an Arawakan language. The Manasí spoke Chiquito, a Macro-Ge language. These Arawakan dialects were very different from those of the primitive Campa, Amuesha, and other Indians farther north in the Montaña. These chiefdoms did not form a solid block but were interspersed among riverine horticultural villages and even nomadic forest hunters in the very heterogeneous area of eastern Bolivia.

In horticulture, housing, village composition, and certain sociopolitical and religious features, these Indians resembled the Amazonian people.

252

They farmed without irrigation or terracing, and they made considerable use of wild game, fish, and vegetable foods. They built pole-and-thatch houses which were like those of the Amazon but which were grouped in villages that far exceeded the usual size of the latter. For example, the Mojo were said to have had villages of 400 houses and 1,000 persons.

Like the riverine horticultural villages, the communities were ordinarily autonomous and were led by chiefs whose authority, although hereditary, was greatly augmented if they also possessed shamanistic power. But, like the chiefdoms of the Circum-Caribbean area, these villages showed a tendency toward class structure. There are reports of a

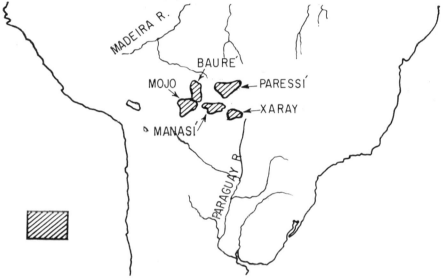

The chiefdoms of eastern Bolivia.

slave class, but this class may have originated after the Indians became slavers for the Spaniards. There was also a tendency toward sociopolitical integration of several villages, especially among the Paressí and Xaray, who are accredited federations of several villages.

Religious patterns combined riverine horticultural and Circum-Caribbean features. The centralization of village religious activities in the men's house, as among the Mojo and Paressí, and in the chief's house, as among the Manasí, is Amazonian; and so is the use of sacred musical instruments which are associated with a men's cult and kept in the religious house secret from women. On the other hand, the prominence of village deities, their representation by idols, the priestly function of the shaman as ceremonial leader, the oracular services of the shaman, and the use of the men's or chief's house as a kind of temple are Circum Caribbean in character.

2. THE MOJO AND BAURÉ

The Mojo occupy a large territory, which extends from the Andean foothills eastward through the Mojos Plains to the fertile riverine lands of the Bauré just west of the Guaporé River. At the beginning of the historic period this region was densely populated, and the inhabitants were tightly nucleated in well-fortified villages, a fact which indicates the great importance of warfare, even though we know little of its nature. A 1715 census set the over-all population for the province of Mojos at 18,000.

This large, sedentary population was supported by cultivation of sweet manioc, maize, sweet potatoes, squashes, gourds, beans, peanuts, and a variety of tropical fruits, including papayas. After the Spanish Conquest, sugar cane, tobacco, and bananas were adopted. Gallery forests, which were not inundated during the rainy season, provided the best farm land. Early Spanish accounts express amazement at the size of the farms and the intervillage roadways with bordering canals that were built across the plains.

Both the Mojo and the Bauré supplemented their harvests by collecting wild plants and by hunting and fishing. On the open plains, they held communal hunts and took large numbers of animals with the help of dogs and fire drives. These hunts were directed by the village chief, who later distributed the kill among the people. Forest hunting was better carried out by smaller parties or by individual hunters, who stalked such game as monkeys and birds with blowguns and poisoned darts.

As among many riverine horticulturalists, jaguar hunting was of special interest. Jaguars, like most carniverous animals in the Americas, were not hunted for food, but, since they are exceedingly dangerous, a hunter who killed one with a spear or bow and arrow achieved very high status. The Bauré sometimes captured jaguars in pitfalls and accorded the privilege of making the kill to the chief. Successful jaguar hunts occasioned ceremonial celebrations; in fact, a jaguar cult was a major social and religious feature among the Mojo.

Both peoples also hunted game with various kinds of traps, and after they obtained horses from the missions the Mojo lassoed game and even jaguars from horseback.

The Spaniards introduced ducks and chickens to the Mojo and Bauré. Wild cattle also became a major source of food, but like most other South American Indians, these people failed to become cattle breeders. No doubt the reason for this failure is that genuine stock raising presupposes exchange in some kind of market economy. So long as the Indians retained an aboriginal culture and a subsistence economy, there was no reason to treat livestock as other than wild game. Later, when South American Indians became sufficiently acculturated and assimilated into the national economies to become cattlemen, they were known as vaqueros, or cowboys, rather than as Indians.

Under the subsistence economy, fish were extremely important. They were taken by millions when the recession of annual floods left them stranded. Fishermen used clubs, spears, arrows, drugs, and baskets, and at night they attracted fish to their canoes with torches. The missionaries attempted to introduce fish nets, but the nets became entangled in the many branches and logs which floated down the streams and had little value.

The native technology of the Mojo and Bauré was superior in certain ways to that of Amazonia, and it shared some of the excellence of the Central Andes. It is very possible that the ample food production supported not only a class of chiefs but special artisans, who devoted full or part time to their crafts. In any event, pottery, basketry, wood carving, weaving, and featherwork were all highly developed in native times and were praised for their quality and beauty by the early chroniclers. Metalworking, however, was probably not native, although objects of gold and silver had found their way from the Andes to this area in prehistoric times and European metal goods later acquired in trade were melted down and recast to make a number of baubles of native design. Smelting of ore seems not to have been practiced at any time.

The rich natural resources combined with intensive farming made possible a dense population. This population was grouped in villages, which formed the basic socioeconomic unit. Mojo settlements were evidently very large, even allowing for exaggeration in the accounts of 400 houses. Where land was inundated each year, these villages stood on high ground where accumulated refuse created artificial platforms. Along the riverbanks, where there were no such high places, sites for cooking fires were built upon elevated, earth-covered platforms. In spots which floods did not reach, houses were arranged around a central plaza. Bauré villages were reported to be larger than those of the Mojo and to be well fortified.

Village members cooperated in cultivating certain fields among the Bauré, and the same may have been true of the great Mojo "farms." The community also cooperated under the chief in hunting and fishing. Palisades, moats, and pitfalls in paths approaching Bauré villages show that warfare was another important factor in consolidating the community.

While each village was largely autonomous, the great causeways with bordering canals that connected Mojo villages obviously required the cooperative work of members of different communities under some kind of authority, however limited and transient. These causeways were built above flood level so as to facilitate foot travel during the rainy season, while the canals could be used for canoe travel. Small streams were crossed by bridges.

Some kind of class structure is indicated in statements that there were "chiefs" whose families constituted a nobility of status superior to that of the ordinary villagers. There may also have been an incipient class of slaves, consisting primarily of captives from enemy groups. Captives were permitted to marry into the village but were held in low esteem. It is difficult to appraise the social role and status of slaves in the Indian villages, however, because the Spanish colonists' demand for bound labor on their farms and in their mines stimulated extensive slaving and may have created a servile class among the Indians that was unknown in native times.

The position of village chief was inherited patrilineally, but the chief's authority depended more upon his personal qualities than hereditary rights. Moreover, it was greatly increased if he was also a shaman. Chiefs were accorded various forms of respect, and they were apparently the only men who had plural wives. The chief was supposed to keep peace within his village, and he probably directed military operations. In order to ensure success in warfare, he observed certain taboos and performed several rites. A chief who had shamanistic power also had important priestly functions in group ceremonies.

These Indians believed in supernatural beings who were manifest in natural phenomena, especially in the sky, and who controlled the weather, crops, and game animals. Andean beliefs are indicated in the concept of gods who inhabit lagoons and trees, in the reverence accorded ancestors, and in the strong attachment of living people to the burial place of the ancestors. A host of minor spirits inhabited the workaday world of the people, and they were the recipients of every morsel of food which dropped to the ground.

The Mojo are remarkable for their jaguar cult and their drinking houses or temples. While the jaguar is feared and attributed supernatural power throughout a great part of the tropical forests and is an important god in the Central Andes, the Mojo made it the central deity of a special cult. Cult members were men who had been wounded by a jaguar and thus became shamans. Furthermore, they conducted rites connected with jaguar spirits, directed the village in magic to ward off impending imminent attacks by jaguars, and throughout life maintained close contact with the cult animal. They also ritually purified a hunter who had killed a jaguar and gave him the secret name of the beast he had killed, a name which he carried thereafter.

The ritual of the jaguar cult and other ceremonies were held in a special house or temple which was built cooperatively by all the men of the village. Women were forbidden to enter this house during its construction, but subsequently they participated in certain ceremonies held in it. The temple housed human trophies, jaguar skulls and paws, and probably also the sacred musical instruments which, as among many peoples of Amazonia, were kept secret from women. The temple has appropriately been called a "drinking house" since a principal ceremonial act was the heavy drinking of chicha as a libation to the deities.

Each village held ten or twelve ceremonies a year, the new moon being considered the best time for them. Quantities of chicha made from many fruits and vegetables were provided for the villagers and their guests from other villages. During a ceremony, the priests adorned themselves in feathers, cut their hair, offered chicha to the gods, and made long orations while the people drank. Female dancers and entertainers were permitted to join the drinking. Disputes that arose between men in the course of the festivities were settled by wrestling.

The ceremonial leaders were not only priests but shamans, that is, men who controlled certain spirit-helpers. As priests, they officiated in the community ceremonies and fasted. They also served as village oracles in answering questions and discovering thieves, but in rendering these services they called upon their spirit-helpers rather than the community gods. In this respect they differed from the principal Manasí shaman-priests, who dealt directly with the major village gods.

The shaman's role as doctor was entirely separate from that of priest. Illness was thought to be caused by spirits or by intrusion of a malignant object into the body. The shaman consulted his spirits who, for a fee, revealed what drugs might relieve the malady; or he massaged and blew smoke on the patient and then sucked out the object that caused the illness.

3. THE PARESSÍ

The Paressí occupied Mato Grosso as far east as the upper reaches of the Paraguay River. Paressí groups warred among themselves, and they raided neighboring peoples, such as the Nambicuara, to take slaves. The history of these people during the eighteenth and nineteenth centuries is one of frequent contacts with white slavers, adventurers, prospectors, rubber gatherers, and finally with Brazilian government officials, settlements, schools, and the communications system. After their territory was officially opened up to exploitation and colonization and the people were put in government settlements at the beginning of the twentieth century, they were quickly acculturated, and some of them were even employed by the government as telegraph operators. Epidemics seem to have been the main factor in the tremendous decline in population.

Aboriginally, the Paressí cultivated extensive fields of maize, beans, and sweet potatoes, and they grew pineapples to some extent. In recent times, they have been moved south from their ancestral habitat to less fertile uplands, where they occupy the gallery forests and shift their fields and settlements periodically. Today, they continue to cultivate a large number of plants, most of which are native. They are skillful hunters, although game is scarce. They use bows, stalking, ambush, fire drives, decoys, imitation animal calls, traps, pitfalls, and hunting dogs. The aboriginal Paressí kept bees, and today they have dogs, chickens, pigs, and ducks. Their fishing resources do not compare with those of the Mojo because the rivers are shallow. Nonetheless, they shoot fish with arrows in flooded areas and use drugs and metal hooks obtained through trade.

The extent of Paressí depopulation and social change during historic times is indicated by alterations in the character of the villages. Native villages consisted of ten to thirty multifamily dwellings, but early twentieth-century villages had only one or two communal houses, each sheltering about six elementary families. Formerly, each settlement had a ceremonial house where idols and sacred trumpets were preserved. Today, such houses are not built.

Native villages were autonomous in most matters, and each was under the dual leadership of a chief and a shaman. As among the Mojo, however, the two positions were often held by the same man. Among the early Paressí, several villages were sometimes federated, and their chiefs owed allegiance to an over-all leader. The chiefs no doubt controlled work parties needed to construct the roads which connected the different Paressí villages, and they were probably military leaders.

In recent times, the sociopolitical structure has been simplified. Federations, or incipient states, have been destroyed, and chiefs are little more than leaders of village ceremonies. The inhabitants of neighboring settlements maintain peaceful trade relations with one another. Since the nineteenth century, some of the Paressí have been attributed a class of captives who performed menial services, such as clearing land and building houses. As among the Mojo, assignment of an economic role to captives probably resulted from the slave trade with the European settlers.

The Paressí resembled the Mojo in their practice of child betrothal. A Paressí man might arrange to marry an infant girl and support her until she came of age, when the marriage was consummated.

The Paressí supernatural world consisted of various spirits which inhabited natural phenomena. The most important were the serpent spirit and his wife. The former was represented by a trumpet and the latter by a flageolet. Both instruments, together with other god's images or symbols, were kept in the sacred men's house, which women were barred from entering. There is no evidence that these sacred instruments were associated with ancestors of kin groups, as they were associated with localized lineages among many peoples of the northwest Amazon or clans among the Mundurucú. Paressí society was much less kin-based than the tropical-forest villages. Ceremonies for the serpent spirit, however, resembled many rites among the nomadic hunters and gatherers and the tropical-forest villages in its exclusively masculine nature. Although the serpent was a community deity, it was propitiated in the men's house or temple by offerings of meat, which the men consumed during the ceremonies. In these ceremonies, men danced with the trumpet and flageolet, stamped, sang, and drank large quantities of manioc chicha. Unlike the Mojo, they excluded women from the proceedings.

Shamans were primarily curers. They were believed to be endowed with the power of flying, and possessed a great store of knowledge. In treating sickness, they blew tobacco smoke on their patients and administered medicinal remedies.

The dead were buried with food and their possessions in their huts, which were then abandoned. The relatives mourned and fasted. Souls of the deceased had to traverse difficult routes to their final resting places in the sky.

4. THE MANASÍ

The Manasí formerly inhabited about fifty villages in the Mamoré Basin, and their culture was much like that of the Arawakan Mojo and Paressí. Today, the Manasí have disappeared as a cultural entity.

The Manasí were good tropical farmers, but, like their neighbors, they also hunted, fished, and gathered wild plant foods. Their subsistence, however, was more adequate than that of tropical-forest villages, for it supported chiefs and priests who grew no food and performed few or no productive functions.

A Manasí village consisted of a number of extended households, which were under the leadership of a head chief and several subordinate chiefs. Early Spanish sources list the following social statuses: chiefs, priests, shamans, subordinate leaders, and common people. While the chiefs apparently constituted a hereditary class, shamans probably achieved status through visionary experiences. There is no record that the Manasí took slaves for exchange in trade or had a slave class in their own society.

Chieftainship in the village was inherited in the male line. A chief had a polygynous household, and his principal wife exercised much authority over the other women of the village, while his young heir apparent bossed the village youths. To succeed his father, the young man had to lead a successful war expedition. The succession to chieftainship, however, took place gradually, since the son relieved the father from time to time of various duties until he was in full charge. The retired chief, however, retained his former prestige throughout life. The final induction of the young man to full authority was celebrated with a great deal of ritual.

A chief had considerable regulative power in Manasí society. It was his duty to chastise wrongdoers. Hunters and fishermen had to obtain his permission to leave the settlement. The common people addressed him in very formal language. The chief organized lay ceremonies, such as drinking bouts, and sent messengers to invite guests to participate in them. He and his family occupied a large house which stood in the village plaza and dominated the settlement. This edifice, rather than a special men's house, served as the place for village meetings and as the temple. The common people built this house, they tilled special fields for the chief's family, and they offered him their first fruits and a share of their fish and game. At his demise, the chief was buried with special pomp and general mourning.

The Manasí clearly present a case in which the ruling family, and possibly a small upper class of chiefs, could be maintained and perpetuated as hereditary institutions because of food surplus. Among the Manasí, probably more than among the Mojo or Paressí, families and possibly classes with specialized, noneconomic status and role had begun to emerge. While the Manasí chiefs were not comparable to the large hereditary classes that constituted bureaucracies of priests and rulers of the Central Andes, they were very similar to the emergent hereditary classes among the chiefdoms of the Circum-Caribbean area.

Manasí religious patterns are significant because they were organized partly around important community gods who were worshiped in a temple cult and served by priests. The separation of priest and shaman is somewhat clearer here than among the Mojo and Paressí, and it is much clearer than among the tropical-forest villages. The Manasí had four major gods who were manifest in natural phenomena. The identity of these is not specified, except that one was the thunder god. The foremost of these gods was the "avenger god," or "Our Father," a vindictive being, who judged the people and punished them with disease. The three other principal deities interceded on behalf of human beings. Secondary to these four gods were innumerable spirits of the dead. The major gods occupied the important places in the temple, while the lesser spirits stood in front of them. Another god of considerable importance, whose role in religion seems somewhat separable from the major quadrumvirate, was the god of the river spirits, who was also worshiped in the chief's house or temple.

Although the village chief was evidently not necessarily a priest or shaman, his religious importance in the community is indicated by the use of his house as temple and assembly hall. During ceremonies, part of the house was partitioned off for feasts and religious rites. The gods entered this sanctum and made their presence known in a fearsome manner by shaking the house, whereupon they were given offerings of chicha. Only "high priests" dared to enter the sanctuary and receive the major gods, for ordinary shamans risked death in facing them. The way in which the priests confronted the major gods, however, resembled certain patterns of shamanism in that the priests were carried away by the deities and subsequently returned safely to the temple just as ordinary shamans were carried away by their spirit-leaders. This suggests that the high priests were as much shamans as their less potent colleagues and that they differed from the latter in their ability to deal with major gods as well as with their tutelary spirits. Moreover, this practice is in the basic pattern of the Mojo and Paressí, among whom the priest consulted the gods as an oracle; that is, he served as an intermediary between the people and supernatural beings but did not lead ceremonialism in supplication of deities with whom he held no intercourse personally. He directly faced the gods and asked them about the weather, harvests, hunting and fishing prospects, and the outcome of proposed war expeditions. When the communion or séance of the priest and the gods was finished, special food was offered to the gods.

The more ordinary class of shamans was distinguished from the priests or special shamans in that the former had no role in public ceremonies. Both kinds of shamans, however, were trained in similar ways and related to the supernatural beings in the same manner. The principal feature of the training of any shaman was his ascent into the sky, which prepared him to deal effectively with supernatural beings. The high priests, like the chiefs, however, enjoyed much higher social and economic status than their humbler colleagues, since they were given part of the commoners' harvest, could eat the food offered to the gods, and lived in houses built by the villagers. While we do not know whether these priests or higher-class shamans formed a hereditary class, they were obviously a privileged class supported by their fellow villagers.

Manasí religion had complex beliefs about death and the hereafter, although an ancestor cult was absent. Manasí death observances were fitted to the temple religion. At a funeral, the relatives of the deceased assembled in the temple, where the priest called forth the soul of the dead person for purification and then "carried the soul on his back" to the Land of the Dead, since the route was devious and dangerous. Souls of persons who had died in different localities went to special places in the hereafter.

ten

FARMERS AND PASTORALISTS
OF THE SOUTHERN ANDES

The southern Andes was separated from the Central Andes by a broad belt of desert running from southern Peru and northern Chile across the mountains into northwestern Argentina. The Atacameño lived in small settlements at the few sources of water in the most arid part of this belt, the Atacama Desert. Their culture showed strong influence from the Central Andes in many specific features, but, owing to their sparse population, they could not support Central Andean social, political, and religious patterns.

South of this desert belt, the country becomes rainier, merging into tola-heath puna of the highland and scrub steppe, or monte, east and west of the highland. Optimum conditions for farming and herding are provided by the mediterranean climate of central Chile, which was occupied by a numerous Araucanian population. Between the Atacameño and Araucanians were the Diaguita, who extended from the coast across the Andes into Argentina and inhabited a country of steppe land and small fertile valleys. Just south of the Argentine Diaguita were the Huarpe, who were at the limits of farming and seem to have been more like the hunters and gatherers. The Araucanians were distributed as far south as the island of Chiloé, the southernmost limit of aboriginal and modern plant cultivation in Chile. South of Chiloé, the archipelago becomes extremely rainy and cold, and it supported only a sparse population of shellfish gatherers. The Diaguita and Araucanians were influenced by the Central Andes, although less strongly than the Atacameño.

All of these Indians were classed in the *Handbook* (volume 2) as

"Southern Andean" because their culture elements were drawn principally from the Central Andes. But they differed from the Central Andean states and empires and from the Circum-Caribbean chiefdoms in their village autonomy and in their lack of hereditary classes, a priest-temple-idol cult, and federation or conquest. While the historic people had a tendency to prestige groups based on wealth, it is doubtful whether this was aboriginal. The Araucanians were very similar socially to the lineage and multilineage tropical-forest village farmers, and they even shared thatched houses, wooden mortars and pestles, and other traits with the latter.

Since so very little is known about the aboriginal culture of these people, typological classification is not now warranted. Some of the Diaguita seemed to have had incipient features of chiefdoms, but most of the societies belong in a very broad category of settled, farming village people. It is impossible to place them in a more adequately defined subcategory.

1. THE ATACAMEÑO: ANDEAN DWELLERS IN THE DESERT OASES

The Atacameño received little notice in early historical sources, and no ethnographic records have been made of their post-Spanish culture. They are known largely from archaeological materials, which are excellently preserved in the dry ground.

The Atacameño once occupied a vast area from the southern border region of Peru to the Chilean province of Atacama, and they extended across the Andes into much of northwestern Argentina. Their greatest concentration appears to have been in the provinces of Antofagasta in Chile and Jujuy and Salta in Argentina. The small groups that survive today have been strongly influenced by Spanish and Aymara culture, and the native language is lost except for a few words recalled by aged informants.

The complete lack of rainfall in the Chilean sector of Atacama territory precluded agriculture except in the few, relatively small oases in Arica, Tacna, and Calama along the coast and in certain favorable locations inland. Along the rather narrow coastal strip, small groups of Atacameño eked out an existence primarily by fishing, hunting marine animals, and gathering shellfish. In the less harsh environment of the intermontane basins of Jujuy and Salta, provinces east of the Andes, farming was more extensively developed.

At best, plant cultivation was precarious and supported only a very sparse population that lived in small local groups. These groups were widely separated from one another, and since the Atacama Desert had little to offer outsiders, they were not often molested by the Diaguita,

Inca, or Spaniards. The construction of fortifications, however, shows they were in danger of attack, and in Argentina the richer resources were an inducement for the Diaguita and Aymara to conquer part of the Atacameño territory. In late prehistoric times, the Inca not only extended their control over much of the Atacameño territory but moved as far south as central Chile. The southern Andes, however, could not support imperial institutions, and the Inca finally withdrew.

Subsistence. The Atacameño were able to farm only at the oases, from which they ran irrigation ditches. Maize, beans, quinoa, squash, calabashes, chile peppers, and a number of other plants as well as types of agricultural implements show influence from the Central Andes. That llama herding was very important to all Atacameño groups in shown by the quantities of llama wool textiles, hides, and bones in archaeological sites. These animals also were used as beasts of burden and for meat. Inland people also gathered wild plant foods and hunted birds and, occasionally, vicuña and guanaco. In historic times, they hunted with the bow and arrow and the sling, but bolas have been found in archaeological sites.

The Atacameño traded widely among themselves, especially between coast and interior and with the Diaguita and Peruvian Indians. Roadways across the desert indicate extensive trade routes.

Excellent products in pottery, basketry, textiles, wood, hide, stone, bone, copper, and occasionally gold and silver are well preserved in great number in Atacameño archaeological sites. The shapes and artistic treatment of the manufactures are so like those of the Diaguita and Inca that it is often difficult to determine their origin. The Atacameño probably copied the styles of Diaguita and Inca trade objects.

Socioeconomic structure and settlements. In so arid an environment, large settlements could not be supported. Archaeological sites show that communities were small and isolated. An early historical source states that each settlement was made up of a group of related families, no doubt a lineage, under the leadership of a "chief," perhaps a kinship elder. Chieftainship, the report continues, passed from father to eldest son. These isolated villages appear to have been autonomous, although linked by trade. Irrigation canals, stone houses, and defensive walls are Central Andean in character, but they were constructed on a very small scale and imply no class specialization or status distinctions.

That warfare, at least defensive measures, was fairly important to the Atacameño is evidenced by the protective walls that generally surrounded Atacameño villages and the choice of vantage points overlooking the cultivated fields as village sites. Moreover, weapons and leather armor are abundantly represented in the archaeological material.

Knowledge of Atacameño religious life, gleaned largely from the archaeological record, discloses an absence of structures resembling temples and objects that might be idols. Burials, however, indicate great concern over the dead and suggest that the deceased were very important in religious observances and ceremonials.

2. THE DIAGUITA: FARMERS OF THE SEMIDESERTS

Diaguita territory lies immediately south of that of the Atacameño, but in prehistoric times the Diaguita had expanded into former Atacameño territory. Most of the Diaguita lived east of the Andes, where they migrated in post-Tiahuanaco times, that is, after A.D. 1000 or 1100. Trade goods found in archaeological sites indicate close contact between the Chilean and Argentine Diaguita. The historic Chilean Diaguita are little known. The best description pertains to the Calchaquí, a subgroup of northwestern Argentina.

Archaeological remains of the Diaguita and perhaps of other culturally similar people of northwest Argentina resemble the Pueblo Indians of the Southwest of North America in their construction of stone-walled houses with adjoining rooms, their ceramic skill, and the general level of their culture. This does not mean, however, that the Diaguita and the Pueblo represent survivals of an early, uniform, inter-American culture stratum. Instead, it means that both peoples were influenced in the building arts, farming, pottery, weaving, and other important features by the high civilizations of the Central Andes and Mexico, but that, living in arid regions which permitted less productive farming, they were organized in autonomous villages which lacked class structure, federations, or other characteristics of chiefdoms and states.

Subsistence and technology. The Spanish chroniclers, although interested primarily in Diaguita warfare, recorded passable descriptions of Diaguita sociopolitical organization and such visible features as dress. They said little about subsistence activities and technology, and we know these largely from archaeological remains.

If the Diaguita practiced irrigation it was on a very small scale. They built agricultural terraces, however, to extend the arable surface of sloping land and to hold the runoff of rainfall from the hills.

The Diaguita raised llamas and possibly vicuñas for wool, which they wove into very fine, many-hued textiles. As in the Central Andes, the people dressed in ponchos and ankle-length tunics. The Diaguita were excellent potters, and they made such Peruvian vessel forms as aryballus and double-spout jars. They cast copper and bronze pins (tupus), crescent-shaped knives, star-headed clubs, chisels, tweezers, and other objects having Peruvian forms, as well as knuckle-dusters, wrist guards, and distinctive forms of their own; and they made bells of gold and silver.

Socioeconomic structure and settlements. The limited sources of water forced a concentration of dwellings and fortifications in small communities. Since many of these structures were built of durable stone and pirca, they are well preserved. The archaeological ruins, together with Spanish chronicles, reveal a good deal about Diaguita social and military organization.

The need for defense brought about two kinds of settlements. The first consisted of an unprotected cluster of houses and a separate military redoubt or fortified retreat, called a pucara. The dwellings were arranged

a   *b*

Prehistoric pottery vessels, northwest Argentina. (After Marquez Miranda, 1939, reproduced in Handbook, vol. 2.)

in streets along streams. When attacked, the villagers fled to the fortifications which were situated strategically on hillsides and consisted of a series of defensive walls built up on terraces. The walls were equipped with loopholes for bowmen, and there were special avenues of retreat. Behind the walls was the permanent bastion, in which the defenders could withstand siege. To ensure a sufficient supply of water, the redoubts were provided with cisterns or wells.

The second kind of settlement was a fortified village which combined features of the hillside redoubts and the farming communities. These villages were fairly large and had granaries, a water supply, and a thick defensive wall.

Warfare. The Spanish sources indicate that each village was ordinarily autonomous, but that there was military cooperation between villages, at least during the time of hostilities with the Spaniards, when powerful leaders gained control. The many fortifications leave no doubt that there was intensive warfare in pre-Spanish times. Reports of torture of captives, head trophies, and status accorded warriors suggest but do not prove incipient class differentiation, for such features were known also to many tropical-forest villages.

During several general uprisings against the Spaniards, most of the Diaguita joined in concerted military effort, although operations by smaller groups were common. The chief gained tremendous authority, but his gallantry was a decisive factor in his ability to control his people.

In fighting the Spaniards, Diaguita military tactics were altered. They used firearms and horses as well as the traditional bows and stone maces, and their armies numbered thousands and included even women and children. This warfare was bitter and uncompromising. Both sides besieged and destroyed the other's towns, laid waste their stores, and burned their fields. When the Spaniards finally broke Diaguita resistance, they sent many to work in the mines in the Peruvian highlands and resettled others as far away as Buenos Aires.

Religion and shamanism. The Diaguita believed that thunder and lightning had supernatural power. It has been thought that anthropomorphic figures represented in petroglyphs, in pottery decoration, and on copper plaques represent deities, but this cannot be verified.

Shamans treated disease, which was believed to be caused by supernatural agencies. They were said to live apart from the ordinary people in special haunts where they drank heavily and often engaged in drunken altercations with one another. In addition to treating sickness, shamans conducted agricultural fertility rites and sacrificed the head of a deer into which arrows had been thrust. The sun was propitiated with an offering of the head of an enemy.

There was great fear of witchcraft, and interfamily feuds followed suspicion of sorcery.

The relatives of a dying person kept watch over his body and drove away the evil spirits. At death, they began ceremonial wailing. They placed food next to the deceased and burned incense, then flexed the body and interred it in a pit or chamber.

3. THE ARAUCANIANS:[1] CHILEAN FARMERS AND PASTORALISTS

The aboriginal territory of the Araucanian Indians extended from the Coquimbo Valley on the southern edge of Diaguita country through the transverse valleys and basin of central Chile. This territory, with its alluvial valleys and mediterranean climate, is much more favorable to farming than the steppes and deserts of the Diaguita and Atacameño farther north. While the Araucanians borrowed such crops as maize, kidney beans, squash, chili peppers, quinoa, oca, and peanuts, it is possible that they should receive credit for domesticating the white potato. Moreover, they had partly domesticated several grains that seem to have been unknown elsewhere.

Agriculture supported a fairly dense population, but the Araucanians had no large nucleated villages, a type which might have been expected. Instead, they were dispersed in hamlets, each usually consisting of a lineage and situated near the cultivated fields.

All the Araucanians had a very similar culture and spoke a common language, but the Spaniards designated them by various regional names. The most common classification distinguishes three divisions, the Picunche, Mapuche, and Huilliche, who occupied the northern, central, and southern zones respectively. The Picunche had been more strongly influenced than the others in material culture and technology by the Central Andes in both pre- and post-Incaic times, but their socioeconomic and religious organization was like that of the Mapuche and Huilliche.

The late Ricardo Latcham, a Chilean anthropologist, observed that the colonial history of the Picunche north of the Bío-Bío River differed profoundly from that of the Araucanians south of this river. Most of the Picunche were absorbed into the Spanish systems of encomienda and hacienda during the first century of the colonial era, whereas the Mapuche and Huilliche remained essentially outside the colonial structure. The Mapuche developed a military and political organization that enabled them to resist Spanish domination longer and more successfully than any Indians in the Americas. They remained independent through the whole colonial period and were subdued and placed on thousands of small reservations only at the end of the nineteenth century. Today, they are gradually becoming intensive agriculturalists.

The aboriginal population of the Araucanians has been estimated at between 500,000 and 1,500,000 at the time of the Conquest. Today, there are probably not over 200,000 Araucanians living on reservations in Chile. Large migrations of Araucanians into Argentina, however, began in the sixteenth century. Many of them sought asylum from military reprisals which followed the failure of their periodic uprisings against the Chilean government. A rather steady stream of Mapuche still cross the Andes to seek better economic opportunities.

The Picunche

The aboriginal habitat of the Picunche is dry in summer and watered by light rains in winter. Rainfall increases from north to south, and at the Bío-Bío River there is a marked change in natural vegetation. Picunche population was sparser than that of the Mapuche-Huilliche, and their small settlements were largely confined to river valleys where irrigation and flood farming could be carried on. Neither the Andes nor the coastal mountains supported farming, although llama herds could be pastured on the slopes of the coastal ranges.

Subsistence. Irrigation agriculture was practiced in most of the Picunche habitat. In the transverse valleys north of Santiago, it was essential to cultivation, while in the less arid region around and south of Santiago it was a supplement to flood farming. In the northern valleys, the Picunche terraced to increase the surface of the valley sides and to hold water runoff.

Weighted digging sticks and rakes were the essential agricultural tools. Llama manure may have been used in aboriginal times, the practice having been introduced along with herding.

Domesticated guinea pigs and llamas furnished meat, although llamas probably served mainly as pack animals and as a source of wool. They were eaten only on special occasions, for example, when they were slain in sacrificial rites. There was a scarcity of fish and game in Picunche territory, but a few fish were obtained from the coast by trade.

Planting, harvesting, and construction of irrigation ditches and dwellings were performed by large, cooperative labor groups, a system known as mingaco. Workers participated by invitation, and the occasions were enlivened by feasting and celebration. While only community members cooperated in planting and harvesting, workers from several communities cooperated in construction of houses and irrigation canals.

Canoes were used only along the coast, and most travel was overland. Llamas were apparently everywhere beasts of burden, but human carriers also transported goods.

Picunche weaving, pottery making, and basketry were well developed and showed strong Peruvian influence. Weapons, like those of Central Andes, included lances, pikes, spear throwers, and bows. The Picunche practiced metallurgy, which they learned in pre-Inca times.

Settlements and socioeconomic structure. Picunche settlements consisted of loose clusters of not over a dozen irregularly grouped houses. They were usually situated along rivers and streams or in easily irrigated land. The houses were generally rectangular and had thatched roofs and wattle-and-daub walls, except in the northern arid region, where they were built of stones and adobe.

Each house was occupied by an extended family which numbered between twenty and thirty persons and was under the authority of a household head. The several households comprising a settlement acknowledged the leadership of a cacique, or chief, whose title was hereditary. Each settlement was politically autonomous.

Each household had rights to cultivated land, but there is reason to believe that surrounding woodland, pastures, and even herds of llama were held in common. The irrigation system entailed cooperation between villages and was extensive enough to require a clear managerial authority in regard to land occupancy and labor, an authority exercised by the cacique or a council.

The Picunche had an incipient status system based partly upon power and partly upon surplus. In addition to household heads and settlement leaders, shamans had considerable prestige because of their supernatural power, while certain individuals enjoyed status owing to their wealth. Below such individuals were the common people of less wealth and influence. In time of hostilities, the power of the cacique was temporarily increased. Although there were no over-all peacetime leaders among the Picunche, several neighboring settlements frequently followed a powerful cacique in time of war. During the Inca and Spanish invasions of their territory, however, the Picunche rose to the occasion in a federated effort only a few times.

The effect of the Inca conquest on Picunche sociopolitical structure is difficult to estimate. We can infer either that the Inca ruled through local leaders or that they established settlements, or mitimaes, of Peruvian Indians, which, together with improved army contacts, facilitated direct control from Peru. In either case, the Inca required gold as tribute from the Picunche. But no deep changes took place, since the Inca rule in Chile was short-lived. Far more drastic changes followed the Spanish colonization of Picunche territory.

Warfare. The Picunche cannot have been very warlike in aboriginal times, for they were disunited at the time of the Inca invasion and were rather easily conquered. They fought in small local groups and were no match for the professional soldiers of Peru. After the arrival of the Spaniards, there is a single recorded instance of a general uprising in the Santiago region, after which the Picunche resorted to guerrilla warfare. The Picunche living in the Santiago region, however, joined forces, and armies of several thousand under single leadership raided the Spanish garrison for several years. Eventual capitulation to the Spaniards demolished any trend toward regional unification among the Picunche.

Religion and ceremonialism. Religion was essentially shamanistic. Shamans were primarily curers and sorcerers, but they functioned at public ceremonials. The office of shaman passed from father to son, but there were also some female practitioners. This may indicate that the role was sometimes achieved through being cured supernaturally or through a strong calling, as well as through heredity.

The colonial Picunche

In 1536, Diego Almagro reached Chile, fresh from Spanish victories in Peru, and explored the territory as far south as the Maule River. The expedition ended in fiasco and returned to Peru with dismal reports of

Chile and its inhabitants. In 1540, Pedro de Valdivia invaded Chile and established Santiago in the Mapocho Valley. One of the most remarkable aspects of the colonization of Chile is the rapidity with which the Picunche were subjugated by the Spaniards, while the Mapuche who lived south of the Bío-Bío River put up a belligerent, long-continued resistance. In north central Chile, the conquest ended in 1544, and those Picunche who had not been killed or fled south were placed under the encomienda system. In this system, divisions or repartimientos of Indians were assigned to the care (encomienda) of individual Spaniards (encomenderos) who had the duty to see to their spiritual welfare and the privilege of exacting tribute. But the system was abused and perverted in many ways.

After encomiendas were granted around Santiago, intensive gold mining was begun with the labor of encomienda Indians, and an attempt was made to extend the conquest south of the Bío-Bío. Between 1544 and 1562, the use of Indians taken from their villages to work long periods in the mines had disastrous effects. Death from overwork, maltreatment, and widespread starvation decimated the population. Meanwhile, heavy crop levies placed on Indian settlements at the very time when their manpower was depleted undermined the aboriginal agricultural economy. Flight, alcoholism, and violence were evidence of physical, psychological, and cultural distintegration.

As new Spanish settlements were founded south of the Bío-Bío River, extensive grants of Mapuche Indians in encomienda put thousands more to work in the newly discovered gold deposits. But numerous rebellions and skirmishes with the Spaniards flared up among these southern Araucanians during the first ten years of contact, and by 1562 warfare was so intensive as to halt the founding of new towns and the discovery and exploitation of gold deposits in that region. Thereafter, northern central Chile was the main area of peaceful colonization, while the territory south of the Bío-Bío remained a frontier zone for several centuries.

Under the mining encomienda, the bulk of the Picunche population had not been brought into intimate contact with Spanish culture. Except for the demands of mita, that is, labor for public works, aboriginal culture was still functioning in most of northern Chile, especially in the regions remote from the centers of Spanish culture. With the depletion of the placer mines in northern Chile and the steady diminution of the Picunche population, mining declined and the encomenderos turned to agriculture and herding. Food production was stimulated by the need to support the troops fighting in the south. During the last four decades of the sixteenth century the establishment of the encomienda as an agrarian institution brought the Indians more directly under Spanish influence, especially in the regions around La Serena, Santiago and, to a lesser extent, Concepción. The Picunche were put to work on farms, in households, and in workshops (obrajes). They were acculturated in various ways depending both on their proximity to the Spaniards and the kind of economic arrangements into which they were drawn.

Indian depopulation continued inexorably, even though mitayos, that is, encomienda Indians, were brought in from Cuyo and captives were taken from south of the Bío-Bío River to replace the dwindling Picunche. As the number of Indians allotted the encomenderos declined, so did the value of the encomienda as an exploitative device in colonization. Shortly after its inception in Chile, the encomienda deviated somewhat from the ideal form of indirect rule, custodianship, and extraction of tribute previously described. Relatively unrestricted by crown authority, it became a system of enforced but unpaid and unregulated labor services of the repartimiento Indians.

During the last decade of the sixteenth century, gold mining nearly ended in Chile, and the encomenderos spent most of their time on their rural holdings. Their need for labor became ever greater, and they used every means to acquire as many Indian workers as possible.

The Picunche rural workers were put under Spanish, Negro (slave and free), and mestizo supervision, and the Indian caciques, or chiefs, ceased to function as intermediaries between the Indians and the Spaniard. The Indian settlements broke up under an emerging peonage system, and aboriginal social, economic, and religious activities disappeared.

After 1600, Spanish settlers were granted land in the remoter areas where Picunche communities still survived, but they received no Indians in encomienda. These farmers and ranchers pushed the last free groups of Picunche from their land. No longer tied to their own settlements, these Indians, together with runaway encomienda Indians and mestizos who felt closer to the Picunche than to the Spaniards, constituted a displaced, disoriented, and rootless segment of the population. Most of these people found employment on the farms and ranches that had sprung up over the central valley of Chile; others became laborers in the Spanish towns. They formed the rank-and-file workers of Chilean society and carried the burden of production through the remainder of the colonial era.

In Chile, as in Latin America generally, there was no strong barrier between races. Widespread miscegenation between the Spaniards and the Araucanians began with the first years of colonization, and by the early decades of the seventeenth century a large portion of the population had mixed ancestry. The mere fact of race mixture exempted a mestizo from encomienda service, endowed him with free status, and often opened his way to participate in special crafts or other nonagricultural labor. Mestizo heirs of the encomenderos formed the bulk of the creole aristocracy, and other mestizos became overseers on the farms and ranches or worked at skilled trades in the towns. They also swelled the ranks of the rural and urban working class. The social status of mestizos was determined by the extent to which they were Hispanicized and by their kinship ties with the landed class.

On the whole, indoctrination in the Catholic religion had little effect on the Araucanians, because the encomenderos generally neglected this obligation and because the colony had very few qualified missionaries before the Jesuits arrived in the last decade of the sixteenth century. Although Santiago was called the "Rome of the Indies" because of its many churches, monasteries, and convents, and although the Jesuits are reputed to have conducted true agricultural and handicraft schools for the Indians, Catholic proselytization came too late and with too little force to have much effect on the Araucanians. Apparently, the mestizos were converted no more easily than the Indians during the first century of colonization.

By 1635 Chilean colonial culture had taken form, and subsequent events had little effect. Belated attempts to settle the few remaining Picunche on reservations continued until 1752, but then failed. Taking captives and holding slaves had been declared illegal in 1674, and in 1791 the remaining encomiendas were incorporated into crown holdings. These measures elicited little protest from the encomenderos because the growth of the mestizo population had created an abundance of free labor that made it useless to hold forced Indian labor in the encomienda system.

The political revolution of 1818, which led to Chile's independence as a republic, had little effect on the inquilino, or tenant farmer, population. The Picunche had ceased to exist as a cultural minority.

The Mapuche and Huilliche

The history of the Mapuche and Huilliche was very different from that of the Picunche, for their native population was many times greater than that of the Picunche, and the Mapuche survive in modern times as distinctive ethnic groups. The difference is understandable as the result of successful resistance to Spanish armed might, which did not subjugate and place them on reservations until three-quarters of a century ago.

The many involved discussions of geographico-political divisions among the Mapuche-Huilliche should be considered only in the light of war-time alliance among the Indians during the colonial period. The early Spaniards, confronted with implacable and seemingly unconquerable Indians, constantly tended to ascribe them native groupings and chiefs which, in fact, did not exist. The Araucanians had no aboriginal political divisions greater than autonomous local groups or lineages. The three or four larger geographical subdivisions of Araucanian territory, representing longitudinal strips along the Andean foothills, the central valley, and the Pacific Coast, together with the general area south of the Toltén River, were designated in various and inconsistent ways and had no fixed or significant boundaries, no political cohesion, and no substantial ethnic unity. All Araucanians between the Bío-Bío River and the region around the town of Valdivia refer to themselves as Mapuche ("people

Araucanian farm at Lake Budi in Chile. (Photo by Louis Faron.)

of the land"). Coastal Mapuche refer to themselves this way, but are called Lafquenche ("people of the coastal region") by Mapuche living to the east in the central valley and the Andes. Likewise, the sub-Andean Mapuche are referred to as Puelche, but call themselves Mapuche. In a sense, therefore, these regional designations hold today, but seem never to have had the political significance accorded them by some of the earlier ethnographers.

Mapuche population and territory are much smaller today than in aboriginal and colonial times, but the Araucanian language is still widely spoken, especially among the older people, who rarely speak Spanish. There is conservatism also in other aspects of their culture, but the mounting impact of economic ties, transportation, and education, notwithstanding the comparative isolation of the Indians in southern Chile, has opened the way to national political, social, and religious influences. The more highly acculturated Mapuche should be classified not as Indians but as an emergent peasant population; for they differ from the Chilean peasants who live among them mainly in their retention of certain vestigial socioreligious patterns.

Subsistence. The aboriginal Mapuche and Huilliche subsisted principally upon cultivated plants, but used game, wild seeds, and fish traded from the coast. They farmed forest glades or cleared timbered

Araucanian plowing for wheat, a European-introduced crop, which is broadcast without further soil preparation. (Photo by Louis Faron.)

land by slash-and-burn techniques to cultivate a large variety of crops, of which maize, potatoes, beans, squash, chile peppers, and quinoa were most important. In the south, especially on the island of Chiloé, potatoes were a better crop than maize, for they grow best in cold climates. The Araucanians cultivated fairly permanent fields, although they periodically allowed them to lie fallow to replenish the soil.

The residential group cooperated in clearing land, planting, and harvesting. Women played an important role in planting and harvesting and did almost all the cultivation during the growing season. It is only in relatively recent times that men have concerned themselves to a great degree with agricultural work.

The aboriginal diet was predominantly vegetarian, for game was scarce and fish apparently did not appeal to the Indians of the interior. Hunting, trapping, and fishing were more important to the coastal Indians, especially those of Chiloé, where farming was least rewarding.

The Mapuche and Huilliche kept domesticated llamas and possibly guinea pigs. Llamas were so numerous in aboriginal times that the people could be considered herders as much as farmers. The llama was highly valued and figured importantly in almost every sphere of aboriginal culture. Its meat was consumed mostly when it was sacrificed on ceremonial or festive occasions. Its wool was woven into ponchos, blankets, and other clothing. It was used as a pack animal, since canoes were relatively scarce except near and along the coast and rivers. The llama was given in payment of the bride price. During the historic period, status was somewhat measured by wealth in llamas. Although llamas were still herded by the Mapuche and Huilliche as late as the end of the eighteenth century, they were largely replaced by horses, mules, sheep, cattle, pigs, and barnyard fowl introduced by the Spanish colonists. Horse meat became a staple, and mare's meat is still regarded as a supreme delicacy by the Mapuche.

Food was stored indoors in bins or in woven, basketlike granaries and outdoors in elevated platforms. Onions and garlic, both of European origin, and other herbs and spices were hung up to dry in the house for daily use. Jerked meat was both sun-dried and smoked.

Women prepared food in various ways. They boiled or roasted maize or made it into flour to be used in soups, bread, and beverages. They combined it with meat and other vegetables in soups and stews or in dishes of beans and potatoes to which some grease was added. These traditional dishes are still favored among present-day Mapuche.

Today, the Mapuche try to set aside one-third of a harvest as seeds for the next season's planting, one-third as a reserve or cash crop, and the remaining third as food for the year. Although the pre-reservation Araucanians were probably able to carry out this plan, difficulties under the reservation system, which went into effect in the latter part of the nineteenth century, prevent its being realized. Agricultural techniques are inefficient, plant diseases are rife, and soil depletion is unchecked.

Manufactures. Many manufacturing techniques have virtually disappeared in modern times, although the Mapuche and Huilliche were once quite skilled in making baskets, cordage and netted goods, fine blankets colored with native dyes, pottery, and stone- and woodwork. Placer gold was mined before the Spanish Conquest, but the Indians did not know how to smelt. Silversmithing was probably developed in the late eighteenth century and reached a high degree of excellence during the next century. Today, baskets, textiles such as ponchos and small rugs, and cordage are manufactured in many, if not most, Mapuche households. Other skills are retained by a few specialists who, however, serve an ever-diminishing native market. Indians living close to Chilean towns sometimes make tourist goods for sale in the market or railroad station.

Transportation. Water travel was relatively unimportant in native times, since most of the Indians lived in the interior valleys, which have few navigable rivers. Three types of craft used in colonial times were

Araucanian potter in Temuco Province. (Photo by Louis Faron.)

the dugout canoe, plank boat, and reed balsa. The planked canoe, a dugout with raised sides, is one of several South American features that may have resulted from Polynesian influence. The reed balsa, a bundle of reeds tied together to form a raft, is an Andean-type craft mainly used on lakes in the deserts, where trees are absent, but also known on the coast. Sails probably came into use as a result of Spanish influence.

Most aboriginal travel was by overland trails. Human carriers transported goods in fiber bags supported by a tumpline, but llamas also served as burden carriers. The introduction of Spanish horses revolutionized transportation and greatly increased the mobility of the Mapuche and Huilliche. Spanish riding gear was copied and modified by the Araucanians, who soon became expert riders and excellent cavalrymen in time of war.

Sociopolitical structure and settlements. There was regional variation in the structure of Mapuche-Huilliche dwellings and in the number of occupants, but everywhere substantial pole-and-thatch houses were built. A household usually sheltered patrilineally related families, some of which were polygynous. In the larger dwellings, each nuclear family

Araucanian fisherman in dugout canoe with trident spear, Temuco Province, Chile. (Photo by Louis Faron.)

had its own compartment for sleeping and cooking, but the household seems to have cooperated in most economic matters.

Houses were not usually clustered in compact communities. In the best farming regions, where cleared farm land was limited, houses were necessarily closely spaced, but each patrilineage, whether living in a single house or divided among several nuclear family houses, was autonomous. Where timberland had to be cleared for farms and in regions of llama pastures, settlements were composed of small clusters of related households. Residence seems to have been patrilocal for the greater part of recorded Araucanian history, and society was organized along patrilineal lines.

Blood feuds and intersettlement raids contributed to the lack of territorially cohesive sociopolitical units among the Mapuche-Huilliche. During the colonial period the formation of smaller and more isolated settlements was furthered by the tremendously disruptive effects of the initial attempt to enforce the encomienda system among the Mapuche, the continual raiding for slaves who were transported to northern Chile, and the Mapuche's retreat and dispersal before marauding Spanish troops.

Settlements, that is, patrilineal lineages, were autonomous in time of peace. Each controlled its own affairs, defended its farm lands and pastures against trespass, and avenged death and sorcery by means of the blood feud. Each was led by a kinship head whose authority was limited both by a council of household heads and by the tendency for dissatisfied and recalcitrant members to split off from the residential group. Regional federation for war, which seems clearly to have been a postcontact phenomenon, brought an amalgamation of settlements and an organized military hierarchy into being which enabled supreme military commanders to deploy large numbers of troops in synchronous attacks along a wide front.

Within the Araucanian settlements there was some social stratification based on both kinship status and wealth, although the latter is probably postwhite. Kinship heads were called lonko, and they were accorded some respect and authority. But even within their households a disaffected party could circumvent their authority by leaving the residential group. Indeed, it seems that the bellicose periods of the colonial era caused a general tendency for factions to split from their parent lineage groups and to dissolve the social ties which had bound them together.

The lonko initiated the agricultural labor and other cooperative, or mingaco, ventures of the settlement or lineage. The lonko began the mingaco by inviting other families of the lineage to work on his projects, then feasted them. After this, each family, under the direction of its own head, continued the cycle until the particular activity had been completed. A lonko did not levy tribute from the other households of his settlement, although in time of need he requested gifts and was provided with food. Since his prestige depended partly upon his largesses, it was customary to grant his requests for food so that he could meet his traditional obligations.

Another title of distinction is ulmen, which means "wealthy man." In aboriginal times an ulmen was usually a lonko, since lonkos were in a position to garner more wealth than most of the other household heads within the lineage. During the colonial period, other men might become ulmens by acquiring wealth in herds and crops, and be accorded a measure of respect and authority. They were not politically powerful in lineage councils, although their opinions carried more weight than those of ordinary household heads and certainly more than those of konas, the ordinary males of the kin group.

When the reservation policy of 1866 was instituted, certain lonkos acquired greater power and were now appropriately designated caciques, or chiefs. They acquired military power, they retained the authority of the peacetime lonkos, and they held title to the land for everyone on the reservation. This condition became crystallized under the modified reservation policy put into effect after 1884.

Since warfare between the Araucanians and the Spaniards so vitally affected most spheres of aboriginal culture, it is difficult to reconstruct precontact economics. Communal ownership of fields not actually in use and of pasture land seems to have been customary, but the Mapuche defended territory rather than farm land and pasture land as such, since there was certainly no scarcity. During most of the colonial period, the Mapuche-Huilliche seem frequently to have shifted their fields because warfare kept them on the move. Inheritance of land, therefore, was no issue. Herds and movable goods, however, seem always to have been owned by individuals and inherited patrilineally. During the Republican period, when the Mapuche were more settled, and especially after their movements were restricted by reservation life, land ownership became a vital matter. Another fairly recent change is that men have taken over farming from women. During the unsettled colonial period, when farming was devoted primarily to subsistence, it was left to women while men concentrated on warfare or prepared for military life. Since the Mapuche have been pacified and settled on small reservations, farming of field or cash crops has become the principal occupation of men, while women now engage only in the small-scale cultivation of vegetable gardens.

Family structure and marriage practices have also changed since aboriginal times. The patrilineal lineages have become larger and stronger since the reservations afford no new lands where they can bud off. But many former features have largely disappeared. Polygyny was once widespread, lonkos especially having large polygynous households. There was a system of wife grading in which the principal wife had a measure of authority over others and ran the household. The sororate, sororal polygyny, the levirate, and the marriage of brothers of one household to sisters of another were all practiced, though apparently with different frequency at different periods in Araucanian history.

Today, most of these traditional practices have declined in importance, and monogamy prevails.

The bride price is now a token payment in such home-manufactured goods as ponchos, rugs, blankets, silver jewelry, and animals. Dramatized bride capture is still occasionally practiced. Elopement occurs rather frequently, especially when the groom is unable to accumulate a substantial bride price, but it is generally followed by a traditional ceremony after the bride price has been accumulated. Virginity is not highly prized, and premarital sexual activity is unrestrained. Promiscuity, however, is frowned upon by a girl's parents.

Warfare. In aboriginal times and during all the colonial period, there was internecine feuding among the Araucanians because of trespass, murder, and other wrongs against settlements and individuals, but there was no warfare for territorial aggrandizement. Organized warfare developed only in colonial times, and most information on the subject concerns hostilities against the whites. In addition to the high order of politico-military development among the Mapuche-Huilliche already described, the most significant change was the adoption of cavalry. Araucanians quickly acquired horses from the Spaniards and developed great mobility and striking power, which enabled them to engage in rather successful raids against Spanish garrisons and to fight a dilatory war for several centuries.

The Araucanians took captives in war whom they sometimes adopted into the local settlement group or used as drudge laborers. Usually, however, they killed captives, displayed their heads as war trophies, and made their long bones into flutes.

Religion and ceremonials. The native Araucanians perhaps believed in a supreme deity to whom they prayed in public ceremonials and propitiated in private prayer and upon whom shamans called for supernatural assistance. While the central concept of a creator god seems to be definitely aboriginal, many supplementary beliefs and practices observed in postcontact times certainly represent accretions from Catholicism.

In daily life, the Mapuche-Huilliche were more concerned with a number of lesser spirits than with the Creator. Shamans called upon their spirit-helpers to combat these evil spirits, to cure illness, and to ward off or discover the cause of death. In his curing rite, a shaman went into a trance, massaged or manipulated the affected parts of the patient, and blew smoke and water in four directions over the patient's body. He also drummed on a tambourine and practiced ventriloquism, transvestitism, and sleight of hand. These shamanistic practices, though typical of Siberia, are known elsewhere in America only in the Arctic. Why any of these, let alone the whole complex, should occur in South America only among the Araucanians is inexplicable.

The Araucanians had no shamanistic societies, although shamans fore-gathered in special ceremonies. The role of shaman was formerly passed from father to son, but today more women than men are shamans, and the neophyte is usually a daughter or close female relative of the prac-titioner. Apprentices are recruited in a number of ways, important among

Female Araucanian shaman with tambourine, gourd, silver orna-ments, and special carved pole. (Photo by Louis Faron.)

which is curing them of disease and instilling in them a belief that they have been called into service. At the machitun, or special ceremonials held by shamans, the neophyte demonstrates newly acquired ability before the group of seasoned shamans.

Death was attended by complex mourning and burial ritual, which involved ceremonial wailing, tearing of the hair, driving away evil spirits, shamanistic autopsy, temporary preservation of the corpse, consumption and libation of great quantities of alcoholic beverages—chicha and wine in post-Spanish times—and the gathering of a great number of relatives and friends of the deceased. Cist and urn burial were formerly practiced. Later, it was traditional to inter the corpse, at least, that of an important person, in a canoe or hollowed log. Today, the deceased are buried in a cemetery in a conventional type of coffin. The modern funeral ceremony, though laden with Catholic ritual, preserves a good deal of the flavor and beliefs of traditional observances.

The dead are believed to enter into a spirit world in which existence mirrors that on earth. The aboriginal conception about the abode of the dead is not clearly described in our sources. The conception of the after-world today clearly includes many Catholic concepts.

NOTES

1. This chapter is based on the historical research and field work of Louis Faron.

eleven

FARM VILLAGES OF
THE TROPICAL FORESTS:
GENERAL FEATURES

1. INTRODUCTION

As a culture area the tropical forest shared many features with the
Circum-Caribbean area, especially technological devices which were
useful in the humid, warm lowland forests. These features include
thatched houses, hammocks, dugout canoes, loom weaving, pottery, subsistence on fish and other animal life of the rivers, and cultivation of
tropical root crops and other plants. The rain-forest people, however,
differed fundamentally from those of the Circum-Caribbean area in their
lack of states, social classes, and a temple-idol cult. This difference is
explainable in part by the superior productive processes in the Circum-
Caribbean area, where the environment, although somewhat like that of
the tropical forests, supported a denser population, permitted surplus
production, and made possible the development of local states, craft
specialists, and ruling classes. In the tropical forests, too little food surplus was produced to permit occupational specialization and social differentiation. Instead, a simple village type of society prevailed, based
on shifting horticulture and exploitation of river resources.

The distribution of this type of culture coincides to a remarkable
degree with that of the tropical rain forests as defined geographically.
It was found throughout most of the Amazon Basin; it extended up the
tributaries of the Amazon, where the jungle finally narrows to gallery

284

Varieties of tropical-forest-village culture. The numbers correspond to the sections in Chapter Twelve. (1) The Guianas. (2) The Island Carib. (3) The Tupinambá. (4) The Tupí-Guaraní. (5) The Chiriguano. (6) The Amazonian Tupí. (7) The Montaña. (8) The Juruá-Purús Rivers. (9) Eastern Bolivia. (10) The northwest Amazon. (11) The eastern Colombia lowlands. (12) Enclaves in the Circum-Caribbean area. (13) Eastern Brazil.

forests fringing the rivers; it occurred in a strip down the coast of Brazil almost to the La Plata Delta; and it existed in Paraguay and portions of Bolivia. In the low, humid forested areas of Colombia, Central America, and most of the Lesser Antilles, it constituted enclaves within the Circum-Caribbean area.

The tropical-forest people were divided among many linguistic families. Caribans lived in the Lesser Antilles, while Arawakans and Caribans were the main groups in the Guianas and in lowland Venezuela. Tupian-speaking people predominated on the lower Amazon (the Mundurucú, Parintintin, and others), on the coast of Brazil (the Tupinambá), in Paraguay (the Guaraní), and even on the flank of the Bolivian Andes (the Chiriguano). Many of the tribes of the Montaña, where the Amazon Basin is rimmed by the foothills of the Andes, had a tropical-forest culture: the Panoans, the Kawapanans, the Jívaroans, and others. The Catukinans on the Juruá and Purús Rivers in the southwest portion of the Amazon Basin and a large number of linguistic groups of eastern Bolivia also shared features of this culture. Tropical-forest people found within the Circum-Caribbean area included the Goajiro of the arid Goajiro Peninsula of Colombia—people who are cattle breeders today— and several Arawakan and Cariban groups in eastern Colombia, especially in the llanos, or plains, west of the Orinoco River and in the mountains immediately west of Lake Maracaibo. The best publicized of these are the Motilón, who still avoid contact with Europeans. On the low west coast of Colombia and the southern coast of Panama, the Chocó today retain much of their native way of life. In Central America, where the culture was predominantly Circum-Caribbean in type, the Lenca, Paya, Mosquito, and several Chibchan groups were essentially like the tropical-forest peoples.

The tropical-forest culture is best understood in terms of its adjustment to the humid, hot lowland rain forests, which its distribution followed very closely. This is an environment in which whites have lived with difficulty. Native Indian life in this area did not support a large population, and it did not lead to any achievements which would popularly rank it as a civilization. But it did entail a considerable number of solutions to the problems of living in the tropics, which have been adopted by whites and Negroes. In the dryer and higher altitudes, such as the highlands of Venezuela, Colombia, and Central America, the tropical-forest features were replaced by a culture more closely related to that of the Andes.

The wide distribution and great uniformity of this culture have been explained in two quite different ways. First, several anthropologists have postulated that it was carried by migrations of Arawakan-speaking people

throughout the rain-forest area. Some scholars even assume that Arawakans contributed this culture to the early inhabitants of Peru, Central
America, and Mexico, where it formed the basis of the high civilizations
which developed much later.

The theory that the Arawakans were the bearers of a distinctive culture
confronts several serious difficulties. The Arawakans are not culturally
the same everywhere. Such seminomadic Arawakans as the Amuesha and
Campa of the Montaña in eastern Peru differ profoundly from the tropical-forest Arawak of the Guianas and even more greatly from Circum-
Caribbean Arawak of the Greater Antilles. At the same time, the Arawakans of each local area resembled their neighbors, who represented
many other linguistic groups—Cariban, Tupian, Panoan, etc.—far more
than their linguistic kin in more remote places. They are very widely
distributed, and there is little doubt that they helped spread many traits
to tribes with which they had contact. But so did the almost equally
widespread Tupian- and Cariban-speaking Indians. Moreover, the tropical-forest culture was the product of many peoples and not the invention
of the Arawakans. Since much of the Circum-Caribbean material culture
and many village-level social features were very similar to those of the
tropical forests, such linguistic groups of the former as the Chibchans,
Timoteans, and others may even have contributed to this culture.

2. HISTORY

The prehistory of the tropical-forest peoples can be reconstructed only
in the most inferential and uncertain manner. Native legends are almost
entirely mythological in character and deal with the celestial bodies. The
Indians lacked a sense of history and took no interest in genealogies.
Even those societies whose principal religious activity centered in a cult
of the dead were concerned with ancestors in a general sense and not
as identifiable individuals. There is no group whose oral history extended
back more than one hundred years.

Archaeology of the tropical forests, in sharp contrast to that of the
Andes, as yet provides little historic depth to the cultural picture. Sites
are difficult to find in the heavy rain forests, and they contain few
imperishable objects other than pottery. Houses, hammocks, stools, baskets, mortars and pestles, bows, arrows, blowguns, spears, canoes, and
textiles were all made of vegetable materials. Owing to the predominance
of deep topsoil throughout the area, objects of stone were extremely
rare, while stone construction was almost unknown. Archaeological sites
are by no means absent, and they hold promise of throwing a great deal
of light on tropical-forest prehistory. As yet, however, comparatively little

archaeological research has been done in the area. Clifford Evans and Betty Meggers are doing important work in the tropical forests, but the area is huge.

The culture history of the tropical-forest people can be inferred only from the distribution of linguistic groups and of cultural features. The

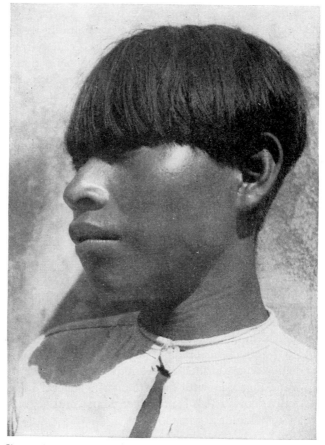

Chama Indian of the Iquitos region, upper Amazon. (Courtesy of Abraham E. Guillém.)

linguistic evidence, together with some oral history, permits the reconstruction of certain migrations but does not necessarily reveal which groups invented or spread the more important cultural features. Three languages are extremely widespread: Arawakan, Cariban, and Tupian. Arawakan is found largely north of the Amazon, and presumably it originated somewhere in this area. But the Taino and Sub-Taino of the Greater Antilles speak Arawakan, and apparently, according to Carib tradition, Arawakans occupied the Lesser Antilles prior to the Carib invasions less than a century before the Spanish Conquest. Arawakan-speaking Ipuriná, Campa, and others were found on the headwaters of the Purús River in southwestern Brazil and the Ucayali River in eastern Peru. The Guaná of the north Gran Chaco and the Tereno of Paraguay are the southernmost Arawakans. The Arawakans are perhaps the most widely distributed of any linguistic group, and they were the most diversified culturally. While no doubt they introduced many cultural traits throughout the areas of their migrations, they were obviously not the primary bearers of the tropical-forest type of culture.

The Carib were distributed principally north of the Amazon in the general area of the Guianas, which was probably their center of dispersal. They may have spread their patterns of warfare and cannibalism rather widely, but the Carib south of the Amazon were not so warlike.

The Tupians or Tupí-Guaraní–speaking Indians were exceedingly widespread south of the Amazon. While most of the dialects of Tupí-Guaraní are remarkably similar and imply fairly recent dispersal, there are some deviant languages, such as that spoken by the very primitive Sirionó of Bolivia, who separated from the main stock long ago. Most Tupian-speaking people can be accounted for by fairly recent migrations which, thanks to the researches of Alfred Métraux,[1] are known in some detail. An important motivation for many extremely long migrations was the search for the Land of the Grandfather, the mythological sky god, which is explained in later pages. From a center of dispersal which may have been south of the lower Amazon, where the largest block of Tupian-speaking people exist today, the migrations went in several directions and continued until the latter half of the sixteenth century. The Tupinambarana traveled up the Amazon to the Madeira River which they followed to its headwaters in Bolivia, then came back downstream to the island of Tupinambarana in the Amazon. Similar migrations probably carried the Omagua up the Amazon to the vicinity of the mouth of the Juruá River, and the Cocama still farther to the Ucayali River.

Some Tupians evidently cut across eastern Brazil to the Atlantic Coast, but one group, the Amoipira, stopped in the interior on the São Francisco River. Other migrations apparently carried Tupians down the coast of Brazil, where they were found in a thin strip from Ceará in the north to Porto Alegre about 2,000 miles to the south. These coastal people have different local nàmes but are collectively known as Tupinambá.

One group of Tupians continued to the Río de la Plata, while others turned inland to become the Guaraní of Paraguay. This migration to Paraguay was probably in very late prehistoric times. Still later, even during the Portuguese conquest of Brazil, some Guaraní continued westward across the Gran Chaco to the very frontier of the Inca Empire in Bolivia, where they became known as the Chiriguano.

Far less is known of the migrations of other groups, but the diversity of languages found at the headwaters of the principal rivers, such as the Madeira, Juruá, Purús, Tapajoz, Tocantins, Negro, and other tributaries of the Amazon, and on the upper Orinoco and Paraguay Rivers suggests a general drift upstream and final isolation in the more mountainous country. This accords generally with the presence of hunting-and-gathering nomads around the periphery of the Amazon and in the watersheds between it and other river systems. The characteristic features of the tropical-forest culture were as much riverine as silvan, and they seem to have been water-borne, whether they were passed from one group to another or carried by migrations, like those of the Tupians. In

Frame of Macuna pole-and-thatch house, Apaporis River. (From Theodor Koch-Grünberg, "Zwei jahre unter den Indianern," Berlin, 1909–1910.)

the more rapid and smaller streams at the headwaters of the rivers, where canoe navigation was difficult or impossible, these features fade out.

The ultimate source of tropical-forest culture is still highly conjectural. Since most of its principal technological features—pole-and-thatch houses, maize, beans, yuca, sweet potatoes, and several fruits, dugout canoes, palisaded villages, basketry, ceramics, bark cloth, and others— are shared with the Circum-Caribbean area, it is possible that they were derived from that source. Their use in a tropical-rain-forest environment, however, would entail distinctive cultural-ecological adaptations and different sociocultural organization. The archaeological research of Clifford Evans and Betty Meggers in the Guianas disclosed no evidence of settlements such as might have been established by people with a Circum-Caribbean culture moving along the coast and rules out the Guianas as a route by which the tropical-forest culture was introduced to the Amazon. On the island of Marajó in the mouth of the Amazon, however, they excavated the site which has long been famous for its elaborately modeled pottery and found clear indications of a culture alien to the area. The ceramics and the huge platform which evidently served to raise the village above the swamps were apparently made by a people who arrived from upstream with a culture wholly unlike that of the general area and who completely disappeared before the arrival of Europeans.

This evidence suggests that, while the Marajoara culture did not necessarily contribute much to the local culture, some features of the tropical-forest culture may have been introduced by more advanced people coming down the rivers at different times. Evans and Meggers consider that the Marajoara culture came from the west down the Amazon.[2] Since the Marajoara art style has certain striking similarities to the painted designs of the Panoan people of eastern Peru, it is possible that they came directly down the Amazon.

Many tropical-forest traits, however, may simply have diffused or been passed along from one local society to another. To understand the nature of tropical-forest culture, it is far more important to recognize that, whatever the origin of each item of culture, the crucial features became the basis of a culture adapted to slash-and-burn farming, riverine fishing, and hunting in an environment that imposed many serious difficulties on all activities and that prevented development of a dense population, large towns, and permanent settlements compared to those of the Andes and Circum-Caribbean areas.

3. CULTURAL-ECOLOGICAL ADAPTATIONS

The general structure of the tropical-forest culture differed from that of the Circum-Caribbean area and the Andes not only in its far greater simplicity—in the much smaller number of elements—but in the special ways in which social, religious, and political patterns were affected by cultural-ecological adaptations. Literature on this area usually describes the people primarily as horticulturalists, who characteristically farmed by means of the slash-and-burn method—the only way of dealing with the large trees and the rank vegetation—and who grew such tropical crops as sweet and bitter (or poisonous) manioc, sweet potatoes, a kind of yam (*Diascorea*), beans, maize, peanuts, and several palms.

These crops, however, provide predominantly starchy foods, and while no adequate analysis has ever been made of the diet, there is little doubt that the people had a need for protein foods, which were obtained principally by hunting and fishing. The importance ascribed hunting and fishing, however, involves a rather crucial and interesting problem regarding cultural and physiological factors as determinants of behavior. Certain anthropologists have maintained that men devoted much time and effort to fishing and hunting in order to escape the drudgery of farming and to gain prestige in these more vigorous and enjoyable masculine activities. According to this view, fishing and hunting were culturally prescribed masculine roles—occupations which attained importance through circumstances of previous generations—and not activities resulting from immediate and obvious needs. While it is undeniable that any system of sexual division of labor and of roles and statuses tends to become traditional in a situation like the present one, it is nonetheless necessary to explain how the pattern developed in the first place. It is circular reasoning to say it is traditional. Any society will exploit wild resources to some extent, 'and when cultivated foods provide a badly unbalanced diet for which hunting and fishing can compensate, it is quite possible that the craving for meat, rather than mere tradition, led men to hunt.

The vast system of tributaries that make up the Amazon system is replete with fish. While major rivers present difficulties to fishing, owing to their size, to the presence of driftwood, which makes use of nets impractical, and to lack of quiet pools where fish poisons can be effectively used, the innumerable small tributaries in this area of high rainfall offer very rewarding opportunities for taking fish with poisons, traps, spears, and arrows.

Game, on the other hand, is dispersed in the forests, and hunting involves certain hazards as well as difficulties. Food animals, such as deer or peccary, are not easily found. Monkeys, which live in trees, are a major food animal, but they are not easy to shoot.

Since hunting and fishing were crucially important to these people, whatever the ultimate explanation, it is incorrect to think of the dwellers in the tropical rain forest as merely farmers. The population was largely concentrated along the rivers and coasts. Vast tracts between rivers had few inhabitants, and these people had a much simpler culture. The tropical-forest Indians were as much riverine and coastal people as they were forest dwellers, as much boatmen as farmers. Rivers and coasts, moreover, were lanes of transportation which made it possible to bring foods in quantity to central points and thus to maintain large villages. Canoes were crucial in communications, and they helped to spread the typical features of this culture. On the smaller tributaries of the Amazon and the Orinoco, especially above the rapids which impeded navigation, the more characteristic features faded out. Large villages, loom weaving, ceramics, and canoes, for example, were absent, and many of the people were and still are nomadic hunters and gatherers.

The typical subsistence activities were remarkably similar throughout the immense area of distribution of this culture. The slash-and-burn method of farming was fairly standard. In order to grow crops it was necessary first to clear patches in the dense tropical vegetation. Lacking iron tools, the Indians used stone axes—which were evidently obtained through trade from distant places—to encircle the trunks, kill the trees, and, if possible, fell them. After this, they burned the dead vegetation and planted crops between the dead trees and stumps. Men helped prepare the plots, but where hunting or warfare were important, women carried out the onerous task of cultivation and weeding.

Because the soils of this area leach rapidly and the plots are invaded by weeds, the yield of any plot decreased seriously after three or four

Yagua men, upper Amazon, using stone axes. They are covered with fibers for protection against insects. (Courtesy of Paul Fejos, Wenner-Gren Foundation.)

years, when it was necessary to clear a new one. The new plot might be accessible from the village, and the village therefore could be permanent or semipermanent. But if all the land within access of the village had been used too recently, both plot and village had to be moved.

The plant domesticates of the tropical-forest area were much the same everywhere, except that bitter manioc, which yields farinha, a flour that can be stored, seems to have had a fairly limited distribution in pre-Columbian times. Aboriginally, it was used so far as we know, in the Amazon Basin, in part of the area north of the Amazon, probably in the Antilles, but doubtfully in Central America. In early post-Columbian times, however, it spread rapidly into Central America as well as to many Indians in the south, perhaps including some on the upper Paraguay River. Bitter manioc, because it was desiccated and preserved, acquired importance in the Amazon after European occupation because it supplied farinha, which became the principal provision for expeditions and the staple food of settlers. Today, both bitter and sweet manioc are the source of tapioca.

Perhaps one deterrent to the aboriginal diffusion of this plant is that it contains deadly prussic acid, which must be removed before it can be eaten. The aboriginal treatment was first to shred the root into a pulp on a board studded with stones or thorns or against a roughened pottery slab. The juices were then squeezed from the pulp, the most typical device for this purpose being a long, basketry cylinder, known as a tipití, one end of which was suspended from overhead while the other was attached to a lever which, when pressed downward, elongated the basket, narrowed its diameter, and compressed the pulp. After this, the pulp was either toasted in the native form of cakes, known as beiju, or dried to form farinha. Tapioca from the juice might be added to the farinha. While the manioc was ostensibly squeezed to remove the poisonous prussic acid, it is probable that cooking would have expelled the acid in any event. Possibly the Indians did not know this. The cakes and flour could be stored or consumed at once.

In addition to food crops, these forest people grew certain other useful plants including calabashes, *Bixa* (a red dye also known as urucú, anatto, and achiote), *Genipa* (a black dye), cotton (used mainly for hammocks, woven bands, and body ornaments), arrow reeds, and fish drugs. They drew heavily upon wild species, and collected many wild fruits and nuts, including Brazil nuts, which became a trade commodity for European goods. The tropical-forest Indians adopted several plant domesticates from the Europeans. These included sugar cane, which filled a deficiency in the native diet, and bananas. They did not, however, take over rice, no doubt in part because their soils were not suited to it, in part because it entailed more work than manioc, and in part because they already had ample starchy foods.

The principal animal foods came far more from the rivers than from the forests. The Indians caught innumerable species of fish, captured turtles, river mammals such as manatees and dolphins, and caymans (often erroneously called alligators), and gathered turtle eggs, which were laid by the hundreds of thousands in the sandy shores of the rivers. They took fish by several devices which were very widespread: drugs, baskets, nets, weirs, traps, multipronged arrows, harpoon arrows, and hooks. In the smaller tributaries, drugs derived from a large number of wild and cultivated plants were mashed and put into pools. The stupefied fish floated to the surface, where they were easily removed from the

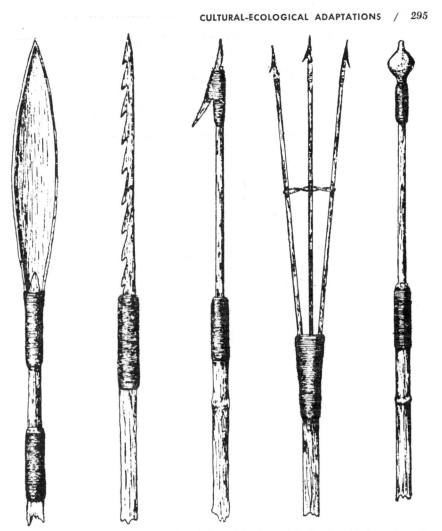

Types of tropical-forest arrow points. Left to right: lanceolate bamboo blade and serrate rod for game hunting, barb; triprong fish arrow; knobbed head for birds. (From Handbook, vol. 3.)

water. The drug did not make them inedible. Fish poisoning must be a very old practice, for it is used in all parts of the world. Several hundred species of plants containing fish drugs were known in South America. The Indians also took fish by means of multipronged arrows shot from canoes or from the riverbanks. Nets were considerably less useful than other devices since so many areas had driftwood or swift currents.

Hunting was a major pursuit, even if the take was not as rewarding as in the Gran Chaco and the pampas. Game included deer, peccaries, tapirs, monkeys, armadillos, anteaters, sloths, agoutis, pacas, capybaras, and various birds. The hunters used spears, traps, arrows, and blowguns. The arrows were often 5 feet long, and bows had a proportionate length, probably because they were commonly made of chonta palm, which has little resiliency, although some hardwood bows had equal length. Arrows intended for large game were tipped with long, sharp lanceolate or

Yagua man shooting blowgun. (Courtesy of Paul Fejos, Wenner-Gren Foundation.)

rod-shaped, pencillike heads and were usually made of bamboo. Bird arrows often had knobbed heads or short crosspieces near the tips so as to increase their striking surface and prevent their sticking in trees, and fish arrows often had tripronged or harpoon points.

A special hunting device characteristic of portions of this area, particularly the northwest Amazon, and used also in southeast Asia, was the blowgun. This weapon is effective only if the dart is poisoned. In South

America, the common poison was prepared from certain vines, especially *Strychnos toxifera*, which contains a violent poison. The slightest wound caused paralysis and rapid death. There is no question that the blowgun was used in prehistoric South America, but Stirling, who examined Spanish references to it, suggests that it may have spread very widely in post-Columbian times.[3]

Another hunting device was the spear thrower, or atlatl, which was known early in the Andes. It consists of a stick about 3 feet long, one end of which engages the butt of the spear and the other, grasped in the

Cubeo widening dugout canoe by means of heat. (Courtesy of Irving Goldman.)

hand, serves as an extension of the arm to give more leverage. The spear thrower was known in the Upper Paleolithic period in Europe, and it was very widespread in native America. In South America, its distribution was spotty, and it was being replaced by bows and blowguns, both of which were invented more recently. At the time of the Spanish Conquest, the spear thrower was still a major weapon in the Montaña, in the Juruá-Purús area, and in certain other localities.

An important auxiliary used in gathering wild foods was the climbing ring. When collecting palm fruits and honey, a man put a loop of rope around his feet before placing them against the tree, to facilitate climbing.

Transportation devices were crucial in tropical-forest life. The stability, size, and composition of any community depends upon means of moving people to the foods and foods to the people. The more backward or nomadic people on the unnavigable headwaters of rivers sometimes made crude bark canoes but no dugout canoes. For land transportation some of these people plaited crude temporary containers of palm leaves. The more characteristic tropical-forest villages used dugout canoes on the main rivers and specially woven carrying baskets when traveling overland. Around the Caribbean Sea the people were expert navigators and voyaged in large ornamented ocean-going canoes with built-up sides and sails. Elsewhere, the canoes were simple hollowed logs. In the absence of metal tools for canoe construction before postwhite times, a tree was felled by hacking at it with a stone ax and then hollowed by alternately burning and chopping out the charred wood. When steel axes could be obtained in trade from the Europeans, the construction of dugouts became easier, canoes were made much larger, and many Indians began for the first time to make such craft. Historical evidence shows that in response to this improvement in transportation the size of communities increased.

4. SOCIOCULTURAL PATTERNS

Tropical-forest society was based on kinship and community groups. Subsistence techniques in this environment barely provided enough food, particularly proteins, to meet daily requirements, and it was impossible to accumulate surpluses that could support full-time occupational specialists or ruling classes. Multivillage states and class-structured societies like those found among the Circum-Caribbean and Andean peoples were absent throughout most of the area, although there was slight social differentiation among certain atypical groups mentioned subsequently.

Community types

The size of the community depended upon the over-all density of the area and the possibility of concentrating the people in communities. The average population density of about 0.5 to 1.0 person per square mile is only a fraction of that found in the Andean area of high civilization—about one-twentieth or one-thirtieth—and the communities were very small as compared with some of the Andean cities. In parts of the tropical forests, such as in the northwestern Amazon, transportation facilities were poorly developed because of the difficulty of river communications. The village often consisted of one large, thatched house which typically sheltered a single patrilineal lineage; that is, an old man, his sons and daughters-in-law, and his sons' sons and wives from other communities. Ordinarily this local lineage was exogamous and patrilocal, that is, the wife was brought to the husband's house. These kinship community groups consisted of perhaps 100 people or less. Probably some communities had four generations, but the sense of kinship must have begun to diminish in such cases.

Where resources were richer and communications were better developed, as along the Amazon proper and the coast of Brazil, some communities were much larger. They consisted of several lineage houses and

Naravute house. Such multifamily dwellings often constitute the entire tropical-forest village. (Courtesy of the University Museum, Philadelphia.)

numbered as many as 2,000 or 3,000 persons. The Amazon River, according to the accounts of the Carvajal expedition, which first descended the river from the Andes to the Atlantic Ocean in the sixteenth century, was bordered almost continuously by large houses. Even allowing for exaggeration, there was probably no clear boundary between one village and the next. Where houses were grouped in what may be called communities, the lineage or household was often more important sociologically than the village, for it retained many economic and social functions.

Throughout much of the area, houses were clustered and consolidated in communities because of warfare. The need for protection against raids was met by crowding the houses within palisades, and such villages were more clearly defined and undoubtedly larger than they would have been otherwise. But there were limits to the village size. The slash-and-burn method of farming required frequent shifts of farm plots, and since the people could not travel an unlimited distance to reach their fields, village size was restricted by the need to cultivate plots within a radius of only a few miles. In many instances, the village had to be moved at intervals to more fertile land.

Certain strictly traditional or noneconomic factors also affected the nature of the village. In many regions, the family houses were built around a central men's house. Men slept, ate, and spent most of their time in this house. In communities consisting of several lineage houses, there was a headman, whose house was ordinarily located in the center of the village. In some societies the death of an inhabitant, especially of the headman, caused the house or several houses comprising the community to be moved. Only the large multilineage villages on major rivers were fairly permanent.

Kinship

Kinship was the basis of society throughout most of this area, and the kin group was nearly everywhere a patrilineal lineage. Every individual felt primary allegiance to his father's relatives. In the Guianas, the Antilles, and perhaps some of the enclaves within the Circum-Caribbean area there was a matrilineal tendency, which may be related to matrilineal organization of most Circum-Caribbean cultures. But this was atypical of the tropical-forest Indians, who had every gradation from localized, exogamous, patrilineal lineages to nonlocalized patrilineal clans.

Exogamous, nonlocalized clans or sibs may originate from localized exogamous lineages where certain conditions are present. When members of a localized lineage marry exogamously, that is, into other local lineages, they really marry outside the locality as well as outside a fairly small group of known relatives. If the lineage becomes so large that a portion of it buds off to form a new community, the knowledge of relationship between the communities will eventually be lost and the community members will intermarry. On the other hand, myths of descent from a common ancestor, ceremonies, and other features may perpetuate belief in kinship after new communities have been established, even when actual relationship is no longer traceable. In this case, exogamy continues with reference to fictitious relationship in the male or female line.

The first stage in such potential clan development was represented in many parts of the tropical forests. In the Montaña, many communities consisted of a single patrilineal lineage occupying one large house. In the northwest Amazon, among the Tucanoans, Witotoans, and neighboring people, the community also consisted of a single patrilineal lineage, which, however, traced its descent from mythical ancestors. All male members of the community belonged to a secret society, which held initiatory rites that celebrated the return of the "ancestors." These northwest Amazon communities were locally exogamous, but they were not true clans since the belief of relationship did not extend outside the community.

In an expanding population, however, where new communities bud off but retain the fiction of common descent with other groups, true clans have emerged. Several clans may later combine to form a single large community.

Such development occurred farther down the Amazon among the Mundurucú, Parintintin, Tupí-Cawahib, and several other Tupian peoples. The Mundurucú, for example, were divided into a number of patrilineal, exogamous clans whose members were found in many Mundurucú villages, while each village had several such clans. The fiction of relation was maintained through the belief that the members of each clan were descended from a plant or an animal. As in the northwest Amazon, these ancestors were thought to be embodied in sacred trumpets which women and uninitiated boys were not allowed to see or touch.

While this development of clans cannot be constructed from direct knowledge, the presumed stages are all present in the tropical forests. It is difficult, moreover, to imagine any alternative that would explain the nonlocalized clans. Once clans had developed, however, they could readily spread from one society to another through intermarriage, provided the communities were large enough to consist of several lineages.

Matrilineal descent and local exogamy were characteristic of the Guianas and portions of the Greater Antilles, but it is not certain that true, nonlocalized clans occurred. The Arawakan-speaking peoples in this area were matrilineal, and so were the Antillean Carib, Goajiro, Cágaba, and Patángoro of Colombia. Whether this matrilineal descent originated locally or was diffused from the Circum-Caribbean peoples is not clear.

Political institutions as such were little developed in the tropical forests, for the communities had few functions which required extensive civil controls. The communities which consisted of a single lineage occupying one large house, as in the western Amazon, were ruled by the elder of the kin group. In the larger communities along the Amazon River and south along the coast of Brazil, a special man was chief. Most often, this headman or chief was the shaman, whose authority and prestige were based more upon respect and fear inspired by his supernatural powers than upon prescribed or hereditary office. While a shaman's main function was to cure illness, he often conducted village religious rites and performed other community functions.

Social structure

The tropical-forest tribes were characteristically structured along lines of kinship, and most interpersonal relations were governed by kinship, as among the simpler peoples to the west and among all the more nomadic people. Sex dichotomy was manifested not only in the division of labor but, in some areas, by segregation of men in a special house. These societies also stressed age differences, which represented in part the change of occupations and roles as persons grew older. Structuring along class lines was largely precluded, because few, if any, societies had the food surplus to support an upper class, specialists, and a form of state organization which hereditary classes apparently presuppose. Moreover, allegiance to lineage members precluded division into different classes, for this would have cut across kin relationships and created conflicting loyalties. In warfare, there was no way in which individuals could acquire permanent and hereditary status through exploits. Although many of the tropical-forest warriors sacrificed male victims and in some cases ate them in a quasireligious rite, they usually married their female captives. Unlike the warriors in the north Andean chiefdoms, they did not acquire a large group of servants who helped raise their economic position, and they did not display the trophies of captives who had been sacrificed in state religious rites to raise their prestige.

A few tropical-forest societies, however, seem to have had the seeds of a class structure. Among the Tucano, there is said to have been a serflike class of Macú war captives. It is also reported that the Omagua, the Manao, and the Quijo of the upper Amazon kept captives as slaves. But these data come from sources which were written after many Indians had begun to take slaves for the European settlers. While the nature of this slavery is not clear, very possibly it was a result of the slave trade. In the same way, a class of slaves seems to have developed among the sedentary village farmers of eastern Bolivia who also sold captives to the Spaniards. Very probably a new economy was emerging, in which warriors devoted most of their time to capturing slaves whom they traded to European settlers for metal goods. To compensate for the manpower withdrawn from subsistence activities, they retained enough captives to carry on farming, hunting, and fishing. Among the Arawak of Guiana, captives formed a loose kind of lower class called Macú. The frequent use in the Guianas of the term Macú in referring to Indians in the area between the Orinoco and the Amazon River suggests that the primitive hunting-and-gathering people who lived throughout this area may have been generally subservient in some way to the more developed tropical-forest people.

Among the Guiana Carib, captives were subservient to chiefs, but they were not a hereditary true lower class. A Carib's son-in-law, prior to setting up his own household, also entered into this class while carrying out his bride service for his future father-in-law. Farther south, in the northeastern part of the Chaco, the Tereno had what appears to have been a somewhat endogamous class consisting of chiefs and warriors and another endogamous class of common people.

The tendency toward status differences just mentioned by no means implies a true class structure. The most clear-cut instance of class difference occurred among the Goajiro in the semiarid open country of Venezuela after they acquired cattle from the Spaniards and livestock became the hereditary basis of distinctions in wealth and status.

Sex differences throughout the tropical forests largely entailed occupational specialization. Women customarily cultivated the fields, although men felled the trees and assisted in certain phases of the harvest. Women cared for the houses and children and did the cooking. They were rarely organized in associations or societies. Men hunted, fished, helped somewhat in the farming, and carried out a raiding type of warfare. In some areas, they belonged to a secret society, and in others they lived in a special house.

Men's secret societies have a rather spotty distribution from the northwest Amazon to southeastern Bolivia, and they differed from place to place. In the northwestern Amazon, among the Tucano and the Witoto, all boys of the local lineage were initiated at the age of puberty through secret rites into the status of adulthood. A somewhat similar initiatory rite was found among certain societies of southeastern Bolivia. A special house was built for men among several groups, particularly among the Tupian peoples of the lower Amazon, but this house entailed no secret organization or initiation ceremony.

Life-cycle observances

Certain characteristic observances were held at different points in the individual's life cycle. The Amazon area is famous for the practice of couvade at birth. This custom is based on the belief that the infant has a stronger supernatural bond with his father than with his mother. After the child is born, the father confines himself to his hammock for a certain number of days and refrains from all activities so as to avoid evil influences which might affect the child adversely. The mother, meanwhile, arises from her childbed and carries on her normal work.

At the age of puberty, both boys and girls are usually subjected to certain rites, the details of which vary considerably throughout the area. The rites for girls are usually intended to ensure their physical well-being as well as to celebrate their transition to womanhood. According to the local culture, she may be whipped, required to dance, scarified, have her hair cut, have her clitoris excised as among the Sáliva and in the Montaña, or be given drugs. Puberty rites for boys are somewhat less common than those for girls, and they tend to consist of initiation into the status of manhood. Certain tribes may merely cut the youth's hair, pierce his nose, or circumcise him (Sáliva), but in the lower Amazon and in the Guianas, he is subjected to more rigorous treatment in which he must prove his physical courage and his skill. For example, he may be tied in a bed of ants or forced in other ways to endure ant bites. He may be required to show his skill in hunting and his fortitude in going without food for a certain period. In some areas the initiatory ceremonies are formal and involve a secret religious society of the kind previously mentioned.

The tropical-forest emphasis upon the individual during different phases of his life extends to his treatment at death, which also varied. Some groups practiced simple burial in the earth, and a few performed reburial, that is, exhumed the bones and reinterred them after the passage of some time. In a few areas, particularly among the Tupians, the body was buried in an urn. Cremation was occasionally practiced. Among some of the Indians of the Montaña as well as among the Antillean Carib, the cremated ashes of the deceased were mixed with chicha, a native beer made from various fruits and vegetables, and ceremonially drunk by the survivors. Funerary cannibalism was practiced by the Tarairiu and Aparai. In contrast to the Andean peoples, desiccation of the corpse was not known except among the Atorai.

Death ceremonialism, although commonly a private family affair, was often a group observance. In the northwest Amazon, the Guianas, and elsewhere, the local group held a community mourning ceremony. It is perhaps no accident that in the northwest Amazon the men's cult was closely connected with the spirits of the ancestors which were believed to return to the group during the initiation and funeral ceremonies. In neither case, however, was their deification of the deceased comparable to that in the class-structured Andean tribes. The spirits were not identifiable individuals, and they did not form a hierarchy of gods. They were simply ancestors or forebears in a general sense who were worshiped in a community cult.

Warfare

Warfare was never carried out for such group purposes as conquering land or exacting tribute, and capture of slaves was almost certainly a post-Columbian response to the Portuguese slave trade. The objective of most fighting was to avenge previous wrongs and hostilities, to take captives for cannibalistic rites, or to take human trophies. The nature of warfare changed after the whites came, when it acquired an economic motive and raids were carried out on a large scale to provide captives who could be sold as slaves. Dislocation of the native groups also often brought them into violent collision with one another.

The cannibalistic rites will be described in greater detail in a later chapter dealing with the distinctive features of the several subareas in the tropical forests. Among some of these groups, especially certain of the Tupians and Carib, cannibalism was developed to a great extreme. Captive men might be adopted into the society and female captives even married only to be sacrificed and eaten some years later. In fact, the progeny of these women might also be eaten. Cannibalism was also practiced among the Záparoans, some of the northwest Amazon peoples, the Guiana Arawak and Carib, the Patángoro, the Guaporé River people, and the Canichana. Elsewhere in the tropical forests, it was largely absent.

The preservation of human trophies made from war victims had a limited distribution in this area, and the kinds of trophies varied in the different localities. The shrunken whole heads made by the Jívaro of Ecuador have been much publicized, although the Jívaro were not unique in this practice. Scalp taking was known in the Gran Chaco and Guianas, and the practice of making the long bones of the body into flutes and skulls into cups was fairly common. The Arara not only took the head but flayed and preserved the entire skin of the victim.

Warfare had an important effect upon the settlement pattern in that it forced the people to live in tightly nucleated, palisaded villages. Some of the Amazon and coastal villages consisted of several hundred persons divided among lineages, each occupying a large house.

Religion

From a functional point of view, religion may be considered under three principal headings: shamanistic performances, wherein the shaman controlled a spirit which served primarily to cure sickness but was also ascribed general power for good or evil; ceremonialism dedicated to purposes of group or village interest; and beliefs in magic and in supernatural beings with which every individual was concerned. The particular ritual elements and the various ways in which supernatural beings were conceptualized were adapted to these broad purposes.

There was group ceremonialism among the tropical-forest people, but it was developed only to a limited degree, especially as compared with the Circum-Caribbean and Andean civilizations. Moreover, the ceremonies had a large variety of local purposes. In the northwest Amazon, among the Witoto and their neighbors and among the Achagua and Sáliva, the principal group ceremony was the initiation of boys into the men's society or ancestor cult, where the ceremony was carried out by

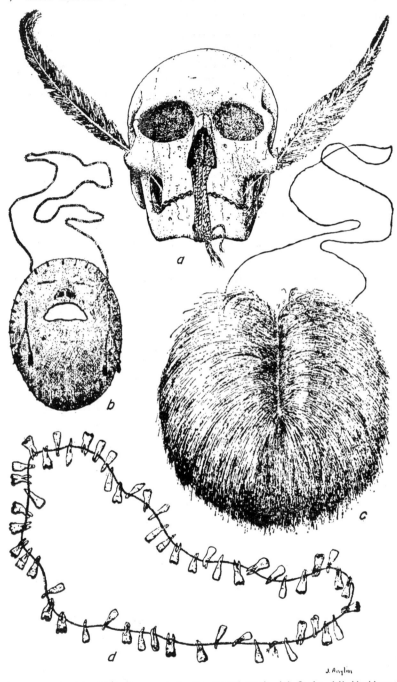

Arara war trophies. (a) Human skull. (b) Gourd mask. (c) Scalp. (d) Necklace of human teeth. (From specimens in Museu Paraense Emilio Goeldi, Belém, Brazil.)

the localized lineage or household. The ceremony itself, as well as the sacred musical instruments and other paraphernalia used in it, were taboo to women and children. In the Juruá-Purús River area, the tribes had feasts for nature spirits which were conceived as male beings. Here, too, the sacred musical instruments used in these feasts were taboo to women and children. The Tacana had a priest-temple-idol cult, but it operated during a boy's initiation ceremony and thus had a very different function from the Andean state cults.

Many groups had harvest ceremonies—the Tupian Mundurucú, Maué, Tenetehara, and Guaraní, the Tarairiu, and the Chaké. The Manao and the Panoans of the Juruá-Purús River region held fertility rites and the Achagua and Sáliva celebrated first fish ceremonies.

The Tupian Indians had a very important religious belief, often known as the "grandfather cult," which involved little ceremonialism but deeply affected their lives. Although this cult seems to have developed in pre-Columbian times, it had a messianic aspect in that it offered the hope of a better life in the future world in the Land of the Grandfather, who was identified with thunder or other celestial beings. This belief led many Tupian groups to make very extended migrations in the hope of reaching this land. While such migrations occurred in aboriginal times, the extreme disruption of native life after the whites came gave a new incentive to finding a place where life would be better. In many parts of the world, a messiah has arisen among native peoples when their way of life has been threatened by Europeans and promised a restoration of aboriginal conditions through religious means. In the case of the Tupí, the mythological Grandfather took the place of the living messiah while the Land of the Grandfather held hope for happier conditions.

There are very few cases in the tropical forests where a special leader or priest was in charge of group ceremonies, and none in which the leader held hereditary or markedly superior status. Usually, the rites were under the charge of a shaman, who held no religious office but possessed supernatural power that was acquired personally, as will be explained later.

Supernatural beings were conceptualized in a great many ways throughout the tropical forests, but several main categories predominated. The beings believed to have greatest influence on human life were the spirits of the bush and rivers, which were generally thought to be malignant and were carefully avoided. Celestial beings, usually identified with the sky, sun, moon, stars, and clouds, were known mainly in mythology and had little connection with or influence on everyday life and human affairs. The Tupian Grandfather, or sky god, was an exception in that he was the center of group interest and aspirations.

The general pattern of shamanism found among the tropical-forest people was basically like that in other parts of the world, although it contained a number of slightly distinctive local elements. The shaman possessed supernatural power in that he controlled a nature spirit, a human ghost, or some other being which enabled him to cure the sick, to cause sickness, and to perform certain miracles. Ordinarily, the shaman used his power on behalf of individuals, a function that was very different from his direction of group ceremonialism.

Sickness was believed to be caused by a foreign object having entered the patient's body or by loss of the soul. In the former case, the shaman removed the intrusive object, and in the latter he found and restored the soul. In the course of his treatment, the shaman imbibed drugs, especially in the northwest Amazon, where an extraordinary variety of drugs and narcotics were found in wild plants, he smoked tobacco, and he resorted to special procedures which distinguished his performance in particular localities.

In causing illness, the shaman used various forms of witchcraft. One widely held belief was that he could turn himself into a man-killing jaguar.

In addition to causing and curing sickness, the shaman sometimes divined the cause of past events and prognosticated future events by consulting his spirit-helper. In this respect, he functioned somewhat like the priest of the Circum-Caribbean area, except that the latter served as an oracle who consulted a village or state deity and that he did so for group purposes.

A large number of ritual elements were widely though differently distributed in the tropical-forest area and were used variously in the initiatory ceremonies, the cult of the ancestors, the harvest, fish, and first-fruit ceremonies, and others. In each case, their functional significance differed. Some of the more characteristic elements were the ant ordeal, taking snuff, gashing the body to make it bleed, whipping, cutting the hair, playing sacred trumpets which some groups identified with the ancestors, and the use of the scratching stick instead of the fingers upon ceremonial occasions.

The various contexts within which these rites were used may be illustrated by the ant ordeal, in which a person is subjected to swarms of biting ants. Among the Rucuyen and certain Tupians south of the Amazon, young boys submitted to the ant ordeal to prove their manhood. The Andaquí used the ordeal to test warriors prior to a battle. The Sáliva required that a new chief undergo this rite. The Arawak included the ant ordeal in their death rites, while certain other peoples in the Guianas incorporated it in hunting ritual. Whipping, another widespread ritual element, was part of the girls' puberty ceremony among the Macusí and certain Montaña tribes. Among the Guayupé and Sae, whipping made young men into warriors. It initiated boys into the tribal cult of the dead among the Yurimagua, but was a feature of the harvest festival of the Chaké.

5. MATERIAL CULTURE AND TECHNOLOGY

As explained previously, the technological knowledge of the tropical-forest people was much like that of the Circum-Caribbean area, except that the former lacked many of the techniques and manufactures of the latter. The tropical-forest people knew nothing of metallurgy in any form, stone architecture, sculpture, construction of roads, bridges, and large cities, and other features dependent upon a stable and highly organized population. Most of the manufactures were rather specifically adapted to the requirements of hot rain forests.

Clothing and adornment. The people were fairly skilled in weaving on the heddle loom but, owing to their warm climate, made little use of what may properly be called clothing. Instead of using dress, they adorned and decorated the body in a great many ways. Woven ornaments included arm and leg bands and occasionally waistbands and breechclouts. Genuine garments were limited to the cushma, a flowing, ankle-length robe used in the Montaña, and the tipoy, used especially in Bolivia. Both of these were undoubtedly adopted from the Andean peoples only a few miles to the west.

Almost everywhere, the tropical-forest Indians inserted ornaments in their ears, nose, and lips, the last in some cases being so numerous that one group of the upper Amazon which wore a dozen or more long plugs sticking out through the lips and cheeks was known as the Barbudos, or "bearded ones." Tattooing and body painting were also very common, and depilation of body hair was widely practiced. Featherwork was extraordinarily well developed in certain areas. In order to produce feathers of desired colors, they used a process known as "tapirage." A bird, most often a parrot, was deplumed and the body rubbed with certain irritants which caused feathers of different colors to grow out.

Head deformation was practiced to a limited extent in the Guianas, among the Island Carib, and in the Montaña. The filing of teeth has been reported among a few tribes of the western Amazon and the Guianas, but it is quite possible that this was introduced by Negroes.

Basketry. Three techniques of basket weaving were known in this area, and these were used for a variety of forms that served special purposes. The first is the coiled or sewed technique, in which the weft spirals outward from the center as a continuous element and is sewed together with a stitchlike warp. This method was known in a few scattered localities and seems to have had a very early, perhaps Andean, origin. The second

Paint rather than clothing adorns many tropical-forest Indians. Bora, northwest Amazon. (Courtesy of Paul Fejos.)

and more characteristic technique is the "true weave" or "in-and-out weave," which makes a checkerboard pattern in its simplest form but can be varied to form twilled patterns. With three sets of strands it becomes a hexagonal weave. This was used for mats, basketry containers, carrying

Vertical loom used to weave robes, bands, and hammocks. Macoa or Motilón woman, Venezuela. (Courtesy of the University Museum, Philadelphia.)

baskets, tipitís or manioc squeezers, and other forms. A temporary basket, however, was sometimes woven from a section of a palm leaf. Among some of the less developed groups, this primitive basket was the only kind made.

The third technique is the twined or finger-woven basket, in which the weft consists of two strands which are passed over and under a warp strand and are twisted around each other between each warp. This was limited to the northwestern Amazon and the Guianas. Like the coiled weave, it appears to have been an old technique which was replaced nearly everywhere by the much simpler and more efficient true weave or twilled technique.

Loom weaving. A large number of the tropical-forest tribes wove upon a heddle loom, which, because it has best been described among the Arawak of the Guianas, has often been called an Arawak loom. There is no reason to believe, however, that the Arawak invented it; in fact, many Arawakan-speaking peoples do not use it. The heddle loom consists of a frame upon which the weft strands are wound. Heddles are attached to the weft strands in order to separate them so that the shuttle bearing the warp can be passed between them. This loom is distributed from the Guianas to the upper Amazon and south to the Tupí-Cawahib, the Mbayá, and the Guaraní. It is basically the same as that used in the Circum-Caribbean and Andean areas, and there is little reason to doubt that it originally came from these more developed areas, where it was invented 3,000 or more years ago. In parts of the Montaña, the belt loom, an Andean type, was also found.

The tropical forests used domesticated cotton and sometimes wild cotton for textiles, but they never used wool, either of domesticated or of wild animals. The principal woven products were bands, hammocks, and, near the Andes, the cushmas and tipoys previously mentioned. Decoration of cloth was fairly simple, being limited largely to woven-in stripes of different colors. Near the Andes, however, designs were characteristically painted on the finished cloth. Perhaps this was a poor imitation of the elaborated woven and brocaded designs found in textiles of the Central Andes.

A twined or finger weave was used for textiles only among some of the Tucanoans and a great many of the Tupians. This is a more primitive weave in that such mechanical aids as the heddle cannot be used, and as in twined basketry, the weft must be passed through the warp elements with the fingers.

Netting had a somewhat scattered distribution and was found in the Guianas, northwestern Venezuela, Bolivia, and among the Achagua and Sáliva, and others, that is, principally among Indians who lack the heddle loom.

Bark cloth. A number of the tropical-forest people in some of the more isolated and less developed regions of the western Amazon, eastern Brazil (Carajá), and Central America manufactured cloth from the bark of special trees by a method almost identical with that used in the Pacific and Southeast Asia. The bark was stripped from the tree, softened, and separated into layers. The layers were then placed crosswise upon one another, moistened, and pounded with a special mallet until they became amalgamated. This crude cloth was often painted and dyed. The manufacture of bark cloth is quite old, since what are clearly bark cloth beaters have been found in archaeological sites in South and Central America. It is probable that such cloth was the ancestor of the paper made by the aboriginal Mexicans.

Bark cloth was used for masks and occasionally for garments, but principally it afforded a poor substitute for woven textiles. For this reason it was found largely among people who lacked loom weaving. Where

Cubeo manufacture of bark cloth. Man in center pounds short log to loosen its bark; man at left strips bark from log; man at right stretches bark. (Courtesy of Irving Goldman.)

both techniques were known in the same group, poor men who had no wives to weave true cloth used bark cloth instead.

Pottery. Pottery containers were manufactured by most tropical-forest Indians. The skill with which the pots were made and the artistic merits of their decoration did not compare with the ceramics of the Circum-Caribbean or Andean areas. A few of the people of the lower Amazon and its tributaries and some of the Tupí-Guaraní painted their pottery rather crudely. Modeling, incising, and use of stuck-on decorations were somewhat more characteristic of the area than painting. This plastic treatment links the lower Amazon with the Circum-Caribbean area.

Certain unusual styles in ceramic modeling and plastic decoration have been found in prehistoric sites on the island of Marajó at the mouth of the Amazon and, somewhat differently stylized, in the region of Santarém and beyond, farther upstream.

In addition to ceramic containers, considerable use was made of painted gourds and of gourds and calabashes which were decorated by pyrograving.

Houses. The characteristic house was constructed of a frame of poles and covered with thatch, providing a reasonably dry shelter in the hot, humid climate. House size differed greatly. Houses designed to shelter extended lineages were enormous vaults, which were 100 to 200 feet long and 50 to 60 feet high. Those built for single families were little more

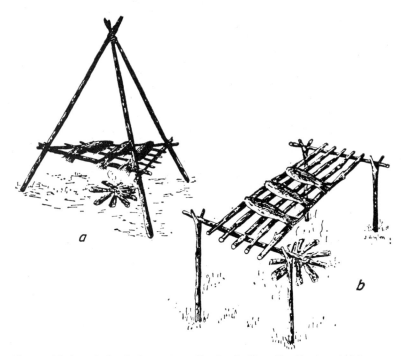

Types of babracots for drying and roasting food. (From Handbook, vol. 3.)

than double lean-tos. Interior arrangements in a house depended upon the nature of the society occupying it. Commonly each family had an area divided off from others by vertical mats.

A characteristic item of household furnishing was a twined or netted hammock. The hammock was used throughout most of the area for sleeping, although it afforded no warmth on chilly nights. In certain peripheral parts of the area, it served only as a cradle. Most houses were provided with carved wooden stools. Among a few groups, the privilege of sitting upon these stools was accorded only to dignitaries. This feature is reminiscent of the Andes, where elaborately decorated thrones were used by the heads of states. Status differences in the tropical forests were too trivial to make special seats an important feature. Every house had characteristic utensils for preparing food: wooden mortars and pestles to crush the various wild and domesticated vegetables, a babracot —a kind of grill made of wood—for cooking and smoking meats and fish, a manioc squeezer or tipití, storage pots and baskets, and cook pots.

It is rather surprising that little protection was found against the mosquitoes that infest this area. Body grease and paint, although usually applied ornamentally, served this purpose somewhat unsatisfactorily. The Yagua and some of their neighbors on the upper Amazon covered the body with an enormous number of fibers which hung loose from the neck to the ankles. Most of the rain-forest people simply endured the ravages of mosquitoes and other insects. Protection from mosquitoes while sleeping was equally absent. The Otomac and some of the Montaña groups constructed mosquito shelters inside the big house, but others did nothing except hover in the smoke at night when they could not sleep.

Rubber. Rubber, made from the sap of trees of the genus *Hevea*, is generally known to have been an aboriginal product within this area. Possibly the tropical-forest people were the first to discover the useful properties of this sap, although a kind of rubber was made from other latex-yielding plants in aboriginal times as far north as Mexico. Moreover, not all of the tropical-forest peoples extracted rubber.

The number of articles made from rubber was quite limited: finger rings and figurines made of solid rubber, and hollow syringes and balls. The syringes were used for enemas, and the balls for games. To make the syringes and balls, layers of rubber were spread over a core of clay. When the clay dried, it was broken into powder and removed through a hole which was then sealed over.

Musical instruments. The tropical-forest peoples had a fairly impressive list of musical instruments of different kinds and for different purposes. Gourd rattles were characteristically, though not exclusively, used by shamans. These, interestingly, have become the maracas of modern dance bands. Trumpets, some of them 6 or 8 feet long, generally had a special role. They were employed in the secret cult of the ancestors in the northwest Amazon, but were also used by the Otomac in festivals and the Sáliva during funerals. Panpipes were very widespread and must have been introduced at an early period, since they have been found in archaeological sites dating 2,000 to 3,000 years ago in both Mexico and Peru. Other musical instruments included several kinds of flutes, clarinets, oboes, jingles, and stamping tubes. The last were long, hollow bamboo sticks one end of which was thumped on the ground.

A particularly interesting item is the signal drum, a large, hollowed log which was used to send messages over considerable distances. Both the construction and the use of this drum were similar to those of signal drums found in Africa and parts of the Pacific. The signal drum, like bark cloth and the blowgun, which also have Old World parallels, had a distribution from Central America through Colombia, western Guiana, and a few northwest Amazon tribes. It is entirely possible that all three

Bora signal drums. (Courtesy of Paul Fejos, Wenner-Gren Foundation.)

features had an Old World origin, although their antiquity in America seems to antedate the possibility of trans-Pacific transportation.

6. SUMMARY

The tropical-forest culture is clearly linked with the Circum-Caribbean in a number of features. Both areas used pole frame and thatched houses, hammocks, heddle looms, basketry, pottery, bark cloth, rubber, dugout canoes, hollow-log signal drums, the babracot, and poisoned arrows. The tropical-forest peoples of the north portions of the area shared with the Circum-Caribbean a village organization which had strong matrilineal tendencies and village chieftainship. Both areas palisaded their villages against attacks. The Circum-Caribbean peoples, however, had state organization, a priest-temple-idol cult of varying degrees of development, knowledge of metallurgy, construction of roads and bridges, use of irrigation (but not on the Central Andean scale), social classes consisting of overlords, commoners, and perhaps slaves or captive laborers, and national warfare, all of which were almost entirely absent among the tropical-forest peoples. The features which the Circum-Caribbean culture possessed and the tropical forest did not were those which made the Circum-Caribbean cultures somewhat like the Central Andes. That the Circum-Caribbean culture should share so many features with the tropical forest is probably explainable by fundamental similarities in environment. These features are largely absent in the arid and high Central Andes.

This portion of the volume has characterized the general pattern of the tropical-forest culture, enumerated the distinctive elements, and suggested both historical and cultural-ecological explanations of these characteristics. Within the area of the tropical-forest cultures, there were certain local divisions or subareas that had their own distinguishing characteristics. These subareas differed in part because of their unequal access to the more inventive centers and in part because of the effects of local cultural-ecological factors. Subsequent chapters will consider separately: (1) the Guianas; (2) the Island Carib; (3) the Tupinambá; (4) the Guaraní; (5) the Chiriguano; (6) the people of the Amazon, most of whom were Tupian-speaking, and the somewhat less developed Tupian-speaking Tapirapé and Tenetehara; (7) the Montaña lying along the eastern flank of the Andes, an area that was extremely varied culturally, although the Panoans, Jívaroans, and Cahuapanans had most of the cultural traits typical of the Guianas and the lower Amazon; (8) certain semi-marginal or nomadic peoples within the Montaña, who lacked many of the characteristic traits and who include a northern group consisting of Záparoans, Pebans, and Western Tucanoans and a southern group including the Panoans and certain Arawaks who lived in the mountains away from the main streams; (9) the northwest Amazon; (10) eastern Colombia and lowland Venezuela, where the tropical-forest type of culture was found among the Arawakan Achagua, the Cariban Piritú, and the Sáliva; (11) tropical-forest peoples of the eastern Colombian lowlands; (12) village enclaves among the Circum-Caribbean chiefs; (13) the eastern Brazilian highlands, an area of simple people, probably recent nomads turned farmers.

These various subareas were distinctive for three basic reasons. First, natural resources and possibilities for exploiting them led to differences in population groupings and occupational specialization. Second, contacts with neighboring cultures introduced special features here and there. Third, owing to the intricacies of diffusion, many culture elements of wide distribution were used locally in innumerable combinations, as different as those caused by the turn of a kaleidoscope.

NOTES

1. Alfred Métraux, *Handbook*, vol. 3.
2. Clifford Evans and Betty J. Meggers are carrying out a long-range plan of archaeological research in the tropical forests. See "Preliminary Results of Archaeological Investigations in British Guiana" (Abstract), *Proceedings of the International Congress of Americanists*, vol. 31, São Paulo, 1955. Also, Betty J. Meggers and Clifford Evans, *Archeological Investigations at the Mouth of the Amazon,* Bureau of American Ethnology Bulletin 167, 1957.
3. Matthew W. Stirling, *Historical and Ethnographical Material on the Jivaro Indians,* Bureau of American Ethnology Bulletin 117, 1938.

► twelve

VARIETIES OF
TROPICAL-FOREST VILLAGES

1. THE GUIANAS: MATRILINEAL SOCIETIES

This area includes British, French, Dutch, and Brazilian Guiana, and part of Venezuela. Much of the territory, especially that near the coast, is extremely swampy, but there are no major rivers comparable to the Orinoco or the Amazon. The native cultures of the Guianas have largely disappeared owing to the settlement of the country near and along the coast at a very early date by escaped Negro slaves, the "bush Negroes," who introduced an African culture which is retained even to the present day. The area also has other foreign ethnic minority groups, including a small enclave of Malaysians. The settlement of the Negroes pushed the Indians back into the interior, where some readaptation of their aboriginal way of life must have occurred. The principal recent studies of the native Indians of this area include excellent analyses of the material culture made by Roth, Gillin's ethnographic account of the Barama River Carib, and Simpson's report on the Camaracotó.[1]

The subsistence basis. The cultivated fields consist of one to two acres which are cleared communally by the members of the village and then worked by women. The plants cultivated are much the same as those in other parts of the tropical-forest area, except that they included certain native fruits such as the avocado. A characteristic dish was the "pepper pot." This is a kind of hunter's stew consisting of a large number of plant and animal ingredients seasoned with pepper and perpetuated by constant additions to the pot so that its contents are never quite exhausted.

Settlements. The present-day settlements of the area range between 30 or 40 and 200 persons, but it is very possible that in native times, when villages were built on the coast and had access to sea foods as well as to river and agricultural resources, they were considerably larger.[2]

Transportation. Water transportation on the coast was well developed, which helped make possible fairly large aboriginal communities. Dugouts were built with an extra gunwale which gave greater seaworthiness. It seems probable that in native times sails of woven mats were used. Transportation on land depended solely upon human carriers, who used baskets and traveled along well-marked paths, but not roads, and who crossed streams by means of logs.

Social features. Communities generally consisted of several lineages, and they tended to be matrilineal owing to a strong preference for matrilocality. The Arawak of the coast, like those of the Antilles, had nonlocalized, matrilineal clans. Not all communities, however, were matrilineal. The Arawakan Palicur and the Cariban Aparai and Wapishana had nonlocalized patrilineal clans. Since such clans were not characteristic of the Guianas nor of the Circum-Caribbean area to the north, they probably are explainable as an intrusion from the region to the west, nearer the Amazon Basin, where the Indians were characteristically patrilineal.

One factor making for matrilineality was the unusually strong development of bride service. The prospective bridegroom lived with and served his future father-in-law for several years before marriage. In some cases, especially among the Caribans, the sons-in-law together with male captives from foreign groups came to form a kind of servile class under the control of the father-in-law. Among the Rucuyen, sons-in-law formed permanently matrilocal members of such a class, which has been called "peito."

Life cycle. There are few data on the details of socialization among these or any tropical-forest peoples which would contribute greatly to an understanding of the formation of the adult cultural personality. Most data pertain to the ritual observed at key points in an individual's life and only secondarily give some idea of how the youth was trained for adulthood.

The couvade was very strongly developed in the Guianas. Young children began to learn adult skills through playing with toy implements and weapons of the kinds they would use later. At the onset of their menses, girls were secluded from the village, and among the Macusi, they were also whipped. Adolescent boys were forced to endure the ant ordeal and to prove their readiness for marriage by showing their ability to work, to hunt, and to build houses. When a death occurred, the village held a mourning ceremony during which the people were whipped in order to drive away evil spirits. A drinking bout concluded the ceremony. Disposal of the body varied with each group. Some buried in the ground or in an urn, some cremated, and some mummified.

Warfare. Warfare was very prevalent in this area, particularly among the Carib whose practice of cannibalism gave their name to this custom. Although captives were eaten or in some cases kept as members of the peito class, the purpose of warfare was not nationalistic in either an economic or a religious sense.

Prior to an attack, the war party performed certain rites of excitation, which included invocation of the jaguar spirit, taking of putrid substances, and individual boasting of war exploits. In making an attack, the warriors assailed a village before dawn using arrows and occasionally blowguns. It is worth noting that this is one of the few cases in which the deadly blowgun was used in warfare. Nearly all other tropical-forest people limited it exclusively to hunting. The war arrows used in this and other areas, however, were frequently poisoned with substances other than curare. They were no doubt as lethal as blowgun darts, although slower to take effect. For defense against attacks, some villages were palisaded and protected by traps placed on the paths approaching them.

These wars were motivated primarily by desire for revenge and to take captives for cannibalistic rites. In post-Columbian times, however, many of the Indians carried out raids to take slaves who were sold to the whites as plantation workers.

Human trophies were aboriginally used to a limited extent. The head of a slain captive was kept for a short time, and the long bones were made into flutes.

Religion. Although religion in the Guianas functioned on a village level and centered primarily in beliefs in nature spirits, in limited group ceremonialism, and in shamanism, there is slight evidence of an incipient temple-idol cult. An early account of the Carib mentions that a stone idol was kept in a temple in a manner suggesting the Circum-Caribbean tribes.

The principal religious emphasis in the Guianas was shamanism, which involved very elaborate curing rites. While working over his patient, the shaman sat upon a special carved bench and shook a rattle which contained crystals. He also took a tobacco drink and smoked cigarettes to induce a proper emotional state, then blew upon his patient, from whom he eventually pretended to suck out the objects that had caused disease. In addition to curing illness, a shaman could also foresee the future and give advice based on this knowledge. He served as a seer, however, only for individual persons and not for the society as a whole. The only community service rendered by the shaman was to make fertility magic, to promote the growth of manioc.

2. THE ISLAND CARIB: MARITIME WARRIORS AND CANNIBALS

The Island Carib occupied all of the Lesser Antilles and part of the island of Trinidad. According to oral tradition, they had set out from the mainland of Venezuela and within less than a hundred years prior to the visit of Columbus had conquered all of these islands. Extremely warlike, they were still expanding at the time of the discovery, when they were raiding the Arawak of Jamaica. It is probable that the Arawak had been the predecessors of the Carib in the Lesser Antilles.

After the Conquest, the Carib population declined rapidly even though Europeans did not really colonize the Lesser Antilles until between 1650 and 1700. Meanwhile, a very interesting group known as the "Black Carib" developed on the island of St. Vincent, where shipwrecked Negro slaves had intermarried with the native Carib Indians. This group finally moved to the coast of Honduras.

A peculiar feature of the language of the Lesser Antilles is that Carib was spoken only by the men, while the women spoke Arawak. The reason for this undoubtedly is that the Arawak had been the principal object of Carib raids and that male captives were killed but the women were taken as wives. The segregation of the sexes and the slavelike status of these women, as described below, were sufficient to preserve the language differences.

Subsistence. The subsistence of the Island Carib is notable first for the cultivation of more fruit crops than was common in other tropical-forest areas. These fruits included pineapples, papayas, and guayavas. Second, the Carib were seafaring and coastal people and did a good deal of fishing. They refused, however, to eat manatee, turtles, and all land animals except agouti and lizards. Since game was almost absent on these islands, this taboo could not have worked a serious hardship.

The Carib were essentially maritime people. They were expert navigators, and to judge by early accounts, they made some of the best canoes in native America. The canoe hull was hollowed from a log, and the sides were built up by the addition of planks. Some of the largest canoes, which held as many as fifty persons, were fitted with two or three masts and sails made of mats or woven cotton. It is possible that use of planked sides, masts, and cotton sails was introduced by Europeans, but the weight of the evidence indicates that these were native inventions. These canoes were highly polished, their sterns elaborately carved, and the entire vessels adorned with paintings.

Social structure. Island Carib society evidenced internal conflicts, since it was subject to several rather irreconcilable influences. The village was usually described as "small," which apparently meant about 100 or 200 persons. In the center of the village was the men's house, where all males slept, ate, and were attended and waited on by the women. The extent of masculine dominance was probably unequaled in native South America. Women dressed and fed their husbands, cleaned the men's house, and cultivated the fields, in addition to keeping their own houses and rearing their children. The women's houses surrounded the men's house.

Since the traditional rules called for residence in the wife's village after marriage and since the villages were quite small, they must frequently have consisted of a matrilineal lineage which was exogamous. An exception to the rule of matrilocality was the village chief, who was in charge of communal fishing and land cultivation. The chief remained in the village of his birth and presided over his sons-in-law, who were subservient to him.

Two factors introduced confusion into these marital arrangements. First, the Carib were polygynous, and it seems that plural wives were not necessarily sisters, for a man might have wives in different villages. Second, captive Arawak wives were introduced to the village of the husband's residence, and while they did not necessarily share the houses of the wives born in the village, they found themselves outsiders if the village were a matrilineal lineage. That the women's language was Arawak, however, shows that captive women had completely outnumbered the original Carib women. The segregation of males in the men's house and the complete subordination of women to a slavelike status would help preserve different languages between the sexes. It is unfortunate that more precise information concerning these strangely conflicting practices is not available.

Warfare. Warfare was the overwhelming interest of the Island Carib and constituted the core of their cultural values. There was no hereditary class of warriors; in fact, war operations were very individualistic. All men lived to fight and gain prestige by their exploits. Warfare had the ultimate objective of taking male captives to supply victims for cannibalism and female captives as additional wives.

A war chief controlled the men of an entire island. To be eligible for this status, he had to have inherited a caracoli—a crescentic ornament made of a gold-copper alloy. These caracoli were originally made in Colombia and were traded to Venezuela, where the Carib evidently captured them from the mainland Arawak.

Prior to a raid, the warriors excited themselves by drinking chicha, the native beer, and eating preserved human flesh. Attacks were always intended to surprise the enemy, whose village was raided at dawn. Fire arrows were first shot into the thatched houses, then the men attacked with clubs, javelins, and arrows poisoned with certain vegetable ingredients. If the attack succeeded, some of the enemy corpses were eaten on the spot. The captives were brought home, and the men were bound for five days before they were killed according to fixed procedure which included several means of torture. First, they were placed in the men's house, where they were thrust with burning brands and cut in various places, after which pepper was rubbed into the wounds. Then they were shot with arrows, beaten to death with a club, and cooked. The victim was expected to shout defiance at his tormentors. Courageous warriors received the victim's heart, and other men ate the remainder of the body, except that the chiefs were presented the fat, which they preserved for later use.

During the cannibalistic rites, the war chiefs boasted of their valiant deeds. Afterwards, a warrior took the name of the enemy he had killed.

Female captives, though sometimes referred to as "slaves" and treated as such in many ways, were given to the warriors as wives. Despite their subservience to men, they did not constitute a hereditary class of slaves, since their children were born free.

Human trophies were of comparatively little interest to the Island Carib, but bones of the victims were sometimes kept.

Religion. While the Island Carib had no community rites for village spirits or idols, individuals were believed to have beneficent familiar spirits or guardian spirits, to whom they made offerings. Shamans had spirit-helpers, which were good or evil. Spirits gave the power to cure, prophesy, cause trouble, and influence the outcome of warfare.

One aspect of the shamanistic rite was unusual in this type of culture. The shaman performed in the men's hut, where he made offerings of food to his supernatural power, which might enter and speak through an old woman. It is not clear whether this is the more common pattern of possession of the shaman by the spirit-helper or whether it is some sort of oracular rite like that of the Circum-Caribbean peoples. Suggestive of the latter is the belief that a spirit might also speak through a cotton figurine and that the hair and bones of the shaman's ancestors contained such spirits.

Life cycle. The couvade was very prominent among the Island Carib. At the time of childbirth, the mother merely fasted briefly. When his first child was born, the father, however, complained of labor pains and then lay in a hammock in a special hut and observed food taboos for forty days. After this he dieted for six months, scarified himself, and rubbed pepper into the wounds in order to make the child courageous.

A growing child was trained by his parents for adult life appropriate to its sex. At puberty, both sexes were scarified and required to fast three to four weeks. A boy was subjected to rites designed to prepare him for the role of a warrior. Pepper was rubbed into his wounds, and he was required to prove his skill in wielding a club and to show his fortitude when his father beat him. An adolescent boy entered the men's house, where he lived and slept thereafter. He was given prostitutes instead of having access to women of his own group.

3. THE TUPINAMBA: PATRILINEAL VILLAGES OF CANNIBAL WARRIORS[3]

A previous section has explained how many Tupian-speaking groups stimulated by the messianic Grandfather cult had migrated widely in late prehistoric and early historic times in search of the happy Land of the Grandfather. Some of these migrations carried a group of Tupians to the coast of eastern Brazil, where they became known collectively as the Tupinambá. Distributed along some 2,000 miles of coast from Ceará in the north to Porto Alegre in the south, they bore such local names as the Potiguara, Caeté, Tupinambá, Tupinikin, and Guaraní. The last name is also applied to their linguistic and cultural kin of Paraguay.

Prior to the Tupian migrations, the coast of Brazil was apparently occupied by very primitive and little-known groups speaking languages of the Ge-Pano-Carib family. These people were collectively called "Tapuya," a Tupian word meaning "enemy." A few of these survived on or near the coast at the time of the Conquest. Archaeological evidence found in the sambaquís, or shell mounds, shows that the Tapuya or their predecessors had some cultural affiliations with the rather primitive people found in the famous caves of Lagoa Santa in Brazil.

Subsistence. The combination of intensive farming and coastal fishing is probably responsible for the dense Tupinambá population and the unusually large villages. The Tupinambá grew five varieties of bitter manioc as well as several varieties of maize and other tropical-forest staples. They managed exploitation of riverine and coastal fishing by using dugout and bark canoes and log rafts. The use of ocean resources kept the Tupinambá close to the coast. Despite their distribution along more than 2,000 miles of coast, they apparently penetrated only a very few miles into the interior.

Social structure and settlement pattern. The basis of the Tupinambá community was the extended patrilineal family which made up the household and which was patrilocal after marriage. Each household had some thirty to sixty families, or 100 to 200 persons. Four to eight of these communal houses were built around a plaza in the center of the village. The villages therefore consisted of 400 to 1,600 persons and were among the largest in the entire tropical-forest area. Owing to the extremely warlike nature of the Tupinambá, who carried on continued hostilities against their fellow Tupinambá, villages were protected by double palisades.

Despite the fact that many women were captured in warfare and taken as wives or concubines, their children did not become free tribal members as among the Carib. These children might be reared for several years, but their ultimate fate was to be eaten.

Warfare. Tupinambá warfare was in some respects a more bloody pursuit than that of the Island Carib. It consisted of continued assaults that pitted Tupian communities against one another. The purpose of a raid was to avenge previous raids and to take victims for cannibalism and thus

The Tupinambá attack a palisaded village. (After Hans Staden, "Warhaftige Historia und . . .," 1557.)

afford individual warriors a chance to acquire prestige. Warfare was constant and constituted the principal emotional outlet. It is related that warfare was so highly regarded that, when certain of the Tupinambá were taken captive by the Portuguese and put to work on plantations, they protested bitterly that such a fate was not proper for a Tupinambá warrior. They much preferred the dignity and glory of being the victims of torture and cannibalistic rites to the humiliation of becoming slaves.

Before carrying out an attack, various magical rites were performed and omens observed, after which the warriors set out accompanied by their women. They first besieged the enemy village and shot incendiary arrows at the houses. When engaging the enemy face to face, they used bows and arrows and clubs. After a successful raid, they cut off the heads and genitals of the enemy they had killed and brought the captives back to their own village, insulting them on the return trip. At the village, they exhibited the captives, who meanwhile pretended extreme contempt for their captors.

The time for the torture and eating was set for a later date. Until that time, a captive was dressed like the villagers and allowed to move freely about the community, although a rope around his neck signified his status. Captives did not attempt to escape and return to their own villages, for their capture so ruined their status that this would have been unthinkable. Until the cannibalistic rite, they were not ill-treated, although they were periodically jeered at and forced to cleanse things that had been contaminated by a recent death.

Chicha was prepared for a drinking bout, to be held at the time of the sacrifice. The portions of the victim to be eaten by various people were allotted to them in advance. When all was ready, the prisoner was decorated and joined the villagers in general singing and dancing. He was killed by means of a special club but until then was permitted to throw missiles at his slayers. In some cases, village women had been allowed to marry the captive. These wives wept during the killing, but then joined the cannibalistic banquet. The victim's blood was drunk and the flesh eaten by everyone except the executioner. The relish with which this was done seems to contrast with Carib cannibalism. The latter might be described as essentially ritualistic, whereas Tupí cannibalism, like that of the Patángoro and certain other Colombian groups, also involved a genuine enjoyment of human flesh.

After the sacrifice, the executioner took a new name and was ritually purified lest the ghost of the victim find and injure him.

It is interesting to note that the Tupinambá had similar rites for a slain jaguar, the hunting of which had ritual importance to many of the tropical-forest peoples.

The term "slave" has been used for captives of both sexes who might be kept alive for some time, during which they were fairly well cared for, given spouses, and accorded all the privileges of the village except that they had to work for their masters. This term is inappropriate, however, because the eventual fate of every captive was to be slain and eaten. The same fate awaited even children of marriages between villagers and captives.

It is perhaps a significant corollary of the violent and excessive behavior entailed in these war activities that the Tupinambá placed great value upon smoothness of manners and cooperation between members of the community. It is said that quarrels were avoided so carefully that any serious misunderstanding might lead a person to run amok, destroy property, and perhaps even burn down his own house and that anger

Tupinambá cannibalistic victims were boiled in large pots or their arms and legs roasted on babracots. (After Hans Staden, "Warhaftige Historia und . . .," 1557.)

often led to suicide by eating earth. Possibly there is a nexus between the behavior toward fellow villagers and that toward members of other communities in that warfare provided an outlet for hostilities which accumulated within the village but were so severely suppressed that any lapse led to destruction of one's property and even the taking of one's own life.

Although the Tupinambá were more violent than the Island Carib in their war patterns, the effect of warfare upon relationships between the

Tupinambá burial ceremonies within a palisaded village. (After Hans Staden, "Warhaftige Historia und . . .," 1557.)

sexes was very different. The Island Carib, despite being somewhat matrilineal, accorded men status far superior to that of women, married captive wives, and permitted their children to be free members of the community. Tupinambá men had no such superior status and, in fact, lacked any kind of men's house or special men's organization, but female captives, even though temporarily married, were always sacrificed eventually and so were their children. Despite a strong tendency toward patrilineality among the Tupinambá, the women had far better status than their sisters among the Island Carib.

Religion. The Tupinambá believed that several supernatural beings were important to mankind. They feared various evil spirits and ghosts.

They identified the thunder god with the Grandfather, or culture hero, around whom centered the messianic movements previously mentioned. Among most tropical-forest tribes, celestial phenomena were little more than characters in mythology, but the thunder god of the Tupí was not only the culture hero but later became identified with the Christian God.

These supernatural beings were symbolized by painted images which were hung on poles and given offerings. Some reports may be taken to mean that the Tupinambá also made wax images which they kept in sacred huts, a practice much like the temple-idol complex, and that they used sacred rattles which were kept in special places away from the eyes of women and were given offerings.

The aboriginal messianic movement which led the Tupí to migrate so widely has been mentioned. Following the wars with the Portuguese, they developed a new form of revivalism very similar to those which occurred among North American Indians and many other native people throughout the world after they had been subdued by invaders but had not yet lost their aboriginal culture. After their subjugation, the Tupinambá believed that by reaching the promised Land of the Grandfather they could achieve immortality, regain their youth, and lead such an idyllic life that the very digging sticks used to cultivate the fields would work by themselves untouched by human beings. In many communities, the people stopped work and danced, hoping to reach that golden land.

4. THE GUARANÍ: SOUTHERN TUPIAN MIGRANTS[4]

Guaraní is the name given the Tupí of Paraguay. They were one of the Tupinambá groups of the southern Brazilian coast who migrated inland to what is today the republic of Paraguay. The Guaraní language is still spoken by the contemporary peasant population of nuclear Paraguay, that is, the region of the fertile plains along the Paraguay River in the general vicinity of Asunción, the capital, and many inhabitants of Asunción speak Guaraní as well as Spanish.

The migrations that took the Tupinambá down the coast of Brazil and the Guaraní to Paraguay, carried the Chiriguano all the way to the flanks of the Andes in Bolivia, where they were in immediate contact with the Inca Empire, whose frontier they were raiding in the fifteenth century. In pre-Spanish times, the Guaraní of Paraguay had only remote contacts with the Andes, from which they were separated by the Gran Chaco, but objects of gold and silver, which obviously originated in the Andes had found their way eastward to Paraguay and south to the La Plata River in such quantity that the latter took its name from the silver encountered there by the Spaniards. The Spanish conquest of Paraguay was largely motivated by the hope that what later proved to be a land almost devoid of minerals might be the fabulous El Paititi, or El Dorado, the source of unimaginable wealth in precious metals.

Subsistence. There was little about the aboriginal Guaraní subsistence to distinguish it from that of other tropical-forest people, except that mate, or Paraguay tea, as it is known in other countries today, was a native plant domesticate in this area. Mate is the national drink of modern Paraguay, and it is enjoyed by people in the modern world.

Social structure and community. The basic social structure of the aboriginal Guaraní villages was like that of the Tupinambá in that each village consisted of four to eight large houses and each house sheltered as many as sixty families that were related through the patrilineal line. The members of each household were apparently exogamous, as among the Tupinambá. That is, a man could not marry a woman of his own household, but might marry one of another household within the same village. Our sources suggest that there were also nonlocalized, patrilineal sibs. Each village had a civil chief, but he controlled few activities, and the shaman had more power than he.

The war patterns were very similar to those of the Tupinambá, but the Guaraní were not given to the excesses of the Tupinambá. The purpose of warfare was to take captives who were ultimately destined to be sacrificed and eaten. A captive man was given a wife, but after several months or a year, he was ceremonially killed. While being tortured, the victim was permitted to pelt his captors with stones and to boast of his courage. As among the Tupinambá, the victim took great pride in proving his courage and exhibiting bravado by hurling insults at his captors, who were tormenting him and beating him to death. The *coup de grâce* was delivered by children who crushed the captive's skull with a copper axe and then dipped their hands in the blood. Anyone who touched or ate the corpse took a new name, probably to prevent the ghost of the deceased from identifying him and harming him.

Religion. Among the Apapocuva-Guaraní, the shaman directed a sacred dance that was designed to ensure a good harvest, ward off danger, and guarantee the successful outcome of any collective enterprise.

Shamans were the principal religious and civil authorities. Their power came from the spirits of their own ancestors. While invoking this power, a shaman performed sleight of hand tricks, sipped mate from a small gourd container through a tube, smoked cigars or pipes of tobacco, and drank chicha. In addition to curing the sick, the shamans served as seers by consulting special bones which they kept in hammocks. Although the Grandfather cult had been a factor in Guaraní migrations, it acquired a revivalistic character after the Spaniards came to Paraguay. The movement was led by shamans, but it incorporated certain Christian elements such as belief in the Redeemer. The movement was designed partly to stir the people to revolt against and expel the Spaniards. It also held that the world would be destroyed by flood or fire and advocated migration eastward to the "land without evil."

The Guaraní today. The Guaraní, thanks to the efforts of Elman Service and Helen Service, are among the few South American Indians whose post-Conquest cultural change has been reconstructed from historical documents and whose present-day way of life has been thoroughly studied in the field.[5]

Most of the 1,000,000 or so people of nuclear Paraguay—the more densely populated region of the Paraguay River centering in Asunción, the capital—speak Guaraní. While many of these people also speak Spanish, a popular belief holds that a Guaraní culture as well as language has been perpetuated in Paraguay. A very strong cultural nationalism in Paraguay has made the Guaraní its symbol. Even the intellectual class of the country not only eulogize the Guaraní language but claim that Guaraní culture survives today and, in fact, that the peasants of Paraguay are Guaraní in race.

The Services found that the Paraguayan peasant has virtually no Guaraní culture. He is largely self-sufficient in that he grows practically all of his own food and meets many of his household and daily wants through his own manufactures, but he depends upon European plants such as oranges, wheat, and sugar cane and European animals such as cattle, pigs, horses, and chickens as much as upon native crops. He uses hammocks, drinks mate, and sometimes builds a house like that of his ancestors, but all other features of his culture are of Spanish origin. This culture differs from what is thought of as typically Spanish in that the poverty of the people precludes the well-known patterns of the upperclass Spanish subculture.

The aboriginal Guaraní were Hispanicized remarkably fast. At the Spanish conquest of Paraguay, the Guaraní comprised a fairly sparse population of subsistence farmers who were unable to produce a surplus to support groups of specialists and ruling classes. The Guaraní villages were based on kin groups in which individuals were essentially equal. Paraguay had little mineral or other wealth to induce Spanish settlement, but a few Spaniards remained there and married into these native kin groups. They established polygynous families, and sometimes had as many as twenty or thirty wives. They and their biologically mixed descendants retained the Guaraní language but were Hispanicized in virtually every other feature.

In the course of time the peasants began to produce certain cash crops in limited quantity for an outside market. Owing to Paraguay's isolation from sea-borne communications and the restrictions on trade through

Asunción with the outside, the importation of manufactured goods was quite limited. The peasants today have comparatively little use for cash and depend largely upon their own efforts. Attempts to create internal industries arc hindered by the lack of capital, the weakness of the local market, and the difficulty of finding workers. The peasants work for cash only long enough to finance a feast or buy a desired object, and then return to their subsistence economy.

The Paraguayan family today is no longer polygynous, but owing to the infrequency of civil or church weddings, the prevailing consensual unions arc very loose, and marriage ties are easily broken. Since children remain with their mothers, the contemporary Paraguayan peasant family, like that of impoverished peoples in many places in the world, tends to be matrilineal.

In native times, interfamilial and interpersonal ties were based on extended kinship relations in the patrilineal line. Today, actual kinship ties have been replaced by the Spanish ritual kinship bonds known as compadrazgo, or co-parenthood. These bonds, although presumably cemented through Catholic ritual, may be established without Church assistance. They serve to create close relations between compadres, that is, the parents and godparents of a child. Each person has many compadres among individuals of other classes and occupations.

Within the Paraguayan peasantry there is some slight inequality of wealth, which creates a range of differences in social status. Even the richest people, however, are unable to support the more typical Hispanic upper-class way of life. Few engage servants or laborers. Few can give their children more than two or three years of local primary schooling. Few are able to cultivate the arts, philosophy, and a regime of gracious living. Affluence is displayed principally in fiestas which are more lavish than those given by poor people. But there is no clear division between an upper and a lower class. The poorest members of the community are welcomed to the fiestas of the richest. Wealth is only comparative, and all the peasants share today what is substantially a lower-class Hispanic mode of life.

Religion in rural Paraguay is also characteristic of lower-class Spanish culture. The Catholic Church is not strongly developed, and many communities rarely see a priest. While religious belief is nominally Catholic, it really is a community, or folk-level, form of Catholicism, in which the cult of the saint predominates. There are household, village, and regional saints, each with his special festivals and religious brotherhood. These function in the absence of a Catholic priest. No features of aboriginal Guaraní religion and few, if any, native magical beliefs have survived.

The significance of the so-called Guaraní cutlure to contemporary Paraguay is little more than symbolic. An intense cultural nationalism underlies a strong political nationalism, which has been manifest in the several violent wars fought by this nation in the past century. Identification of this culture as Guaraní has given it emotional significance, but it is actually Guaraní only in language. Even the Guaraní language seems destined to play a minor role and someday disappear, for Spanish is becoming the language used in national functions such as government, business, and education. The present bilingualism, therefore, marks a developmental phase which has been found in other countries and still exists to a considerable extent in highland Ecuador, Peru, and Bolivia. Bilingualism is found where rural, ethnic, or lower-class subcultures survive in strength. It gives way to Spanish where national influences begin to outweigh distinctive local patterns.

Paraguayans ascribe much importance to the strong Guaraní racial element in the population. It must be stressed, however, that this element is Indian. There is no such thing as a distinctive Guaraní race.

5. THE CHIRIGUANO: RECENT MIGRANTS TO THE SOUTHERN ANDES

The Chiriguano were descendants of the Guaraní who, according to the calculations of Alfred Métraux, had migrated in four principal stages between 1471 and 1526 from Paraguay to the flank of the Andes. The last stage was recounted by certain shipwrecked Spaniards who had been part of it. The purpose of the migration is not at all clear, although the search for the land of the ancestors may have been one factor and the opportunity to raid the rich people of the Andes may have been another. During their migration across northern Paraguay and the Gran Chaco, the Chiriguano absorbed some of the Arawakan-speaking Chané.

The Chiriguano culture had the basic Tupian tropical-forest pattern, although a few elements were acquired from the Andean civilization. The native culture of the Chiriguano has been only sketchily reconstructed from contemporary records. The modern people, who number about 20,000, were studied in 1928 by the late Baron Erland Nordenskiöld of Sweden. This study, however, was concerned principally with material culture, and it was handicapped by the fact that the Chiriguano were by then strongly Europeanized.

The native Chiriguano village consisted of several large houses, each probably sheltering a lineage. Owing to the intensity of warfare, each village was palisaded. Modern villages, however, show the influence of recent changes in that the houses are much smaller, each being occupied by only two or three biological families. Aboriginal social structure seems to have been based on the patrilineal lineage, although bride service sometimes led to permanent settlement of a young man in the household of his father-in-law.

The Chiriguano retained the Tupian patterns of warfare previously described. It is said that when they were passing through the country of the Chané in the sixteenth century, they killed and ate as many as 60,000 of these Indians. Chiriguano children shot the captives to death with arrows. In more recent times, no doubt because new economic patterns gave value to labor, captives were retained as slaves. A somewhat distinctive feature of the native warfare was that the heads of captives were kept as trophies and periodically taunted.

Although the basic nature of Chiriguano society, village structure, warfare, and religion was not altered by contact with the Andes, a number of Andean culture elements were borrowed. Among these were masks, dances, clowns, dice games, gambling, coca chewing, manufacture of certain Andean pottery styles, beds built of planks on a slightly raised platform, cushmas, sandals, and tipoys, the last as a woman's garment. As in other areas near the Andes, adoption of the platform bed relegated the hammock to a place for resting during the day or to a cradle for infants.

6. TUPIANS OF THE AMAZON RIVER: VARIATIONS OF PATRILINEAL SOCIETIES

The general distribution of the Tupí-Guaraní–speaking peoples, together with historical evidence concerning their migrations, suggests that the Amazon or the region immediately to its south was perhaps the principal point of dispersal of this language group. Since, however, the Portuguese conquest of Brazil was water-borne and the more developed Tupian groups were coastal and riverine, the white invaders absorbed most of the Tupian peoples along the coast of Brazil and the Amazon River at a very early date. The Tupians not assimilated into European society were displaced so that they migrated and blended with other tribes. For these reasons, comparatively little is known about the Tupian peoples of the Amazon.

It is only recently that genuine ethnographic studies have been made of any Tupians within this general area. The late Kurt Nimuendajú obtained limited information concerning various small and more or less acculturated tribes of the lower Amazon, Charles Wagley and Eduardo Galvão studied the semi-marginal Tupian-speaking Tenetehara in eastern Brazil, and more recently Robert F. and Yolanda Murphy studied the Mundurucú of the Tapajoz River. In all cases the aboriginal culture is greatly changed, and many of the people have been assimilated into the rural Brazilian or caboclo population.

Several Arawakan groups scattered along the Amazon are no better known than the Tupí.

Starting at the mouth of the Amazon River, the Aruã, an Arawakan-speaking group, occupied Marajó Island at the coming of the Portuguese. These people are virtually unknown except by name, having been pushed into the interior when the Portuguese and Dutch fought for the mastery of trade in the area. There is no doubt, however, that the rather spectacular pottery and other archaeological remains found on this island

Modern Cocama girl, upper Amazon. (Courtesy of Abraham E. Guillém.)

cannot be ascribed to the Aruã, whose culture was fairly simple. The Manao and other Arawakan peoples in the middle Amazon are of interest because they are among the very few Indians who used the blowgun and curare poison in warfare. They are also unusual in that they took prisoners who were said to have served them as drudge slaves. These Arawakans, however, became slavers for the Portuguese, an activity which may have introduced the idea of slavery to them. According to fragments of information, the Manao had such characteristic tropical-forest customs as the couvade, confinement of girls and flogging of boys at puberty, and the practice of urn burial.

Far better known are the Omagua and Cocama on the upper Amazon. They were canoe Indians, whose villages were strung for many miles along the river. They cultivated many food plants, although bitter manioc was known only to the Omagua, and they raised cotton for weaving, tobacco, and two fish drugs, barbasco and *Clibadium*, which are fairly widely distributed in the tropical forests. Turtles and their eggs were an extremely important source of food in this region, but after the Europeans came eggs were collected in such great numbers for their oil that the turtle nearly became extinct. The Omagua and Cocama took fish by means of harpoons, spears, drugs, bows and arrows, and weirs. In early times, they used spear throwers, or atlatls, for hurling spears and harpoons, but in historic times, they substituted blowguns and poisoned darts for these weapons.

Omagua and Cocama social structure and village life have several interesting features. The household consisted of fifty or sixty persons who, as among so many other Tupian peoples, apparently constituted a single patrilineal lineage. Spanish expeditions of the sixteenth century found the houses closely spaced along the riverbanks, so that village limits were vague, but in some places there were concentrations of more than 200 houses. There is some evidence that the Omagua lineage houses were grouped in dual divisions, or moieties, but the social or religious function of the moieties is not known.

These people are exceptional in the tropical forests for their incipient class structure. The early Spanish writers describe a small group or class of "nobles" or "chiefs" whose members were initiated into their special status at childhood by means of a ritual haircut. After this rite, these individuals were carried about on litters. It is difficult to say whether these nobles constituted a permanent and hereditary superior class based on economic differentiation and surplus production. Since the Cocama are fairly near the Andes, where nobles were carried in litters as one of many evidences of their status, it is probable that palanquins diffused from that source, even though they were absent among most Indians of the Montaña. Among the Cocama, however, this mark of distinction may have been accorded only those individuals who were chosen for status rather than a hereditary class.

A second social class consisted of the common people, and a third of "slaves." The last probably consisted not only of captive women and children but also of men. The Cocama, unlike so many of their Tupian kin in Amazonia, were not cannibals and spared most of their captives, presumably to perform common labor. As among the Aruã, however, this slave class may have resulted from slave raids for the Portuguese colonists.

The Cocama, however, warred not only to obtain captives but to take head trophies, and many of their unfortunate male victims suffered this fate. Ritual aspects of this warfare incorporated features found in other religious contexts in the tropical forests; for example, before a battle each warrior rubbed pepper in his eyes and whipped himself.

The southern tributaries of the middle and lower Amazon were largely occupied by Tupian-speaking Indians, the better known of which were the Mundurucú of the lower Madeira and Tapajoz Rivers, the Parintintín, and the Cawahíb, Cayabí, and others farther up the tributaries. Southward toward the headwaters of the tributaries, the more characteristic features of the tropical-forest culture gradually were lost. Twilled baskets were made by most of the Indians near the Amazon, but the Parintintín and Cawahíb made only temporary containers plaited of palm leaves. Simple bark canoes, instead of dugout canoes, were used on the upper rivers. Loom weaving gave way to finger-twined cotton cloth. All these Tupians made pottery and used bows, lances, spears, clubs, and shields, but they lacked blowguns and spear throwers.

The Mundurucú

The Mundurucú are the best known of the south Amazon Tupians, owing especially to the early observations of the British naturalist Bates and to the recent research of Robert and Yolanda Murphy. Formerly, the Mundurucú village consisted of thirty or more family dwellings and a men's house. Each dwelling was a small matrilineal lineage, since it housed a woman and her female descendants. The Portuguese demand for farinha, or manioc flour, enhanced the importance of these households, for farinha was produced by women. After reaching adolescence, all males slept, ate, and carried on daily activities in the men's house, and visited their family dwellings only for purposes of sex, to play with their children, or to take a between-meal snack. The Mundurucú, however, were divided into nonlocalized, exogamous, patrilineal clans and moieties. The clans bore the names of plants and animals, which were believed to be the ancestors of the clan members and which were represented in ceremonies by sacred trumpets that women and children were not allowed to see or touch. How these clans may have developed from localized, exogamous lineages has been discussed previously. The simplest explanation of the moieties, or dual divisions, is that they were introduced from eastern Brazil, where they were so strongly developed among the Ge-speaking people but had also become part of the social structure of the Tupian Tapirapé and Tenetehara. These exogamous divisions meant that in marriage a man might take his wife from his own village or from another village, provided only that she be of a household, clan, and moiety different from his own.

Village members were bound together by several ties. Men cooperated in clearing the forests for farm plots but left cultivation to women. They associated closely with one another in men's affairs in their special house. The village was also a religious unit in that ceremonies were held for community benefit. Under the village chief, the men made war. Since, however, several villages often joined together in native times in raids for head taking, and later for slaving, which made the Mundurucú feared by Indians over a wide area, there was considerable intervillage cooperation and solidarity.

The native Mundurucú pattern of warfare differed from that of their neighbors largely in intensity. In aboriginal times, Mundurucú warriors raided principally to take head trophies. After killing the enemy, they removed his head, took out the brain, painted the head with urucú, and then laced the lips together and dried the trophy. Female captives, however, were taken as wives of Mundurucú men and their children became ordinary members of the village. If a Mundurucú were slain in battle, his fellow warriors endeavored to bring his head home so that a feast might be given in his honor. Afterwards, the head was worn by a relative. Warfare was the principal means of achieving status within the village, and to be a warrior was a prerequisite to living in the men's house. Slave taking for the Portuguese enormously increased the importance of warfare for its economic and social rewards.

Mundurucú religion was notable for its village fertility ceremonies, which were designed to increase fish and game and further the growth of manioc. These ceremonies were held in a special hut and were led by a shaman who endeavored to propitiate the spirits of the game and fish and who made offerings to the skulls of the special spirits concerned. The ceremonies were oracular in that the shaman, practicing ventriloquism, gave the answers of the spirits to questions put to him. The Mundurucú also held a peccary ceremony in which dancers imitated the young animals while a boar fights off a jaguar impersonator. This ceremony is supposed to protect the people against the greatly feared jaguar. As in the northwest Amazon, the Mundurucú also held special ceremonies in honor of the ancestors of the sib or clan.

Acculturation of the Mundurucú

The rubber trade in Amazonia initiated a series of culture changes which have now run their course among most of the Mundurucú. In aboriginal times, the Mundurucú left their villages, which were located on high ground, and traveled each year during the dry season to fish in the major streams. When the Portuguese created a demand for rubber, they began to collect latex from the wild rubber trees growing in gallery forests along these same streams and to exchange it for manufactured goods, especially hardware such as knives, axes, and pots. Dependence upon trade goods gradually extended to include clothing, food, and many luxury items as well as necessities. Knowledge of native manufactures was lost.

The changed economy completely transformed Mundurucú social life. Constantly in debt for trade goods and ever more dependent upon them, families remained longer on the rivers gathering rubber until, one after another, they left the village to settle permanently along the streams. Today, each family has exclusive rights to tap the trees within a well-defined section of gallery forest. Here it lives in isolation, devoting itself to rubber collecting and to a small amount of farming. Aboriginal village institutions are virtually gone, and the families are loosely related to one another through the trading post with which they deal. The trader is not only their link with the economy of Brazil, but he is their patriarchal leader or patron. The Indians look to him for help and guidance, and they are bound to him through perpetual indebtedness in a system which involves credit but no cash.

Racially, the Mundurucú are still Indians, but culturally they are a special subsociety or subculture of Brazil. Were transportation to be improved, production of additional trade commodities and a system of cash transactions introduced, and other features of Brazilian national culture implanted, they would become like the widespread Brazilian caboclos, or backwoodsmen, whose Indian ancestors have been largely assimilated culturally and mixed racially.

Indians south of the Amazon

The Indians of Amazonia who lived farther south along the lesser tributaries occupied much smaller villages, some of which consisted of only a few houses, each sheltering a single family. These villages had neither men's houses, an ancestor cult, nor clans. They carried on considerable warfare, principally to take trophy heads, but some took victims for cannibalistic rites. Their religious ceremonies were held in honor of ghosts, which is perhaps a variation of the widespread household or sib ceremonies for the ancestors.

The high, arid plateau of eastern Brazil is occupied by a large block of Ge-speaking people most of whom are nomadic hunters and gatherers. Many of the larger streams, however, drain into lower country where agriculture is possible in the gallery forests which line their banks. Two Tupian tribes, the Tapirapé and the Tenetehara, are fairly well known, owing to Wagley's studies of the former and Wagley and Galvão research among the latter.

The Tapirapé are similar to the Tupian peoples in their reliance upon bitter manioc and their manufacture of twilled and woven baskets, twined cotton hammocks, and incised pottery, but they lacked canoes. Socially, the Tapirapé are more like the Ge than their Tupian relatives. Their households are matrilineal, and the houses are grouped around a men's house in the center of the village. Each village is divided into patrilineal moieties which control occupations and sports but do not regulate marriage. Each moiety is divided into three age groups, the members of which have special duties appropriate to their age. Even the men's house is divided into two sections.

Moieties compete against each other in games, particularly in the log race, which is characteristic of the various northern Ge-speaking people. In this race, a member of each moiety carries a log, which is up to a foot in diameter and 6 or 8 feet long, over a well-marked racecourse for many hundreds of yards or even several miles.

The tendency, which is so strong among the Ge, to proliferate various kinds of associations is also manifest among the Tapirapé. In addition to age-graded moieties, a village is also divided into eight associations in which men take membership from their fathers and women from their mothers.

7. INDIANS OF THE MONTAÑA: SEMINOMADIC FARM VILLAGES

The eastern flank of the Andes from Ecuador to Bolivia is known as the Montaña, and its inhabitants are sometimes collectively called the Chuncho. A large number of linguistic groups occur in this area, many of them being found nowhere else, although the very widespread Arawakan language is represented by the Campa and other groups of eastern Peru and Bolivia. The most important linguistic groups are Panoan, Cahuapanan, and Jívaroan, but there are many others.

The area is very mountainous, and the headwaters of the Amazon originate in extremely precipitous canyons cut deep in the Andes. A tropical-forest type of culture is found in the Montaña along the low, warm reaches of the main rivers. Among the more rugged mountains and on the smaller tributaries in the hinterland of the country, the Indians lacked most of the characteristic tropical-forest features and somewhat resembled nomadic forest hunters and gatherers.

The history of the Montaña may be divided roughly into four periods. The first is prehistoric and is itself subdivided. There is slight evidence of Andean influence when the Formative-period culture was rapidly spreading in all directions. Somewhat later in prehistoric times, it is probable that a culture more specifically adapted to the tropical forests spread upstream; the many languages in this area indicate successive

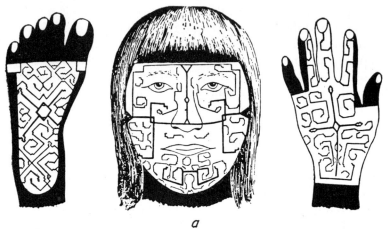

a

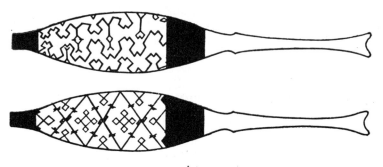

b

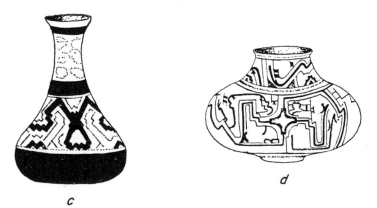

c

d

Art style in the Peruvian Montaña. (a) Body decoration among the Shipibo Indians. (b) Shipibo weaving swords. (c) Piro pot. (d) Panobo olla. (From Handbook, vol. 3.)

migrations. The striking similarity of the art style of the Panoan-speaking Indians of eastern Peru to that of Marajó strongly suggests a direct historical connection between the Montaña and the mouth of the Amazon. Evans and Meggers believe the Marajó people had come down the Amazon, but not necessarily from eastern Peru. The spread of peoples and culture upstream stopped in the deep valleys on the eastern flank of the Andes, where the innumerable linguistic groups became isolated and differentiated from their neighbors. Despite the proximity of the Montaña to the high culture of the Andes, there was surprisingly little influence of the Andean cultures upon the Montaña, except in isolated culture elements such as the belt loom, head deformation, the platform bed, and a few others. The twenty or so miles of steep, rainy, foggy, and cold mountains—the Ceja de la Montaña, or "Eyebrow of the Montaña" —lying between 2,000 or 3,000 feet and 5,000 or 6,000 feet seems to have been a rather effective culture barrier and to have been virtually uninhabited.

The second period of this area is that of Spanish exploration, which lasted from 1532, when Peru was conquered, to about 1643. Whites penetrated the area largely from the highlands. Missionaries and others introduced the Quechua language widely in the Montaña, where it became a lingua franca and supplanted many native tongues. A few towns were founded during this period, but none survived. Nor were any lasting effects made on the Indian culture, although European diseases took a heavy toll.

The third period witnessed considerable white influence on the Indians, owing mostly to the work of the missionaries, first the Jesuits and later the Franciscans and others. This period lasted from about 1643 to 1830, the Jesuits being most influential until their expulsion in 1767.

The missions affected the Indians in several ways. In the first place, the Indians were attracted to large mission villages mostly by the opportunity to obtain steel tools and such new crops as bananas and sugar cane. Second, contacts of different ethnic groups at the villages served to spread many aboriginal features such as the blowgun, the dugout canoe, and the Quechua language. Third, the people were forced to wear more complete dress and to adopt Christian burial. Dress, burial, and other traits of Christian European culture did not last, however, after the Indians fled from the missions and retreated into the forests. But the steel axes upon which most Indians now depended, enabled the people to build better canoes, to travel farther, and therefore to concentrate in large communities.

There were also adverse effects. Hostilities arose among Indians of different groups who had been brought together in the mission villages, resentment against the Europeans resulted from the banning of polygyny, while the Portuguese slave raids which started in 1694 created general warfare throughout the area. This warfare pitted Indian groups against one another for purposes and in ways unknown in aboriginal times. This new kind of warfare, together with European diseases, killed possibly two-thirds of the population.

There resulted a succession of revolts in 1686, 1695, 1704, 1742, and 1767. The Indians massacred the white settlers and expelled or killed the missionaries. In 1767, the Jesuits were ordered out of the missionary field and the Franciscans took over.

Chief, war captain, and judges among modern Canelos Indians. Canes are symbols of authority. (Courtesy of the American Museum of Natural History.)

One of the most interesting of the Indian revolts was that in 1742, which followed a worldwide pattern of messianic movements elsewhere among primitive peoples. The point had been reached when the native culture was seriously threatened, the people were dying, and the whites were definitely beginning to weaken the Indians' hold on the country. A Cuzco-born Indian, who had been educated in Spain, proclaimed himself to be the son of God and a descendant of the Inca Emperor and asserted that he had the wisdom of Solomon and the ability to make mountains fall. Claiming that he was sent by God to restore His kingdom, he commanded a considerable following among the Indians.

The fourth period might be designated Republican or National, since it has lasted from the early nineteenth century, when the Latin American republics were gaining their freedom from Spain, to the present day. During this time, the whites made permanent settlements and began to reduce the Indians in the area to a state of serfdom. Toward the end of this period, starting about 1890 and lasting till 1910 or 1920, the rubber

Shrunken heads, Jívaro Indians, Ecuador. The strings from the mouths, lack of facial hair, and other features distinguish these from the many fakes made for sale. (Courtesy of the American Museum of Natural History.)

boom was a major factor in destroying the native way of life. The production of cash commodities for an external market linked the native people more closely with the larger institutions of the nations.

There are still missions in the area, and to a considerable extent aboriginal culture survives in the more remote and inaccessible mountainous areas. In general, the decline of the Indian population was directly proportionate to their stay in the early missions, where crowding facilitated the spread of smallpox and other European diseases.

The aboriginal culture of the Montaña has comparatively few features to distinguish it from other divisions of the tropical forest. Several items, however, are exceptional. The Muscovy duck was domesticated here, although it was so named after being taken to Russia. A number of highland features in the Montaña include cultivation of white potatoes and use of the llama and alpaca in the higher altitudes, especially the upper Marañón River, and the use of llamas and guinea pigs by the Jívaro. Many of these Indians use platform beds and have relegated the hammock to the role of cradle.

The native social structure is not very well known. Many of the more remote communities consist of a single house sheltering an extended family of fifteen or twenty persons. Some houses have only one nuclear family. The larger villages on the main rivers perhaps comprise one or more patrilineal lineages, as among most of the tropical-forest peoples, although Tessmann believes that matrilineal totemic clans were common to the tribes of the Ucayali River. Tessmann's evidence for this, however, is very unconvincing.

A well-publicized feature is the Jívaro custom of head-hunting. The custom is motivated principally by revenge and by the belief that the trophy head gives the taker supernatural power. Head-hunting is not a form of tribal warfare. The raiding parties attack villages in which they have relatives as often as not. To prepare the head, the skin is removed from the skull and hot sand poured in again and again in order to dry and shrink it, after which the lips are sewed in a characteristic way. Heads taken from unclaimed bodies in city morgues are shrunk in a somewhat similar manner and frequently sold to tourists in South America. These are distinguishable from the Jívaro specimens by the fact that they usually have mustaches or facial hair and that they lack the characteristic method of closing the mouth.

Some atypical people of the Montaña

These consist of two groups, first, the Záparoans and the Western Tucanoans in the north and, second, some of the hinterland Panoans and Arawakans in the south. They differ from the better-known tropical-forest Indians largely in their lack of many of the characteristic features of the latter. All are farmers, but some rely more upon hunting and fishing than upon their crops. Those living on small and rapid streams lack canoes. Their population is fairly sparse, and their villages consist of a single nuclear family or a small extended patrilineal family. In warfare, they are the victims of more aggressive tribes on the larger rivers rather than genuine warriors themselves.

In technological features, certain primitive devices survive in place of the more developed tropical-forest forms. Some of these people use stone and iron pyrite to make fire, grind food in wooden troughs instead of in mortars, and make bark cloth or palm-fiber textiles instead of woven cotton cloth. Most of them make temporary palm-leaf baskets instead of durable woven baskets and use carrying nets in place of carrying baskets. Whereas the Panoans of the Ucayali River make excellent polychrome pottery, most of these backward peoples make only monochrome or crudely incised vessels.

A notable feature of the northern seminomadic groups and of certain of their neighbors in southeastern Colombia is the use of an enormous number of native drugs. Tobacco is used only by shamans, who take it and other drugs to help put themselves in a state of trance when performing their curing and other rites. It is taken in the form of cigars, cigarettes, snuff, pipes, juice, and leaf for chewing. Another plant used by shamans for its magical effect is a species of *Cyperus*. A species of *Banisteriopsis*, popularly known as cayapi, yagé, or ayahuasca, produces hallucinations and eventually sleep. Huanto, a species of *Datura*, is used here as in North America to foretell the future. Guayusa, a species of *Ilex*, and a creeper called yoco (*Paullinia yoco*) serve to sustain a person against fatigue, but are also used as emetics. Finally, coca, obtained in the higher portions of the Montaña, deadens the effects of pain and fatigue owing to its cocaine.

The blowgun, to judge by its distribution in native times, appears to have centered and possibly to have originated somewhere in this region. It, too, depended upon knowledge of a drug or poison, curare, which is derived from a creeper. It would seem that the Indians of this area had acquired a special interest in experimenting with the narcotics, poisons, and other drugs in their native flora and for this reason knew the use of so many of them.

It should be noted that most of these drugs were limited largely to ceremonial use in aboriginal times. In the highland, for example, coca was used in rites and handled only by the priests. In postwhite times, however, it was commonly consumed by everyone, since it fortified against hunger, cold, and fatigue. Similarly, tobacco and certain of the other drugs in the tropical forests were used in native times by shamans to conjure up their supernatural powers, but after the coming of the whites they were used daily by everyone.

8. THE JURUÁ-PURÚS RIVER AREA: SEMINOMADIC FARM VILLAGES

A number of linguistic groups formerly occupied the large territory centering around the Juruá and Purús Rivers, southwestern tributaries of the Amazon. Chief among these were the Panoan, Catukinan, and Arawakan peoples. These Indians largely disappeared following the early exploitation of rubber, which extended up the rivers deeply into this territory.

The Panoan-speaking Indians of this area formed a single large block with their linguistic kin of the Ucayali River of eastern Peru, but they were more like the Panoans of the mountainous hinterland east of the Ucayali River than those of the river proper. Although they subsisted by

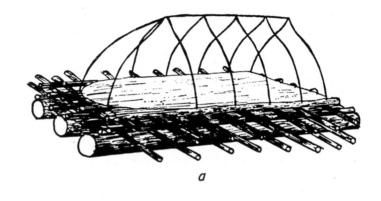

a

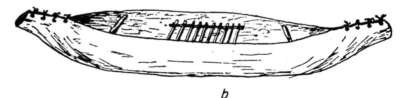

b

Primitive craft on the Juruá-Purús headwaters. (a) Paumarí raft. (b) Yamamadí bark canoe. (From Handbook.)

farming, their social groups were small and impermanent. These Panoans had somewhat extensive puberty observances for girls during which their teeth were stained, their noses were pierced for ornaments, and they were deflowered. Ritual cannibalism of the dead is also reported.

The Arawakan-speaking people also formed a continuous block with their primitive linguistic relatives of the upper Ucayali River of eastern Peru and Bolivia. These Indians depended largely upon fishing and hunting, in which they used the blowgun, spear, and bow and arrow. They manufactured twilled baskets, plain pottery, hammocks, loom-woven bands, and dugout and bark canoes. The use of sacred flutes and bark trumpets that are taboo to women and children in a feast dedicated to nature spirits links them with some of the peoples of the northwest Amazon.

9. EASTERN BOLIVIA: A CULTURALLY MIXED AREA

Eastern Bolivia was one of the most diversified cultural and linguistic areas of any part of South America. In part, this diversity corresponds to the extreme geographical differences: plains in the east and southeast, rain forests in the north and northeast, a large highland area to the west extending to Lake Titicaca in the Central Andes, and the extremely arid Gran Chaco, with its sparse and xerophytic vegetation in the south. In part, the diversity may be explained by the fact that cultural influence had spread up the several major river systems that originate in Bolivia: the Madeira River which flows into the Amazon, the Paraguay River which flows eventually into the Paraná River and empties into the Atlantic Ocean at Buenos Aires, and the Pilcomayo River which traverses the Gran Chaco and flows into the Paraguay River. The many linguistic differences found at the headwaters of most South American rivers strongly suggest that migrations tended to run upstream, where groups became isolated off in areas on the whole unfavorable for culture development of the tropical-forest type. The tremendous linguistic diversity at the headwaters of the Amazon on the Ucayali and Marañon Rivers is paralleled in Bolivia. Despite the fact that the Indians of the Montaña and Bolivia were within only a few miles of the Andean civilization, they acquired comparatively few Andean traits. Many of them were in fact so primitive as to be classifiable as nomads.

In eastern Bolivia on the headwaters of the Madeira River were several groups of Panoan-speaking Indians, including the Sinabo, Chacobo, Caripuna, and Pacaguará, and Tacanan-speaking people, including the Tiatinagua and Araona. Members of other linguistic groups included the Leko, the Moseten-Chimane, and the Yuracare. The Tiatinagua, Leko, Mosetene-Chimane, Yuracare, and the Arawakan-speaking Apolista were on the frontiers of the Central Andean Aymara Indians of Bolivia. In addition to these groups, the headwaters of the Madeira River were occupied by the Móvima, Itonama, Canichana, and several Chiquitoan-speaking peoples. The Chapakura and a number of scattered Chapakuran-speaking peoples were found on the upper Guaporé River, and several enclaves of Bororo-Otukean–speaking groups lived among the Chiquitoans.

Several Arawakan groups, such as the Mojo, Bauré, and Paressí were more sub-Andean than tropical forest in cultural type.

In food-getting activities, special patterns supplemented the fundamental tropical-forest farming pattern. Indians dwelling in the forests used bows and poisoned arrows and blowguns for hunting, while those of the eastern plains used bolas, drives and surrounds, and disguises, devices characteristic of the eastern Gran Chaco and the plains farther to the south.

Technological features were on the whole characteristic of the tropical forests. The people grew domesticated cotton and wove it on a heddle loom, but some of them also made bark cloth. Most furnished their houses with hammocks, carved wooden stools, and mats. They made pots of the fairly simple types found among other tropical-forest people and rubber balls which they used in a game.

Highland influence is represented by the general use of the cushma, or tunic, the Araona use of coca, the Tiatinagua practice of head deformation, and the use of carrying nets as well as carrying baskets. Whereas most of the tropical-forest people wove special fire fans of wild fibers, these Indians, like the highland people, made them of feathers. Among their weapons were slings and clay missiles in which poisoned points were embedded. Although not metallurgists themselves, they acquired a certain number of metal objects through trade with the highlands.

It should be stressed that these varied culture elements acquired from the highlands had no fundamental effect on the nature or type of social structure found in northern and eastern Bolivia. In fact, the social groups were extremely varied. At one extreme, the Atsahuaca and Chapacurans were divided into small family units, each occupying a simple lean-to. Among the nomadic Tupian Sirionó, small extended family units wandered through the forests living on wild game and vegetable foods. The Canichana lived in fortified hamlets of nearly 100 persons. A still more developed community life was found among the Cayuvava where as many as 1,800 to 2,000 persons occupied a single village. According to early chronicles, as many as seven Cayuvava villages were unified under a single chief, an organization representing an incipient state. In addition, the Cayuvava had the Andean feature of a central temple where offerings were made to the gods. For these reasons, they might be included with the sub-Andean chiefdoms of eastern Bolivia. A somewhat similar sociopolitical pattern seems to have prevailed among the Xaray, a linguistically isolated group of the upper Paraguay River, where there were as many as 1,000 persons per village and, according to early accounts, four villages under a single chief.

Most of the linguistic groups mentioned in this area, however, were of an intermediate character in their sociopolitical organization. The Yuracare, for example, had one to several large houses in each village, and it is quite possible that each house sheltered a kin group or lineage. Perhaps in the same intermediate pattern were the Guarayú, Pauserna, and Tacana, who had 100 to 200 people per household. The Tiatinagua with two to eight families per house were not unlike these other groups, nor were the southeastern Panoan-speaking peoples, whose villages consisted of two or three communal houses.

A general feature is recognizable in the diversity of social arrangements. Close as these Indians were to the Andean highlands, none had the basic crops, the systems of irrigation, or the permanent villages to support a high civilization of the Central Andean type. Since all were essentially of the tropical forest in nature, their social arrangements varied according to local resources from seminomadic types, which were found in the less productive mountainous regions and watersheds surrounding the Amazon Basin, to sub-Andean culture types of chiefdoms found in villages of 1,000 to 2,000 persons in the more productive areas. These larger villages acquired certain particular characteristics from the Andes, but none had the basic productive patterns which were necessary for the development of a genuine class-structured society, a state organization, and a priest-temple-idol cult that was integrated with and implemented the state society.

Warfare in eastern Bolivia was of a kind appropriate to the economic and social organization, as we have observed elsewhere in the tropical forests. Most of these societies were quite unwarlike. The Chiquito raided neighboring groups and took captives, whom they permitted to marry into the tribe. The Canichana carried on intervillage raids and took captives whom they ate or kept as "slaves." The offspring of these slaves, however, were free men and did not form a hereditary class of slaves. There was no national warfare carried out for purposes of conquest or tribute.

10. THE NORTHWEST AMAZON: SIMPLE TROPICAL-FOREST TYPES

The northwest Amazon centers mainly on the Uaupés and Caquetá Rivers and includes several linguistic groups, notably the Eastern Tucanoans, Tucuna, Yurimagua, and a number of scattered Arawakan and Cariban people. The best known are the Tucuma, thanks to Nimuendajú,[6] and the Witoto and their neighbors, who were described just after the rubber boom by Whiffen.[7]

This subarea is characterized by patrilineal lineages, each occupying a single house which constituted the community and was strongly integrated by an ancestor cult or men's secret tribal society. It lacked many technological features of the tropical forest. While bitter manioc has been the basic crop in recent times, the Tucuna lacked it natively, and the same might be true of the others. The Indians made poor textiles, many of them woven of wild bast without a loom. They used bark cloth for ceremonial masks, and poor people used it for clothing. Pottery was common in this area, some of it plain and some modeled or painted. The Arawak and Carib employed the loom but made only hammocks on it. The Tucuna made hammocks of netting. The rivers were sufficiently large, however, to permit the use of dugout canoes, which furthered the development of large villages.

The socioreligious patterns are the most distinctive features of these tribes. Among the Tucanoan-speaking peoples, each village consists of

Communal Witoto house. (Courtesy of Paul Fejos, Wenner-Gren Foundation.)

a single lineage which is totemic in that the people believe that they had certain common ancestors with eponyms. Mythology recounts the origin of the ancestors, and ceremonial devotions to the ancestors are part of a ritual in which young men are initiated into the status of manhood. The initiatory rites include a number of features which are associated elsewhere with a very similar ancestor cult. The ceremonies are held secretly, women and children being excluded. The boys are ceremonially whipped and shown the sacred trumpets which are identified with the mythological ancestors. Women and children believe these trumpets to be the voices of the ancestors, who are present at the ceremony. Although the ancestors are not identifiable individuals, who can be traced genealogically, they are impersonated by men wearing bark cloth masks at the mourning rites held for the death of actual people.

A men's tribal or secret society combined with mourning rites is found in many other parts of the world. It is very possible that at a fairly ancient time, before the higher civilizations developed, such men's cere-

Cubeo bark cloth dance masks. (Courtesy of Irving Goldman.)

monialism was more common than it is today. And it is most consistent with a kinship basis of village organization.

The Witoto and some of their neighbors are also organized in communities consisting of a single house that shelters a patrilineal lineage. Although their ceremonialism is not adequately described, they too use sacred trumpets, and the idea of the ancestor cult may well be present, even though Whiffen does not specifically say so. Moreover, Whiffen

Witoto women and children. (Courtesy of Paul Fejos, Wenner-Gren Foundation.)

Witoto men. (Courtesy of Paul Fejos, Wenner-Gren Foundation.)

describes mourning ceremonies which are clearly connected with the kind of socioreligious organization previously described.

The Tucuna, according to Nimuendajú, had thirty patrilineal clans, each of which claims a tree or animal as its mythological ancestor. A given clan apparently is found in more than one place. Moreover, the clans are grouped in exogamous moieties.

11. THE EASTERN COLOMBIAN LOWLAND: SIMPLE FARM VILLAGES

The llanos or plains of eastern Colombia where the streams drain eastward from the Andes mainly into the upper Orinoco River were occupied largely by Arawakan-speaking Indians, although there were several enclaves of other languages, especially Guahiboan-speaking people and members of the Sálivan-Tairoan linguistic family. Lowland Venezuela included many Cariban-speaking groups along with a considerable number of smaller linguistic families of other affiliation.

Since virtually none of these people has been investigated by ethnographers and, in fact, largely lost their native culture a hundred or more years ago, they are known only through fragmentary data gleaned from the early Spanish chroniclers and other contemporary sources. For these reasons we shall devote a few paragraphs to explaining the more interesting features of the few groups about which reasonably reliable information is available.

The Guayapé and Sae. The Guayapé and Sae, who probably spoke an Arawakan language, lived in the southern llanos of Colombia and immediately adjoined the Muisca or Chibcha proper, the most powerful realm or kingdom in the Andean highlands to their north. These groups, though essentially tropical-forest in culture type, are of interest because of several ways in which familiar tropical-forest features were combined with features derived from the Circum-Caribbean peoples of the nearby Andes. As rain-forest farmers, they relied principally upon bitter manioc, but for an undisclosed reason, the Sae did no hunting and, in fact, considered that wild game should not be eaten. They did, however, subsist in part by means of fishing.

The social unit consisted of a village of many houses grouped around a plaza in which the ceremonial house stood. The kinship composition of the village is not known, but the practice of village endogamy in marriage probably indicates that the village did not consist of a single lineage. Each village had a headman who was installed in office in a ceremony in which the villagers carried him around on a litter, an Andean practice.

The Guayapé and Sae engaged in hostilities to a considerable extent. They attacked with a number of weapons, including slings, and protected themselves with hide or leather shields. Both of these are Andean traits. To protect their villages against attack, the Guayapé and Sae erected palisades.

Crisis rites included many observances which are quite widespread in the tropical forests, but here they were found in unusual combinations. For example, at childbirth a man was confined, as is common in the practice of the couvade, but his confinement was terminated by ceremonially whipping him. Whipping was also used in the rites which initiated a boy into the status of a warrior. At death, the Guayapé, like a number of Indians of the Montaña, drank the cremated ashes of the deceased in the native beer, chicha. The Sae ordinarily ate the corpse of the deceased, but a rich person drank the ashes with beer.

Religion had no distinctive patterns except that the sun and moon were prominent in mythology and there was considerable emphasis upon the transmigration of human souls to animals and the transmutation of shamans into animals, especially the jaguar. The idea that a shaman could change himself into a jaguar to kill or injure his enemies, however, is very characteristic of tropical-forest cultures.

The Achagua and Sáliva

The Arawakan-speaking Achagua and the linguistically independent Sáliva also occupied a considerable portion of the very arid plains of Colombia east of the Chibchan-speaking peoples of the highlands. This country was probably quite sparsely settled and was unable to support any intensive cultural development, although the Achagua, who were most widespread and are best known, evidently had a type of tropical-forest culture.

They subsisted primarily upon bitter manioc, which seems to have been aboriginal throughout this general area. An unusual feature of manioc cultivation was that young men were ceremonially whipped when the plants were placed in the ground so that they would not be lazy in later life.

Socially and religiously, the Achagua seemed to have shared some of the basic patterns of the Witoto and Tucanoan-speaking peoples of the northwest Amazon, who lived not far to their south. The Achagua were divided into animal-named lineages, each apparently localized in a single-house community. The lineage was patrilocal and probably exogamous. There is some evidence, however, that some of the villages may have contained a number of houses, that is several lineages, enclosed within a palisade and governed by a chief. Some of the early sources state that "vestal virgins" were concubines of the chiefs, as among the Andean people.

The Achagua had some kind of group ritual that centered around a death ceremony rather than the initiation of boys into the village or lineage ancestor cult as among the Witoto. At this ceremony, sacred trumpets were blown and the deceased were then buried. Subsequently, the corpses were disinterred, cremated, and the ashes drunk with chicha. Achagua religion included several unusual features: belief in a supreme god, belief in gods of the fields, riches, earthquakes, madness, and fire, and the worship of lakes. The Achagua used dance masks on certain religious occasions from which women were excluded. This limitation of the ceremonies to men suggests that they had the character of a man's village society as among the Tucanoans and Witoto, although the evidence is very inconclusive.

The Achagua, although somewhat warlike, were usually victims of raids by the Chibcha of the highland, who captured them for sacrificial victims for their ceremonies. They protected their villages with palisades. When the Achagua killed enemies, they made flutes of the arm- and legbones and drank a potion in which they mixed the dried heart to make themselves brave. The Achagua are one of the very few peoples in South America who poisoned their arrows with the deadly curare which was so widely used on blowgun darts.

The Sáliva resembled the Achagua, but had several additional features of interest. They believed in a Creator as well as in deities of the sun and moon. They sculptured figures of "demons" which were consulted as oracles by shamans, a feature undoubtedly derived from the Circum-Caribbean culture. This general area was noteworthy also because shamans used drugs in divination.

One other detail that deserves mention is the use of strings of shell for money. These shells were traded from the coast of Venezuela, where their use as currency seems to have originated.

12. VILLAGE ENCLAVES AMONG THE CIRCUM-CARIBBEAN CHIEFDOMS

The Betoi. The Betoi, who linguistically have been classed as Chibchan by some scholars and Betoyan by others, more probably spoke a Tucanoan language. They adjoined the block of Circum-Caribbean Chibchan people inhabiting the highlands. The subsistence patterns of the Betoi are characteristic of the tropical-forest culture, and their social organization was based upon the patrilineal lineage of twenty-five or more persons who occupied the single house which constituted the village. Some houses, however, were reported to have been 200 feet long and 30 feet wide and must have sheltered unusually large lineages. The house or community was not permanent, since a new one was built after the death of an occupant. The lineage house was really the quarters of the women and children, for men had a special house in which they held drinking bouts, or chicha festivals.

The Betoi were unusual for the following features: infanticide, which they said they practiced because "woman's life was hard"; the extensive use of drugs, including yopo, by shamans; the belief that shamans could send "demons" to cure the sick; the manufacture of bark cloth; and the use of shell money.

The Patángoro and their neighbors. Several Indian groups, including the Patángoro, who probably spoke a Cariban dialect, occupied the Central Cordillera of the Colombian Andes west of the principal block of Chibchan-speaking Circum-Caribbean peoples. Their culture was predominantly of the tropical-forest pattern, although a great many features, expectably, linked them with the Andes. Their subsistence patterns were based on intensive farming, including many of the fruits characteristic of the Circum-Caribbean area. Typical also of the latter culture was the custom of making salt. The distribution of the manufacture and use of salt in South America corresponds very closely to that of the more developed civilizations and is largely absent among tropical-forest horticulturalists and nomadic peoples.

A Patángoro village was palisaded against the extensive warfare carried out in this general area, and may have consisted of eighty to ninety houses grouped around a ceremonial building. Social organization was based upon exogamous and probably nonlocalized matrilineal clans.

Warfare among the Patángoro and their neighbors shared the extremely bloody features common to many of the Indians of Colombia, although its social significance was distinctive. These Indians fought with bows and poisoned arrows and protected their villages by means of doors contrived as deadfalls to entrap the attackers, sharp stakes upon which the enemy might impale themselves, and boiling water poured down from the walls. All captives were immediately killed and either boiled and eaten or else cremated and drunk with native beer, or chicha. Since it appears that the Patángoro regarded human flesh as an essential food, warfare might therefore almost be considered as a form of hunting.

Several specific features linking these Indians with the Circum-Caribbean culture were the use of head deformation, the construction of bridges made of lianas or vines, the use of platform beds instead of the tropical-forest hammock, and the shaman's practice of concealing himself behind a wall to answer questions. This last practice is a form of oracle but cannot properly be classed as a priestly function such as was associated with the temple-idol cult of the Circum-Caribbean culture. Another interesting detail of this culture, somewhat reminiscent of the Aztec of Meso-America as well as the Chibcha, or Muisca, is that, because the afterworld was regarded as a paradise, suicide was extremely common.

The Goajiro

The Arawakan-speaking Goajiro occupy the arid peninsula of the same name in Colombia. They are exceptional, if not unique, among South American Indians in their adoption and breeding of European livestock while still retaining an aboriginal culture. In the Gran Chaco and pampas, the Indians hunted wild cattle as if they were game but did not breed them. The Goajiro had cattle by 1550 and soon acquired horses, sheep, goats, pigs, fowl, and burros. This economy relegated farming, hunting, and fishing to a minor role.

Goajiro society was based on some thirty nonlocalized, matrilineal, animal-named sibs. These were subdivided into somewhat nomadic groups—encampments or rancherias—which were also animal-named, and lived in simple movable shelters owing to frequent shifts from one pasture to another.

Since wealth in cattle has become the basis of status and since members of the rancheria theoretically own property in common, some rancherias have gained higher standing than others. Cattle wealth has also created internal conflicts. The aboriginal social system required close relations between a man and his sister's son, the avunculate, and property passed from uncle to nephew. There is today, however, individual ownership of livestock, despite theoretical community ownership, and a man evades the traditional pattern of inheritance by giving livestock to his own children before his death.

While there are feuds amongst the Goajiro divisions and loose cooperation in repelling invaders, there has been no genuine group warfare carried out to take territory, people, or tribute and no permanent organization or class of war leaders. Religion has always been limited to shamanism and belief in mythological celestial beings and bush spirits.

Lacking military, religious, or economic cooperation that might consolidate local groups or rancherias into larger units, social controls are on a clan basis. The authority of clan chiefs and rancheria chiefs, however, depends upon their personal wealth.

Wealth pervades many other aspects of Goajiro culture. Children are often sold; extravagant bride prices must be paid the girl's maternal uncle; and funeral feasts are an occasion for wealth display, when as many as a thousand cattle may be sacrificed.

In addition to clans, shamanism, and mythology, other aboriginal features survive: breechclouts, bows, pots, weaving, games, and musical instruments. But the Goajiro depend heavily upon trade, exchanging salt, cattle, milk, cheese, hides, pearls, and logwood for firearms, cloth, blankets, beads, rum, sugar, rice, plantains, tobacco, and hardware. This trade has eliminated many native elements, just as wealth in livestock has transformed social and political patterns.

The northern Caribbean lowlands

The Caribbean coast, or "Mosquito Coast," in Nicaragua and the adjoining portion of Honduras is a flat, hot, humid region of rain forests and occasional swamps. Its principal inhabitants were the Paya, Jicaque, Sumo, and Mosquito, who spoke a variety of languages. Although these people adjoined chiefdoms and abutted the Maya on the north, they seem clearly to have been tropical-forest villagers. While warfare was strongly developed and cannibalism was practiced, there is no clear evidence of hereditary classes, chiefs who controlled several villages, or a temple cult. Many other tropical-forest Indians were warriors and cannibals but lacked chiefdoms. There are many cultural elements of South American and Meso-American origin in this area, but the diminution of federations, class structure, and state institutions noted in the south Caribbean lowlands continues here. While knowledge of the native culture of these lowlands is extremely thin, it is probable that aboriginal Indians had no state institutions.

Subsistence today and in the past has followed the Central American pattern previously described. In recent times, these Indians have adopted bitter manioc from South America and plantains from the Old World. Dependent to some degree upon trade relations with the outside, the Jicaque grow maize as a cash crop, while several groups have begun to raise cactus in order to produce cochineal, a dye-producing insect.

These Indians continue to gather wild foods, hunt, and fish. Guns have replaced bows and arrows and spears, but communal hunts sometimes last several days. Torches and dogs are used in rousing game. Fishing with hooks is women's work, but fishing with drugs, bows and arrows, spears, traps, and torches is the men's task. The Sumo lasso young crocodiles, and all groups take sea turtles and manatees. Fish are sun-dried and meat is smoked for preservation.

Pigs, sheep, goats, cattle, horses, and cats have been acquired from Europeans, but many wild birds are kept in captivity and tamed, and native bees are kept for their honey. Live turtles are penned in shallow pools for future use.

Foods are prepared by boiling, broiling, and roasting and are liberally seasoned with sauces of red pepper and salt. These are aboriginal practices, but maize tortillas and a mash made from green bananas and palm nuts, which can be kept six months and is made into a bread, are recent innovations.

Today, the people trade for many goods. Their own products are limited to utility wares, which do not compare in quality and quantity with aboriginal products. Transportation and trade with the outside, however, are still carried on by means of dugout canoe or human carriers who use tumplines.

The Mosquito formerly lived in villages of 100 to 500 persons, but Sumo villages were smaller. A lineage, if not clan, organization is indicated by the use of commodious communal houses, each sheltering an extended family.

In aboriginal times, chiefs and shamans had great power, but there is no evidence that they constituted hereditary classes or controlled multi-village chiefdoms. While the Indians were undoubtedly warlike in native times, their war chiefs were elected by a council of elders. The position was not hereditary, although among the Sumo it could pass to a man's nephew or stepson. The Mosquito federated into a tribal unit only under British control. The federation chief wore a silver or gold breastplate and carried a special staff as insignia of office. Both insignia are probably of European origin.

The manner of burial of Mosquito and Sumo chiefs was much like that of neighboring chiefdoms. Among the Mosquito, retainers, slaves, and sometimes a shaman were said to have been interred with the chief, while important persons among the Sumo were buried with gold and clay masks. There are also reports of mummification of chiefs. The reference to retainers and slaves shows status but not necessarily the pattern found among the chiefdoms. Moreover, several death practices specifically resemble those of many tropical-forest people: abandonment or killing of seriously ill persons; abandonment of a village after death; burial in a canoe; and female infanticide.

Most information about native warfare pertains to external features rather than organization and authority. All Sumo and Mosquito men were considered potential warriors and were arranged in ranked military orders that were distinguished by special insignia. They underwent rigorous tests and dietary restrictions and celebrated special ceremonies during their training. Some puberty ordeals and tests, although required of all boys, were preparatory to military training.

These people believed in a large number of malevolent nature spirits, who inhabit caves, deep water, and similar places. It was the primary function of the shaman to placate these spirits and to dispel their hold on sick people. The Sumo, Mosquito, and Paya have a concept of an otiose sky deity known as "Our Father" (possibly a belief of European origin), and the sun, moon, stars, especially the Pleiades, and other celestial phenomena entered native myths and theosophic ideas. These gods seem not to have affected people in their daily lives. There were no temples or priests, and the mythological beings were not supplicated.

One of the few ceremonies recorded was an anniversary mourning rite held to appease evil spirits and help the soul of the deceased.

Most modern Sumo and Mosquito villages have a practicing shaman whose chief duty is to cure illness. The better to grapple with the spirits of evil, the shaman enters a trance, dances, sings, and prays over painted sticks and carved figures. Shamans also lead group ceremonials in time of epidemic disease and prognosticate the success of hunting (and formerly war) parties. In daily affairs, they are influential and respected.

13. THE EASTERN BRAZILIAN HIGHLANDS:
HUNTERS AND GATHERERS WHO TURNED FARMERS

In eastern and southern Brazil and a portion of northern Paraguay, there is a large block of Indians, most of whom speak Ge languages, who fundamentally resemble the tropical-forest-village type, yet differ from it in three important ways. First, although these Indians have been small-scale cultivators in historic times, there is good evidence that they were formerly nomadic hunters and gatherers. For this reason, many authors and the *Handbook* contributors class them as marginal people. Second, they are essentially landsmen who did not use canoes and who failed to make fullest use of riverine food resources. Third, while their villages are independent sociopolitical units, each is divided into a number of kinship divisions, moieties, age grades, associations, and sexual dichotomies unequaled in South America. In some areas, each village was divided into several pairs of moieties which in turn were subdivided into a complex system of age and occupational associations. This complex structure, however, is an intensification and formalization of, rather than a departure from, the fundamental kinship, age, and sexual basis of society which predominates among the more primitive people. A comparable complexity is to be found perhaps only among the Australian aborigines. Such structure tends to be minimized, suppressed, and even obliterated by the institutions of a multicommunity state.

These features are most developed in that solid block of Ge-speaking people of the highlands of eastern Brazil. Since, however, the Ge-speaking Caingang, who are somewhat separated from their linguistic kin and live to the south, together with the Bororo of the upper Paraguay River share these features, they must be considered members of this general subtype.

The eastern Brazilian Ge include: the Northwestern Ge, who in turn include the Timbira (Canella and Apinayé), Northern Cayapó (Pau d'Arco and others), Southern Cayapó, and Suyá. The almost identical Shavante, Sherente, and the now-extinct Shacriaba, along with several groups known as the Acroa, formed the Central Ge.

Caingang is the generic name for a number of peoples who make up the southern branch of the Ge-language family—the Guayaná, Coroado, Caagua (Caingua), and others. Since these peoples share many cultural characteristics, they may be described as a unit. They occupy a large territory in the plains and forests of southeastern Brazil in the states of São Paulo, Paraná, Santa Catarina, and Rio Grande do Sul. Their population has been greatly reduced since contact with the whites who colonized this part of Brazil, but formerly the Caingang possibly numbered between 5,000 and 10,000.

The Bororo, who speak an isolated language, occupy an extensive territory along the upper reaches of the Paraguay River and its affluents, just north of the canoe-dwelling Guató. They consist of a western and an eastern division. Several Bororo villages have become extinct in historic times, and the population seems to have shifted somewhat since contact with whites.

Archaeology shows that much of the northern sector of the Ge area in eastern Brazil was formerly occupied by a people who were different from the Ge. The latter appear to have migrated from the southern sertão into the steppes and gallery forests farther north. They dominated the area, although several Tupian-speaking groups maintained themselves on the rivers in historic times, owing no doubt to the great mobility their canoes gave them. The Ge were not rivermen.

Because of its general infertility and unattractiveness, this area continues to be little known today. It is only partially settled by Brazilians, and some of the Indians are openly hostile to Europeans. Our only knowledge of these Ge people comes largely from several monographs by the late Kurt Nimuendajú, a German ethnologist who lived among the Indians of the Amazon and eastern Brazil from 1906 until his death in 1946.

At the beginning of the nineteenth century, the Apinayé, Shavante, and Sherente were estimated at 12,000 persons. Warfare with Indian and white groups combined with European diseases, however, have seriously reduced their numbers. Recent estimates give the Apinayé a population of about 160 and the Ramcocamecra branch of Canella only 300.

Subsistence. Although the Ge area of eastern Brazil consists of relatively arid and unproductive uplands, which today are used primarily for cattle grazing, most groups had access to the extremely important gallery forests. Along the main rivers, seepage provides water to narrow fringes of land which can produce crops as well as forests, whereas only a short distance away rainfall is insufficient to support either trees or crops.

While the adoption of domesticated plants was seemingly the factor that enabled the Ge and Bororo to live in permanent villages, cultivation was recent, and it has remained secondary to hunting and gathering among most of these people. The Ge of eastern Brazil adopted bitter and sweet manioc, maize, sweet potatoes, and yams, but in contrast to the riverine village horticulturalists, whose principal crop is manioc, the Ge depend more upon sweet potatoes and yams. The Bororo acquired manioc and maize from their Indian neighbors and rice from the Europeans. Methods of cultivation follow the usual slash-and-burn pattern, wherein men clear the fields and women cultivate, harvest, and carry home the crop.

Since, in contrast to most of the riverine horticultural people, plant cultivation is not well developed and river resources are scantily exploited, all of these people devote much time to hunting and gathering. The eastern Brazilian Ge leave their villages to spend long periods in the steppe and then return to their villages at harvest time. Bows and arrows are the principal weapons, but they employ various methods of hunting. In communal hunts, they frequently fire the grass to drive the animals. To take deer, they post hunters in trees where the animals pass. Armadillos are clubbed. Dogs were unknown to these Ge in native times, and traps were little used.

The Bororo hold a collective hunt after a shaman has prognosticated a favorable time and place. Their principal game includes tapirs, peccaries, rabbits, various birds, and jaguars.

Caingang hunting likewise includes some ritual. Peccaries, tapirs, and deer are hunted communally, the first with the assistance of dogs, which drive the animals toward hidden bowmen. Tapir and deer are also tracked and often driven into a stream, where they can be shot or clubbed to death. Birds are caught with spring-pole traps or are lured by decoys.

Despite the general lack of canoes, fish are an important food, and they are taken by means of several widespread techniques. All groups use the multipronged fish arrow. In addition, the Ge use scoop nets, and they and the Bororo use fish drugs. The Bororo employ weirs, nets, and harpoons to take fish and harpoons for landing caymans.

Subsistence upon natural foods also includes plant and animal species. Everywhere, wild honey, plants such as pine nuts, palm fruits, and various nuts and seeds, and larvae are crucially important, and in some localities they probably supply more food than cultivated crops. The Caingang use the climbing ring, a typical riverine horticultural trait, to ascend tall trees to gather honey and birds' eggs.

The Ge and Bororo waste little food. The latter roast game in its skin and eat all of it, even though they have to grind the bones in a mortar. Sometimes, however, they boil the intestines in pots. The eastern Brazilian Ge, who lack pots, broil their meat on babracots or bake it in earth ovens. The Caingang cook in a similar manner.

The community. Among these people, concentration of the population in large communities was hindered by the lack of good transport facilities, which prevented food from outlying fields and hunting grounds from being brought to a central location. Goods were carried overland in baskets by women. There was a general absence of canoes. Some of the Ge along the Tocantins, Araguayá, and upper Xingú Rivers adopted crude bark canoes and dugouts recently, but this has apparently contributed to community enlargement only to a minor degree.

The Ge of eastern Brazil are extraordinary for their construction of roadways which lead in fairly straight lines outward from the villages as much as 10 miles. While the larger of these roads are used for races in which contestants carry heavy logs, smaller roads lead to farming sites and hunting grounds.

Villages among the Ge and Bororo are fairly permanent, although not necessarily inhabited continuously throughout the year. The eastern Brazilian Ge may abandon their village seasonally to trek after game, while the Bororo move away from the rivers to higher ground during the rainy season. House structure shows some influence from the more permanent dwellings of the riverine horticultural villagers. The aboriginal Caingang lived in rude huts. The house was divided into four dwelling quarters, one each for a nuclear family. The Caingang later constructed a substantial gabled house, which may have originated from two lean-tos. In the modern houses, platform beds and hammocks are replacing the older beds of skins, branches, and bark strips. The native Caingang village had four to six huts and 80 to 100 persons.

Among the eastern Brazilian Ge and the Bororo, the house arrangement within the village reflects certain features of social organization. The Ge village contains several hundred persons whose houses are characteristically placed in a circle or semicircle around a ceremonial plaza, in which the bachelors' or men's house sometimes stands. The dwellings, moreover, are grouped according to the moiety membership of their occupants, but the particular nature of such grouping varies locally according to the kind of moiety organization.

The Bororo village also consists of a circle of dwellings around the men's house. The houses are grouped according to clan and moiety affiliation. They are arranged in a northern and a southern half, and, crosscutting these moieties, they are placed with reference to what are called Upstream and Downstream divisions.

The Bororo dwelling is built by men, but following the matrilineal principles, it is owned by the women of the several families who are related through a female lineage within the clan. In the house, each nuclear family has its own fireplace and platform beds.

The men's house in a Bororo village is in the center of the dwellings.

It is the workshop, club, and ceremonial center for all men of the community, and it is also the dormitory for bachelors. Women are strictly excluded from this masculine headquarters.

Social patterns. It is unusual but not inconsistent with the manner of life of people such as the Ge and Bororo that their social structure, being based primarily upon age, kinship, and sex, should develop fairly complex arrangements. Among these people, there is a combination of moieties, or dual divisions, clans, and associations, or age and sexual groupings. These take innumerable forms and combinations among the people under discussion, and there is even a difference in descent since some societies are matrilineal and others patrilineal.

In eastern Brazil, exogamous matrilineal moieties are found among the Pau d'Arco, Canella, and Apinayé, while patrilineal moieties characterize the Sherente. Except among the Apinayé, these moieties are exogamous and thereby prevent marriage with another member of the moiety. Marriage among the Apinayé is regulated by four exogamous marriage classes. Assignment of youths to the various age grades is described below.

A Bororo village is divided into exogamous, matrilineal moieties known as Weak and Strong, which in turn comprise four to seven clans having animal and plant eponyms. There is no evidence that the eponyms are regarded as ancestors as in much of Amazonia, and even the initiation of adolescent boys into the secret of the bull-roarers seems to be entirely disassociated from any kinship group. In certain villages, the Weak and Strong moieties are crosscut by an Upstream and a Downstream moiety. The clans have special rights regarding manufacture and display of such things as ceremonial bows, arrows decorated with the clan emblem, and penis-sheath designs and ownership of personal names, dances, and songs.

Exogamous patrilineal moieties are found among the Sherente of eastern Brazil, who are also divided into six age-graded groups and four men's associations, which carry out special hunting and sporting activities. Caingang villages are also divided into exogamous, patrilineal moieties, which are subdivided into two or four sections that also regulate marriage. A child, although born into his father's moiety, is assigned to a section at the time his body is first ceremonially painted with colors indicating sectional affiliation.

Since not all moieties among the Ge are exogamous, it seems that diffusion of the concept of dual and other divisions did not carry all the features of the moiety complex. The Canella, for example, have three pairs of nonexogamous moieties, which are identified by natural phenomena and which engage in sporting events, have personal names, and are divided into four age classes. The Apinayé have four exogamous marriage classes, but their matrilineal moieties are not exogamous and have the principal function of competing in log races. The Apinayé are also divided into four men's age groups.

Boys and girls are organized into the age-graded groups which are prevalent among Ge-speaking peoples. While the pattern of age-grading links the Ge with the tropical-forest peoples near them, the great complexity of the age groups is a distinguishing feature. The Apinayé divide males into four groups: boys who have not been initiated to adult status; warriors between the ages of fifteen and twenty-five years; mature men who have passed through warrior status; and elders no longer active in log racing. The Pau d'Arco system is similar to that of the Apinayé, but includes both sexes and has a modified series of grades, which, in the case of men, is based on their status as husbands and, in the case of women, on their position in relation to parenthood and household status. The Northern Cayapó, Sherente, and Timbira have similar arrangements of female age grading.

Among the Sherente and Canella young unmarried men are segregated into several age and status groups. These in turn are linked to four men's associations connected with hunting, sports, and formerly with warfare. The Sherente provide bachelors with quarters in the plaza, where the young men sleep and organize for their participation in group activities. Canella youths, although lacking the bachelors' house, take up positions in the central plaza, where they sleep when weather permits. The groups are spatially arranged according to moiety affiliations and further segmented to correspond to associational cleavages.

The men's associations of the Canella and Pau d'Arco have important ceremonial functions in collective hunting and ownership of buriti and babassú trees, which are defended by the associations against unauthorized exploitation. The Sherente associations play an integral part in certain ceremonial activities and used to have well-defined roles in the conduct of warfare. The Sherente have a women's society which functions especially in a naming ceremony for boys, during which men enact a sham killing of a woman in a ritual attempt to intimidate the females.

Since none of these communities consists of a single lineage, marriage is ordinarily regulated by membership in moieties, clans, classes, or groups rather than by residence.

The Apinayé, Canella, and Northern Cayapó are strictly monogamous, and the Sherente predominantly so, although the latter permit polygyny and have institutionalized leviratic marriage. The sororate is recorded only for the Apinayé and is not compulsory. The Timbira groups do not allow cousin marriage. The Sherente practice cross-cousin marriage, the preferred form being to the mother's brother's daughter's daughter. The avuncular relationship is important in all groups mentioned.

Postmarital residence is generally in the wife's house and has been described as permanent among all groups except the patrilineally organized Sherente, where it is always a temporary arrangement. The Sherente couple move to or near the groom's father's house after the first year or so of marriage. Parent-in-law avoidance is widely practiced among the Ge, but the restrictions on behavior diminish after children are born and the marriage is firmly established.

Bororo marriage is regulated by moiety exogamy and preferential unions between certain clans. It is celebrated by a group ceremony. Kinship terminology suggests that a preferred form of marriage is with the father's elder sister's daughter and with the father's younger sister. A man might also marry his stepdaughter. Polygyny is preferably sororal. Postmarital residence is in the wife's household.

Caingang marriage, too, is usually monogamous, although polygyny and polyandry are sometimes practiced, the former being the privilege of older and more important men. Wives are usually much younger than their husbands, and custom even permits a man to take a prepubescent wife who remains in her home until she reaches adolescence. Occasionally, a man takes as second wife his stepdaughter, his wife's sister's daughter, or his own sister's daughter. Cousin marriage is prohibited, but sexual relations between cousins are not uncommon, and a cousin may continue to be a man's concubine after his marriage.

There was also a class of "wantons" among some of the Ge peoples, best described for the Canella, Sherente, and Apinayé. Wantons were women who did not marry but who had sexual relations freely with warriors and bachelors in the men's house. They generally became wantons owing to premarital sexual intercourse which failed to lead to marriage. Nimuendajú describes how these young girls were forcibly dragged into the plaza by older men and, after having their hair clipped, were forced to spend the night with them. This took place on the day the youths were initiated into warrior status.

Leadership. Although these communities consist of several moieties and other groups, there are few cooperative village endeavors that required leadership that is not kin-based.

In eastern Brazil, the village headman occasionally inherits his position, but his authority is greatest where it is based upon religious power. In all matters, he generally shares responsibility with a council of elders. The Caingang chief tends to inherit position in the male line, but he too has little authority. He leads collective ventures and receives honor at community feasts. His prestige depends upon looking after the welfare of the people and generosity in distributing gifts, but he seems not to receive any surplus from his followers to facilitate his largess. Among the Bororo, the chief's authority depends upon his persuasiveness in daily affairs and upon influence in ritual and warfare, but he has no coercive powers. Murder, for example, is settled through blood feuds of the kin groups concerned.

Warfare. In aboriginal times, warfare contributed little to village integration or leadership because it was largely a matter of feuds or inter-village raids. There was no territorial or economic conquest, and there were no warrior societies.

The Northwest and Central Ge, however, carried on hostilities among themselves and against the Tupians, while later they fought the whites and mestizos. Their characteristic weapon was the bow and arrow, but they also used lances, clubs, and stone axes. Surprise attacks were the principal tactical operation among all groups, but the Timbira did not hesitate to make a stand against the Neo-Brazilians when their numbers were equal to those of the enemy.

Warfare was waged by the entire group of active males, with special roles being assigned to age and associational segments among them. In feuds among the Canella, a maternal uncle and nephew organized revenge parties. Otherwise, a council of elders decided who would lead the raids.

It was not customary to take prisoners or human trophies. Enemies were killed whenever possible. However, the Sherente and Pau d'Arco took child captives, and the latter also took women. Reports of cannibalism among these people are based on inconclusive evidence.

It was customary for a warrior who had killed an enemy to go into retreat for a period which varied from ten days (Apinayé) to one month (Sherente and Canella). The warrior observed restrictions on food and activities. A ceremonial bath, decoration with falcon feathers, and announcement of his valiant exploit in the central plaza marked the end of ritual penance.

Aboriginal war among the Caingang was waged not for conquest or booty but only to avenge murder. In blood feuds, male enemies were killed and decapitated, but women and children were spared for adoption into the victorious group. Feuding was highly patterned, community members being assigned special roles and organized in standard ways. Disputes within the community were also settled in a highly stylized manner. Contestants fought in mock battles and were careful not to kill each other. Warfare against the whites was much less regularized. It depended a great deal on the element of surprise and allowed the individual free action in battle.

The Bororo used to raid their neighbors, the Cayapó, Guaná, and Guaycurú. They fought principally with the bow and arrow but also used clubs, club-swords, and knuckle-dusters.

Life cycle. The Northwestern and Central Ge of eastern Brazil practice the couvade at the birth of a child. That this custom is found here but not among the other people under discussion is evidence of influence from the river horticultural villages of the tropical forests. The couvade requires a series of dietary and behavioral restrictions. All men who have had sexual intercourse with the mother must observe these taboos no less than the husband. The purpose is to assure the well-being of the infant.

Dietary and behavioral restrictions are also in force during girls' puberty rites among all Ge-speaking groups. There is a general notion of impurity associated with the initial menstruation, which continues at all periods throughout life and forbids menstruating women to have sexual intercourse, practice horticulture, wear decorative dress, and engage in certain recreational activities.

At childbirth, among the Bororo, both parents abstain from certain foods. In one region, food taboos are extended to the entire group, although those imposed on the parents of the newborn child are more severe and last longer. At puberty a boy receives a penis sheath, which symbolizes his adult status and entitles him to share in the men's secret knowledge. He is shown the bull-roarer and witnesses secret rituals from which women and children are excluded.

At the approach of death a Canella man strives to return to his maternal house to die. After death, the corpse is prepared for burial by special friends of the deceased, who pluck his eyebrows, cut his head hair, and paint his body with urucú. A volunteer gravedigger buries the corpse in a sitting position near the maternal home. Later, secondary burial is performed. Secondary burial was also characteristic of the Apinayé, Timbira, and Sherente. In all three groups there is the widespread belief, manifest in the care taken in burying the dead, that the earth should not come into contact with the corpse.

Bororo observe elaborate death rites. The corpse is secluded from women and children, while relatives ceremonially gash themselves and utter long mourning chants. They wrap the deceased with his personal possessions in a mat and bury him. Special food and dress restrictions are then imposed on the surviving kinfolk. After provisional burial, the mourners hold a hunt, which culminates in a communal eating of the catch. More bloodletting and chanting follow, after which the flesh is removed from the corpse and the bones are kept in the men's house for a time, where they are painted and decorated with feathers according to clan colors. Finally, the bones are given secondary basket burial in a deep stream. During the funeral rites it is felt opportune to initiate several young men into the men's society. At the initiation ceremony, bull-roarers are brought into play and exhausting dances are performed.

Ceremonies and religion. The Ge as a whole share similar beliefs concerning celestial deities, animism, and magic, although emphasis differs among the various groups.

The most important celestial beings are the sun and moon, of which the sun was dominant. Creation myths are common to all groups, and the Apinayé derive their moiety organization directly from the sun. The Canella publicly pray to the celestial deities for rain, good harvests of domesticated and wild plants, and for hunting success. The Eastern Timbira and the Apinayé observe a four-day ceremony at harvest time in which supplications are made to the sun, but also seek individual visions to induce hunting success. Among the Sherente the sun and moon do not figure in personal vision quests, their powers being mediated through other astral deities.

The Caingang's supernatural world centered in ghosts and many kinds of spirits, which inhabit natural phenomena such as trees, mountains, and animals. Some spirits are considered friendly and may become a person's guardian and helper, but others are malevolent and should be avoided. The Caingang believe that animals are controlled by a master spirit who governs their increase. To avoid antagonizing this spirit, hunters do not slaughter wantonly.

Most ceremonies, especially those of the Canella, have little religious significance to the village as a whole and are more functions of the social segments such as moieties, clans, and associations and their secular, festive activities. Ceremonies are extremely complex in their details, but share the following general attributes: singing and dancing, relay racing, clowning, and a sham enactment of communal hunting.

The Great Feast of the Sherente is connected with the foregoing beliefs. It is designed to prevent drought and is observed only by males, who are arranged into two major groups, with a small body of elders forming a third. The main groups alternate in fasting and looking after the requirements of the participants. Rigorous fasting lasts for three weeks, and the men lose a considerable amount of weight. Physical exhaustion is no doubt conducive to the group visions at the end of the fasting period, even though the visions are highly stylized. A group hunt, a log race, a prayer to the sun, and individual vision quests succeed one another in that order. Afterwards, one of the leaders receives a special message from the sun, mediated by a star in Orion, which grants rain and admonishes that the people abandon white man's clothing. After moiety meetings and a concluding ceremony, the people disperse to carry on their regular activities.

It is felt that ghosts assist the dying by guiding their souls to the place of the dead, which is situated somewhere on the earth's surface rather than in the sky or in an underworld. Among the Apinayé, ghosts assist the living by imparting special knowledge about magic and medicine.

The greatest communal rite of the Caingang pertains to a cult of the dead, and it is the time when children are assigned to sections of their moiety. The main purpose of the ritual is to sever connections between the living and the dead. During the ceremony, which occurs when the maize crop is green, the various moiety sections or subgroups wear distinctive facial paint and are led by relatives of the deceased. After a funeral rite there is group drinking and revelry. Among the Apinayé, as well, there is a connection between a boy's initiation and mourning for his dead parents. A person's surviving ceremonial partner is privileged to decorate and bury his corpse, arrange for secondary burial, and be the chief heir of his possessions.

Both the Apinayé and the Sherente believe in soul loss as the cause of illness, a belief which is absent among the Canella, who, however, regard supernatural contact with the dead as a major protective measure for the living.

Shamanistic curing is not highly valued or often resorted to, since friendly spirits impart curative knowledge to ordinary individuals without special calling. Most people attempt to effect cures by means of traditional medicinal remedies. If a shaman is consulted, he is paid only if successful. Apinayé shamanism is more developed than in the other groups and suggests, in its approximation to shamanistic practices among tropical-forest peoples, a strong influence from neighboring Tupian groups.

Among the Caingang, shamans communicate with spirits to learn the best course of action for the community. They also cure illness, but this is a minor function, and they do not receive fees for their treatment. Both shamans and ordinary persons practice divination in a number of ways.

Bororo religion involves two sets of animistic beliefs concerned respectively with the souls of dead shamans and the souls of departed tribesmen. The shaman is possessed by the ghost of a shaman and cures through the powers imparted by him. Cigar smoking, sucking out the infectious object, and, especially, the "consecration" of choice bits of food for his spirit-helper characterize the shaman's activities. The other set of spirits, ghosts of ordinary people, continually visit their community to eat, drink, and dance, foretell the future, cause illness, and so forth. These spirits commune with the living through special mediums. Actually, the shaman mediates both sets of spirits, but apparently the Bororo make a conceptual distinction between the two activities and sets of beliefs.

NOTES

1. Walter Roth, *An Introductory Study of the Arts, Crafts, and Customs of the Guiana Indians,* Bureau of American Ethnology Annual Report 38, 1916–1917. John Gillin, *The Barama River Caribs of British Guiana,* Papers of the Peabody Museum of Archaeology and Ethnology of Harvard University, vol. 14, no. 2, 1936. George Gaylord Simpson, *Los Indios Kamarakotos: Tribu Caribe de la Guyana Venezolana,* Revista fomento, Año 3, nos. 22–25, 1940.

2. Clifford Evans and Betty J. Meggers believed on the basis of archaeological evidence that the settlements were small, lacked palisades, and were not built on mounds or platforms. See Betty J. Meggers and Clifford Evans, *Archeological Investigations at the Mouth of the Amazon,* Bureau of American Ethnology Bulletin 167, 1957.
3. See Alfred Métraux, *Handbook,* vol. 3.
4. *Ibid.*
5. Helen and Elman Service, *Tobatí, a Paraguayan Village,* University of Chicago Press, Chicago, 1954.
6. Curt Nimuendajú, *The Tukuna,* University of California Publications in American Archaeology and Ethnology, vol. 45, 1952.
7. Thomas W. Whiffen, *The North-West Amazons: Notes on Some Months Spent Among Cannibal Tribes,* London and New York, 1915.

thirteen

NOMADIC HUNTERS
AND GATHERERS:
GENERAL FEATURES

1. INTRODUCTION

It has been customary to classify the nonfarming Indians of South America as marginal or hunting-and-gathering people. Marginal is meaningful in terms of culture elements; for most of these societies were remote from the centers of inventiveness, and they received comparatively few of the traits found among the more complex cultures. Marginal, however, is a misleading designation of cultural types, for it implies that a society is only a poorly developed imitation or copy of a fully developed form that has culminated or climaxed in the center of the culture area to which the society is peripheral. Cultural types are total sociocultural systems rather than agglomerations of elements originating in certain centers. The nonfarming Indians are marginal only in the sense of sharing a very small number of elements with the complex cultures. This is a negative characterization, a statement of their lack of many elements and patterns.

At the time of their discovery, the nomads lived in regions that were economically marginal, inferior, or relatively unproductive, such as swamps, deserts, and other hinterlands. Here they avoided their more powerful and warlike neighbors who inhabited the arable lands along the principal river systems, and they were off the main stream of culture diffusion.

Varieties of nomadic hunters, gatherers, and fishers. The numbers correspond to the sections of Chapter Fourteen. (1) Archipelagic shellfish gatherers. (2) Plains hunters and gatherers. (3) The Gran Chaco. (4) Forest hunters and gatherers. (5) Aquatic nomads.

The nomadic hunters and gatherers as a whole are distinguished from other South American Indians by the over-all simplicity of their patterns and by their lack of many technological and social features found elsewhere in South America. Because they lived in unproductive environments, their simple food-getting techniques supported only sparse populations, which were segmented into small, scattered and undifferentiated social aggregates. These people were nomadic in that they lacked permanent habitation sites and frequently moved in search of food. Their travels, however, were normally restricted to fairly well defined and limited territories of a few miles extent. In aboriginal times, none migrated on the huge scale of many of the pastoral nomads of Asia, although the Tehuelche moved long distances after obtaining horses.

The nomadic hunters and gatherers do not represent a single type. In aboriginal times, the predominance of hunting or of food collecting and the organization of the people for carrying out these activities in the different environments produced several very unlike types, and in historic times the introduction of the horse to certain areas resulted in the development of additional types. The principal types are: archipelagic shellfish-gathering families of southern Chile, a people dispersed in small family clusters; plains or pampean hunting bands of Argentina and Patagonia, who were organized in patrilineal lineages; forest hunters and gatherers who occupied portions of eastern Brazil and constituted enclaves around the headwaters of the Amazon Basin and other scattered areas but who are too little known culturally to be placed with certainty in any well-defined type; predatory horse nomads whose warring bands developed in the pampas and Patagonia after the Spanish Conquest; and aquatic nomads or canoe people of certain swampy areas.

The nomadic hunters and gatherers were distributed largely through those areas which are unfavorable to the cultivation of domesticated plants, especially in the southern portion of South America. The Chilean archipelago south of the island of Chiloé is too cold to permit farming, and it lacks an abundance of fish comparable to that which supported large, permanent communities on the northwest coast of North America. Throughout Patagonia and the pampas and into the plains of the eastern Gran Chaco and part of Mato Grosso, the country is either too arid for cultivation or it is covered with sod lands that resisted dibble-stick cultivation. Some areas, such as the upper Paraguay River and the Orinoco Delta, are excessively swampy. Portions of eastern Brazil are high and arid. A few of the forest hunters and gatherers who lived as enclaves in Amazonia carried on some slash-and-burn horticulture, like their village neighbors; but they had no access to riverine foods, and they lacked the canoe transportation which supported fairly permanent villages among the latter. These hunters and gatherers lived between the principal rivers, not along them.

The common characteristic of the diversified environments of the nomads was a low food productivity when exploited by aboriginal technology. These areas had the sparsest population of South America, their exploitation required frequent movement of the people, and they supported social groups which had only a simple level of organization. Except for these features, the nomadic hunters and gatherers are not distinguished as a whole from other South American Indians by special characteristics. Other people hunted, collected wild products, and fished to supplement farming and animal breeding, while some of the hunters and gatherers engaged in small-scale farming. The difference was in population density, relative importance of the kinds of subsistence activities, and the nature of the organization of the people necessary to carry out these activities. The nomads had a sparse and scattered population. They depended principally upon wild plants, animals, and fish. Those who farmed had, in most instances, borrowed plant domesticates fairly recently and used them as relatively unimportant supplements to wild foods.

The organization of these simple societies primarily reflects the demands of their food quest. Food collecting is individualistic and competitive, whereas hunting and fishing may be cooperative in different ways, depending upon the nature of the game or fish and the methods of taking them. The subsistence patterns entailed a number of different cultural-ecological adaptations that strongly conditioned the nature of the social groupings and many basic aspects of the entire culture. In analyzing these adaptive processes, we are concerned with those environmental features which are important in relation to the technology rather than with the total environment.

The relationship of man and nature changes dynamically either when new techniques are introduced to the society or when the society migrates into a different environment.

A probable case of prehistoric change caused by migration is that of the Northwest and Central Ge Indians of eastern Brazil, who had formerly been nomadic hunters and gatherers in the arid areas before they moved into the gallery-forest area—the lower valleys where forests fringe the rivers—which permits tropical horticulture. In the gallery forests, they adopted farming from neighboring tropical-forest villages and settled in larger and more stable communities than formerly. They also developed more complex sociocultural structures.

An example from post-Conquest times of how technological innovations change the culture type is seen among the pampean and Patagonian

Indians and certain people of the eastern Chaco. After receiving horses, the aboriginal, territorial patrilineages of the pampas and Patagonia became multilineage predatory bands which were not restricted to territories. Some of the Chaco Indians practiced small-scale cultivation in aboriginal times but, upon acquiring horses, practically abandoned horticulture for nomadic horse bands which subsisted by raiding the Spaniards and their livestock. In both areas, horse nomadism brought about changes in band size, social composition and structure, and political organization. Wholly new sociocultural types evolved, although many aboriginal culture elements were retained.

Among the Sirionó of Bolivia, the Guayakí of Paraguay, and perhaps the Warrau of the Orinoco Delta, adaptations entailed by migration to new environments brought deculturation, or culture loss. In contrast to the pampean and eastern Chaco peoples, subsistence activity among the Sirionó and the Guayakí did not become more productive through the introduction of European techniques. These Indians retreated from the white settlers and their powerful Indian neighbors to inaccessible regions, where they largely abandoned horticulture to rely on a predominantly hunting-and-gathering subsistence. Other enclaves of nomads isolated in the tropical forests and interfluvial regions may also have experienced a similar deculturation. Deculturation owing to forced movement in post-Conquest times to unfavorable environments also occurred among many chiefdoms in the Circum-Caribbean region.

The nomadic hunters and gatherers spoke languages belonging to all three main families. The Warrau, Mura, and several nomads of eastern Colombia are of the Macro-Chibchan family. The people of the Chilean archipelago, Patagonia, the pampas, and the upper Orinoco River and scattered groups of seminomads in the western Amazon belonged to different subfamilies of the Andean-Equatorial family. The only family not found among the Central Andean Indians is Ge-Pano-Carib. Except for some of the Venezuelan chiefdoms and the tropical-forest Carib and Panoans, this occurred principally among the hunting-and-gathering people: the Charrua in Paraguay, the Mataco, Guaycuruan, and others of the Gran Chaco, the Huarpe in western Argentina, the Guató of the upper Paraguay River, the Nambicuara, the Ge and Carajá of the east Brazilian highlands, and the Camacan, Mashacalí, Purí, Coroado, Malalí, and others near the Brazilian coast.

2. HISTORY

The prehistory of most nomadic hunters and gatherers is highly conjectural, since oral histories lack appreciable depth and accuracy and few archaeological investigations have been made. Moreover, archaeological materials are limited to a few artifacts of stone, bone, and shell, which afford little idea of the total culture. House remains are rarely found, although shell mounds or refuse middens were left by these people on the coasts and rock shelters and other camp sites are occasionally discovered.

In some instances, archaeology suggests movements of people. For example, pottery remains found in Brazil in the territory occupied by the historic Ge-speaking Cayapó and Timbira, neither of whom knew ceramics, indicate that these peoples are relatively late arrivals in a region once inhabited by a fairly numerous pottery-making and presumably horticultural people. Nimuendajú suggested that the Cayapó moved into this region from the southern steppes, displacing the former inhabitants. It is supposed that the Tupian-speaking, canoe-using Yuruna and Shipaya later entered the territory and were able to defend themselves into historic times against the Cayapó, who lacked canoes. These Ge-speaking groups probably learned plant cultivation from their Tupian neighbors along the larger rivers and in the gallery forests to the north and west.

In many cases, linguistic distributions suggest prehistory. Since most of the nomadic hunters and gatherers belonged to linguistic groups not found among their neighbors, it may be inferred that they had long remained in isolation. This isolation was increased by pressure of the more warlike village people, who gradually forced the nomads into the less productive hinterlands. On the other hand, the Sirionó began a westward migration in prehistoric times, and since they are surrounded by people with a more advanced culture and different languages, they probably split off from the other Tupians a long time ago. It is possible, however, that post-Conquest Indian dislocations and movement drove them into greater isolation and caused them to abandon horticulture. The Sirionó have even lost, or else never had, the knowledge of making fire.

The Guayakí represent another case of deculturation in historic times. They once practiced cultivation, but when pressures from whites and hostile Guaraní Indians forced them into the forested hinterlands of the Caaguazú Hills, they became primarily hunters and gatherers who, like the Sirionó, live in small nomadic bands which are ever on the alert against attack. The Warrau of the Orinoco Delta may have had farm villages or even chiefdoms before they retreated into the inaccessible swamplands, where they abandoned farming.

Where archaeology affords important stratigraphy, or time depth, it supports the assumption that the simple culture of the nomads endured a very long time in these isolated areas with comparatively little change.

The most impressive time sequence has been established by Junius Bird, Lothrop, and others in the region of the Strait of Magellan and

Beagle Channel, where carbon 14 dating shows that the lowest cultural levels date from 6000 to 7000 B.C. (Palli Aike Cave, Chile: 8639 years + or — 900). Bird[1] found five levels, which were distinguished by types of projectile points and other artifacts but otherwise indicated no significant changes that might affect the nature of society. The earliest level contained remains of a people who probably hunted the now-extinct giant ground sloth, and the latest period had artifacts very similar to those of the historic Ona Indians. Farther south, in the region of Beagle Channel, the stratigraphic sequence is of comparable length, but there appears to have been even less change in the hunting-and-gathering economy over the millennia. While Patagonia and the pampas lack stratigraphic studies comparable to those made in Tierra del Fuego, Bird's evidence suggests that a basically similar hunting-and-gathering culture had also persisted in these areas during a long period, even though new societies may have moved into the area.

Since features that were formerly widely distributed as part of an archaic culture may survive in peripheral or isolated areas, it is interesting to note that ceremonies which initiate youths into the formal status of manhood and at the same time sharply differentiate men from women and children were very conspicuous, although not unique, among certain nomadic hunters and gatherers. Such ceremonies are found among other simple societies in widely scattered parts of the world.

Some particulars of the culture history of the Gran Chaco can be surmised from the distribution of culture elements. The Chaco was a kind of cul-de-sac where early features from many sources were preserved. For example, in this area and in parts of the Central Andes, there were certain games and gambling practices that are known widely in native North America but were not found elsewhere in South America. These were possibly survivals of some early inter-American culture. More recently, the Chaco borrowed from the Andes and the tropical forests. Andean influences were strongest on the western fringe of the Chaco among such peoples as the Chaná, Chiriguano, and Tonocoté, who were in contact with the Inca in both prehistoric and historic times. Andean traits include the spade, eyed needle, poncho, wooden spoons and bowls, and such trade objects as pottery vessels and metal ornaments.

Tropical-forest influences were introduced from the east, and the Guaraní were no doubt among the principal purveyors of these influences. Tropical-forest traits in the Chaco include loom weaving, feather ornaments, the gourd rattle, mortar and pestle, certain crops such as sweet manioc, and use of urucú and tobacco. These are most numerous along the borders of the Chaco and, owing to environmental limitations, diminish among the bush-dwelling nomads of the central Chaco and the pampean Indians to the south.

According to the cultural historical age-area hypothesis, many features of the hunting-and-gathering people are interpreted as marginal survivals of an early Pan-American cultural substratum which has been replaced elsewhere by a more developed culture. It is pointed out that such elements as earth ovens, brush houses, fringed skin garments, and many others have a "split distribution," that is, occur principally among nomadic groups in far northern and southern latitudes of the Western Hemisphere but not in between. Undoubtedly, many traits are very old in America and have survived only among the simpler peoples. Thus the use of tubes for ritual drinking of water and special sticks, in place of fingers, for scratching louse bites during certain ceremonies have no obivous appropriateness to the local way of life. One may suppose, therefore, that these arbitrary practices probably had a single, early origin from which later survivals were somehow derived. It is not difficult to imagine, however, that such traits as brush windbreaks, fur clothing, skin and bark containers, and many others which are also found in the extreme north and south were simple and obvious solutions to local needs; that is, they were cases of independent invention.

Whatever the history of particular inventions, there is no doubt that the social patterns of the hunters and gatherers were locally conditioned by the adaptive processes of cultural ecology. Differentiation of cultural types began shortly after epipaleolithic people entered the New World and began to disperse through a variety of environments. Although all Indians remained hunters and gatherers until 2500 or 3000 B.C., their organization for collecting seeds, shellfish, and other foods, for fishing, or for hunting special kinds of game was different in each case. The nomadic hunting-and-gathering peoples encountered by the Europeans represent some of the types that may result from these adaptations, but none is a survival of an archaic American type that was uniform from the Arctic shores to Tierra del Fuego.

3. SUBSISTENCE PATTERNS AND SOCIAL FEATURES

Among the nomadic hunters and gatherers, the organization of the people for subsistence purposes was a major determinant of the essential features of social organization, and it strongly conditioned most other aspects of culture. The low productivity of the environments limited the population density, while the lack of food surpluses together with poorly developed transportation prevented the settlement of large population aggregates in permanent communities.

Despite typological differences between the nomads, all tended to be structured along lines of kinship, sex, and age. Even the larger bands consisted of several lineages or extended kin groups. The elementary families comprising the lineage or band were organized in fairly cohesive units to cooperate in the food quest, in ceremonial and festive activities, and when the occasion arose, in defense of band territory or in reprisal for sorcery. Social and occupational classes were characteristically absent, however, and there were no priesthoods or full-time secular leaders having more than advisory powers.

Despite these general similarities, there was considerable diversity among the societies of nomadic hunters and gatherers; for the nature of the small, dispersed, and mobile groups depended very directly upon the methods of obtaining food in each environment. These may be subsumed under three principal types, whose social features directly reflect organization for subsistence purposes.

The simplest socioeconomic structure is the autonomous, elementary, or nuclear family; that is, father, mother, and children. Next in complexity and size is the unilineal band, which is organized on either patrilineal or matrilineal principles and is characterized by local exogamy. The third level is represented by the multilineage or composite band, which consists of several unrelated lineages.

The elementary family was the basic sociopolitical and economic unit among the Chono, Alacaluf, and western Yahgan of the Chilean archipelago. The Guató of the upper Paraguay River were also organized in largely autonomous elementary families. The Nambicuara of the southern Mato Grosso seasonally dispersed into individual family groups for subsistence purposes.

Unilineal bands, that is, societies consisting of lineages, were found among the Ona, Haush, and eastern Yahgan, who were patrilineal, patrilocal, and exogamous, and among the Guayakí and Sirionó, who were matrilineal, matrilocal, and exogamous. It is probable that the aboriginal Patagonian and pampean Indians were organized in patrilineal bands, much like those of the Ona, although their early acquisition of horses brought about multilineage bands. The Guahibo, Chiricoa, and possibly, the Purí-Coroado seem also to have been organized into patrilineal bands in aboriginal times.

Multilineage bands were widespread in the Gran Chaco. In the western Chaco, the component lineages tended to be matrilineal and matrilocal. Social groups composed of several unrelated families or lineages were also found among the Bororo and Caingang, both of whom had matrilineal moieties. The Warrau were also matrilineally organized.

Family units. Reliance principally upon shellfish in the Chilean archipelago (Chono, Alacaluf, Yahgan) caused a sparse population, fragmentation in family units, dispersal along the intricate shorelines of the innumerable islands and the mainland, and littoral nomadism in small bark canoes. Land foods were unimportant.

The critical ecological fact is that shellfish gathering in the archipelago is necessarily competitive rather than cooperative, and since resources are meager, individual familes had to forage in isolation. Many primitive hunters and fishers fragment in family groups for food gathering during a portion of the year yet associate with one another sufficiently long during other seasons to develop permanent, multifamily bands or communities. The Chono, Alacaluf, and Yahgan had no access to important quantities of game or fish. Multifamily assemblies were possible only for brief periods and at unpredictable times when a stranded whale or a seal herd was found. These were occasions for important ceremonies, but they entailed no permanent social units larger than the family, and they lasted only until the surplus was consumed, after which the families had to move out again in search of food. Sometimes these ceremonies were planned in advance, but their fulfillment depended strictly upon the chance availability of a food surplus and not upon setting aside stores for the occasion.

It should be stressed that the isolation of these families did not mean lack of motivation for associating with one another—visiting, gossiping, games, songs, and other purposes of social intercourse. It was a sheer practical necessity.

Another important feature of this family nomadism is that it followed no traditional or fixed routes, nor was it confined to clearly delimited areas, except among some of the Yahgan. This may be attributed to the somewhat erratic occurrence of shellfish. A corollary of the absence of territorial rights was the absence of group warfare. Hostilities were limited to skirmishes when one family trespassed on a shellfish bed being exploited by another, but fights were avoided if another solution could be found.

The Guató represent a case in which families were independent of one another most of the year, when they lived in canoes and exploited river resources; but, owing to a richer environment than the archipelago, they were able to remain together for a few months in semipermanent shelters along the riverbank. Defensive warfare contributed to cohesion within each of three regional divisions of the Guató.

Patrilineal bands. The cultural ecology of the Ona, Hausk, and eastern Yahgan, and probably the Tehuelche, Poya, Querandí, and Charrua brought about multifamily, patrilineal hunting bands even though the population density was only 0.1 to 0.2 persons per square mile, a figure smaller perhaps than in the archipelago. The crucial feature was that cooperative hunting of guanaco, rhea, and various small mammals yielded greater returns than individual hunting. Since these animals occur in comparatively small herds—very unlike the great migratory herds of bison or caribou in North America—and since human mobility was limited by foot travel, band hunting rights to well-bounded territories were claimed and defended against trespass. Collection of wild plant foods did not offset the sociological effects of hunting. Owing to the sparse human population, these bands numbered only about 40 to 100 persons. Since hunting was the principal activity and men remained throughout life in country they knew well, the bands consisted of nuclear families related through the male line. Wives were taken from other bands.

Composite or multilineage bands. After the Spaniards introduced horses and cattle to the pampas, Patagonia, and the Gran Chaco, the cultural-ecological adaptation was drastically altered. Horse nomadism permitted far greater mobility, new hunting methods, and vastly better transportation; livestock which ran wild provided a new source of food; and the Spanish settlements offered wealth that could be raided. In the pampas and Patagonia, the aboriginal hunting territories were too small for mounted nomads, and the native foot bands amalgamated into much larger bands of hunters and raiders which roved over ill-defined areas. The horse bands often numbered as many as 500 persons, and a Tehuelche band of 1,000 was observed in 1849. Each band consisted of several lineages, but their size and composition fluctuated as one or another chief attracted or lost followers. The older kinship basis of leadership was replaced by authority based on ability and persuasiveness and extending over several unrelated kin groups.

Band solidarity was enhanced by warfare, for population movements and amalgamations caused by expansion and confusion of band territories brought Indian groups into conflict with one another. There were hostilities even between the pampean Indians and the Araucanians, some of whom had been forced eastward across the Andes. Meanwhile, expansion of Spanish settlements threatened Indian occupation of the pampas at the same time that it provided new wealth that could be taken in raids.

Among the guanaco-hunting peoples, several bands sometimes joined together for social and religious ceremonies. But this activity entailed no hierarchy of religious specialists or hereditary classes. Since warfare also failed to create special classes, socioeconomic cleavages within the band followed lines of kinship, sex, and age.

Matrilineal bands. Matrilineal bands are the counterpart of patrilineal bands but differ in the line of descent. They occurred among forest people who collected wild vegetable foods, hunted, and fished. Woman's role in the collection of vegetable foods was certainly a factor in causing matrilineality. Oberg, however, has offered a more complicated hypothesis.[2] He reasons that, since matrilineal bands are more closely spaced territorially than patrilineal hunting bands, the band or kinship head, who is a male in both kinds of bands, has access to and control over his sons who reside matrilocally with their wives' bands. Since the patrilineal bands are patrilocal, a leader's sons are under his immediate control. While we really do not know the distance between bands, it seems likely that interband kinship bonds would be stronger where the sons live in their wives' bands than where wives live in their husbands' bands.

Examples of matrilineal bands are found among the highly nomadic forest Guayakí of Paraguay and the Sirionó of eastern Bolivia, both of whom subsist by a simple hunting, gathering, and fishing economy. Bands range from 30 to 100 persons among the Sirionó and are smaller among the Guayakí. The kinship elders are band leaders. Matrilocal residence is strictly observed; husbands come from neighboring bands to reside with their wives. The bands travel as a unit, often sharing a common shelter at successive camp sites. Society is kin-based, and cleavages follow lines of relationship, sex, and age. Hostilities are carried on to avenge sorcery and exploitative trespass, but there is no warfare for territorial conquest or to take captives.

The Gran Chaco was extremely varied culturally and environmentally, but unfortunately most of its aboriginal people are too little known to place any of them confidently in a sociocultural type. While plant cultivation had a fairly general distribution in aboriginal times, most of the Indians depended in varying degrees upon wild products. There was a general contrast between the dry western area, where the xerophytic scrub supported little game and the people depended primarily upon seasonal harvests of wild seeds, especially the algarroba, and the wetter east, where cultivation and fishing were more productive.

The western Indians shifted camp periodically, especially when their waterholes dried up and forced them to find new ones. These bands seem to have been matrilineal and to have claimed territorial rights over gathering, hunting, and fishing areas, but their pre-Spanish composition is not clear. We do not know whether they consisted of single, exogamous matrilineal kin groups, like those of the Sirionó and Guayakí, or of several lineages. There were probably considerable changes in band structure during early colonial times, when, as in the pampas, formerly independent lineages amalgamated in larger units under the pressures of warfare from the Spaniards and from marauding groups of nomadic horse Indians. During the colonial era, most Chaco peoples had multilineage bands, which, among the foot Indians, numbered between 50 and 200 persons.

Chieftainship in the western Chaco was strengthened in postcontact times, but it was rarely hereditary. In the case of multilineage bands, leadership was based on such personal qualities as courage, wisdom, generosity, and often possession of shamanistic powers. In post-Conquest times, owing no doubt to the ceaseless warfare following the advent of the Spaniards, some chiefs had authority over several bands.

It is doubtful whether certain aboriginal groups of the eastern Chaco, especially the Guaycuruans, should be classed as hunters and gatherers. Since fish were available along the main rivers and cultivation was fairly productive, settlements were larger and less mobile than in the west. Little is known of native residence patterns and kinship structure among the Guaycuruans. Early sixteenth-century evidence indicates that, even before acquiring horses, the Mbayá resembled the chiefdoms in that they had established suzerainty over the agricultural Arawakan Guaná, which implies that the Guaná produced sufficient crop surpluses to contribute to the support of their conquerors. Acquisition of horses tightened the Mbayás' hold over the Guaná but did not make the Mbayá more nomadic. In post-Spanish times, Mbayá household heads came to constitute an endogamous upper class in a rather rigidly stratified society.

The Abipón, Mocoví, Toba, Lengua, and others practiced limited cultivation in aboriginal times, but they depended on wild foods to the extent that they had to shift their settlements seasonally to follow the ripening of seeds and the replenished hunting grounds.

Although the native food quest carried out on foot (except among the canoe-using Payaguá) operated to keep resident groups relatively small, the acquisition of horses by the Indians of the Chaco grasslands radically changed subsistence patterns and social and political structure. The mounted Guaycuruan Indians roamed larger territories, virtually gave up horticulture, and carried on predatory raids against Spanish settlements, herds of cattle, and other Indians. The intensification of warfare created classes of military leaders and warriors. While there may have been an aboriginal tendency toward warrior classes, if the Mbayá are indicative of a regional pattern, predatory horse-nomadism quickened its development and crystallization.

Groups of little-known composition. The enclaves of nomadic hunters and gatherers scattered in the steppes, llanos, unproductive coastlines, deep interfluvial forests, and swamps—Southern Cayapó, Purí-Coroado, Guaitaca, Macú, Mura, Shiriá, Waica, Guaharibo, Yaruro, Guahibo, and Chiricoa—though little more than names, apparently differed from their neighbors, the tropical-forest village farmers. They lived in small, wandering bands of unknown but probably simple composition, residence rules, and kinship relations.

The Yaruro occupy the banks of several tributaries of the Orinoco River in eastern Colombia and Venezuela and depend largely on river resources. They venture into the forests and llanos only occasionally, to hunt armadillos, deer, and other game. They represent an extreme of mobility, seldom spending more than a night or two at the same camp site.

The Macú, Shiri, Waica, and Guaharibo are nomadic forest dwellers who inhabit parts of the Amazon Basin that are unfavorable to cultivation. The less acculturated groups among them continue to use stone axes and are without canoe transportation.

The Guahibo and Chiricoa are similar in many ways to the Macú, Shiriana, and their neighbors, but they hunt in the savanna lands of eastern Colombia and move seasonally according to the harvest of wild seeds. River resources provide them with only supplementary foods.

With few exceptions, the forest hunters and gatherers make little use of the rivers. Their subsistence is mainly derived from land resources, and transportation is confined mostly to human carrier and foot travel. They tend to avoid the major rivers for fear of more powerful horticultural peoples found along them.

With the notable exception of the Mura, none of these nomads were warlike. The aboriginal habitat of the Mura was along the lower Madeira River, whence they spread northward in warlike waves, overrunning the river-dwelling farm people in their path. Although the Mura might in the past have practiced cultivation and occupied riverine settlements, they are known in the historic period as predators who stole their food from farm settlements encountered in their expeditions. They were good canoemen, like the Yaruro, and fully exploited the rivers for fish, mammals, and turtle eggs. They used bark canoes, however, until they learned to make more substantial and larger dugouts from the settled horticultural peoples. Since their pacification, the Mura have tended to merge with the Neo-Brazilian population along the Amazon.

4. MARRIAGE AND THE FAMILY

The function of sexual unions varies in certain ways in different levels of culture. In modern, industrial societies marriage is usually formalized by a civil and/or religious ceremony; for it is a social contract and it involves property rights, inheritance, and birth records for state purposes. But some classes, such as landless and illiterate workers, may often be content with consensual unions or common-law marriage, which is an informal, readily dissolved union.

Although the term "marriage" is conventionally used to describe sexual unions among primitive people, it must not be understood to have the same meaning as in legally sanctioned sexual partnerships in modern nations. In some ways, primitive marriage is more like modern common-law or consensual unions. Yet even this category is too broad; for the nature of marriage and the family depends upon which cultural activities are carried out by the family and which by the band, village, or larger sociocultural unit. These marriages resemble consensual unions in that their dissolution entails no complicated divorce procedures that must follow state laws. But they are not necessarily unstable, and many potent forces serve to perpetuate them.

Rather fundamental differences in marriage and the family follow the level of the sociocultural unit to which the family belongs. Among the shellfish gatherers of the Chilean archipelago, the family carried out nearly all cultural activities in isolation. It was the autonomous pro-creational, economic, educational, and political unit. It cooperated with other families only briefly during sea hunts and initiation ceremonies. These family functions affected the choice of spouses, the nature of polygyny, and remarriage.

In the choice of a spouse, the principal prohibition among the shellfish gatherers was marriage to a known relative. Since kinship was rarely reckoned beyond three generations, however, this prohibition probably did not extend beyond first cousins. While polyandry was reported only among the Yaruro, most hunters and gatherers permitted polygyny.

Among the archipelagic people, marriage constituted the strongest bond between families, since the families were not linked together in larger bands or villages. Related families traveled together when possible, helped one another, and found pleasure in one another's company. The levirate and sororate, therefore, had special importance to such people, even though these customs also occur in more complex societies. Here, marriage with the brother of a deceased husband or the sister of a deceased wife perpetuated bonds between two families. Similarly, polygyny was typically sororal, that is, it meant marriage to two sisters. Marriage to a woman and her daughter by another man was also permitted. Both sororal polygyny and marriage to a mother and daughter naturally limited the number of spouses. Food production also had limiting effects, for few men could support a large number of wives.

Within the limitations of these patterns, the stability of unions was affected by the desire for children. A certain Guató man was said to have successively married all his wife's sisters before obtaining the number of children he desired. Postmarital fidelity was also a factor in permanency of union, and promiscuity, especially on the part of the wife, was disapproved.

While avoidance of near relatives was the principal determinant in choosing spouses among the shellfish gatherers, all the people organized in lineages practiced exogamy with reference to their lineage or extended kinship group. Where the residence group consisted of a single lineage this meant that local exogamy was required. But marriage into another lineage or band was not always random, and preferential forms of marriage were common. Among the matrilineal Bororo, for example, the preference for marriage with a cross-cousin—the father's sister's daughter—meant marriage into the father's lineage and original residence group. A similar pattern is suggested for the Nambicuara and was probably fairly frequent elsewhere. Such marriages served to strengthen the ties between both particular families and particular bands.

In these lineage-based societies, the individual family lost a certain amount of its autonomy and found greater security in sharing many activities with related families. In all cases, however, division of labor was based upon sex rather than class or group specialization. Women tended children, cared for the household, gathered wild foods, and transported camp gear. Men made their weapons, hunted, and fished. In the few cases of farming, men did the heavy work and left the routine drudgery of cultivation to the women.

Authority patterns followed family groupings and specialization. The father controlled the nuclear family, while the kinship elder was in charge of community activities of the lineage. The only true specialist was the shaman. Classes of warriors and captives were either entirely atypical, for example, among the Mbayá of the Chaco, or they were post-Conquest. So also were chiefs of such multilineage mounted bands of predatory warriors and hunters as those of the pampas.

5. RELIGION

Religion involved four principal kinds of concepts and practices among the hunters and gatherers: life-crisis beliefs and rites; shamanism; belief in supernatural beings; and magic.

Life-crisis rites began with birth and ended with death. Childbirth was always a fairly simple family affair. In the case of death, however, the entire local group mourned the deceased, especially if he had been a headman. Disposal of the dead varied: cremation among the Guaharibo, Awcicoma, Caingang, and occasionally the Toba; urn burial among the Purí-Coroado; secondary burial among the Charrua, Chaná, Bororo, Mataco, and others; burial in mounds among the Caingang; and direct earth burial.

While puberty rites were also usually of concern primarily to the family in the case of girls, the archipelagic Indians, the Ona, the Tchuelche, and some of the pampean and Chaco people held initiation rites which brought several bands together. In some cases, especially among the Ona, this ceremony inducted boys into the status of manhood and emphasized sex differences. In other cases, the ceremony marked the transition of both boys and girls into adulthood. Whereas most religious observances served individual or family purposes, these initiation rites involved the larger group and imparted ethical concepts regarding proper adult behavior to the initiates.

The shaman performed important functions among all hunters and gatherers, except the Sirionó and Guayakí, who are reported to have no such specialists. Typically, the shaman served individuals rather than groups. His principal function was to cure supernaturally caused sickness, which he accomplished with the assistance of his spirit-helper. He massaged his patient, sucked out the malignant object supposed to have caused the illness, and blew water or tobacco smoke over the patient. The Caingang and Botocudo were unusual among these people in ascribing illness to soul loss rather than intrusion of a foreign object into the sick man, and the Purí-Coroado were exceptional in that their shamans conjured ghosts and sky spirits to cure illness since they had no spirit-helpers.

Beliefs in supernatural beings took several forms. The Ona, Tehuelche, and Puelche believed in a supreme being, although they were not monotheistic. This being had little importance in the affairs of people except that he was blamed by the archipelagic Indians for epidemics. Some of the people of the Chaco and elsewhere made the stars and other natural phenomena characters in mythology, but they did not venerate them as objects of religious worship. Among celestial phenomena, the Pleiades were important, especially where farming was carried on, because their annual appearance at a certain place in the sky marked seasons of the year.

People were more interested in bush spirits and ghosts of the dead, which they feared, than in high gods or celestial beings. Ghosts or ancestors, who were not, however, identified as the ghosts of particular individuals, were probably of general importance. They were ritually impersonated by the Bororo and Caingang, who also held elaborate funeral ceremonies.

The hunters and gatherers carried out a good deal of magic, often as a means of manipulating supernatural beings. For example, the Chaco feasted and prayed in order to control the weather and sickness; many forms of magic were practiced by the Sirionó to further their subsistence activities and to dissuade evil spirits from doing them harm; and a widespread shamanistic function was to predict future events and find lost objects.

Some of this ceremonialism involved the whole local group, which made the occasion recreational as well as religious through drinking and feasting. Where leadership was required, it fell usually to the shaman, whose supernatural power gave him great influence over all activities of the group. But there was no case in which an organized group supplicated a supreme being for common purposes under hereditary classes of chiefs except among the Warrau, whose priest-temple-idol cult is discussed in Chapter Fourteen, section 6, as a probable survival in a deculturated society.

6. TECHNOLOGY AND MATERIAL CULTURE

All the hunters and gatherers were similar to one another in two general respects. First, they had comparatively little material paraphernalia, such as weapons, textiles, clothing, ornaments, buildings, and the like, owing as much to their inability to transport numerous objects in their nomadism as to their lack of inventiveness and their remoteness from the sources of inventions. Second, many of their manufactures were made by fairly simple techniques which were invented long ago and which, though found also among other Indians, were superseded by better techniques in most societies.

To judge by archaeological stratigraphy as well as from culture element distributions in South America, it is probable that heddle-loom weaving replaced netting and finger twining, that dugout canoes followed bark canoes, that checkerboard, twilled, and other forms of woven basketry came later than coiled basketry, that the wooden fire drill was invented later than the strike-a-light of flint and iron pyrite, that the bow and arrow and the blowgun succeeded the spear and spear thrower and the bolas, that pot boiling and the babracot came after stone boiling and the earth oven, and that wind instruments were later than percussion instruments. The older forms are not universal among hunters and gatherers, but they are found more frequently in these than in other groups.

In addition to the many survivals of older techniques, however, certain hunting-and-gathering people, especially those who lived near advanced societies, borrowed from their neighbors and each therefore possessed a somewhat distinctive inventory of cultural objects.

Weapons of hunting and warfare. Although bows and unpoisoned arrows were used by all nomadic hunters and gatherers at the time of white contact, the archaeology of Tierra del Fuego shows that they were acquired in late prehistoric times and that they replaced bolas, which had been used earlier. Bolas were probably never universal in the Americas, but they have a spotty distribution from Alaska to Tierra del Fuego and evidently are quite old. It is interesting that the introduction of the horse gave a new value to bolas. Two or three balls joined by cords could be swung from horseback to ensnare cattle, guanacos, and other large game as effectively as the lasso, which the Spaniards introduced. The bolas rather than the lasso became typical of the horse nomads of Patagonia, the pampas, and parts of the Chaco.

The spear and in some groups the spear thrower, or atlatl, survived from pre-bow times. As in the case of the bolas, the spear acquired a new function among the horse Indians. Long lances were used in warfare as among the Spanish cavalrymen, and they tended to replace the bow.

A third weapon that is also probably older than the bow is the sling, which occurred down the Pacific Coast from Colombia to Tierra del Fuego, but had fairly minor importance to the nomads.

While various stratagems were used in hunting, such traps as spring poles and deadfalls are found mainly in Amazonia, where a few forest nomads may have borrowed them. There was a wide distribution of such fishing devices as spears, harpoons, harpoon arrows, weirs, and nets, while the archipelagic people also used knives of mussel shell, poles to dislodge shellfish, clubs, and bird snares. The use of fish drugs and fishhooks, however, was more characteristic of the tropical-forest village farmers and these devices were found among only a few of the forest enclaves of nomads.

Domesticated animals and plants. Domesticated animals played a minor role in aboriginal subsistence. Dogs aided some of the archipelagic people in driving fish, but it is not certain that they were pre-Columbian in the southern portion of the continent. It is interesting that, while the Patagonian and pampean Indians depended primarily upon the guanaco, they never domesticated it, although the Andean Indians had domesticated its relatives, the llama and alpaca, at a very early period. The steamer duck was partly domesticated in southern Chile.

Cattle and horses were introduced to the nomads of the grasslands and Patagonia by the Spaniards and had a revolutionary effect upon the culture. None of these societies, however, became stockbreeders until they were thoroughly assimilated into the cash economy of the republics, and it is doubtful whether they practiced horse breeding, important as horses were to them.

The nomadic Indians of the southern latitudes lived beyond the limits of farming by aboriginal methods. Some of the enclaves of forest nomads, however, adopted small-scale cultivation as a supplement to wild resources, but practically none learned to grow bitter manioc and process it with the tipití.

Fire making. With the possible exception of the Sirionó, all nomads knew how to make fire, but the people of the Chilean archipelago and Patagonia used flint and iron pyrite to strike a spark by percussion. This presumably old method survived also among a few village farmers of Amazonia, but all other South American Indians used friction between two pieces of wood, a method of nearly worldwide distribution. In the Americas, friction was created by twirling the hard point of a drill in a socket in softer wood.

Food preparation. Methods of preparing food relate partly to the absence of such techniques as roasting on babracots and boiling in pots, although these were sparsely present among a few forest enclaves. To roast food, the nomads usually placed it directly on the fire or in earth ovens—preheated holes covered with earth and coals. The Chono placed heated stones in a bark container to boil food.

Condiments were rare, and most of the nomads used no salt. In the New World, a diet of cultivated vegetable foods has a high correlation with use of salt, while a diet of animal foods seems accompanied by an indifference to salt. In the Andes and the Circum-Caribbean area, where plant food was consumed more than meats, salt was not only a major trade item but often had ritual significance. Among the tropical-forest farmers, salt seems to have had less importance, though pepper was a major condiment; but whether this can be ascribed to lack of access to salt or to lack of dietary need is not clear. A number of tropical-forest people used ashes in lieu of salt. The nomadic hunters undoubtedly derived sufficient salt from meat, but some of the Chaco Indians, who depended largely upon plant foods, traded salt from the highlands.

Containers: pots, baskets, and skin. It was once believed that only settled village farmers make pots. This is not literally true, for in South America many nomadic hunters and gatherers learned ceramics. The distribution of pottery, however, shows clearly that the nomads were late borrowers and not inventors of it. The people of the Chilean archipelago and Tierra del Fuego and the Antillean Ciboney had no knowledge of ceramics, and the same was probably true of the Nambicuara, Mura, and Botocudo. Since ceramic vessels add to the burden of a nomadic people, pots were ordinarily made with little care and fall into Willey's categories of "crude" and "simple." People who had to leave much of their heavy gear when they moved their camp site would hardly expend great effort on it even if they had the leisure and skill to do so.

Occasionally in the history of inventions, earlier techniques are more difficult and time-consuming than later ones. This seems to have been true of basketry, since the technique of coiling or sewing is earlier archaeologically in Peru than the much simpler twilled weaves. Coiling was largely limited to the west coast, although other techniques were introduced to the Central Andes. The only technique of southern Chile and Tierra del Fuego was a primitive form of the coiled technique, known as "half-hitch coiling," used to make loosely woven baskets for gathering shellfish.

The simpler forms of woven basketry—that is, where the strands pass over and under one another, as in checkerboard and twilled weaves—are distributed throughout the tropical-forest village cultures and are shared by the nomad enclaves within them. But this technique also seems to have two principal developmental types: the temporary containers of palm fronds, woven when needed and as quickly discarded, and the carefully woven and decorated baskets made of prepared strands. The nomads used the former more often than the latter method.

The two main basketry techniques—the coiled and the woven—failed to penetrate the hunting areas of the pampas and Patagonia, where the

Toba spinning yarn, Gran Chaco. (Photo by Alfred Métraux, courtesy of the University of California.)

people used skin containers and even boiled by placing water and hot stones in them. The use of skin for many purposes, such as house covers, clothing, and containers, is one of many parallels between these people and the bison-hunting Plains Indians of North America.

Fabrics. The manufacture of textiles by a twined or finger weave, that is, by twisting a pair of weft elements over each warp, was earlier archaeologically than heddle-loom weaving in Peru, although it is reported in recent times only among the Chaco, Guató, Sirionó, and some eastern Brazil peoples. The heddle loom, although found throughout most of South America, was known to few nomads: the Sirionó, Nambicuara, and Chono. The Tehuelche apparently adopted it in the historic period from the Araucanians.

The limited occurrence of the loom among the nomads relates in part to the lack of garments in the warmer areas, the use of hide or fur robes in the cold climates, and the general absence of domesticated cotton fibers. The Chaco, however, natively wove cotton goods and in historic times used sheep's wool.

Netting is a very old technique, and it was used for fish nets in nearly all places where nets were effective. Netting was very well developed in the Chaco, especially in making bags which were used in lieu of baskets for transportation and storage. A few nomads who had adopted hammocks netted rather than wove them—Charrua, Mashacalí, and people of the Orinoco River. This distribution seems rather random, and it represents the chance combination of an old technique with a new cultural object, the hammock. Here and there, netting was also used for other purposes.

Clothing and ornamentation. In the cold southern latitudes, the body was protected by skin robes. While skins were also used in the northern portion of North America, the latter area differed importantly from South America in that the Indians tanned the hides and furs and cut and sewed shirts, dresses, and other attire. Tailoring of either skins or textiles was not practiced in South America, and tanning was probably unknown.

While full-length textile body coverings were used in the higher Andes, woven attire among the forest-dwelling nomads, as among their village neighbors, consisted of ornamental bands rather than garments.

Body adornment included ear-, nose, and lip plugs—though these were absent among the archipelagic people—featherwork, arm and leg bands, necklaces, paint, tattooing, and headdresses. These took many forms, but in general they served to distinguish bands or lineages, sex and age groups, and associations, and were never badges of status.

Dwellings. The temporary shelters used by most of the nomads hardly merit the name "houses." The Nambicuara, Guahibo, Guanahatabey or Ciboney, and others were said to lack houses altogether, sleeping entirely without shelter or under a simple windscreen. Most groups used caves or rock shelters if they were available. More adequate shelters were erected in ways that are found in many parts of the world. First, a domed hut of bent-over poles covered with leaves, brush, grass, or hides was made in the Chilean archipelago, the Chaco, and a few other places. The Patagonian and pampean toldo of the post-Columbian horse period is a larger hut built on the same principle. Second, a conical hut of poles supporting one another—fundamentally like the tipi and Canadian forms of conical pole huts—was known to the Yahgan. Third, a single or double lean-to was built by the Ona, Guató, Purí-Coroado, and others.

The larger and more permanent pole-and-thatch house of the tropical-forest type occurred only among some of the nomads who were in contact with the village farmers, for example, the Bororo and Warrau.

Miscellaneous knowledge. The nomads seem originally to have lacked musical instruments, except rhythm beaters. The archipelagic people had only sticks to beat time, while the people of the Chaco, the Bororo, and others used more complex rhythm beaters and rattles. In the course of time, however, the more northerly groups borrowed a variety of trumpets, flutes, Panpipes, and other wind instruments from their neighbors.

The use of chicha, an intoxicating beer, and tobacco was also unknown to the more southern hunters, but had been borrowed by some of the Chaco and forest nomads from their neighbors.

NOTES

1. Junius Bird, *Handbook,* vol. 1.
2. Kalervo Oberg, "Types of Social Structure among the Lowland Tribes of South and Central America," *American Anthropologist,* vol. 57, no. 3, part 1, pp. 472–488, 1955.

fourteen

VARIETIES OF NOMADIC HUNTERS AND GATHERERS

1. FAMILY SHELLFISH GATHERERS OF THE CHILEAN ARCHIPELAGO

The Chono, Alacaluf, and Yahgan Indians occupied the whole Chilean archipelago from the Guaitecas Islands to Cape Horn. This is a rugged, wind-swept, cold, and mountainous region with hundreds of islands, fiords, and channels. The annual rainfall ranges from 80 inches in the north to 120 inches in the south, and the average temperature is 32°F in winter and 50°F in summer. The country is covered by a dense, almost impenetrable rain forest, which is a formidable deterrent to overland travel and which, together with the cold, prevents farming. The rugged topography and almost complete dependence upon ocean resources made canoe transport vital to subsistence. Martin Gusinde called the people of this region "canoe nomads."

Considerable ethnographic information has been collected by anthropologists and travelers on the culture of the Yahgan and, to a lesser extent, of the Alacaluf. Least is known of the northernmost people, the Chono, who became extinct in the nineteenth century. The Alacaluf and Yahgan are almost extinct today, having a combined population of about 200 persons. In aboriginal times, they probably numbered no more than several thousand, and the Chono considerably less. Today, the surviving Alacaluf and Yahgan are greatly acculturated.

These three peoples shared a majority of cultural traits and had very

397

similar subsistence patterns, social structure, and magicoreligious beliefs and practices.

Subsistence. Crop cultivation is possible only in the northern portion of the archipelagic region, around the Guaitecas Islands. The Chono who lived here adopted potatoes in aboriginal times from Araucanians of the island of Chiloé, and in post-Spanish times they raised maize and barley on a small scale. Their farming was sporadic, however, and did not greatly affect the more important subsistence patterns of shellfish gathering and marine hunting. The Yahgan, Alacaluf, and most of the Chono had no choice but to subsist by food collecting.

None of these people were pastoral in pre-Conquest days, and it is not certain that they even had dogs.

The archipelago is comparatively poor in fish, game, and wild food plants. Moreover, the difficult terrain hinders exploitation of land resources. The principal foods were shellfish, sea mammals, and birds. The subsistence economy was geared primarily to the exploitation of a large number of shellfish beds, which required frequent movement of the people along the shores. Shellfish were gathered by women, principally along the beaches and from boats offshore. The Indians speared shellfish in water up to about 2 fathoms, but in deeper water divers, especially women, brought them up in baskets held between their teeth to waiting boats. Among the Yahgan, the women's role in diving for shellfish completely eclipsed that of men. It is difficult to say whether this division of labor followed the common pattern wherein women collect wild foods while men hunt or whether it is a tribute to women's greater fortitude and better insulation in withstanding the icy waters, which range from 40°F to 50°F. Children, too, were food producers. Almost as soon as they learned to walk, they scoured the tidal beaches for mollusks and sea urchins which they promptly cooked and ate.

The families recognized the need for conservation and avoided exhausting the shellfish beds. As the yield of each bed diminished, the people moved to the next gathering ground. To judge by observations in the historic period, families did not follow the same routes each year but varied their itinerary and sometimes wandered far afield from their usual territory. Furthermore, chance finds of such temporary food surpluses as dead or beached whales, seal whelping grounds, or bird rookeries caused abeyance of shellfish gathering. At such times, normally isolated families assembled in large aggregates to gorge while the food lasted. A certain haphazardness in the annual rounds is suggested, and it seems to have depended upon the erratic occurrence of such surpluses and the unpredictability of the yield from shellfish beds in successive years.

While women dove into the chilly seas, men hunted sea mammals and marine birds, but the yields were meager. The most plentiful bird species were cormorants, steamer ducks, geese, swans, petrels, and penguins. The Indians hunted these in a number of ingenious ways. They took cormorants with the aid of torches and clubs at night, while they roosted, and lured other species by live decoys or by imitating their whistle, then captured them with pole snares. If the hunters exercised great care, they might take nearly all the birds roosting on a rock ledge or an islet. Sometimes parties of hunters rushed upon roosting birds and clubbed large numbers to death. Such operations, however, could not be repeated frequently at the same place without risk of exterminating the birds.

Hunters generally harpooned sea lions in the water or killed them with clubs on shore, but they sometimes caught them in nets and traps. They used harpoons to hunt porpoises. To take coypus and sea otter, they were aided by dogs, which held them at bay in the rocks until hunters killed them with long poles. Dogs even helped drive fish into shallows or into nets. Dying whales were assailed by many canoeloads of hunters, who harpooned them and dragged them ashore. Whaling was very dangerous, and it not only failed frequently but often brought death to some of the hunters. Dead, beached whales attracted many Indians, but since they were sometimes putrid by the time they were discovered and eaten, it is likely that the Indians were occasionally poisoned.

It has been asserted that these Indians fell far below the cultural level of the Indians of the northwest coast of North America because they were not exposed to influences like those which reached the latter from Asia. Actually, they were no farther from the Andean civilizations than the Indians of southern Alaska were from the high cultures of Asia. It is more to the point that fishing is of relatively minor importance in the economy of southern Chile. Compared to the northwest coast of North America, where the surplus provided by abundant yields of littoral and riverine fishing permitted the highest cultural development of all nonagricultural peoples in the Western Hemisphere, the fish resources of the archipelagic region are decidedly meager. That fish have always been unimportant is attested by the scarcity of fishbones in archaeological sites. The absence of a predictable surplus prevented the archipelagic people from maintaining large, permanent settlements and a society with social classes and specialists. Although whales and large herds of seals provided temporary abundance, storage of surpluses each year was impossible because of the erratic occurrence of those foods and the absence of techniques for preserving them.

Plant foods were scarcely utilized by the archipelagic people, and land game provided only a small and insignificant part of the diet.

Food was prepared in simple ways. The Chono boiled food in bark buckets by placing hot stones in them, but this practice was not known to the Yahgan and Alacaluf. Meat and shellfish were generally cooked directly on the coals.

The inventory of tools, weapons, and other gear was limited to the barest necessities, owing in part to difficulties of transporting them in the small canoes. These included the implements used in the food quest, coverings and sometimes frames for their small, domed huts, a few simple tools for manufacturing weapons and for preparing food, skin clothing, and sundry items for personal adornment. They made baskets which were distinctive for their half-hitch coil and bark vessels to hold drinking water and to bail the leaky canoes. Many simple implements were improvised when needed and then thrown away.

Transportation. Since the difficulties of overland travel together with the dependence upon marine foods made canoe travel essential to survival, it is surprising that Yahgan and Alacaluf canoes were small, treacherous craft made of bark. The Chono, however, are said to have used canoes with built-up plank sides, similar to the Araucanian canoes, and the Alacaluf adopted plank boats during historic times. In the nineteenth century the Yahgan learned to make dugout canoes from a Brazilian Indian who had chanced to travel far from his native land. Today, the Indians use dories obtained from the whites.

Men manufactured the native canoes, but women paddled, steered, and managed them, and maintained the constant fire on the clay hearth. They took fire from site to site in their canoes to avoid rekindling new fires, since these were made with a strike-a-light of flint and iron pyrite which few families owned.

Sociocultural structure and settlements. The dependence upon shellfish required not only constant movement from one beach to another but split the society into units of elementary or nuclear families. Sometimes, if the food supply permitted, two or three families traveled and camped together.

There were no permanent settlements. At each of the sheltered beaches, which are rare in the region, the family spent a few days gathering shellfish, repairing their spears, harpoons, clubs, slings, bows and arrows, camp gear, and canoes. They dressed skins with a shell scraper to make fur capes and crude moccasins, their only clothing. At the better sites, they left pole-hut frames which could be used by other families.

When the shellfish had been depleted, the family or families moved on to the next camp site, carrying their gear, the skin or bark house covering, and sometimes the house poles in their canoes. The itinerary was dictated by the hope of finding food rather than by any concept

Alacaluf camp showing temporary nature of the huts. (Courtesy of Junius Bird.)

Frame of Alacaluf house. (Courtesy of Junius Bird.)

of boundaries or territorial rights, except among some of the Yahgan. The only reason for avoiding a site was that a member of the family had recently died there. If, however, a family attempted to exploit a site already occupied by another family, a fight ensued.

The eastern Yahgan of Navarino Island and Beagle Channel seem to have had larger and more permanent settlements, owing no doubt to their access to guanaco. In this area, Lothrop found large, prehistoric refuse mounds containing pit houses, built probably somewhat like the conical pole-and-brush houses of the southern Ona, although the culture at these sites otherwise resembled that of the western Yahgan.

The organization for subsistence entailed family autonomy in most activities. The family was the basic social, political, economic, and educational unit. It surrendered sovereignty only temporarily during collective whale and seal hunts and initiation ceremonies, but even on these occasions it did not necessarily associate with the same families. In daily life there was no leader above the family head, and there were no formal structures such as lineages, sibs, or territorial divisions. The web of kinship relations constituted the only permanent ties that extended outside the immediate family circle. That these were slightly weighted on the paternal side is suggested by the close bonds between a man and his brother's son. This was somewhat counterbalanced, however, by the practice of bride service and bride payment among the Alacaluf and Yahgan.

The Chono, Yahgan, and Alacaluf were usually monogamous, although polygyny was permitted. One form of polygyny was marriage to a widow and her daughter at the same time. The levirate and sororate, although not required, served to maintain close ties between two families. A man had to avoid direct speech and close personal relations with his wife's parents, especially his father-in-law, throughout life. Similar restraints were at first imposed between the wife and her parents-in-law, but these were relaxed after the birth of children.

Ceremonialism and religion. In the absence of gods which were supplicated for community purposes, two religious forms were dominant: crisis rites, including birth, puberty, and death observances; and initiation ceremonies. The former concerned mainly the individual and his family; the latter affirmed sex and age status and temporarily involved large groups of families.

Birth ceremonies were very simple family affairs. The Alacaluf father stood guard outside the confinement hut during childbirth but helped out if other assistants were not available. After delivery, the umbilical cord, placenta, head hair from both parents, parrot feathers, and a live coal were wrapped in a skin and buried under the hut. The mother and father then fasted for a few days.

Yahgan practices were similar to those of the Alacaluf. Both parents observed food taboos before and after the birth; the mother took sea baths daily after delivery; and the father observed the couvade for several days during which friends and relatives cared for the family's needs. These people assembled, however, as much for commemorative and ceremonial reasons as for practical purposes.

A girl's puberty observance was brief and relatively simple. During her first menses, the Alacaluf girl fasted while confined in a special hut. The Yahgan girl fasted, had her face painted, received counsel from an older woman, and eight or ten days later bathed in the sea. A feast then followed.

The initiation ceremonies marked the passage from youth to adulthood, and they were attended by a large number of families. These ceremonies were not regularly scheduled, however, since they depended, first, upon chance acquisition of sufficient foods, such as a stranded whale, and, second, upon whether a group of neophytes had reached the appropriate age. Their function, therefore, consisted more of recognition of age and sex status, temporary renewal of bonds between families, and religous-recreational activities than of consolidating social units of fixed membership.

In their recognition of age status and sexual dichotomy, these ceremonies were not unique. A formal grouping of men is found in many cultures, and a secret men's society is found in different parts of the world among many simple societies. In South America, a similar organization occurred in several places, for example, in the northwest Amazon. While this ceremony occurred in typical form among the Ona, sex distinctions broke down in the Yahgan rite, during which both boys and girls were initiated, and somewhat in the Alacaluf rite. Bird sees in these rites two streams of influence: an older initiation rite involving festivities in a special house and a more recent "ghost rite" which involved impersonation of ancestors and was diffused from the Ona.

The best descriptions of these ceremonies deal with the rites of the Yahgan, which are similar to Alacaluf and Ona ritual. Our scanty information about the Chono suggests that they had similar rites.

The Alacaluf initiation ceremony began with the preparation of scaling clubs and shellfish poles in a special hut, where the men painted their faces and engaged in mummery, singing, and dancing. After the weapons were ready, the men went to the sealing grounds and the women sought shellfish. The success of the hunt must certainly have determined the duration of the ceremony. Women were admitted to certain phases of the ceremony, but their main task was to gather shellfish, cook the seal meat, and prepare the green hides.

The men next built a second large ceremonial structure in which they and the young men slept, prepared ceremonial paraphernalia, sang, and danced. The older men told stories and instructed the neophytes in men's work and proper adult behavior. While this instruction imparted moral precepts, society was too loosely knit to have had a genuine ethical system. The youths learned age status and masculine behavior rather than social ethics in the broadest sense. The males were painted according to their ritual and adult status, which followed a rough age-grading that distinguished neophytes, boys who had passed through the rite previously, and men with more ritual experience. No such age distinctions were made among women.

Women were admitted to the ceremonial house before being humiliated by a ritual dousing with water, but they were excluded from watching the special feathered dancers who performed at night, and they were the target of a masked spirit impersonator who ran among them clubbing all he could reach. Toward the end of the ceremony, men and women changed roles, the men going to the women's quarters and the women staying in the ceremonial house. Both sexes spent the last night in the ceremonial house, after which the families dispersed to resume their food search.

The Yahgan ritual climaxed the vocational and moral training of boys and girls and was a precondition to marriage; but since all people who had previously passed through the ceremony were permitted to participate, it contributed much to social solidarity among normally independent families. The rite was led by an elder and, like the Alacaluf initiation ceremonies, was held only when the need arose or a temporary food surplus was available. It has been said that ceremonies lasted from several days to several months, but the maximum duration is questionable. Very likely some ceremonies were held for fairly long periods in historic times when the people chanced upon a wrecked ship or foregathered to exploit the generosity of exploration parties, such as the crews of the *Adventure* and the *Beagle*.

The leader of the rite was assisted by a mentor and guards. Each candidate wore a special costume, carried a painted staff, and had three sponsors. The candidates observed a series of endurance tests, drank water through a bird-bone drinking tube and used a scratching stick (both are very widespread New World ritual practices), were temporarily tattooed, and were given vocational and moral instruction. Most of the ritual consisted of special dances and songs. Then followed a mock battle between the sexes and a feast, after which the assembly disbanded.

Only initiates were considered full adults, and only boys who had passed through the rite twice were admitted to the mysteries of the kina ceremony, which was often held just after the conclusion of the initiation rites.

The Yahgan kina ceremony was more strictly in the pattern of a men's secret society, and its similarity to the Alacaluf yinchihaua and the Ona klóketen ceremonies indicate an interchange of ritual among these peoples. The kina ritual symbolized a mythical period when women domineered the males and controlled society through impersonating spirits, after which men discovered the hoax, usurped spirit impersonation, overthrew the women, and dominated the society. Men enacted the myth in spirit disguises and terrorized women and the uninitiated.

Apart from the ceremonials, Alacaluf and Yahgan religion involved a belief in supernatural beings which ranged from familiar spirits to a supreme deity. While the supreme deity of many South American Indians was an otiose being who was indifferent to human affairs, the Alacaluf and Yahgan prayed to their high god for food, health, and good weather, but they railed against him when they felt he had brought undue trouble or pain.

When a person died, the Alacaluf painted the mourners' faces black, beat on the outside of the deceased's hut, and buried his effects with some food and live coals. The Yahgan fasted, painted and gashed their bodies, and lamented while special mourning speeches were delivered. The mourners directed their anger at the supreme deity and hurled invectives at him. The deceased's personal possessions were cremated along with the corpse.

Shamans did not officiate in any rites or ceremonies. Their chief function was to cure illness, which they did by massaging the patient and sucking out the disease-causing object with the aid of their spirit-helpers. They could also cause sickness by capturing the souls of their victims. Their familiar spirits enabled them to control weather, assist hunters, and predict the future.

2. BANDS OF HUNTERS AND GATHERERS OF THE STEPPES AND PLAINS

The Ona of Tierra del Fuego

In aboriginal times a similar culture type probably extended from the Ona of Tierra del Fuego through Patagonia and the pampas. Since the mainland Indians were almost entirely unknown until after they acquired horses, it is best to discuss them separately.

The Ona are known in considerable and vivid detail thanks to the excellent volumes of description and photographs by the Austrian anthropologist Father Gusinde.[1] They comprised two major groups, the Shelknam and Haush, who differed slightly in dialect and culture. The Shelknam were composed of a northern and a southern division, between which there was some traditional enmity. The Europeans found the Ona in all the island of Tierra del Fuego except the southern coast. They occupied about 20,000 square miles and were estimated at about 2,000 persons. Preemption of their land, the introduction of European diseases, and a policy of extermination carried out with a ruthlessness rarely paralleled in European contact with native people decimated their numbers in the nineteenth century. Today, less than 50 Ona survive, and they seem destined to extinction or absorption among the whites in a very few years.

The southern part of Tierra del Fuego is heavily wooded, but becomes prairielike in the central and northern sectors. Like Patagonia and the pampas, it supports guanaco and other game. Ona culture was more like that of the Patagonian hunters than the sea-food gatherers of the Chilean archipelago, the eastern Yahgan excepted.

The Ona depended entirely upon wild foods, of which tuco tucos, a small rodent, and guanacos were by far the most important. They hunted guanaco with bow and arrows, and were assisted by dogs which, however, they may have acquired from Europeans. Less important game included foxes and other small land animals. The coastal Indians also took fish, shellfish, seals, and birds. Wild plant foods had negligible importance, although fungi as well as meat were dried and stored against times of want.

The division of labor was almost entirely on a sexual basis: men hunted, fished, made weapons, and performed the heaviest work around camp; women cared for the children and the household, gathered shellfish, dressed skins, made baskets, and transported household equipment on their backs when the family moved to new hunting grounds. Bowyers, who were paid for their work, were apparently the only specialized artisans, but even they were unable to subsist solely by their specialty.

The southernmost Ona, like the eastern Yahgan across Beagle Channel, lived in fairly substantial conical huts made from branches and tree trunks, but the Ona of the northern and central plains set up windbreaks of guanaco skins fixed to flimsy pole uprights. These portable shelters suited nomadic hunting life, and they were similar to those used by the Patagonian and pampean nomads.

The elementary family was an integral part of the larger lineage or patrilineal band, which had 40 to 120 members. The band consisted of relatives in the male line, that is, sons and grandsons, who took their wives from other bands. It was led by the elder of the lineage, whose authority was limited and modified by the counsel of all the adult males. Each band claimed hunting rights in a well-defined territory which, according to Gusinde's information, averaged about 400 square miles, and it defended these rights against trespass. This contrasts with the absence of territorial rights among the archipelagic peoples, except the eastern Yahgan. Interband contacts among the Ona were infrequent but involved hostilities arising from exploitative trespass and cooperation deriving from intermarriage and ceremonial participation.

Ona bands were patrilocal and exogamous. Marriage between blood relatives was prohibited, and wives were generally taken from distant bands. Monogamy prevailed, but polygyny, sororal polygyny, and the levirate were common. Polygynous men acquired prestige through being able to support several wives. There was no bride price or bride service, but postmarital residence was usually matrilocal for a short time, after which the couple went to live permanently with the husband's band.

The Ona, like the Yahgan and Alacaluf, observed the onset of a girl's puberty by simple rites. There was a feast, and the girl was painted, secluded, and instructed about proper adult conduct by her elders.

The Ona klóketen rite, however, was a full-fledged initiation of boys into manhood. It involved secrets that were revealed only to men, physical ordeals, and strong distinction between the sexes. Adult men, especially shamans, wearing masks and special costumes, paraded before the assembled bands in the guise of supernatural beings and threatened women and children. In this sexual dichotomy, women and children were supposed to believe that the masqueraders were really spirits, and any woman who knew the truth about the pretense kept it to herself. In the end, the spirit impersonators revealed their identity to the young males undergoing initiation and swore them to secrecy.

The ceremony was not only one that stressed sex differences but one that emphasized age contrasts in distinguishing men from boys. During the ceremony the young men fasted, underwent physical endurance tests, such as lying naked in the snow for twenty-four hours, and were restricted in their usual activities. Meanwhile, their elders gave them intensive instruction in their adult roles.

The ceremony ended in a great feast, after which the participants resumed their regular hunting activities. If several bands had assembled for the ceremony, they departed for their own territory.

The Ona believed in a supreme deity who punished errant human beings by inflicting disease on the entire group but who otherwise remained aloof from human affairs. Individuals apparently prayed to this god, offered him bits of food, and tried to propitiate him in other ways. The supreme deity was believed to have established traditional behavior and order among people and to punish transgressors; that is, he was a culture hero, but he was not thought to be the Creator.

Shamans not only functioned in the klóketen rite, but they served as curers and sorcerers and helped the group in hunting and warfare. Their supernatural helpers were the spirits of dead shamans, and the supreme deity played no role in their supernatural practices. Shamans trained their sons in their traditions and lore, which were always inherited in the male line.

Hostilities between bands resulted merely from revenge against trespass, murder, and sorcery. Skirmishes involved few participants, and sometimes disputes were settled by wrestling matches or bow-and-arrow duels.

Patagonian and pampean peoples

The Tehuelche, Puelche, Querandí, and Charrua were the most numerous and historically the best known of the nomadic peoples inhabiting the guanaco region on the continent. The Tehuelche occupied the wind-swept, arid, brush-covered steppes of the Patagonian tableland from the Strait of Magellan to the Río Negro, while the Puelche and Querandí inhabited the flat, grassy pampas which extend north to the Río de la Plata. The Charrua lived in the grasslands north of the Plata not far from the tropical rain forests.

The Patagonian and pampean Indians numbered some 36,000 persons, and their density of 0.12 per square mile was the sparsest in South America. Since the military defeat of the Indians in 1883 and the opening of southern Argentina to white settlement, native culture has virtually vanished. Argentina today is said to have few "Indians," but Indian racial characteristics are abundantly evident in the gaucho and other rural populations, especially in the west and south of Argentina.

During the first half of the eighteenth century, three important factors affected the Indians of the pampas and Patagonia. First, several thousand Chilean Araucanian Indians migrated across the Andes into the pampas in order to escape Spanish pressures. Second, there was sustained contact with whites which entailed hostility in military encounters but peaceful relations at mission stations. Third, and perhaps the factor of greatest importance, the Indians acquired horses from the Spaniards whose cattle began to run wild throughout their country.

The aboriginal or prehorse culture of this area is little known except for very brief comments made by members of Magellan's and subsequent expeditions. While many native traits obviously survived until much later times, one can only suppose that aboriginal socioeconomic organization resembled that of the Ona.

In aboriginal times, the Patagonian and pampean Indians practiced no agriculture and had no domesticated animals, except possibly the dog. Although farming was practiced nearby in northwest Argentina and the Andes, it was inhibited in the south by the unfavorable climate and in the north by the heavy grasses of the pampas, which could not well be cultivated without an animal-drawn plow.

Tehuelche hunting rhea and guanaco with bolas. (After George C. Musters, "At Home with the Patagonians," London, 1871.)

These Indians subsisted principally upon guanaco, rhea, and numerous smaller animals. Prehorse hunting methods included stalking with guanaco decoys, rhea disguises, and bows and arrows. These techniques continued in use among the southern Tehuelche and Ona foot nomads but were abandoned by the northern Tehuelche and Puelche when the horse was introduced. The mounted Indians employed large-scale surrounds, caught the rhea and guanaco with bolas, and killed them with spears.

Wild plants, roots, seeds, and berries were gathered, but meat was the mainstay. Dried or smoked, it was pounded and mixed with fat to make pemmican, which could be stored a long time. Water resources were not important to these peoples, although the Charrua did some fishing and the Querandí are said to have made a kind of "flour" from pulverized fish.

Model of Tehuelche toldo, or skin shelter. (Courtesy of American Museum of Natural History.)

The Tehuelche and Puelche had no canoes, and the Querandí and Charrua made only limited use of them. In prehorse times, women transported the camp gear from one hunting camp to another.

Aboriginal social units probably consisted of patrilineal bands like those of the Ona. Owing to the possibility of covering more territory and carrying more goods on horseback, the mounted bands became much larger than the patrilineal bands. They comprised 100 to 120 persons among the Puelche and as many as 500 among the Tehuelche. These mounted bands, however, were composed of rather independent patrilineages, who might change band affiliation. Each lineage consisted of several families who lived together in their own toldo, or skin-covered pole shelter. Among some of the Tehuelche, who received horses most recently, moreover, patrilineages continued to claim rights to their hunting territories after affiliating with larger mounted bands. It is probable, therefore, that the mounted bands were amalgamations of previously independent lineages.

The multilineage mounted bands functioned as collective hunting and warring units. They normally hunted within very broad areas over which they had some sense of proprietorship, but these areas had no definite boundaries comparable to those of the smaller, unmounted Ona bands. Owing to the great mobility and changing membership of these bands, it was impossible that any band should confine itself to a fixed territory. Competition for hunting resources rather than territory brought the bands into frequent collision with one another, and competition increased when the Araucanians migrated into the area from Chile.

Warfare took the form of predatory raids against the Spaniards, defense against punitive expeditions, and hostilities between Indian groups. It became a major factor in group cohesion and contrasted sharply with aboriginal interband feuds which resulted from woman stealing and murder and led only to small-scale hostilities. Early reports that captured women and children were sometimes used as drudge labor and at other times adopted into a family may or may not reflect aboriginal practice. The capture and incorporation in the local society of members of other societies has been widely reported in South America, but it was certainly intensified, if not originated, by taking slaves for European settlers.

Leadership of mounted bands directly reflected band functions. A capable and influential chief, or cacique, attracted families to himself so long as he was successful in hunting, warfare, and predatory raids, but the families felt free to join other leaders and often did so.

Within the band, each patrilineal lineage was probably exogamous. A man paid a bride price and took his wife, or, if he could afford it, his wives, to his own toldo or tent. That caciques preferred to marry into the family of another cacique indicates a trend toward, but by no means the achievement of, hereditary status.

The aboriginal Querandí and Charrua bands were fairly small and averaged about fifty persons. Like the Patagonians and pampean Indians, the local groups of Querandí and Charrua adopted horse nomadism in early post-Spanish times and allied themselves with powerful leaders. Their competition with neighboring Indians and organization in predatory bands were much like that in the pampas and Patagonia.

But the Charrua and their neighbors had a number of peculiar features not found elsewhere in the pampas. From the tropical-forest Indians, they may have adopted such practices as making drinking cups of the skulls of their war victims and slaying captives at the death of a chief. On the other hand, such ritual elements as skewering the arm and cutting off finger joints as signs of mourning and the quest by an individual for a supernatural vision are out of character in South America yet resemble the Plains Indians of North America. These elements invite speculation concerning their local invention or inter-American diffusion. But they have very minor bearing on the nature of the hunting bands.

At a girl's first menses and at childbirth, the Tehuelche and Puelche erected a special hut where a shaman sang and let the woman's blood, while mares were slaughtered, old women sang, and men danced in feathered headdresses. The Puelche girls' puberty ceremony was celebrated by a large assemblage of people, spirit impersonation, and ritual whipping.

After a death, the survivors mourned and mutilated themselves. Charrua men skewered themselves from wrist to shoulder, and both men and women chopped off finger joints. The Tehuelche gashed themselves and cut their hair to demonstrate grief.

The Tehuelche and possibly the Puelche believed in a supreme being who, after creating the world, remained otiose. The Querandí have been described as "supreme atheists," but little is known of Querandí and Charrua religion and birth and puberty ceremonials. All these peoples believed in good and evil bush spirits. The shamans cured sickness with the assistance of spirit-helpers, and among the Tehuelche and Puelche, they played important roles in the ceremonies.

In the processes of their acculturation as horse nomads, the Indians of the pampas and Patagonia present provocative parallels to many North American Indian horsemen of the Great Plains. The people of both areas acquired horses in such numbers that their subsistence habits and their social groups were deeply affected before they had borrowed European culture through direct, face-to-face contact with whites. Local groups amalgamated in larger, mounted hunting bands. The authority of the kinship elder was superseded by that of the successful war leader. Subsistence upon native animal and plant resources was supplemented and in many cases replaced by predatory raids on the new settlers. The new power of the chief, the temporary and unstable amalgamation of formerly independent groups, and the predatory activities were short-lived. Military defeat and assimilation as subcultural groups of cowboys, or Gauchos, in the new colonies and nations soon followed.

While the general direction of acculturation was parallel, there were also interesting similarities as well as differences in detail that followed horse nomadism. Whereas North American Indians adopted most Spanish accouterments for horses, e.g., bridle, saddle, and lariat, the pampean

Indians used bridles and saddles but devised their own "toe stirrup"—that is, a stirrup for the big toe—and used bolas of native origin in addition to lassos. On the other hand, the South Americans became remarkably similar to the Plains Indians in development of pemmican, use of horsehair in human coiffure, and many other details. These secondary effects of nomadism were certainly not diffused between mounted North and South America.

3. THE HUNTERS, GATHERERS, FISHERMEN, AND FARMERS OF THE GRAN CHACO

The aridity and lack of resources of interest to Europeans in the Gran Chaco delayed its exploration with the result that few early accounts of its inhabitants were written, and it has received little attention from ethnologists. Dobrizhoffer's book on the Abipón, written in 1784, is undoubtedly the best complete description of any single Indian group.[2] Forty years ago, Baron Erland Nordenskiöld, the Swedish anthropologist and authority on South American Indians, made several trips to the Chaco. But being a museum man primarily interested in technology and cultural objects, he recorded little of social culture. Métraux's account in the *Handbook* was drawn from hundreds of sources, most of which were written after horses were introduced to many of the Chaco people and European pressures and culture had affected all of them in some degree.

Today, few Chaco Indians, except in the extreme northwest, retain any appreciable amount of native culture. The Indians of the eastern and southern grasslands are now rather completely Hispanicized, while those of the scrub forests have changed greatly through acquiring livestock, working at tanneries, or living at mission stations. The small remnant of people with native culture in the northwest is being pushed into ever more restricted and less productive lands through recent expansion of the white population. According to Juan Belaieff, their Paraguayan friend and anthropologist, the number of these people is decreasing rapidly, even though epidemic diseases are not a major cause. As among many primitive peoples who suffer loss of lands and too rapid white impingement, depopulation seems to be caused by decline of the birth rate, which itself is perhaps linked psychologically to the traumatic impact of European contact.

Environment and resources. The Gran Chaco, though more varied than the pampas, is generally arid and covered with xerophytic scrub, but it is traversed by several major rivers. Wild vegetable foods were the basis of subsistence everywhere, but these were supplemented to an important degree in certain localities by seasonal runs of fish in the principal rivers, by hunting, especially in the plains of the east and south, and by small-scale farming, except in the extremely arid regions away from rivers.

The Chaco is a low-lying plain which is drained southward from Mato Grosso by the Paraguay River and to the southeast by the Pilcomayo, Bermejo, and Salado Rivers, which originate near the Andean foothills. The southern Chaco becomes grassier and merges with the pampas, while northward along the Paraguay River in the east it becomes warmer and wetter and merges into the tropical forests.

In the Chaco, most of the wild vegetable foods were supplied by the thorny bush, whose innumerable species often reach tree height. The more important edible species include pod-bearing algarroba (*Prosopis alba* and *Prosopis nigra*), tuscas (*Acacia moniliformis*), fruit of the chañar (*Gourliea decorticans*), mistol (*Zizyphus mistol*), and cactus fruits, but the pith, shoots, fruits, seeds, and fermented sap of palms were eaten, while wild rice and a few tubers provided additional food, especially in the east. Honey and larvae were also important wild foods.

The Pilcomayo, Bermejo, Salado, and Paraguay Rivers provided the best fisheries. The first three vary considerably in volume between seasonal flood and ebb, and they follow capricious routes through part of their courses, meandering and even seeping underground in places. In the rainy season, they overflow to form swamps and lagoons where fish are stranded in the subsequent dry season. Fish were taken, according to circumstances, by means of dams, weirs, nets, baskets, wooden and bone hooks, harpoons, spears, and bows and arrows, but fish drugs, so common elsewhere in South America, were not employed. Some of these methods were cooperative, some were used by individuals.

Until recently, the Chaco, especially the eastern and southern grasslands, had considerable amounts of game such as guanaco, rhea, and many smaller animals. This accounts for the Andean-given name Gran Chaco, or "great hunting" area. While game was undoubtedly far more abundant than in the cold, high Andes, it was secondary in the Chaco to vegetables and fish. Moreover, game seems to have been reduced in numbers after the Spanish Conquest.

The reduction of game was partly compensated by sheep, cattle, and horses, which the Spaniards introduced. Although the eastern and southern Chaco Indians adopted the horse and formed mounted bands and although many groups herded sheep, none became genuine cattle breeders like the Goajiro Indians of Venezuela. The thousands of animals which escaped Spanish ranches and became wild were hunted as game. Use of the horse, however, radically altered patterns of hunting, warfare, and socioeconomic groups, especially among some of the Guaicuruan-speaking people.

Farming seems principally to have been a supplement to other food-getting activities and did not tie people to the land in permanent settlements. The gardens, planted each year before the bands set out in search of wild foods, could rarely be tended carefully and continuously.

There were several local types or subtypes of Chaco Indians. In the higher land between the western Chaco and the Andes lived the Tupian Chiriguano and the Arawakan Guaná, recent migrants who carried a culture derived from the tropical forests. To the east of the Chaco lived the Tupian Guaraní, also tropical-forest village farmers, who comprise the basic population of modern Paraguay.

The Payaguá of the Paraguay River were essentially rivermen, and they have been described as "pirates," while the Mbayá of this region were depicted by early sources as overlords of the Guaná, from whom they exacted a portion of their farm harvest as tribute. Both cases suggest incipient aboriginal class structure that could have been maintained only by surplus production. The Chaco seems an unlikely area for such a structure, even in the more fertile eastern portion, but there is no doubt that class or status distinction existed after the Indians acquired horses, and it may have had some basis in native times.

After the horse was introduced to the Chaco, the Indians became rather clearly divisible into foot and equestrian, or horse, tribes.

The foot Indians

The foot Indians included Zamucoans (Zamuco and Chamacoco) of the northeast; Matacoans (Mataco, Chorotí, Ashluslay, Maca, Lengua-Enimago) of the central Chaco from the Paraguay River west along the Pilcomayo and Bermejo Rivers; the Lule-Vilelans of the western central Chaco; Tupians (Tapieté) of the northwestern Chaco; and Mascoians (Lengua, Kaskihá), who were settled along the Pilcomayo River in east central Chaco.

In the western Chaco, aridity, soil salinity, and exceedingly hot summers—the hottest in all South America—together with plagues of locusts and foraging animals discouraged farming. The cultivated plant species and the shovel-shaped digging stick used in this region had been adopted from the Andes. Seasonal fishing in the Bermejo, Pilcomayo, and Salado Rivers was a vital supplement to wild foods. Indians inhabiting the arid interiors traveled to these rivers during the great fish runs, which lasted two to three months. It is not clear whether fishing rights of any kind were claimed in aboriginal times. In post-Spanish times, many bush-living peoples, such as the Matacoans, either settled on the rivers in defiance of the permanent inhabitants or obtained permission to remain and fish during the season. Mounted Indians, including perhaps some who had previously fished very little, also visited these rivers.

The task of gathering wild plants, including algarroba beans, many fruits, and various roots and seeds, was women's work, while men collected honey, palm fruits and pith, nuts, and sprouts and hunted. Guanaco and rhea were most abundant in the southern Chaco, while deer and peccaries were more common in the grasslands in the east and

Taba-Pilagá camp shelter, Gran Chaco. (Photo by Alfred Métraux, courtesy of the University of California.)

north. These were taken by means of surrounds, drives toward a fence or enclosure, stalking, disguises, and animal calls. Before the adoption of horses, game was killed with bows and arrows and short spears and sometimes with bolas and several kinds of traps. Magical charms and shamanistic ritual were believed to enhance hunting success. Feral cattle, sheep, goats, horses, and other livestock introduced by the Spaniards proliferated on the pampas and increased the meat supply.

Most of the Chaco peoples had an occasional small surplus. They smoked fish or dried and left them in the sun on roof tops. They dried locusts, which they fried in their own grease before eating. They sometimes kept vegetable foods in special granaries, but more often merely set them aside in a corner of the dwelling. Food was prepared either by boiling, broiling, or baking in earth ovens.

The foot Indians carried their household goods in netted bags. While the many types of netting evidence considerable skill in elaborating a simple technique, the bags were not a highly efficient means of transportation. In Spanish times some Indians adopted burros rather than horses for transportation; for this animal can thrive in arid country. The Guachí and the Payaguá used canoes, but other Chaco Indians had no watercraft, except that beer troughs and bullboats, or coracles, were used as ferries to cross rivers.

Most groups of Chaco Indians moved seasonally to meet the demands of a gathering-and-hunting economy. Houses, therefore, were limited to such simple types as brush windbreaks and lean-tos, which can easily

European-influenced, pole-wall Mataco house, Gran Chaco. (Photo by Alfred Métraux, courtesy of the University of California.)

be constructed of local materials, or several kinds of portable pole-and-mat huts, some of which had separate compartments for individual families.

The Chaco Indians seem to have been strongly matrilineal, but it is not known whether aboriginally any groups had been divided into territorial, exogamous, and matrilocal lineages which were the counterpart of the localized patrilineal bands of the Ona of Tierra del Fuego. There was a tendency after the Spanish Conquest for local groups to amalgamate in larger bands. These bands numbered 50 to 200 persons and comprised several extended families. Our sources intimate that bands had some kind of territorial rights, and state that they were under the nominal leadership of a chief whose limited authority was based on his skill, wisdom, and courage and often on his position as the group elder or shaman. Selection of band leaders seems not to have followed any immutable pattern, and the position was not inherited.

Band members usually married inside the band but outside their own lineages. Newlyweds generally lived at least temporarily with the wife's family, when the husband was often exploited by his parents-in-law. Divorce was easy and seems commonly to have been initiated by the wife.

Among the Mataco, Toba, Chamacoco, and others, the bands or lineages were named after animals, natural objects, parts of the body, and so forth, but there is no evidence that these eponyms were considered to be ancestors as in the Amazon, that they were held sacred, or that they were objects of food taboos.

The main motives for hostilities were resistance to exploitative trespass, revenge against violence or witchcraft which had resulted in the death of a group member, the capture of women and children, and, especially after the introduction of European cattle, pillaging both traditionally hostile Indian groups and Spanish settlers. Ritual excitation was common preparatory to battle, and a victory was celebrated with feasts in which head or scalp trophies were displayed and extended drinking bouts held. Male enemies were seldom spared, but captive women and children were incorporated into the group.

At pregnancy, both expectant parents began to observe various food and work taboos which they maintained until the child was considered sufficiently developed to be safe from supernatural harm. There were, however, few rites attending childbirth. Mechanical abortion and infanticide were common, especially among unmarried and deserted women. To deliver twins was considered an evil omen.

Both boys and girls underwent initiation rites. In some cases, boys went through several stages of initiation and gained full adult and warrior status when blood was extracted from their genitals. Some of the rites resemble those of the Yahgan in that the youths were given moral instruction after which spirits were impersonated by masked men. The secret of the masks was revealed to the initiates, who were sworn under pain of death to keep it from women and children.

Treatment of adolescent girls varied considerably in detail. On the Bermejo and Pilcomayo Rivers, girls' puberty rites were attended with singing and dancing designed to protect the girls from evil spirits, which were impersonated by some of the dancers. In many groups, the ceremony lasted a month, during which the initiate remained in isolation and observed a special diet. In others, the people merely chanted over the pubescent girl for a few days and then confined her to a corner of the house. Pubescent girls were allowed sexual liberty and often took the initiative in love affairs.

All Chaco groups had a great fear of the spirits of the dead and began burial arrangements as soon as death seemed imminent. Sung laments and dances accompanied funeral activities. These were performed mostly by relatives, although other members of the group often participated. The corpse was usually given simple earth burial in a cemetery, where the grave was ritually cleaned and food offerings were made; but secondary burial was practiced by some peoples. The house of a deceased was burned, and his property was usually destroyed rather than interred with the corpse. Sometimes the entire village was burned. These ceremonies concluded with a drinking bout.

In contrast to the southern guanaco hunters, the Chaco peoples did not believe in a supreme being of any kind. While they believed that celestial bodies sometimes affected human beings, these bodies were largely characters in mythology and not objects of worship. The Indians were principally concerned with ghosts and bush spirits, which they thought brought disease and other misfortune and were dealt with by shamans. Shamans also worked in other ways for the general welfare of the local group. The Chaco Indians regarded a spirit as good only if it were under the control of a shaman or at the command of a person to whom it had appeared in a vision.

Chanting and shaking a gourd rattle were considered the two most effective means of controlling spirits so as to ward off danger and ensure good fortune. Drum beating had the same ritual effect, although it was less widely used. Deer-hoof rattles, bull roarers, whistles, and ritual dances, which were performed until the people were exhausted, were all considered efficacious in coercing supernatural beings. Individuals or small groups as well as entire communities might use these means. Charms, amulets, and scarification provided additional security to most Chaco peoples. Certain collective rites, usually led by a shaman, were designed to bring good harvests and abundant game.

The primary function of a shaman was to cure illness which was thought to be caused either by the intrusion of a malignant object into the patient's body or by the loss of his soul. The shaman cured illness of the first kind by sucking out the object and spitting it from his mouth, or by blowing on the patient. In the case of soul loss, he sent his familiar spirit to recapture and restore the soul. A shaman often inherited his calling from a male kinsman, but since it was believed that his power came from a spirit, it was necessary that his soul be abducted by the spirit in order for him to become a bona fide shaman. An apprentice shaman, moreover, had to observe other shamans at work in order to learn their tricks and procedures, and he was required to fast, go into a retreat, and chant special lore. Finally, in the presence of other shamans and members of the band, he proved his professional adeptness. Women knew much magical and medicinal lore, but they were rarely shamans.

In addition to curing, a shaman performed oracular functions for his community and for individuals by obtaining knowledge from supernatural beings about mundane affairs. His secular influence and prestige were usually great, and often he was leader of the local band. The shaman's position, however, was an uneasy one. Since illness and violent death were attributed to malevolent shamans, an unsuccessful practitioner might be killed in revenge for his supposed ill deeds.

Bands of horsemen

Most of the mounted bands of the Chaco spoke Guaicuruan: Abipón, Mocoví, Mbayá, and some of the Toba. The Guaicuruan Pilagá and others among the Toba, however, did not become horse Indians, and the Payaguá remained canoe people. Except for the Mbayá, who expanded along both sides of the northern Paraguay River, the Guaicuruan horse nomads centered between the Pilcomayo and Bermejo Rivers west of the Paraguay River. After acquiring horses they began an expansion which eventually encompassed thousands of square miles. They moved south and southwest, coming into contact with hunting-and-gathering Indians along the western border of the Chaco. They also clashed with the Spaniards, whose towns and estancias along the Paraguay River they continually raided.

Before obtaining horses, these peoples were culturally similar to neighboring groups such as the Lengua and other Mascoians and Matacoans, who lived along the western side of the Paraguay River and along the Pilcomayo and Bermejo Rivers. They practiced some horticulture, but depended heavily on collecting wild plant foods and hunting. In the eastern Chaco, torrential seasonal rains make the rivers rise and inundate the land, causing swamps, but fishing was always important in season. The limited cultivation was devoted to maize, beans, squash, gourds, sweet potatoes, and sweet manioc, all tropical-forest plants. Tobacco was also grown, and sugar cane, introduced by the Spaniards, became important.

The prehorse Mbayá had conquered the sedentary horticultural Guaná, an Arawakan group who lived east of the Paraguay River, and made them vassals. The Guaná provided them agricultural produce, manufactured goods, and menial labor, while the Mbayá in turn protected the Guaná against incursions from other warlike groups.

After horses provided greater mobility, eastern Chaco Indians ranged much more widely to find fresh pasturage for their large herds and new gathering and hunting grounds. They also engaged in incessant predatory raids to take loot from Spanish settlements and to steal crops from other Indians. These new nomadic habits caused the near abandonment of horticulture, while gathering techniques were modified since women could ride out to more distant grounds. Hunting techniques were also altered significantly, and raiding for food became of vital importance in the economy. Rheas, guanaco, deer, and peccaries were no longer stealthily approached on foot but deftly surrounded on horseback, killed in larger numbers, and driven more efficiently. Other methods appropriate to hunting on foot, such as fire surrounds, fence drives, and disguises, were not abandoned, but the horse greatly increased the effectiveness of large-scale surrounds.

The hundreds of thousands of semiwild cattle which had spread throughout the southern Chaco plains and the country east of the Paraguay and Paraná Rivers around the Spanish settlements were freely killed. Since the Indians bred no kind of livestock, they met their need for horses through theft. It is said that in a single raid a man might return with four hundred horses, easily escaping the armor-encumbered Spanish cavalry, which bogged down in crossing the Paraguay River and the marshes of the eastern Chaco.

Horses were of paramount importance in transporting household equipment and portable rush-mat huts from one camp to another. Mounted women led horses piled high with family belongings which were held in netted bags or rolled up in rush mats.

The Mbayá, owing to the tribute in farm produce and services supplied them by the Guaná and to improvement in their own farming which followed the example of the Guaná, were able to occupy comparatively permanent settlements. Horses enabled them to raid at great distances, but they returned to their headquarters. Their villages, like the tropical-forest settlements of their vassals, consisted of sturdy pole-and-thatch houses carefully arranged in a semicircle around a central plaza.

Other horse Indians, in contrast to the Mbayá, tended to roam as much as, if not more than, formerly, for they sought new hunting grounds and pasturage for their ever-increasing herds. Their settlements and shelters, therefore, continued to be temporary in nature and easily moved, although horse transportation permitted them to be larger, as among the Abipón.

Although incipient class stratification among the Mbayá was undoubtedly pre-Spanish, the acquisition of horses and the intensification of warfare and raiding solidified class distinctions. There was, however, a major difference between the Mbayá and other mounted Indians. The former had incorporated an entire population of conquered people into their sociopolitical structure, whereas the Abipón and Mocoví merely absorbed prisoners taken in skirmishes and had no mechanism for subjugating whole tribes. The division of Mbayá society into nobles, warriors, serfs, and slaves, however, probably reflects the influence of equestrian warfare. The nobles were divided into the blood nobility who inherited titles and those upon whom titles were bestowed for their lifetime only. Among the former, there was a further distinction between the members of an aristocratic lineage and those of less exalted ancestry. Distinctions were manifest in various ways; for example, the main stages in the life of a chief's son were celebrated with public ritual, games, and drinking bouts. The authority of even the most powerful leaders, however, was moderated by a council consisting of lesser chiefs, distinguished warriors, and old men.

The warrior class was second in importance to that of the chiefs and nobles, and it enjoyed special privileges. Although membership originally was no doubt achieved through personal exploits, it had become hereditary.

The third class was comprised of the Arawakan Guaná serfs, over whom the Mbayá chiefs extended their control through marriage and conquest. The Guaná produced for their Mbayá masters, the nobles, whom they addressed as their "lords," but they called Mbayá commoners simply "brother." They looked to the Mbayá for protection against warlike Chaco peoples such as the Zamucoans and the Lengua.

Captured and purchased slaves made up the fourth Mbayá class. These slaves were kept in perpetual and hereditary servitude, although their offspring could achieve free status through marriage with Mbayá, probably of the warrior class. This class included captive Indians from throughout the eastern Chaco and the forests of Paraguay and also some Paraguayan mestizos. The main source of slaves seems to have been the Chamacoco. Possession of a large retinue of slaves greatly augmented the prestige of the noble class, and servants were conspicuously displayed to demonstrate their owner's grandeur.

Among the Abipón and Mocoví, warriors belonged to military societies. Although all outstanding fighting men were eligible, they were admitted to the society only after undergoing a ritual ordeal. Among the Abipón, since warriors' wives shared their status, it would be more appropriate to call this a warrior class than a society. The members spoke a special dialect which symbolized their superiority to the common people, and they wore distinctive clothing and ornaments.

While the Guaicuruan tradition of warfare probably existed in precontact days, it became intensified owing to such new objectives as the capture of horses and cattle, the plundering of Spanish settlements, the capture of slaves, and the increased prestige of warriors. It also became more highly organized, was conducted over larger territory, and involved elaborate tactical maneuvers, huge victory celebrations, a change in weapons from bows and arrows to long Spanish-type lances, the employment of cavalry, and the formation of military alliances (Abipón, Mocoví, Toba) against the Spaniards. The horse Indians became magnificent cavalrymen. They attacked on horseback, deployed into several striking forces, hung from their horses in such a way as to avoid missiles, and sometimes concealed themselves entirely by hanging under their horses bellies.

While these class-structured societies strongly resembled the chiefdoms described in Chapters Six to Nine, there was a fundamental difference in their development. In the northern Andes, Central America, Venezuela, and the Antilles, the chiefdoms developed in aboriginal times on the basis of surplus farm production and dissolved soon after the Spanish Conquest. In the Gran Chaco, native subsistence supported only small nomadic bands and a few settled village people. The basis of what might be called post-Spanish chiefdoms was less the wealth produced by the Indians, except in the case of the Mbayá and Guaná, than that introduced by the Spaniards, especially livestock, while the means of acquiring it, horse nomadism, was also of Spanish origin.

The Chaco also exhibits a range of variation that suggests developmental stages. Among some groups an individual gained transient prestige for war exploits. The Mocoví had a society of warriors whose members were inducted with much ritual. One suspects that this society may have grown partly from a men's tribal society, which was originally like that found elsewhere in South America but which had acquired important military functions. The Abipón warrior group had characteristics of a social class rather than a society. The Mbayá classes seem to have become so fixed by heredity as to resemble castes; for neither sex nor outstanding exploits were prerequisites for admission.

We do not mean to imply any sweeping generalizations about class development except that hereditary class or caste status must rest on a productive surplus. Otherwise, status groups may originate in diverse ways. A servile class may arise from individual captives, from conquered populations, or from persons who failed to gain prestige. A warrior class may develop from a men's society, or it may crystallize around successful individuals. At the same time, a men's society, as among the chiefdoms of eastern Bolivia, may be transformed into a local religious cult rather than a warrior class or society. In short, certain formal structures may acquire new functions while particular functions may be served by different forms.

The several life crises observed by the horse Indians differ from those celebrated by most of the other Chaco Indians in the elaboration and intensification of certain aspects of the ceremonies. The significance of these is their tendency to bolster the developing class structure among the Abipón and Mbayá. Thus ritual at the birth and childhood of nobles was designed to distinguish them from commoners or nonwarriors. Puberty initiation underscored the importance of the warrior element and its connection with nobility. The rites for a chief's daughter were elaborate public affairs and required much preparation. Marriage was ceremonially arranged between families with a view to affirming social prestige in the class hierarchy.

Rivermen: the Payaguá

The Payaguá, a Guaicuruan people, were expert canoemen. Known to the Spaniards as river "pirates," they inhabited the marshes and streams along the upper Paraguay River from which they made forays. They were principally seed gatherers, especially of wild rice, which they harvested from their canoes. In post-Conquest times, they practiced horticulture and lived in rather substantial settlements along the rivers. Their large dugout canoes were capable of carrying forty men, and their boating skill was acknowledged by the Indians and Spaniards alike.

A strong class tendency like that noted elsewhere in the eastern Chaco is evidenced by their treatment of chiefs, who were carried in litters (an Andean trait), had their lips pierced, and were accorded other evidence of their status and the purity of their blood lines.

4. FOOT NOMADS OF THE FORESTS

Small groups of hunters and gatherers were scattered in remote places among the more developed riverine horticultural villagers. Since these groups exist today comparatively unchanged, it is best to describe them in the present tense. Living in inaccessible places, such as the headwaters of the tributaries of the Amazon or in the deep forests between the main rivers, they have had few white visitors and are comparatively little known.

The culture of these people probably varied somewhat in food getting, especially in the use of canoes by some and its absence among others. The foot nomads are described in the present section and the "aquatic nomads" in section 5. The former include the Sirionó of Bolivia, the Guayakí of Paraguay, the Nambicuara of Mato Grosso, the Purí-Coroado and Guaitacá of the Brazilian coast, the Macú of the deep jungles between the main rivers north of the Amazon, the Guaharibo, Shirianá, and their neighbors on the Amazon-Orinoco watershed, the Guahibo and Chiricoa of eastern Colombia, and the Guana-

hatabey, or Ciboney, of the western Antilles. Of these, only the Sirionó
are really known, thanks to Allan Holmberg, who spent a year traveling
the deep forests with them and fully depicted them in a monograph.[3]

Nearly all the forest hunters and gatherers, both foot and aquatic,
cultivated a few domesticated crops in historic times; but since farming

"Tapuya" or forest nomad of eastern Brazil. To left is spear thrower.
(From Handbook.)

is comparatively recent among them, usually postwhite, and since it is
a supplement to hunting and gathering wild foods, it has not required
permanent settlements. Some nomads, like the Sirionó, do not even
remain with their farm plots during the growing season.

Nomadism entails many similar practices. When traveling overland,
women carry the baggage in baskets suspended from tumplines and
care for the children while men hunt. Hunting and fishing are the men's

principal tasks, while collecting vegetable foods, cooking, and camp tending fall to women. Bows and arrows are everywhere the principal hunting and fishing weapons. Owing to constant travel and the limitation on what women can transport overland, shelters are crudely improvised of locally available materials at each camp, while paraphernalia for cooking, eating, sleeping, and meeting other biological essentials as well as for religious and recreational activities are necessarily very limited.

Owing to the sparse and dispersed food resources, the human population density is low, and social aggregates are small. The basic social

Camacan dance, eastern Brazil forest nomads. (After Prince Maximilian Wied-Neuwied, "Voyage au Brésil," Paris, 1822.)

units are either nuclear families or extended families or lineages, and such interpersonal relationships as marriage, leadership, and ceremonial groupings are primarily controlled by kinship. Since, however, these nomads are enclaves within large areas of fairly sedentary and often warring riverine villages of fishermen and horticulturalists, many of them have become somewhat militaristic in self-defense. Some, such as the Mura, have even gained a reputation as fighters. Food getting rarely requires cooperation between localized lineages and usually is best carried on by the nuclear family, but warfare has often brought otherwise independent families, lineages, and bands into cooperation.

There seem to be several social types which were brought about by cultural-ecological adaptations. Although all these people are migratory hunters, fishers, and gatherers, some are predominantly overland travelers, whose bands live by hunting and collecting, while others are aquatic nomads, whose society is usually split into family units, each traveling in its own canoe. The aquatic Guató and Mura spend much of the year dispersed in family canoes. When Mura families assemble, the local "band" is apparently an extended family. The aquatic Yaruro and Warrau are also divided into lineages or bands which seemingly are matrilocal.

The foot people who lack canoes split into nuclear families less readily than the canoe Indians. Their social units consist of extended families, which in the case of the Sirionó and Guayakí are known to be matrilineal.

The frequency of matrilineality among these forest nomads probably reflects the economic importance of women in gathering wild foods, and it contrasts with the prevalent patrilineality of the riverine horti-cultural villages. Whether territorial and property rights are involved in this matrilineality is not known.

While marriage is ordinarily monogamous, polygyny is practiced by leading men. Polygyny is usually sororal; that is, plural wives are sisters. This is related to the sororate, wherein marriage after the wife's death is with her sister. The levirate, wherein marriage after the husband's death is with his brother, also occurs. These practices strengthen the bonds between families and bands. Cross-cousin marriage, which most groups practice, has the same effect.

The Sirionó of Bolivia

The Sirionó occupy the dense tropical forests of eastern Bolivia. They speak Tupian, and form a linguistic and cultural enclave in a region of more advanced Mojos-Chiquito groups, having separated from their Tupian kin long ago. In recent years, a number of attempts have been made to induce the Sirionó to become settled farmers near missions and government stations, but these efforts misfired, and disease has decimated their population. Today, there are probably less than 3,000 Sirionó, widely scattered in small bands in the deep jungles.

The Sirionó are essentially hunters and gatherers, although some now practice desultory small-scale slash-and-burn horticulture. According to Holmberg, they take more than forty species of game and eat many varieties of wild plants, especially palm cabbage, which is available the year around. Hunting, however, is rarely cooperative. Individuals stalk and shoot game with bows 7 to 8 feet in length and unpoisoned arrows 8 to 10 feet long. They say that the long arrow embedded in an animal makes escape more difficult and retrieving easier.

The annual food quest follows a rather regular pattern. In the dry season, the Sirionó may clear a patch of forest to plant maize, sweet manioc, and sweet potatoes. Lacking canoes, the group then moves on foot in search of game and wild plant food and visits the clearing from time to time only long enough to care for the field. It returns to harvest and store the crops in large palm baskets, and then resumes its travels through the forest. It crosses rivers either on rude bridges of felled trees or by swimming. The people carry a firebrand from one camp to the next, for the Sirionó say they have forgotten how to make fire.

The Sirionó build flimsy, temporary shelters of poles lashed to tree trunks and covered with palm leaves. The huts are generally quite large, however, and shelter 30 to 120 people. One such shelter constitutes the temporary settlement of the band.

Each band is matrilocal and matrilineal, and it consists of a number of nuclear families related through the female line. The different bands, however, seldom come into contact with one another during the year. The band tends to be exogamous, although there is no fixed rule. A man, however, preferably marries his mother's brother's daughter.

A band leader has little authority. He is respected for his wisdom and may make suggestions about hunting trips and band movements, but his advice is not always followed. His major prerogative is that of occupying a central position in the large house, and he always heads a polygynous family. He must, however, perform the round of daily tasks that fall to all adult males.

The precarious existence of the Sirionó allows for little elaboration of ceremonialism or recreational activities. From time to time, the Sirionó let their blood in a sort of rejuvenation ceremony. More frequently, they dance for relaxation during the long tropical nights. When maize and wild honey are abundant, they make chicha, the native beer, and men hold a drinking bout during which they smoke pipes and sing. Such revelry often culminates in fighting, which may continue until the chicha is consumed.

A child is born openly in the communal house. At birth, the couvade is observed, and there is ritual purification in which the new parents walk into the forest scattering ashes, then return to their compartment in the large house bringing kindling for a new fire, which signifies new life. The practice of teknonymy, that is, addressing the mother and father as the "parent of so-and-so," reenforces this notion of a new life.

At about the age of puberty, but not necessarily at the first menses, a girl goes into the forest for six weeks in the company of several old women and a hunter, who require that she observe food taboos, ceremonially bathe, sing, and have her hair cut. The puberty ceremony is prerequisite to approved sexual activity.

The Sirionó are very unusual in their lack of true shamans, who cure or perform sorcery. They considered the moon to be a culture hero, who gave them maize, manioc, and other features of their culture. They fear spirits of the dead as evil, and in order to ward off the spirits' malevolence while curing illness, they rub and chant over the skull of a dead person. To ensure an abundant supply of game, they observe a number of taboos; for example, a hunter abstains from eating the meat of an animal he has killed.

Sirionó bands do not war against each other, and they shun hostile contacts with other groups. Since much of the territory they formerly inhabited has been preempted by their more powerful neighbors and by whites, the Sirionó bands survive today only in the deep forests to which they have withdrawn. Their history is one of defensive retreat, and they have no military activities on which to base status.

The Guayakí of Paraguay

The Guayakí live a nomadic life in the forests of eastern Paraguay, where they have eluded white contact to the extent that few persons have observed them in their native surroundings. Under pressure of white colonization, they have retreated into the barely accessible Caaguazú Hills, where an estimated maximum of 500 persons have managed to survive punitive expeditions and epidemic disease. The Guayakí are one of the least known and least acculturated groups in this part of South America. They speak a Tupian dialect closely related to Guaraní.

In a never-ending search for game, wild food plants, and suitable fishing places, the Guayakí keep continually on the move, seldom remaining in a camp for more than one night. They travel entirely on foot and hunt principally with bows and arrows but also use traps and pitfalls to catch large animals, such as tapir and jaguar, while they club small animals to death. Both men and women participate in coati hunts, which are sporting events. They take fish with bows and arrows, dams, and poisons.

Upon finding a grove of pindo palms or wild orange trees, the Guayakí camp nearby until they exhaust the supply of fruits. At large groves, several bands may remain together for a few days.

The Guayakí now practice no horticulture. It is possible that they formerly cultivated maize, only to give it up when the semisedentary life it entailed became too hazardous in the face of constant threat from whites and Guaraní Indians. The Guayakí make pets of many wild species including coati, but these animals also provide a reserve food supply and are eaten in time of want. The Guayakí are reported to have domesticated "wild pigs," which probably means that they also kept tame peccaries. Like many primitive people they eat certain larvae, but they are very unusual in that they conserve the larvae in decaying tree trunks, a practice suggesting native American beekeeping.

Although the Guayakí seldom remain in any camp more than a day or so, unless deterred from moving by heavy rains, their fear of hostile Indians and whites causes them to take much precaution in selecting their camp sites. They avoid camping on river shores, because the running water might prevent them from hearing an approaching enemy, and prefer to camp in the deep forest where they erect a fence of branches as a defense against jaguars and make a clearing which minimizes the chance of surprise attacks by enemies. In these camps, they construct temporary huts of bent branches covered with mats or palm leaves.

The Guayakí are said to be organized into autonomous matrilineal bands of about twenty individuals each. These bands rarely come together. Band leaders have only advisory powers, resting on prestige acquired by hunting and fishing ability. The bands range in overlapping hunting grounds, and the notion of trespass seems to be unimportant. A trapped animal or a cache of larvae in a palm tree, however, becomes band property and is respected by other bands. Hostilities are held at a minimum.

Residence is said to be strictly matrilocal, but it may be that only the son-in-law of a band leader lives with the latter's band.

As for Guayakí religion, it is said that the Indians fear malevolent nature spirits, but we do not even know whether they have shamans.

The Nambicuara of Mato Grosso

The Nambicuara were once estimated at 20,000 persons, and they inhabited a large area in the southern Mato Grosso. Epidemics have reduced the present population to about 2,000. The Nambicuara habitat is an infertile plateau of sandy soil covered by scrubby xerophytic growth. Agriculture is possible only in the gallery forests along the rivers and streams. Much like the Sirionó, who live to their southwest, the Nambicuara form a relatively simple cultural enclave of nomadic hunters and gatherers in a region of more complex cultural development.

Subsistence activities differ sharply during the rainy and the dry seasons. During the latter, the Nambicuara move about in the bush, where men hunt large game while women and children gather wild plants and catch small animals and insects. In the rainy season, they move to the gallery forests to settle in temporary camps, where the men clear small garden plots by a simple slash-and-burn method and plant maize, manioc, beans, gourds, cotton, and tobacco, the last being smoked avidly by both sexes. They also fish with traps, drugs, and arrows.

The Nambicuara had no domesticated animals until they came into contact with whites in the twentieth century, although they seem always to have had a great number of pets, such as monkeys and parrots. Today, they have dogs and chickens; and, while there are horses and cattle in their country, the Indians hunt only the strays with bows and arrows as if they were wild game. They have not become horse nomads.

While traveling during the dry season, each nuclear family builds a rude shelter. The encampment consists of several huts erected without settlement plan. These dry-season bands are probably kin groups led by an elder.

During the rainy months, Nambicuara settlements are more stationary. Each recognizes a headman, often a shaman, whose authority, however, is limited and depends on the good will of or his kinship ties with the individual family heads.

The Nambicuara bands share a common language, despite dialectic differences, and a generally similar culture, but these have not brought about any sense of solidarity or "nationalism." Bands from different regions sometimes skirmish with one another, and sometimes they trade. But they have not consolidated as a sociocultural unit.

A man often marries a widow and her daughter. Cross-cousin marriage is preferred, and sometimes the arrangements for betrothal are made between the boy's father and maternal uncle while the potential spouses are still infants. The girl's puberty rite is a precondition to marriage and is considered the first step in the marriage ceremony.

The Nambicuara believe that there are a number of bush spirits which take animal form, especially that of the jaguar. Death is attributed to these spirits. Thunder is the most powerful spirit and provides men, especially shamans, with revelations and visions. Shamans possess great supernatural power, which they use in curing, when they employ "thunder arrows," and in leading group ceremonials. In the ceremonies, which are held at the beginning and the end of the dry season, men play sacred flageolets. Women are not allowed to observe the performances.

The Purí-Coroado

The Purí and the Coroado once formed an ethnic unit, but they separated several centuries ago, allegedly because of a blood feud between two families. Linguistically and culturally these offshoots were very closely related and are treated together here. The Purí-Coroado ranged the forests and mountains of eastern Brazil, near the coast, where they lived in scattered family groups which subsisted by hunting and gathering. Numbering perhaps 6,000 at the beginning of the nineteenth century, they quickly declined after contact with whites, and today only a few families survive.

Traditionally hunters and gatherers, the Purí-Coroado practiced no agriculture and had no domesticated animals until the beginning of the nineteenth century, when they came under strong white influence. Even then, the Coroado, who took up cultivation of maize, bananas, and beans, are said to have been only indifferent farmers and continued to depend heavily upon wild foods. The Purí raided the fields of the Coroado and other Indians as well as those of white colonists, a tactic which engendered continuous skirmishing between the nomadic Indians and the colonists. Fishing is seldom mentioned in the sources describing early

Coroado and Purí shelters, eastern Brazil. (From Handbook.)

colonial or native culture, and it was probably of secondary importance, for these people lacked any kind of watercraft.

The Purí built rude lean-tos of palm fronds, and the Coroado made a slightly more substantial modified lean-to. These flimsy structures were occupied by extended families, one or two of which comprised a band of about forty people. Band members cooperated in hunting, and several bands united to carry out war against a common enemy or to defend themselves. They celebrated victory with feasts and displayed human trophies taken in battle.

The kinship groups were led by an elder whose authority was symbolized by elaborate dress, but whose actual powers were quite limited. The elder and successful hunters apparently were the only men who took extra wives.

The Purí-Coroado conceived the world to be filled with spirits, some of which were intractable and malevolent and some of which could be summoned by shamans to divulge information about future events. The shamans worked themselves into a state of mind to conjure their spirit-helpers by copious tobacco smoking. The shaman's principal role was to cure illness.

The Guaitacá

These Indians occupied the coastal region north of Rio de Janeiro, and although their aboriginal number is not known, they are said to have been in control of the fertile grasslands north of Lagoa Santa. They held off the Tupinambá and the Portuguese until 1630, when they were defeated and brought under Portuguese rule. Today, the descendants of the Guaitacá are fully acculturated Neo-Brazilians.

Aboriginally, the Guaitacá depended on hunting, gathering, and limited cultivation. Those living along the Atlantic shore attacked sharks with short spears, and they used sharks' teeth as tips for their arrows, but it is doubtful that they obtained much food from the sea.

Although the Guaitacá and Tupinambá were continually at war with each other, they periodically arranged a brief truce to trade. After silent barter, both groups dispersed and resumed hostilities.

The Macú of northern Amazonia

Several groups which roam the territory of the Río Negro and the Caiarí-Uaupés river basin have been subsumed under the generic name Macú. Macú, however, is merely a derogatory term used by the riverine Indians to designate the forest nomads whom they consider inferior and hold in a subservient relationship. It is not at all certain whether all the Indians designated by this name speak the same language, and comparatively little is known of their culture. The Macú of the Río Negro, a northern tributary of the Amazon, were perhaps more widely dispersed in the northern Amazon before the Arawakan, Cariban, and Tucanoan peoples expanded in the area. These riverine village horticulturalists brought war, slavery, serfdom, and cultural assimilation or physical extinction to many Macú. Other Macú who occupy a large area between the principal rivers seem to be populous, although their numbers are not known.

Most of the Macú are nomadic hunters, gatherers, and fishermen, who have no canoes. They use bows and arrows, blowguns (perhaps acquired in trade), stone axes, and clubs. They live in flimsy, temporary shelters and, lacking hammocks, sleep on the ground. Those of the Caiarí-Uaupés River, however, now live in rather large horticultural settlements of great communal houses.

The Guiana Macú engage in considerable trade with the sedentary Taulipang and Macushí, through whom they obtain European wares.

The Shirianá, Waica, and Guaharibo of the Amazon-Orinoco watershed

These peoples are even less known than their southern neighbors, the Macú. The Shirianá, who belong to the Macro-Chibchan linguistic family, are essentially hunting, fishing, and gathering nomads, who inhabit the forested regions of the upper Orinoco. Some of them have adopted limited horticulture since their contact with more advanced Macú groups.

All of these peoples have the blowgun, but most of them hunt and fish with the bow and arrow. Habitations are reported to be quite flimsy, temporary, and small and to be round, rectangular, or lean-to in type. These peoples learned to make canoes in relatively recent times from surrounding riverine village horticulturalists. The Shirianá dugouts are fairly long and commodious. Most transportation, however, is by human carriers who use large twined baskets.

These groups characteristically cremate their dead, and the relatives carry the ashes in their travels.

The Guahibo and Chiricoa of western Venezuela

The Guahibo and Chiricoa are two of a number of hunting-and-gathering nomads who occupy a large and unproductive area in the llanos and parts of the forests of eastern Colombia. They are strikingly different from the surrounding sedentary horticulturalists, the Arawakan Achagua. They speak closely related dialects and are practically identical in culture. The Guahibo have been recently estimated at about 20,000.

The Guahibo and Chiricoa depend primarily upon peccaries, deer, and other land animals, but they also gather wild plants, fish, and hunt river mammals. The most common hunting technique is the surround, but deer are stalked from behind brush screens by hunters who smear their arms with a rosin which attracts the animals. The most important single food animal is the armadillo, which is very numerous and is taken from its hole by means of a pointed stick after the savanna grass has been fired. These Indians drug fish or kill them with the bow and arrow and harpoon, practices probably borrowed from the surrounding sedentary peoples.

They travel overland on foot, but use rafts in moving down the rivers. Between April and June, they seek groves of wild plums and travel from one to another as the fruit in each becomes exhausted. The season of palm fruit is the happiest, for people can gorge themselves. During the remainder of the year, armadillos supplemented by wild roots provide the principal foods.

The Guahibo and the Chiricoa use every part of an animal, which they roast directly over the fire. They eat not only the uncleaned intestines of game they kill but intestines which have been discarded by sedentary groups they encounter. They preserve a small amount of meat and fish by smoking it. Like their neighbors, they make a mildly alcoholic drink, or chicha, of fermented palm sap.

These nomads constantly travel, rarely passing more than two or three days in one camp. Unless they carry portable palm-straw mats as house covers, they simply sling hammocks out in the open or sleep directly on the ground. Neither childbirth nor death are reasons to stop a band on the march. The dead are either quickly buried or left exposed to animals. The aged, ill, or wounded, however, are well cared for and are carried by the stronger members of the group when camp sites are changed.

The more acculturated Guahibo now build permanent pole-and-thatch houses and, like the Achagua, practice horticulture.

The largest functioning unit is the band, which is headed by a chief whose authority is inherited patrilineally. The band is divided into sub-units of six to eight families which hunt and gather separately.

Trade with the sedentary agricultural peoples in the region is important to the Guahibo and the Chiricoa. The item of greatest value formerly traded by the nomads to sedentary peoples was captive slaves taken from other tribes. The nomads are welcomed by the sedentary peoples as carriers of news picked up in their wanderings, and they in turn quiz the horticultural groups about events which have taken place since their last visit. They usually travel in large numbers to the settlements, where their strength gives them an advantage in trading.

We do not know whether taking captives for trade was a precontact custom, but slaving for the whites became extremely widespread after the Spanish Conquest. The Guahibo and Chiricoa even attacked mission stations and sedentary Indian groups, and their excellent military tactics brought them considerable success. To guard against retaliation at night, they left their fires burning while they stole off into the darkness to sleep at another site.

The Ciboney of the western Antilles

The Ciboney, or Guanahatabey, have special interest not only because they seem to have been the first inhabitants of much or most of the Greater Antilles but because they occupied the area near Florida on the route of possible diffusion between North and South America. On the whole, however, it is clear that the Ciboney could not have been instrumental in the diffusion of the more interesting cultural links between the Circum-Caribbean area and the Southeast.

The chiefdoms of the Greater Antilles and northern South America had not only states or confederations, mounds, temples, idols, priests, and social classes much like those found in the Mississippi Valley and parts of the Southeast, but both areas shared blowguns, certain domesticated plants, and other traits. The Ciboney lacked all of these features and possessed only a simple hunting-and-gathering culture. Even the Arawak, who had a general, if somewhat attenuated, Circum-Caribbean type of culture, probably entered the Antilles too late to have constituted a link between North and South America.

If the Ciboney played any part in diffusion between North and South America, the culture concerned was much simpler and territorially more restricted than that represented by the chiefdoms. Like their nearest neighbors in Florida, the Ciboney were very primitive collectors of wild foods. More specifically, Ciboney archaeological materials resemble certain Florida remains, especially in shell artifacts. This may indicate that the Ciboney originated in Florida or that the Florida materials were left by a people of Antillean origin. While it is not certain that the contact-period Ciboney used canoes, since no traces of them have been found in archaeological sites and canoes are not mentioned in the Spanish chronicles, they must obviously have had fairly seaworthy vessels at one time in order to reach the Greater Antilles, whatever their place of origin. But sea navigation does not necessarily mean that there was a cultural connection between the Antilles and Florida, for it could be argued that the similarity of Ciboney and Florida artifacts is only superficial. The language affiliation of the Ciboney might clinch one of the alternative explanations of their origin, but their language, unfortunately, is unknown.

At the time of the Spanish Conquest, the Ciboney survived in small enclaves, principally in western Haiti and Cuba, but their archaeology shows that they were once more widely spread throughout the Greater Antilles, where they seem to have been the earliest human occupants. The more powerful horticultural Arawak had evidently replaced or absorbed the Ciboney in most of the Greater Antilles, and they were still expanding at the expense of the Ciboney when the Spaniards arrived.

Achaeology provides most of our knowledge of Ciboney culture. Sites yield shells, fishbones, and remains of marine and land reptiles and mammals. Since Cuba and Hispaniola have few mammals and their waters are not rich in fish, wild resources did not afford abundant foods. The sites contain no cultivated plants or pottery. The principal artifacts are chipped stone tools and projectile points, ground stone implements such as axes and stone balls, and shell objects.

The archaeological inventory, as well as the location of habitation sites, shows that the Ciboney were mostly a shore-dwelling people, who inhabited rock shelters and caves, if such living quarters were convenient, or erected temporary shelters in the open in order to live near their food supply. These archaeological sites are small and suggest transient occupation. While the composition and permanence of any local group is not known, early sources report that one encampment at Cayo Redondo had about 100 inhabitants. Such size is probably exceptional, and most encampments must have consisted of one or a few families.

It is impossible to present a general view of Ciboney culture. The Spaniards remarked that they wore nothing but breechclouts and girdles, but they used body paint and crudely fashioned ornaments. Some of the inexplicable and strangely shaped archaeological objects may well have had religious significance, but we do not know what.

5. AQUATIC NOMADS

The Guató of the upper Paraguay River

To judge by archaeological evidence, the Guató have long inhabited the lowlands and marshes of the upper Paraguay River, where, in recent times, they live for most of the year in their dugout canoes. The Guató have been in intimate contact with Neo-Brazilians and appear to be on the verge of cultural extinction. Their culture, therefore, must be described in the past tense.

The most striking feature of the Guató way of life was the amount of time the people spent in canoes in quest of fish and amphibious mammals. They took these with bows and arrows, spears, and hooks. They also hunted land game with the aid of dogs, while women gathered numerous tropical-forest plants, such as acuri, yataba, and an aquatic plant called forno d'agua. In flood season the Guató harvested large quantities of wild rice from canoes. In addition to wild plants, they cultivated a few bananas of European origin and native acuri palms on artificially elevated sites, where the trees could not be damaged by the seasonal floods. Each family owned a stand of acuri palms from which it made a kind of wine. Occasionally, the Guató grew maize and manioc along the riverbanks, but these plants were delicacies rather than staple crops. They also raised a few chickens, which they acquired from the whites.

Meat was generally boiled in crudely finished pots. Cayman tails, fresh maize, and bananas roasted on hot ashes were considered delicacies. The Guató were very exceptional in that men did most of the cooking.

The elementary or nuclear family traveled in its canoe apart from other families most of the year. It lived and slept in the canoe, where a fire was kept on a clay hearth. Since interfamilial activities were rare, the family was the basic social and economic unit most of the time. During a few months each year, however, several families built temporary thatched shelters on the riverbank near one another. They stored their possessions out of reach of sudden floods, which were an ever-present threat.

There were three local geographical divisions among the Guató which occasionally came together in council under the leadership of a chief to organize skirmishes against the Caingang Indians or the whites. Otherwise, the Guató were peaceful, and the elementary families were autonomous in their day-to-day activities.

The Mura of the lower Madeira River

When first contacted by whites, the Mura occupied the right bank of the lower Madeira River, from whence they spread out to the Purús River and the region just north of the Solimões. Chroniclers report that they expanded by raiding and overrunning sedentary horticulturalists who inhabited the lower Madeira River and adjacent areas, killing and multilating their foe but taking no captives. Their maximum extension was reached around 1774, when local Brazilians began punitive raids in an attempt to exterminate them. While the Mura obviously were predatory nomads somewhat more than sedentary farmers, their very small and uncoordinated settlements could not have been a very serious menace to their neighbors.

In the last decades of the eighteenth century, the Mura sought peace with the whites, probably because disease and continual warfare with the hard-pressing and far more powerful Mundurucú had weakened them considerably. In the next century, they joined a local uprising against landed whites, siding with escaped Negro slaves and mestizos, but they were defeated in the period 1834–1836 with great loss of life.

Estimates that the aboriginal Mura population numbered 30,000 at the height of their expansion seem too high. In 1864 there cannot have been more than about 3,000, and their population had dwindled to 1,600 in 1926. Like many other hunting-and-gathering groups, the Mura are verging on extinction as a cultural entity. Most of the Mura now speak Portuguese, although formerly they spoke the lingua geral of the Amazon as well as their native tongue. The latter is surprisingly classified in the Páezan subfamily of Macro-Chibchan, a language group distributed mainly in Ecuador.

The Mura are said to have cultivated maize and manioc, but production was never large in scale or economically important. They raided the sedentary horticulturalists for manioc and other crops rather than attend to cultivation themselves. Their main subsistence came from the rivers, where they caught fish, turtles, manatee, cayman, otter, and other species with a skill that gained the admiration of their neighbors. They fished with a bow and special arrows and took manatees with harpoons.

The Mura were expert rivermen who originally used bark canoes but later learned to make dugouts. In their expansion, the Mura kept to the low, flooded lands and riverbanks, settling only where their canoes would be of greatest advantage to them.

Since the Mura lived for extended periods in their canoes, where they slept on platform beds, the isolated family had unusual social importance, as among the Guató. During part of the year, however, they lived in settlements consisting of a few dome-shaped huts scattered along a lake shore or riverbank. Each hut was ordinarily occupied by an elementary family. Such villages had 45 to 150 individuals in aboriginal times. The Mura appear to have begun to use hammocks in recent times, having learned about them from their tropical-forest village neighbors.

Settlements were loosely integrated under a chief whose authority was quite limited. The reputation of the Mura for warfare suggests that war leaders must have had some importance. But Mura warfare was guerrilla-like, fought by small groups, and it did not permanently bind the people of a large area together. The economic and social life could not in fact support large military organization.

Within the settlements, there were disputes over trespass at family fishing sites, but these were settled by family heads rather than by settlement chiefs.

At puberty, girls were secluded, while boys took parica snuff. These were a precondition to marriage. As soon as a girl reached puberty, her suitors fought boxing matches to determine who would wed her. Marriage was strictly monogamous in aboriginal times, but later, perhaps owing to the capture of women in warfare, every adult man had two or three wives whom he treated as menials. Today, bride service is sometimes required of a suitor.

The Mura are now nominally Christian, and their mythology contains a number of Christian elements interwoven with what may be presumed aboriginal beliefs. Part of the ritual cycle includes the great parica feast —a narcotic-induced ecstasy, dancing flagellation, and a men's drinking bout—as well as several other flagellation ceremonies which are connected with puberty, the full moon, and the preparation of manioc gardens.

Shamanism is concerned principally with curing disease, and the practitioners are highly esteemed for their ability.

The Yaruro of the Orinoco tributaries

The Yaruro differ from their neighbors, the Guahibo and Chiricoa, mainly because they dislike hunting in the savannas and prefer to live along the rivers. They are excellent canoemen and spend much time in their 18-foot dugouts, subsisting on fish and river animals.

Two-man teams, often assisted by a boy, take fish from canoes, usually by means of bows and special arrows. They also take crocodiles, manatees, turtles, and other large animals with harpoon arrows. Turtle and crocodile eggs are important foods, and live turtles are kept in shallow pools to be eaten when needed.

While the Yaruro are reluctant to travel on land, they sometimes explore the forests for hearts and fruits of palm trees, and women gather wild seeds and dig roots. They also take occasional deer and armadillos, but unlike the Guahibo and Chiricoa, they rarely stalk the former or dig for the latter.

In recent times the Yaruro have begun to grow some maize, but like many incipient farmers, they eat it green.

Yaruro cuisine is simple, and the people eat but one meal a day. They eat eggs and roots raw, boiled in crude pots, or roasted. They place crocodiles and turtles directly on the fire until they can be cracked open, then parboil the meat. They are content to eat fish only half cooked.

Unlike their sedentary neighbors, the Yaruro lack permanent settlements. While most of their travel is in canoes, they sometimes move overland, men and women transporting heavy loads in baskets supported by tumplines. On such treks, women are responsible for all household gear and for small children.

Dry-season encampments consist of very flimsy windbreaks, which are occupied only two or three days before the people move on. Rainy-season settlements are more permanent and consist of fairly substantial dwellings.

Today, the few hundred Yaruro who live on the Capanaparo and Cinaruco Rivers are divided into socioeconomic units each of which is an extended, matrilocal family. These local units are crosscut by exogamous, matrilineal moieties, which regulate marriage and which perform complementary ceremonial functions. Headmen of the extended families inherit their authority patrilineally, but the shaman-chief who controls moiety functions succeeds to his position matrilineally.

Marriage is normally monogamous, but instances of polygyny and fraternal polyandry—marriage of a woman to several brothers—are known, and the levirate and sororate are practiced. Moiety exogamy requires marriage with a person in the opposite moiety. In addition, there is some preference for marriage between a man and his mother's brother's daughter.

A widespread form of kinship relation is seen in the restraint required between a man and his mother-in-law, even though these persons are obligated to assist each other.

The Yaruro believe that the moon goddess, wife of the sun god, is the creator of the world and that her son is the culture hero and ruler of the afterworld. Shamans, who may be men or women, derive their power from the moon goddess, whom they depict anthropomorphically on their rattles. In order to go into a trance and become possessed by spirits, they smoke as many as a hundred cigars, take narcotics, and drink quantities of chicha. The spirits of their ancestors and various deities then enter and speak through them. Although the shamans are important leaders of moiety ceremonials, their principal function is to cure illness.

The Warrau of the Orinoco Delta

In recent historic times, the Warrau have been nomadic hunters and gatherers. There is good reason to suspect, however, that they represent a rather extreme case of culture loss, or deculturation, since their generally swampy habitat in the Orinoco Delta and the country eastward to the Pomeroon River is unfavorable even to the slash-and-burn farming characteristic of the riverine horticultural villages. Settlements in the historic period had as many as 200 or 300 people only among those who recently adopted agriculture, and the Warrau today certainly do not seem like a people who ever had states, class structure, or specialization.

Many anthropologists, however, have suspected that the modern hunting, fishing, and gathering Warrau may have moved from some area to the north or west of the Orinoco Delta and that their culture was formerly like that of the riverine horticulturalists but lost certain characteristic features in their less productive modern environment. Johannes Wilbert also believes the Warrau migrated from the west, but thinks they have always been hunters and gatherers. In any event, today they have a priest-temple-idol cult and social classes that are more like those of chiefdoms than the patterns of the nomads or village farmers.[4]

Wilbert found among the Warrau that each of the larger settlements has a temple which shelters a wooden, bone, or clay idol, often with anthropomorphic features, which represents "Our Grandfather," or the supreme being, and which is guarded by jaguars and served by vultures. The supreme being is served by a special priest who differs from shamans. Each temple cult is strictly local, being found only in villages which have a priest. The priest receives special treatment from the villagers, but it is not certain that he holds a hereditary role.

The supreme god, "Grandfather," is regarded as the Creator and also as the cause of sickness, flood, or other disasters. He is placated by offerings of palm flour contributed by each village member, but the priest sanctifies and returns this flour to the donors. The priest lives in a special house and may not engage in arduous labor. Moreover, he is distinguished from the chief. The priest may cure disease by expelling the spirits of a deceased person which the god sends into the patient's body. He uses a rattle, the stones of which represent his spirit-helpers, and he sings. But there is also a realm of pure shamanism in which the priest cannot operate, just as the shamans cannot function as priests. One kind of shaman sings, smokes, and massages the patient to remove special kinds of evil spirits. Still another class of shaman removes disease-causing objects from the body.

This religious pattern of the Warrau, which is so unlike anything known among the nomadic hunters and gatherers, shares some features with the Circum-Caribbean chiefdoms and shows some differences. While it is possible that the Warrau have recently borrowed certain features from Circum-Caribbean neighbors, whom they may have resembled at an earlier time, it is also very possible that, having shifted habitat in pre-historic times, they brought into their present area a general pattern that can no longer be supported. The prehistoric inhabitants of the island of Marajó at the mouth of the Amazon, the Marajoara, also brought a culture that was unlike that of their riverine horticultural neighbors and that could not be supported by the tropical-forest economy. The Warrau may well represent a similar displacement into an area where only deculturation could occur, an area wherein they lost most of their previous Circum-Caribbean features, except the priest-temple-idol cult.

Except for Wilbert's disclosures regarding their religious pattern, the present-day Warrau appear to be an exceedingly primitive people. The Warrau cultivate plantains, sugar cane, watermelons, chili peppers, and bitter manioc, of which only the last two are indigenous American Indian plants. Bitter manioc reached them in post-Columbian times. They still rely largely upon fishing with traps, hooks, drugs, nets, fish arrows, spears, and harpoon arrows and are efficient rivermen in their use of sturdy canoes that hold as many as fifty persons. They hunt with bows, fire drives, bird decoys, blinds, traps, and dogs. A rather fixed hunting pat-tern is suggested in the custom that the hunter leave his game some distance from the village for the women to bring in. The Warrau also depend to a great extent upon the native, undomesticated *Mauritia* palm. They ferment and drink its sap, they pulverize and make its pith into a kind of bread, they eat its fruit, and they make hammocks, aprons, headgear, and other articles of clothing from its fiber. They use many other wild products, such as sweet potatoes, yams, and the larvae of various insects.

Village patterns today are consistent with a society based on kinship rather than on class, and many specific elements link these people with the riverine horticulturalists. The Warrau build simple lean-tos or bee-hivelike houses, and in the swampy regions they elevate the entire village on a single platform made of several layers of tree trunks covered with clay. While the nuclear family is the basic economic unit, the community is a matrilineal, matrilocal lineage.

While Wilbert describes the simple kinship structure of the Warrau as consistent with nomadic hunters and gatherers, he mentions classes of chiefs, priests, shamans, and magicians, and several groups of laborers that functioned only in connection with temple festivals.

Many elements common to the tropical-forest peoples enter into the ritual accompanying the life cycle. After childbirth, the couvade is observed; that is, the mother is confined and ritually purified, and the father must refrain from sexual relations and avoid certain foods for a long period. At puberty, a girl is secluded in a special hut, has her head shaved, keeps to her hammock, refrains from speaking or laughing, and undergoes an ant ordeal before becoming eligible for marriage. At death, a chief's corpse is sometimes allowed to decompose and the skeleton later hung up in the house, after which the bones are placed in a basket and hung in the house.

The main function of the shamans is to cure illness that is supernaturally induced. Their paraphernalia includes a séance hut, a gourd rattle, and quartz crystals. To become a shaman, one must undergo a severe initiation to the order. His initiation requires extensive cigar smoking, which, after ten days fasting, puts him in an unconscious, death-like state. Upon recovery he is ready to practice his skills. Shamans control malevolent spirits, predict the future, and interpret dreams.

Some Warrau features may have been borrowed in historic times from Negroes and from Europeans. For example, certain musical instruments appear to have been introduced from Africa by the escaped slaves, the "bush Negroes," who settled this general area. The concept of the "evil eye," which Wilbert reports, must also be Old World. While the temple cult and priest can hardly be ascribed to European origin, the conceptionalization of the single god and creator as a "white man with fair hair, dressed in a white tunica reaching down to his feet" may, despite the widespread Indian idea of the White God, represent Christian influence.

To conclude this interesting, if somewhat complicated, picture of the Warrau with speculative, theoretical observations, it can be said that one may view the culture history of the Warrau in two ways. First, to follow Wilbert's suggestions, perhaps farther than he intended, Warrau culture may represent three historic layers: (1) a nomadic hunting-and-gathering, matrilineage society, with a very simple technology and shamanism based on the concept of illness caused by an intruded foreign object; (2) tropical-forest farm village accretions, such as plant domestication, dugout canoes, baskets, and spirit intrusion or soul loss as the cause of disease; and (3) the priest-temple-idol cult, with its associated but temporary class statuses derived from a Circum-Caribbean-chiefdom type of culture.

The other view is that it was a Circum-Caribbean or tropical-forest farm-village culture, features of which survive among a people who were deculturated owing to their migration into an environment that permits little farming. While the culture history of any society is normally cumulative, the reverse process is a possibility, as evidenced by the post-Columbian descendants of the Circum-Caribbean chiefdoms.

Both the processes of cultural accumulation and cultural loss may, of course, occur among any people. But to reconcile the confusion of seemingly different points of view, one must return to the fundamental premise that such features as permanent villages, intervillage chiefdoms, social classes, and a priest-temple-idol cult serving state purposes presuppose a productive surplus. A nomadic hunting-and-gathering people, such as the Warrau, might have borrowed superficial features from their agricultural neighbors of the past. But they surely would not have invented these features themselves.

NOTES

1. Martin Gusinde, *Die Feuerland-Indianer*, Mödling bei Wien, vol. 1, *Die Selk'nam*, 1931; vol. 2, *Die Yamana*, 1937; vol. 3, *Anthropologie der Feuerland-Indianer*, 1939.
2. Martin Dobrizhoffer, *An Account of the Abipones: an Equestrian People of Paraguay*, translated by Sara Coleridge from the Latin original of 1784, 3 vols., London, 1822.
3. Allan Holmberg, *Nomads of the Long Bow: the Sirionó of Eastern Bolivia*, Institute of Social Anthropology, Publication no. 10, 1950.
4. We are indebted to Johannes Wilbert of Venezuela for much unpublished information on the Warrau, especially on their religious culture.

▶ **fifteen**

RETROSPECT

AND PROSPECT

This chapter will summarize the story of the South American Indians in broad outline so as to prove perspectives on their past, present, and future.

The first arrival and dispersal of human beings in South America, the invention and diffusion of methods of subsistence in the varied environments, the organization of the people into bands, villages, chiefdoms, states and empires, and the development of technological, intellectual, and aesthetic achievements constitutes a major chapter in human history. While this story cannot be wholly separated from that of Meso-America and North America, since there was widespread element diffusion, the evolution of the several kinds of sociocultural types was indigenous to the southern continent.

The next major chapter begins with the conquest of South America by European colonial powers. The conquest introduced changes which were most profound at the colonial and state levels of culture but which were also felt at the community or folk level. There is, however, such continuity of community culture from pre-Columbian to modern times that a large portion of rural persons, especially in the Central Andes, are classed today as Indians.

The history of post-Conquest South America is divisible into several major developmental eras, each marked by changes in colonialism, in national types, and in the effects of these changes upon the local populations. In the course of this history, the percentage of persons classed as Indians in the national census has constantly shrunk, while the native

445

cultures have changed. A very few Indians survive today as genuinely independent and aboriginal societies. Many more have cultures which, though aboriginal in general character, are strongly modified. The great majority, most of whom live in the Central Andes, are no longer independent but constitute subcultural groups or subsocieties of the modern nations.

Today, the indigenous way of life is being irretrievably lost, and each year more Indians are coming inextricably into the context of the national life of the republics. Meanwhile, the Central and South American republics are themselves being modified by worldwide industrial trends. As these national cultures change, the native groups which constitute subsocieties within the nations are deeply affected.

The acculturation of the Indians—the emergence of new kinds of subsocieties and subcultures—has been studied only in recent years, but its implication for the future can be roughly outlined. Although the Indians will have left a strong biological heritage in the population of many countries—a heritage which, however, is increasingly mixed with that of other races of mankind—and contributed many particulars to modern cultures, such as certain domesticated plants, they are losing their cultural identity. The local groups are coming to resemble whites, Negroes, and Asiatics who have a similar way of life and place in the national cultural systems.

1. THE ORIGIN OF THE SOUTH AMERICAN INDIANS AND THEIR CULTURE

Each year new discoveries modify previous ideas concerning the antiquity of the Indian, his migrations, and the ways in which native cultures developed. Future discoveries will modify many details of the present volume, but the general picture will not be greatly altered.

The origin of the American Indians

America was first populated by fully developed Homo sapiens, or modern man. The New World has no extinct species of fossil man or higher primates from which human beings might have evolved. Whether the first migrants to the New World were racially homogeneous has been questioned, but there is no doubt that they were predominantly Mongoloid in race, that they were derived from the peoples of Asia, and that they migrated to America via Bering Strait. Possibly non-Mongoloid races such as the Caucasoidlike Ainu, who constitute a nearly extinct racial minority in northern Japan, contributed minor strains to the original biological heritage of the Indians, and very likely occasional canoeloads of Polynesians crossed the Pacific to the shores of America.

Any mixture of other races and any trans-Pacific migrations, however, were minor episodes in the story of native American cultural development. North America was first populated at least 15,000 years ago, and probably much earlier, by a simple, nonfarming people who brought elementary techniques for hunting, fishing, and gathering wild foods. Plants and animals were not domesticated in the Old World until about 5000 B.C. and in the New World until 3000 to 2500 B.C. Plant domestication and the evolution of New World cultures were autochthonous, except for a few minor elements that diffused via Alaska and others that may have come across the Pacific.

The dispersal of the first Indians throughout the Americas followed routes which, though not yet fully disclosed by cultural-historical studies, can be partly reconstructed from archaeology, linguistic distributions, and ethnographic types.

General history of South American Indians

South America was populated at least 10,000 years ago, and new finds will undoubtedly disclose earlier dates. Subracial characteristics of the Indians give few clues as to how the streams of migration may have split into lesser currents; for very dissimilar types now adjoin one another in small areas. For example, in Tierra del Fuego the tall Ona of the interior are neighbors of the short Yahgan of the coast. Body height, cranial and facial proportions, and other more detailed physical characteristics follow no territorial pattern that conclusively shows historical migrations. Moreover, the physical variations cannot be related to environment, culture, or other factors; for the Indians have inhabited South America too recently and have moved about too frequently for any such natural selection to have operated.

The three major linguistic families tentatively proposed by Greenberg, however, strongly suggest main streams of population movement, and these accord in part with inferences that can be drawn from cultural data. The Andean-Equatorial family is distributed from northern Peru southward through most of the Andes and the Chilean archipelago to Tierra del Fuego and east of the Andes into the pampas and Patagonia. Although a branch of this family, which includes the Arawakan, moved into the Amazon, the picture is otherwise one of population movement along the Andes, predominantly from north to south. The great cultural variations within this family—a variation which ranges from the high civilizations of the Andes through the village farmers and pastoralists of central Chile to the nomadic hunting bands of Patagonia and the pampas and the family shellfish gatherers of southern Chile—can be explained by three factors. First, the dispersal of the original speakers of this language took place before agriculture was known in the Central Andes.

Second, the more southerly members, especially the archipelagic and Patagonian Indians, were remote from the centers of invention. Third, the southern environments barely permitted subsistence and could not support more advanced features which might have diffused from the Central Andes.

Such far-flung Equatorial members of this family as the Arawakans, who were characterized by a tropical-forest type of culture, seem to have been expanding rapidly and widely at the time of the Spanish Conquest.

The Macro-Chibchan family of the northern Andes of Ecuador, Colombia, and Central America was, with certain exceptions, fairly localized in the area of aboriginal chiefdoms. Apparently this linguistic group had expanded predominantly from south to north, from South America into Central America. Since the original migrations into South America were from north to south, this represents a reversal of population movement. We do not know when the current began to flow northward. Archaeological data show that a few of the many ingredients of the Formative Era culture originated in Meso-America. But culture can diffuse against a slow movement of people.

The Macro-Chibchan family, although predominantly associated with chiefdoms, was not entirely limited to them. The very primitive Warrau of the Orinoco Delta and the Mura of the lower Madeira River also belong to the Macro-Chibchan family.

The Ge-Pano-Carib family is largely confined to the tropical-forest peoples and to the simpler nomadic hunters and gatherers of the southern headwaters of the Amazon, the eastern Brazilian highlands, and the Brazilian coast. No members of this family occupied the Central Andes, and none had chiefdoms. The family must have differentiated east of the Andes at an early period, for most of its members are nomads.

The earliest American culture

Because the first inhabitants of America came during the Palaeolithic or Stone Age of the Old World, they were already equipped with some technical knowledge and with patterns of social life. This original culture, which is sometimes called the archaic culture, is known partly from direct evidence and partly from inference.

Imperishable objects, such as stone implements found in archaeological sites, show that the Indians knew how to chip flint in order to make spear points, skin scrapers, and simple tools for working wood and bone. The scrapers are good evidence that they wore skin robes and perhaps simple footgear, like that of the Patagonians. Charcoal from early sites proves use of fire, which may have been made at first with flint-and-pyrite strike-a-lights, such as those used in the far south and in parts of the Montaña, and later by friction between two pieces of wood.

Since many features are worldwide among nomadic hunters and gatherers or have survived among the South American nomads, they were probably part of the archaic culture. These include cordage, earth ovens, crude shelters or windbreaks of poles with a variety of shapes and coverings, the atlatl for throwing spears, shamanism, crisis rites, belief in nature spirits, and a society based on kinship.

These elements certainly do not exhaust the contents of the original heritage; but we cannot be sure whether many other widely distributed elements were archaic or merely prehorticultural. For example, games of chance, the ritual scratching stick, netting, coiled basketry, men's secret societies, and others are very old, but how old and whether they were once shared by all South American Indians cannot be determined.

2. THE DEVELOPMENT OF SOUTH AMERICAN CULTURES

Although the technological and sociological ingredients of the archaic culture were perhaps available to all South America, the cultural patterns of the early hunters, fishers, and gatherers cannot have been the same in all areas. Particular subsistence techniques were important in the different environments—in the Andes, the tropical rain forests, the savannas, the steppes and deserts, and the cold, rainy southern archipelago. Moreover, the organization of the societies for subsistence—the cultural-ecological adaptations—was necessarily somewhat different among fishermen, food collectors, and hunters. The earliest inhabitants of South America were surely as diversified as the nomadic hunters and gatherers described in Chapters Thirteen and Fourteen.

Once South America was settled, a long series of inventions of diverse origin increased man's control of his environment. Some of these, like the bow and arrow, which was invented in the Eastern Hemisphere, nearly attained worldwide distribution. Some, such as maize, beans, squashes, and other crops, spread widely within the Western Hemisphere. Others were limited to portions of South America; for example, large-scale irrigation, certain plant species, bronze, quipus, monumental architecture, and many others to the Central Andes; certain root crops, pole-and-thatch houses, and hammocks to the tropical rain forests; balsas or dugout canoes to the coasts and rivers; and so forth.

As inventions were made and diffused, cultural-ecological adaptations changed, and new types of societies began to emerge; for new kinds of land use required special forms of cooperation and managerial controls, while productive surplus permitted classes of specialists. Meanwhile, the development and spread of patterns of warfare and religion also affected the societies of many areas. By the time of the Spanish Conquest, the five principal types of societies or sociocultural systems described in the present volume had developed.

The Central Andes

The greatest center of inventiveness and social development was the Central Andes. It is difficult to pinpoint the places of origin of the many elements of the basic Formative Era culture since most of these—domesticated plants, heddle-loom weaving, ceramics, metallurgy, roads, palaces, belief in high gods, priests, idols, temples, temple mounds, and states and empires—were shared with many of the Circum-Caribbean people and with the Maya, Aztec, and others of Meso-America. There seems to have been a lively inter-American exchange of cultural elements during the Formative Era, perhaps before the Macro-Chibchan migrations began to move northward into Central America. To understand the succession of cultural types in the Central Andes, however, it is not necessary to trace each element to its ultimate origin. Central Andean cultural evolution was based upon increasing farm productivity, which soon achieved a surplus that brought technological progress, aesthetic creativeness, and complex social, religious, and political patterns.

The impetus to this evolution was the domestication of plants some 2500 years B.C., which initiated the Era of Incipient Farming. Cultivation of *Canavalia* beans, later of maize, and still later of other crops, probably at first on the moist lands bordering the rivers, permitted settlement in permanent but small villages. Basketry, weaving, and ceramics were established crafts by this time.

The Formative Era brought an impressive list of new crops and the use of irrigation and fertilization, which provided sufficient surplus to support an expanding population, larger communities, and emerging states that were internally differentiated into classes of farmers, artisans, builders, religious leaders, and administrators. Religious centers consisting of mounds and temples became the focal points for clusters of formerly independent villages. Full-time specialists now developed weaving, ceramics, metallurgy, sculpture, and construction of religious edifices, all decorated with stylized art motifs.

The theocratic states reached an aesthetic culmination in the Era of Florescent Local States, but there is evidence that warfare of some kind had begun in this era. To judge by the many pictorial representations, its purpose was probably the capture of victims primarily for religious sacrifice and possibly for slaves rather than exaction of tribute or territorial conquest. The Florescent Era, however, was characterized more by intensification of the many regional aesthetic styles than by militarism or by technological inventiveness.

During this era, population continued to increase as irrigation was expanded, and it reached its pre-Columbian maximum toward the end of this era or the beginning of the following era. Territorial expansion of states probably resulted from the integration of many communities within single irrigation systems. Class differentiation was sharpened, and the rulers became war leaders as well as priests. But the era is noteworthy chiefly because it brought the finest textiles, the most elaborately modeled, molded and painted pottery, the most exquisite work in stone, bone, shell, feathers, and gold and other metals, and the largest temple mounds in Andean prehistory.

The Era of Cyclical Conquests and the empires of that time began when productivity had reached its maximum and local states undertook to conquer their neighbors in order to exact tribute. Militarism in this era differed from that of the Florescent Era in that sacrificial victims and slaves were no longer taken. Animals rather than people were now used in blood sacrifice. Warfare entailed conquest of large territories, whose populations were moved about, regimented, and thoroughly controlled by a strongly bureaucratic government of warriors, priests, and civil rulers. The regimentation in civil and political life was paralleled in the standardization of material culture. Architecture, dress, and even art styles lost distinctive local character and became similar everywhere. Many objects were now mass-produced.

The earliest empires are represented by Chimu on the north coast and probably by Tiahuanaco in the highlands, while the last and greatest was that of the Inca.

The Circum-Caribbean chiefdoms

The chiefdoms of Ecuador, Colombia, and the Circum-Caribbean area did not constitute a major center of inventiveness, but since the northern Andes and Central America lie in the path of diffusion between North and South America, they received many basic productive, technological, and social traits which provided the foundation for a complex, if somewhat distinctive, cultural evolution.

The northern Andes and Central America had a Formative Era culture which must have been more or less contemporary with that of the Central Andes and Meso-America and which seems to have had the same general characteristics. Diffusion of a few particulars of this culture from north to south is suggested by their presence in Central America and Ecuador but not in the Central Andes. But these particulars, which include such elements as napkin-ring-type earrings, do not really affect the larger inter-American picture of Formative features: crop production, a ceremonial complex of temples, idols, and priesthoods, and many technological skills.

Although a Formative Era culture existed throughout much or most of the northern Andes and Central America, archaeology does not yet enable us to subdivide subsequent eras or territorial divisions in a way comparable to that of Central Andean prehistory so as to present an account of how local developments led to the contact-period chiefdoms.

The Circum-Caribbean chiefdoms found at the Spanish Conquest were very small as compared with the empires of the Central Andes; and although based upon surplus production and strongly divided into social classes, they lacked the castelike rigidity of the Inca classes. These differences are explainable by cultural-ecological adaptations and by diffusion. The Central Andean states developed on the basis of irrigation, which required intercommunity cooperation as the systems of canals and ditches expanded. While many of the chiefdoms irrigated, they never developed such large-scale enterprises. In the course of state formation in the Central Andes, the sacrifice of human beings in a temple cult and the waging of war to capture victims were auxiliary factors, secondary to irrigation, in consolidating the people of a state. Among the northern Andean chiefdoms, human sacrifice in the temple-idol cult and warfare to take victims became the major integrating factors. This warfare also served such economic purposes as capture of slaves or concubines and exaction of tribute, but the nature and importance of slaves is in question and tribute implied control of surplus rather than of territory.

Warfare to capture slaves and victims, the temple-idol cult, and human sacrifice had an inter-American distribution and therefore, more likely than not, were acquired by the chiefdoms through diffusion. These factors led to the appearance of strong military and religious leaders whose control over the commoners forced maximum farm production. They also led to political consolidation and class structure. To say that diffusion was involved in the evolution of the chiefdoms, however, is not to depict the process as one of simple borrowing. The process might be called "forced diffusion," since predatory warfare passes from group to group by a kind of chain reaction. The victims of aggression have no choice but to fight or run away. In the areas of the chiefdoms, the settled populations not only fought back but themselves became aggressors and adopted the custom of sacrificing human beings in a temple cult.

In the Greater Antilles, the war patterns were weaker, and human sacrifice was not adopted. The theocratic power of the rulers, however, was sufficient to integrate considerable populations into chiefdoms and to command a portion of the surplus production.

The southern Andes

The peoples of the southern Andes drew heavily upon the Central Andes for a long list of technological skills, such as farming, llama breeding, ceramics, weaving, metallurgy, and construction. The extreme aridity of the north Chilean deserts, however, so limited population density that communities consisted of independent lineages no larger than those found among many nomadic hunters and gatherers. While a reduced number of elements diffused beyond the deserts to the Araucanians of the fertile central valley of Chile, the Araucanian population was vastly denser than that of north Chile. But, in the absence of such politically integrating factors as large-scale irrigation, warfare for tribute, or the temple cult, the Araucanian population remained divided into a large number of small, independent, lineage-based communities.

The tropical-forest farm villages

There was a remarkable correlation between the distribution of low, hot rain forests and independent farm villages. Many features of the tropical-forest village culture were probably derived from more complex Central Andean or Circum-Caribbean culture. These included such plants as maize, beans, squashes, and others and such technologies as ceramics, heddle-loom weaving, and perhaps basketry. Since all these elements are very old and widespread, however, it is hazardous to guess the exact place of their origin.

A considerable number of traits were no doubt invented as the result of improvisations found useful in any hot tropical rain forests. Among these are pole-and-thatch houses, hammocks, babracots, climbing rings, bow-and-arrow types, fish drugs, and various domesticated tropical root crops, fruits, and palms. Other traits of special value in the tropical forests, whatever their place of origin, include dugout canoes, bark cloth, blowguns, fish spears and nets, and traps.

The community type throughout the tropical forests was remarkably homogeneous, and it resulted from a combination of factors that were present everywhere. Slash-and-burn farming in the dense forests supported a comparatively sparse population which was grouped in independent communities. While these communities were larger along the principal waterways, where fish, reptiles, and aquatic mammals contributed to the food supply and canoe transportation facilitated centralization of the people, all were characteristically unstratified socially and based primarily upon kinship relations. Warfare was typically carried out for individual honors or revenge rather than for conquest or tribute. Slave raiding was almost certainly post-European. Religion was based upon shamanism, life crises, and belief in spirits. While community ceremonials were not uncommon, they were typically led by the shaman rather than by a special priest. Neither warfare nor religion could create classes of rulers and specialists, for few if any localities permitted a productive surplus to support such classes.

It is conceivable that the tropical-forest population was still expanding at the time of the Spanish Conquest and that the future might have brought denser populations.[1] It is doubtful, however, that the nature of society would have been greatly altered. The need to shift the farm plots every few years and sometimes to move the villages prevents community stability. Moreover, increase in production may have led to increase in population rather than to a surplus that would support specialists.

Nomadic hunters and gatherers

Viewed in terms of culture elements and the histories of these elements, the nomadic hunters and gatherers are marginal survivors who retain many early or archaic cultural traits and who share comparatively few of the more recent inventions. As we have seen, however, there is reason to question which of the culture elements found among these people were actually derived from a Pan-American archaic culture stratum and which were local inventions made wherever particular improvisations were required—for example, the many simple types of shelters.

All the nomadic hunters and gatherers are similar in two respects. First, they are organized in small groups which are nomadic within circumscribed territories, whose interpersonal relations are based primarily on kinship, age, and sex and whose religion consists essentially of life-crisis rites, shamanism, and belief in spirits. Second, they are similar to one another in their lack of farming, livestock breeding, permanent settlements, multikin social groupings, warfare for conquest, tribute, or capture of victims, social classes, civil rule, a priest-temple-idol cult, and such technological knowledge as ceramics, heddle-loom weaving, metallurgy, basketry, and religious or civil architecture.

These negative characteristics, although undoubtedly common to all the nomadic hunters and gatherers at an earlier period in South American culture history, do not now hold in all cases. Many nomads among or adjoining the tropical-forest or Andean cultures have adopted some farming, ceramics, weaving, house types, and other traits from their neighbors. The important point, however, is that such borrowing has in no instance affected the fundamental simplicity of their society or their essential nomadism. In other cases, former nomads have become settled village farmers—and the whole history of culture development has been one of adoption of farming and transformation of sociocultural types—and they are no longer classifiable as nomads.

But the category of nomadic hunters and gatherers is a far more generalized type than tropical-forest farmers, chiefdoms, or Central Andean states and empires. Since the organization of these simple societies for subsistence—the cultural-ecological adaptation—is more responsive to the exigencies of particular environments than that of the more complex and technologically more highly developed societies, there is a variety of local types or subtypes.

Where wild food collecting is the principal mode of subsistence, as among the archipelagic shellfish gatherers of southern Chile and to a certain extent the wild-rice-gathering Guató of the upper Paraguay River, the nuclear family is the only permanent social unit, and it carries out most cultural functions. Where hunting had more importance than food collecting, as in the pampas and Patagonia, the people were organized in patrilineal hunting bands, that is, extended patrilineal lineages. Among many of the forest nomads, food collecting together with hunting brought about matrilineal bands—small, extended matrilineages that were more or less the counterpart of the patrilineal hunting bands. Another type of nomad is represented by the aquatic people who, like the archipelagic food collectors, tend to live for much of the year in nuclear family units but seasonally assemble in larger aggregates.

These several types of social groupings represent in large measure ways in which people can best be organized for exploiting scattered shellfish, large game, forest foods, or fish and aquatic plants and mammals. But the nomads may have additional sociological complexities, some of them borrowed features. For example, the Ge of eastern Brazil have an intricate organization of moieties and age classes, the Warrau a surprising priest-temple-idol cult, and the Patagonians and archipelagic people initiation ceremonies and, in some cases, a men's secret society. Except for the Warrau cult, these are, however, all variations on the themes of sex, age, and kinship groupings, which are fundamental to all nomads.

3. POST-EUROPEAN CHANGES

When the Europeans discovered and began the conquest of South America early in the sixteenth century, Central Andean civilization seems to have reached the limits of its potentials under irrigation farming. Without knowledge of iron and a system of money, commerce, and investment, production could not have been expanded or wealth increased. Cyclical conquests, during which empires would rise, collapse, then rise again, seem to have been the social destiny of the Andean peoples for an indefinite period unless basically new technologies and patterns were invented or introduced. As it happened, the new features came to the Central Andes with shocking impact from overseas. Among the tropical-forest and hunting-and-gathering people, however, it is entirely possible that, given time, new technologies and forms of production might have appeared and entailed rich cultural development in the future. The course of such development, however, is purely speculative.

The specific effects of the European conquest differed considerably in the various major areas. This is seen in the dissimilar demographic trends among the native people and the present-day proportion of Indians to people of overseas ancestry in the various republics and colonies. It is also manifest in the emergence of new subcultural types—corporate peasants, dispersed peasants, hacienda and plantation workers, farmers, wage laborers, and skilled artisans—under special conditions.

While the subcultural types found in South America today are very different from the aboriginal cultural types, they represent the product of a series of gradual transformations induced principally by the integration of the people in larger colonial and national economies and sociocultural systems. Many of these changes began as the indirect result of European influence before the Indians had direct and sustained relations with Europeans.

Demographic trends

After the European conquest, the trends in racial composition and proportion of Indians to the total population in the major areas of South America differed significantly owing to the interaction of native Indian population and culture, European occupation, and importation of African slaves and other racial and ethnic groups.

Table 4 gives estimates of the number of Indians in pre-Conquest times and in the middle of the twentieth century. It must be emphasized that these figures are exceedingly gross approximations and that their significance lies in the trends they indicate rather than in absolute numbers. The aboriginal estimate is uncertain owing to the practical difficulties of counting Indians and to the frequent tendency to exaggerate their numbers. The contemporary estimates vary widely because of disagreement concerning who should be considered an Indian in the census. This difficulty is greatest in the Central Andean countries, where the proportion of persons of pure European descent is relatively small yet one-third to one-half of the population is classed as mestizo. Since Indian ancestry predominates among the mestizos, they could be classed as Indians on a purely racial basis despite traces of Caucasian intermixture. The United States classifies persons with as little as one-eighth Indian ancestry as Indians. By this criterion, the number of Indians in South America today would be doubled or tripled. Since, however, Indians are identified as persons who "live like Indians," while mestizos are persons who have adopted considerable European culture, there is enormous latitude for disagreement. Estimates of the modern Indian population of Peru and Bolivia vary from 4,600,000 to 7,000,000 —from less than 40 per cent to more than 60 per cent of the total— and for El Salvador from 85,000 to 400,000. Only some 60,000 persons or approximately 4 per cent of the population of Paraguay are classed as Indians, although the country is overwhelmingly Indian racially.

TABLE 4. *Post-conquest Demographic Trends among Indians within Territories of Modern Nations**

Nation	Estimated aboriginal number	Indian population mid-20th century	National population mid-20th century	Approximate percentage of Indians in mid-20th century population
Peru– Bolivia	3,824,000	4,600,000– 7,000,000	11,142,000	37–62
Ecuador	551,000	960,000– 1,900,000	3,500,000	27–60
Colombia	1,157,000	250,000– 840,000	12,033,000	2–7
Panama	225,000	48,000– 82,000	864,000	6–9.5
Costa Rica	120,000	3,000– 8,000	881,000	0.3–1.0
Nicaragua, Honduras, El Salvador	293,000	85,000– 400,000	5,270,000	1.6–7.6
Venezuela	175,000	56,000– 112,000	5,420,000	1–2
Antilles	225,000	Trace	16,560,000	Trace
Chile	1,100,000	40,000– 450,000	6,072,000	0.6–7.4
Guianas	90,000	11,000	600,000	1.8
Brazil	1,988,000	500,000– 1,100,000	55,772,000	0.9–2.0
Paraguay	316,000	60,000	1,496,000	4.1
Uruguay	33,000	Trace	2,525,000	Trace
Argentina	103,000	120,000	18,379,000	0.6

* These estimates concern territories comprising modern nations and therefore do not represent demographic trends with exclusive reference to aboriginal cultural types. Peru and Bolivia are predominantly Central Andean but also include the Montaña and eastern Bolivia. Ecuador includes the Ecuadorian Montaña, which natively had some 51,000 Indians. The area of modern Colombia embraced some 157,000 tropical-forest people as well as 1,000,000 northern Andean Indians. The Central American countries included a minor population of tropical-forest Indians, while the Lesser Antillean Carib were also tropical forest in type. Chile had perhaps 9,000 marginal type Indians in addition to the 1,091,000 southern Andean type. The Guianas and Brazil Indians were predominantly tropical-forest people, and the hunters and gatherers comprised a very small portion of the total. Paraguay, Uruguay, and Argentina were largely hunters and gatherers, except for the few tropical-forest people in Uruguay and the sub-Andean Indians of northwest Argentina.

These differences largely reflect disagreement as to where the line is drawn culturally between Indian and mestizo. Since more Indian culture survives in the Central Andes than elsewhere, a large proportion of the people is classed as Indians.

In addition to white-Indian crosses, there is much intermixture of Indians and Negroes in the tropical lowlands.

For these reasons, it would be impossible to unscramble the racial heritage of each person and assign him to definite categories based upon proportions of Indian, white, and Negro ancestry.

These differences are explainable in terms of certain factors that also brought about the contemporary subcultural types.

In world areas which had a sparse native population of hunting-and-gathering nomads, European colonization exterminated, drove back, assimilated, or confined the native people to limited areas or reserves. In Uruguay and Argentina, as in the western United States and Canada, Australia, and extreme south Africa, the aborigines were too few and too mobile to serve as a labor force. Colonists brought their families, expropriated native land, and worked it themselves. The native people now classed as "Indians" comprise an insignificant fraction of the modern population: 1 per cent in Argentina, only a trace in Uruguay.

In areas which were slightly more densely populated and which had farm villages yet no native surplus production, as in the tropical forests, the Europeans established plantations. Since the comparatively mobile native people faded back from European penetration, labor was provided by slaves who were forcibly retained. The first New World slaves were Arabs from Spain, after which came the great slave traffic from Africa and large-scale slaving among the Indians. We have repeatedly mentioned in previous pages that the European demand for slaves led Indian societies to raid one another, entailed new patterns of military organization, and in many cases introduced a slave class into the native Indian social structure.

The general decline of the tropical-forest population after the Conquest is attributable to several factors: the new patterns of warfare, epidemic diseases of appalling intensity contracted at the missions and new settlements where the people were in close contact with one another, and assimilation of the enslaved Indians with Negroes and Europeans on the plantations. The remaining people classed as Indian —for example, the large numbers in Brazil—are now mostly in remote regions, away from the principal rivers which have been the avenues of European penetration.

The demographic story in Chile is a little different, owing to the exceptional stubbornness exhibited by the Araucanians. Although the native population has been more than halved, the Indians who fought a prolonged delaying action while they retreated to the south and only surrendered toward the end of the last century were put on reservations where, owing to this territorial isolation, which is rare in South America, they retain identity as Araucanians. Besides the reservation Indians, however, large numbers of Araucanians were assimilated long ago into the rural Chilean population.

European occupation of the area of the chiefdoms was much like that of the tropical forests. Although the native population was fairly dense, the villages reasonably large, and the society partly supported by surplus production, there was still territory in the swamps, mountains, and other undesirable regions where the Indians could retreat from the European onslaught. When the Indians fled, following the destruction of their aboriginal chiefdoms, the colonists faced the need of slave labor to work their agricultural holdings. This was especially true of the low, coastal areas, some of which had a tropical-forest culture as well as chiefdoms. In parts of the Colombian and Ecuadorian highland, however, the Indians were more permanently and densely settled, much as in the Central Andes, and the excess population induced by alienation of lands left them no choice but to become hacienda workers. Ecuador and highland Colombia still have large numbers of Indians, whereas Central America and Venezuela have comparatively few.

In the Antilles, which were fairly densely settled, the small islands afforded no refuge. Forced labor and epidemics so reduced the number of Indians that slaves were imported at an early date, and the surviving Indians became thoroughly mixed with other races. Today, they do not exist as an important racial or cultural entity.

The inhabitable portions of the Central Andes were so densely populated, the villages so permanent, and the people so closely tied to their communities that they had no means of escape from the Spaniards. The aboriginal nonfarming class of yanaconas, or artisans, household servants, and the like, was greatly augmented when expropriation of land together with forced cultivation of tribute crops on land still held by Indians reduced the capacity of the land to support the people. This surplus population had no choice but to become laborers for mines, public works, and haciendas. The abuses of labor, especially in the mines, and the ravages of disease among people weakened by food shortages reduced the population sharply after the Conquest. In time, however, as the new economy became established, the native population more than recovered its aboriginal number. Today, nearly 40 per cent of the Central Andean people are classed as Indian, and many more are predominantly Indian in race.

These South American demographic trends have close counterparts in North America and Meso-America. The United States and Canada parallel Uruguay and Argentina in that the aboriginal population was sparse—770,000 in the United States and 230,000 in Canada. By the mid-twentieth century, despite recent increase, it was about half the original number. Including persons of mixed race, it was 395,000 or .02 per cent of the total population of the United States and 165,000 or about .1 per cent in Canada. Mexico and Guatemala, whose main aboriginal population compared culturally with the Central Andes, had some 3,200,000 Indians in pre-Columbian times and today some 6,000,000

Home of modern Peruvian small farmer on homestead colony. (Photo by Louis Faron.)

Indians or about one-fifth to one-fourth of the modern population but nearly double the aboriginal number.

Acculturation in the post-Columbian period

The general trends of Indian culture change after the European conquest are understandable as the interaction of European and native patterns within the context of local environmental and ecological factors. But over the centuries there were also extremely important changes in the European-derived patterns themselves. The impact of a gold-extracting economy upon the Indians differed from that of an agrarian economy, which itself changed fundamentally when industrial trends of the nineteenth and twentieth centuries began to penetrate everywhere.

The first phase of European colonialism was motivated by the desire for gold rather than any wish to settle permanently in South America. The mechanism for extracting wealth was a system of indirect rule, the encomienda, whereby native leaders were charged with collecting tribute in gold and wealth from their people.

The encomienda soon gave way to Spanish ownership of the sources of wealth and to direct rule. Meanwhile, agrarian wealth began to acquire importance, and Europeans settled permanently upon their

Acculturation in the tropical forests: the Macusi of British Guiana. Missionaries are often the first major contact of Indians with the western world. (Courtesy of The University Museum, Philadelphia.)

estates. There were several forms of agrarian estates which, as we have seen, depended upon the local environment, native culture, and aboriginal population density and settlement pattern.

In the sparsely settled areas of nomadic hunters and gatherers, the Europeans displaced the Indians and worked the lands themselves. Prior to their complete displacement the Indians formed predatory bands of horse nomads. After the colonies were thoroughly established, the surviving Indians became absorbed in the rural proletariat; for example, the Gauchos who work the cattle estates of Argentina.

In the more densely settled tropical-forest and Circum-Caribbean areas, agrarian wealth had to be extracted through slave labor and the plantations included large numbers of Indian as well as African slaves. Under plantation conditions, native culture was very rapidly lost. But many Indians in these areas avoided capture. As freemen in the forests with ample land to cultivate, their acculturation took a distinctive course. Their native patterns were changed by indirect European influences rather than by force.

In the early phases of the colonial period, the military organization and probably the social structure of the tropical-forest Indians were affected by slaving expeditions and operations. The societies were also influenced by trade goods, especially steel axes and knives, which enabled them to improve canoes, build larger houses, and clear the forests more easily. And they were affected by missionization and tribal dislocations, which brought different groups into contact, sometimes violently. More recently, the lure of manufactured goods has gradually enmeshed them in the network of commerce, and today they are broadly classifiable as dispersed peasants. This designation signifies an economic dependency upon the larger society through production of cash or trade commodities such as rubber, wild nuts and fruits, and farm crops. Examples cited previously are the rubber-tapping Mundurucú, the caboclos or backwoodsmen of Brazil, and the Guaraní-speaking farmers of Paraguay.

The acculturative effects of the European conquest were different in the densely populated Central Andes. From the very beginning, a large landless population of Indians worked in Spanish mines and on haciendas because they had no other choice. The hacienda laborers, like the household servants and artisans in the towns, were rapidly acculturated to a Spanish way of life. The Indians who retained their lands—especially the people of the small, highland farming communities who are today classed as "Indian"—became linked to the larger society through dependence upon manufactured goods just as the free Indians of the tropical forests did. These Indians are peasants, but since they differ from the dispersed peasants of the tropical forests in that they live in tight-knit, closed, and permanent communities, they are called corporate peasants.

We have so far enumerated five principal acculturational trends: first, direct assimilation—or often extinction—of the nomadic hunters and gatherers; second, enslavement of Indians, who became mixed with Negroes and assimilated to plantation life; third, permissive and gradual acculturation of free Indians, who became dispersed peasants in the areas where slave plantations were established; fourth, employment on haciendas, where Indians were bound to rural estates by lack of alternatives rather than by slavery; and, fifth, surviving Indian communities of free landowners, who became corporate peasants in the areas where haciendas developed.

These five types are broad categories of Indians in the rural areas. While the types intergrade, since peasants may work part time or on shares for hacienda owners and the degree to which labor is bound is variable, they serve to illustrate the basic conditions or causal processes of acculturation. When more comparative analyses of acculturated Indians have been made, we shall surely be able to distinguish significant subtypes and perhaps additional major types.

These types do not take into account the many Indians, such as many of the yanaconas or servant class of aboriginal Peru, who became absorbed into Spanish households or factories and soon lost all traces of Indian culture. They also fail to take into account the new types which are now emerging as the result of world industrial influences. Before examining these last, however, it is well to consider the major characteristics of the previously mentioned subcultural types, for these have embraced the great majority of the Indians since the European conquest.

Little need be said of the directly assimilated nomadic hunters and gatherers or former slaves, for they virtually cease to exist as cultural entities. While some African culture is found in South America, it should be noted that any aboriginal features surviving among slaves are largely those carried by individuals. Where individuals are bought and sold, being torn even from their families, structures such as family types, community organization, and authority patterns cannot be perpetuated. Much of the African culture that survives among Negro populations of South America is either limited to Negroes who have escaped from slavery, for example, the bush Negroes of the Guianas, or it consists of such bits of magic, witchcraft, songs, dances, and folklore as may be perpetuated in a group of changing composition. Culture loss is less on the hacienda than on the plantation, and still less among the dispersed and corporate peasants.

The hacienda

While many diversified productive arrangements are subsumed under the terms "hacienda" and "plantation," we use hacienda to designate a typically paternalistic, preindustrial agrarian estate found in the densely populated areas in early colonial times and in the remote parts of these areas today. The hacienda developed to serve the local needs of the growing towns, and it was not geared to carry out world commerce in a highly competitive market. The hacendado, or owner, has individual title or rights under European grants to his land. His cash production is designed to secure for himself and his family the luxury goods that must be obtained from the outside, often from overseas. Otherwise the hacienda is typically, although not always in practice, a self-contained unit, which meets most of its own needs.

The hacienda worker is bound largely by lack of land of his own and the absence of other employment opportunities. Sometimes, he is bound also by restrictive legislation, which limits his mobility and job choice;

Home of a tenant farmer on an Andean cattle hacienda preserves many native features. (Courtesy of Sol Miller.)

and he may be further bound by continued indebtedness to the hacendado. Fundamentally, his relation to the hacendado is based upon reciprocal but unequal obligations. These outweigh wages, for the hacienda does not operate on a cost-accounting basis and many favors and privileges are granted the worker in lieu of wages. The worker receives land on which to cultivate his own food; there may be local shops for producing clothes and other goods needed by the worker as well as by the hacendado, or the worker may produce these himself; and the laborer is given medical care, family advice, and other forms of aid by his benevolent patron. In return, he may supply children as servants to the master's household and render innumerable special services.

Under this arrangement, the worker's family patterns and indeed a considerable amount of his previous culture may be preserved, provided only that it does not conflict with the larger hacienda pattern. The hacienda, however, insists on conformity within the paternalistic arrangements. The workers remain illiterate, they become Catholics, and they follow the political dictates of their hacendado.

The corporate peasant

In the Central Andes, the isolated communities of corporate peasants are in effect Indian reserves. On the coast, where haciendas were established soon after the Conquest, the Indian as such has disappeared. In the highlands, he has lost much of his land to haciendas, and those who retain land live in compact communities which may be both physically and culturally isolated from the European haciendas and towns. The communities are appropriately designated corporate because they are tightly integrated in many ways. They hold land in common, although each member has rights to cultivate certain plots. They marry endogamously, being fearful of outsiders. They carry on innumerable village ceremonies, many of them taken from the Catholic religious calendar but most of them strongly native in character. These ceremonies not only bind the members together but also have a socially and economically leveling effect. All men belong to cofradías, or religious brotherhoods, and must in turn assume the financial obligation of supporting the ceremonies. Since the cost may dissipate a lifetime's savings, wealth acquired by individuals tends to be spent on the community rather than saved, invested in means of production, and passed on to heirs. Acquisition of private property and individual status based upon wealth are thus almost impossible.

Owing to the limitation of community lands, however, the overflow population must make a living elsewhere. It therefore provides labor not only for the highland haciendas but for the modern coastal farms or so-called plantations.

The in-group feeling associated with corporate-peasant isolation gives rise to local distinctiveness in dress and other overt features. The corporate-peasant culture, however, has a continuity with village culture of aboriginal times as far as family life, farm practices, food habits, and religious and social practices are concerned. But it has also incorporated many Spanish features with aboriginal features and patterned them in what is a new subculture or subsociety of the larger nation.

The dispersed peasant

These peasants are so named because they lack strong attachment to any place or community and their social structure is rather amorphous.

Modern home of the Maué Indians of the middle Amazon. (Courtesy of Seth Leacock.)

Modern Baniwa house, northwest Amazon. (Courtesy of the American Museum of Natural History.)

They represent one or more stages of development which lie between the breakdown of aboriginal society and the complete assimilation of the people into stable rural communities of the modern nations.

In the case of the Mundurucú, who gradually broke away from their native villages to become independent family rubber tappers, there were several distinctive stages of acculturation. The modern Guaraní, on the other hand, are somewhat footloose farmers, who have plenty of land, move freely about cultivating food crops wherever they wish, and work for cash only occasionally and for very special reasons. The crucial factors that distinguish all dispersed peasants from corporate peasants are abundance of land and weakness of community integration. However, as the inevitable desire for cash and what it will buy imbues them, they gradually become caught up in the web of commerce. They gather wild products, raise cash crops, work for wages, or in other ways become more and more like the rural people of European and Negro ancestry.

4. PRESENT AND FUTURE: WORLD INDUSTRIAL INFLUENCES

The final chapter in the acculturation and ultimate assimilation of the South American Indians began when world industrial trends reached massive proportions about a century ago. But this chapter is by no means finished, for the Industrial Revolution, with its scientific and technological progress and its concomitant urbanization and development of mass communications, transportation, and other characteristics, shows no signs of deceleration. Moreover, world industrialization is penetrating to some societies whose members are still primitive hunters, as in remote parts of Amazonia where airfields and other means of communication are being introduced, to other people who are in early stages of peasantry, and still others, who have been plantation and hacienda workers. While it will be many years before the processes have culminated, the acculturation trends that these processes will entail are clear.

With the increasing involvement of South America in world commerce, plantations and haciendas are being transformed into highly capitalized, technologically advanced, and impersonally operated agrarian units, which are run strictly for profit. These are so different from the traditional plantations and haciendas that they are far better designated as modernized farms or field-and-factory combines. Owing to cost accounting, under this type of management the personalized patron-peon relationship is lost, and an owner-employee system based upon wages predominates. Devoted exclusively to monocrops, the laborers are no longer provided with subsistence plots. They feed, clothe, and often shelter themselves from their own wages.

While the trend toward a cash rationale and impersonalized owner-worker relations is everywhere evident, it has not yet run its course. Two features especially evidence lag. First, large agrarian enterprises may offer their workers housing, schools, medical services, and recreational facilities, in addition to wages. This is partly a continuation of the paternalistic tradition, partly a means of attracting workers in areas of labor shortage. Second, the workers still retain subcultural differences that derive from their diversified origins as dispersed or corporate Indian peasants, Africans, Portuguese, Spaniards, Asiatics, and others.

Meanwhile, powerful factors are tending to level these cultural differences. Large family holdings or corporate ownership require a managerial class, which destroys the last vestiges of intimate owner-worker relations. Literacy, union membership, territorial mobility, and urban contacts destroy the attachment of individual families to particular estates and create a national outlook and an awareness of belonging to a labor proletariat. Economic, political, and social goals are sought through group action rather than through individual negotiations with the employer. The extreme of this development is exemplified by the great corporation-owned sugar fields and factories of Puerto Rico, where persons of Negro, Indian, and European descent comprise a homogeneous, unionized class of wage earners.[2]

While these trends are accelerating and accumulating force, it does not follow that all Indians employed on agricultural estates will become culturally homogeneous. They will continue to be employed on agricultural enterprises which have somewhat different internal arrangements because they are devoted to different crops and lie at varying distances from markets and towns. They will still be subject to the somewhat dissimilar influences of the institutions of different nations. And many will work as part-time employees, tenants, and sharecroppers, according to local expediency.

The effect of industrialization upon Indians now classed as peasants will be somewhat different from that upon the employees of agricultural estates. Since the peasants have remained free, their acculturation will be induced rather than forced, even though they have been subjected to certain restrictive legislation in the past. It will be induced fundamentally in the sense that change from production for subsistence as in aboriginal times to production of trade and cash commodities is stimulated by the desire for manufactured goods and the other money-valued adjuncts of western civilization.

The change of native Indians into peasants began in the period of mercantilism, when the lure of hardware was irresistible to people who greatly needed steel axes, knives, pots, and other metal tools and utensils with which to cope with their environments. Later, these people came to want clothing, foods, and innumerable knicknacks and baubles produced by the factories of civilized nations. The desire for what money can buy initiated an irreversible trend that has characterized native peoples throughout the world. In Amazonia, as an earlier chapter showed, the Mundurucú, who were natively subsistence farmers, gave up food crops and devoted themselves almost entirely to gathering rubber, which they exchanged for food and clothing as well as hardware. The Guaraní are on the threshold of becoming cash-crop farmers, and will probably soon cross it.

The sewing machine has reached remote corners of the world. In this Andean highland village, it is among the few machines used, and was obtained through barter. (Courtesy of Sol Miller.)

A cash orientation is striking at the very heart of the corporate-peasant communities in the Andes. As individuals succumb to the enticements of manufactured goods, they desire to expend their incomes upon themselves rather than for community religious festivals, and they seek title to the lands they have worked. Individual ownership and inheritance constitute the entering wedge that has destroyed innumerable peasant communities in the past and seems destined to destroy most in the future.

Moche, the last so-called Indian community on the north Peruvian coast,[3] which has completely individualized land holdings, is now in the throes of losing its land to the far more efficient agricultural estates around it and of disintegrating as a distinctive entity.

Production of cash commodities and individual ownership of land are by no means the sole industrial influences causing contemporary changes. These influences have been intensified during the industrial era owing to the increased volume of cheaply manufactured goods and to vast improvements in transporting and marketing them. But other factors are being introduced concomitantly. The people are gaining access to education, newspapers, radios, medical aid, farm extension instruction,

Schools come to Vicos, Peru. (Photo by John Collier, Jr., courtesy of Cornell University.)

and many other services. They visit towns and cities and experience urban influences in dress, food habits, recreational interests, and fundamental values. They are abandoning traditional legal and authority patterns for systems of law and government derived from Europe, and they are becoming more active members of Christian churches.

In short, they are becoming literate, nationally conscious farmers instead of isolated primitive peasants. Owing to their new outlooks, contacts, and values, many are drawn into urban centers as skilled and semiskilled workers. And since race prejudice as such is comparatively weak in Latin America, those with exceptional ability and education may become artistic, professional, and political leaders. All of these people pass out of the category of Indian, regardless of their race.

NOTES

1. Robert Carneiro has shown in the case of the Kuikuru of the upper Xingú River in particular and the tropical-forest people in general that villages usually had a much smaller population than accessible land would support. ("Slash and Burn Agriculture: A Closer Look at its Implications for Settlement Pattern." This paper will appear in the *Proceedings of the 5th International Congress of Anthropological and Ethnological Sciences.*) While many factors other than production may have limited community size, it is difficult to avoid the belief that the population was expanding.
2. Julian H. Steward (ed.), *The People of Puerto Rico,* University of Illinois Press, Urbana, 1956.
3. John Gillin, *Moche: a Peruvian Coastal Community,* Smithsonian Institution, Institute of Social Anthropology, Publication no. 3, 1947.

INDEX